CHAPTER 9

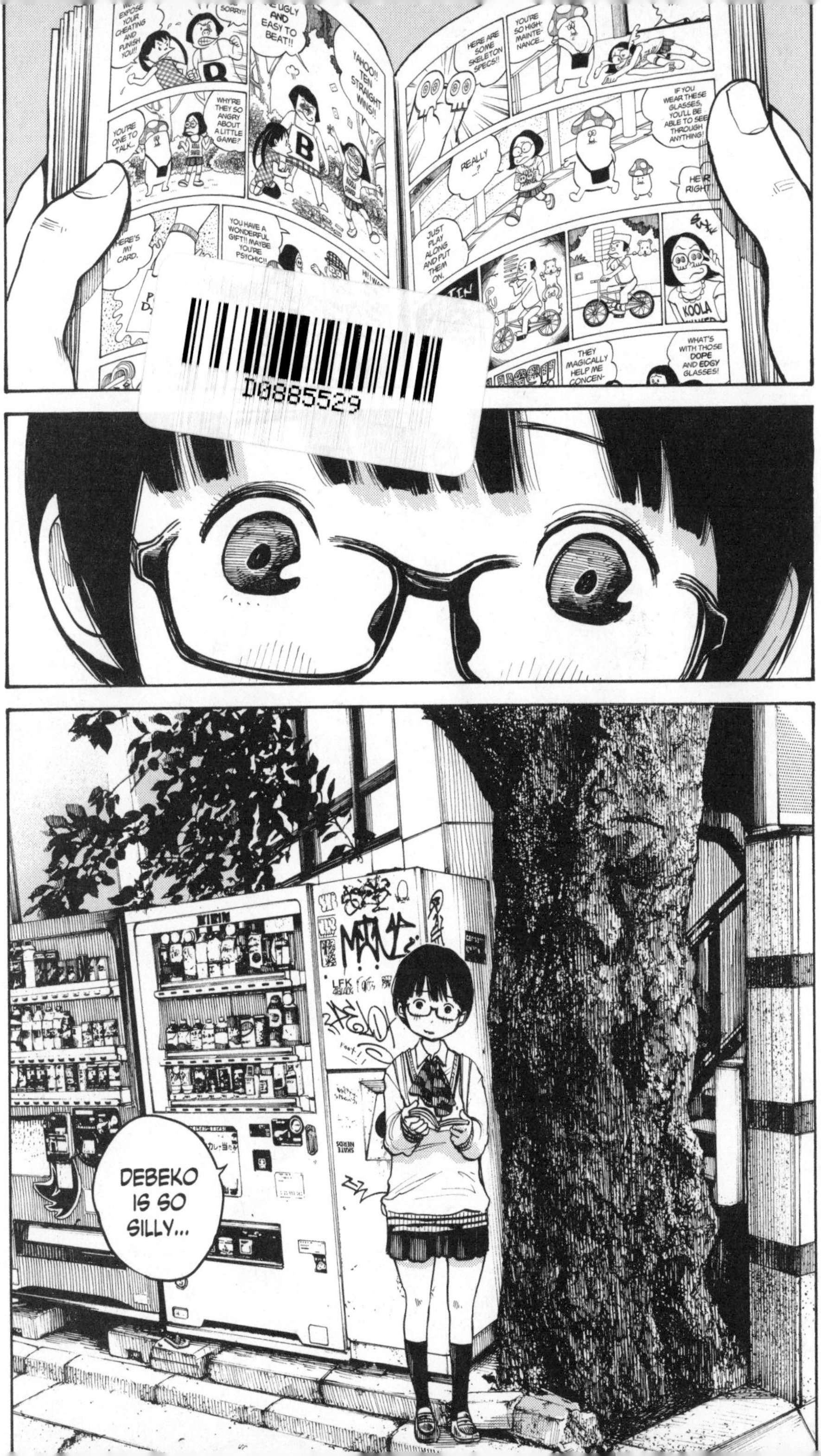
YOU'RE SO HIGH-MAINTENANCE...
HERE ARE SOME SKELETON SPECS!!
IF YOU WEAR THESE GLASSES, YOU'LL BE ABLE TO SEE THROUGH ANYTHING!
REALLY ...?
JUST PLAY ALONG AND PUT THEM ON.
KOOLA
WHAT'S WITH THOSE DOPE AND EDGY GLASSES!
THEY MAGICALLY HELP ME CONCEN-
YAHOO!! TEN STRAIGHT WINS!!
AND EASY TO BEAT!!
SORRY!!
EXPOSE YOUR CHEATING AND PUNISH YOU!!
WHY'RE THEY SO ANGRY ABOUT A LITTLE GAME?
YOU'RE ONE TO TALK.
YOU HAVE A WONDERFUL GIFT!! MAYBE YOU'RE PSYCHIC!!
HERE'S MY CARD.
DEBEKO IS SO SILLY...
SKATE NERDS

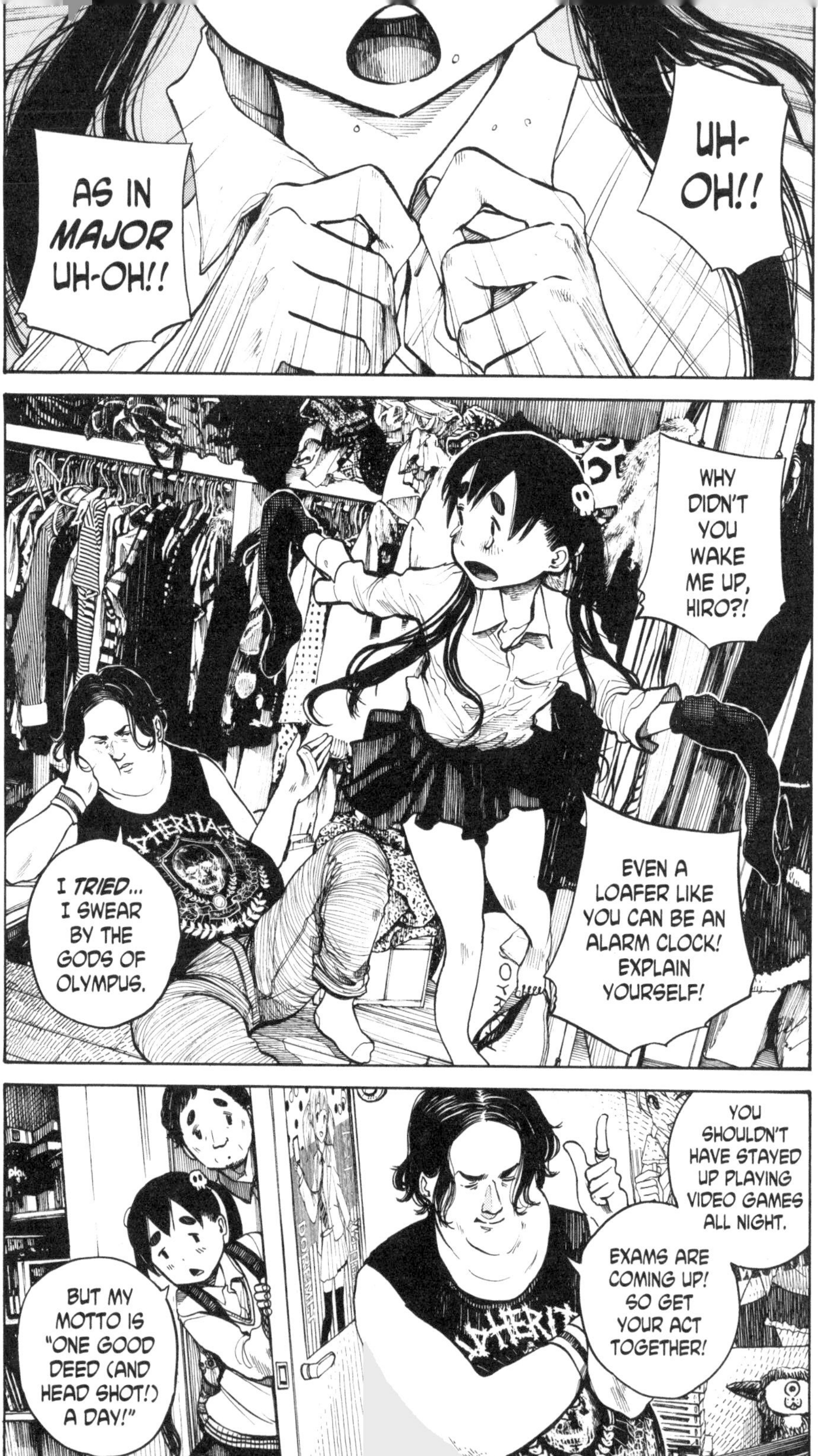
UH-OH!!
AS IN *MAJOR* UH-OH!!
WHY DIDN'T YOU WAKE ME UP, HIRO?!
EVEN A LOAFER LIKE YOU CAN BE AN ALARM CLOCK! EXPLAIN YOURSELF!
I *TRIED*... I SWEAR BY THE GODS OF OLYMPUS.
YOU SHOULDN'T HAVE STAYED UP PLAYING VIDEO GAMES ALL NIGHT.
EXAMS ARE COMING UP! SO GET YOUR ACT TOGETHER!
BUT MY MOTTO IS "ONE GOOD DEED (AND HEAD SHOT!) A DAY!"

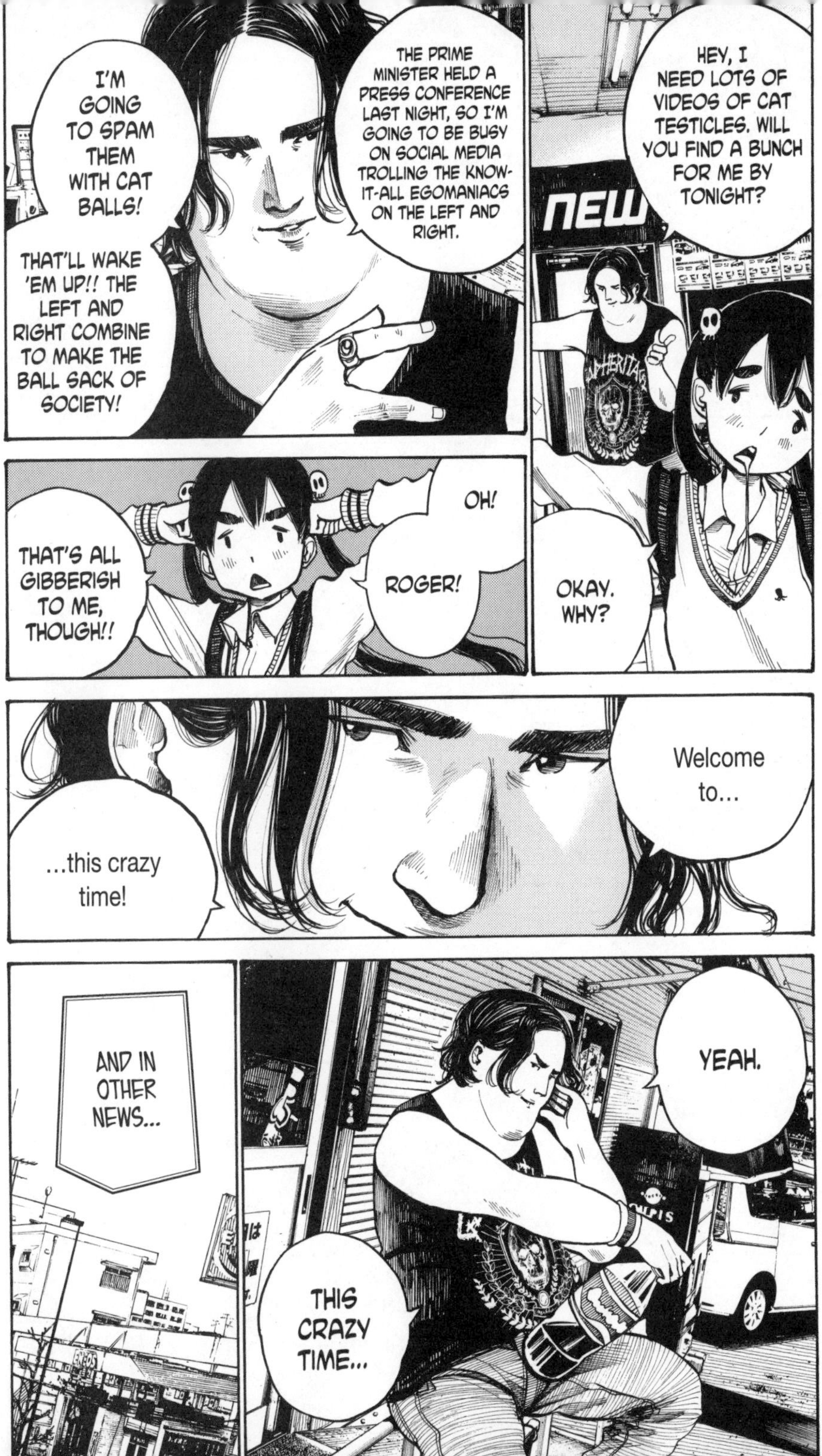
HEY, I NEED LOTS OF VIDEOS OF CAT TESTICLES. WILL YOU FIND A BUNCH FOR ME BY TONIGHT?
NEW
OKAY. WHY?
THE PRIME MINISTER HELD A PRESS CONFERENCE LAST NIGHT, SO I'M GOING TO BE BUSY ON SOCIAL MEDIA TROLLING THE KNOW-IT-ALL EGOMANIACS ON THE LEFT AND RIGHT.
I'M GOING TO SPAM THEM WITH CAT BALLS!
THAT'LL WAKE 'EM UP!! THE LEFT AND RIGHT COMBINE TO MAKE THE BALL SACK OF SOCIETY!
OH!
ROGER!
THAT'S ALL GIBBERISH TO ME, THOUGH!!
Welcome to...
...this crazy time!
YEAH.
THIS CRAZY TIME...
AND IN OTHER NEWS...

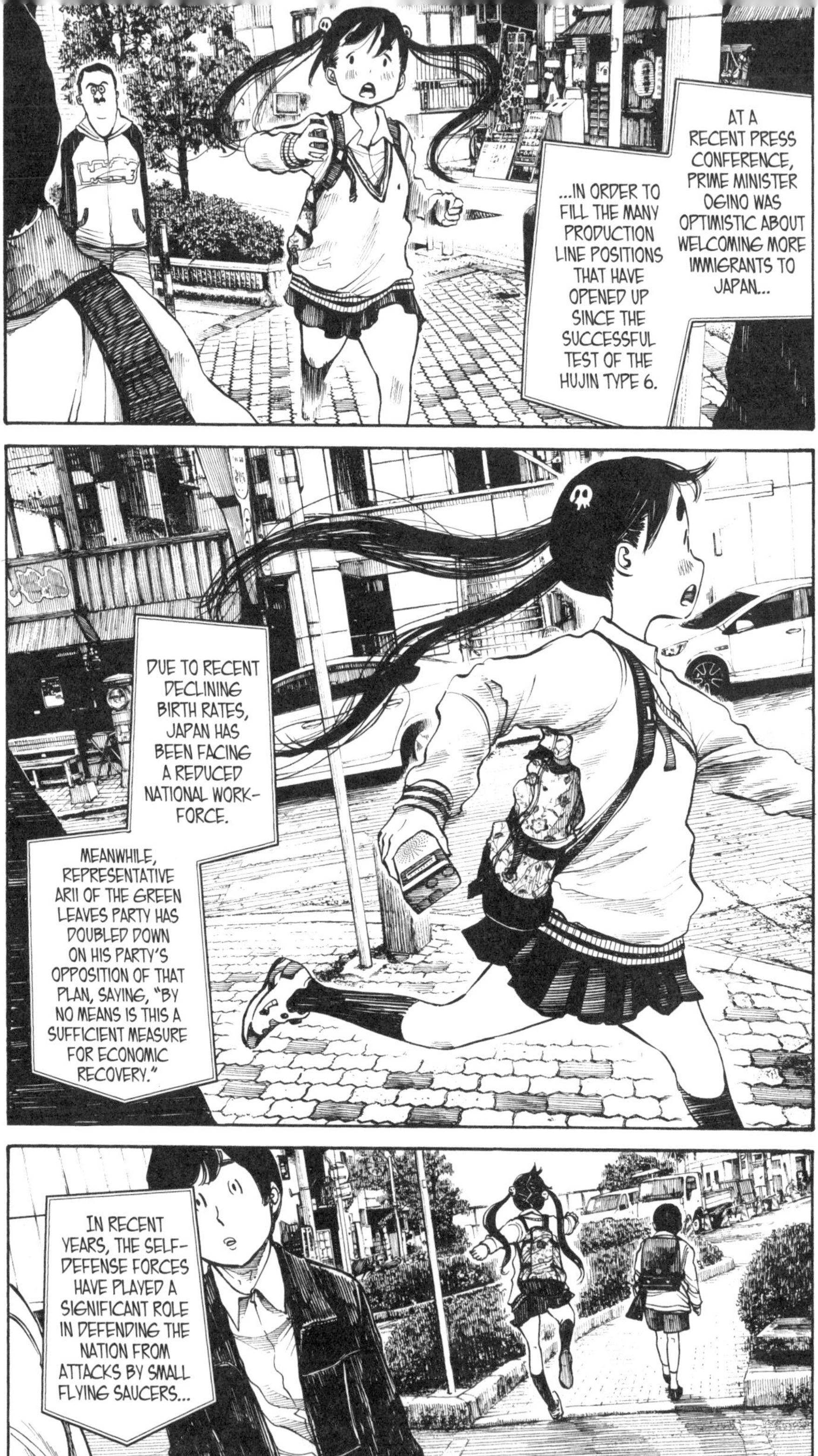
AT A RECENT PRESS CONFERENCE, PRIME MINISTER OGINO WAS OPTIMISTIC ABOUT WELCOMING MORE IMMIGRANTS TO JAPAN...
...IN ORDER TO FILL THE MANY PRODUCTION LINE POSITIONS THAT HAVE OPENED UP SINCE THE SUCCESSFUL TEST OF THE HUJIN TYPE 6.
DUE TO RECENT DECLINING BIRTH RATES, JAPAN HAS BEEN FACING A REDUCED NATIONAL WORK-FORCE.
MEANWHILE, REPRESENTATIVE ARII OF THE GREEN LEAVES PARTY HAS DOUBLED DOWN ON HIS PARTY'S OPPOSITION OF THAT PLAN, SAYING, "BY NO MEANS IS THIS A SUFFICIENT MEASURE FOR ECONOMIC RECOVERY."
IN RECENT YEARS, THE SELF-DEFENSE FORCES HAVE PLAYED A SIGNIFICANT ROLE IN DEFENDING THE NATION FROM ATTACKS BY SMALL FLYING SAUCERS...

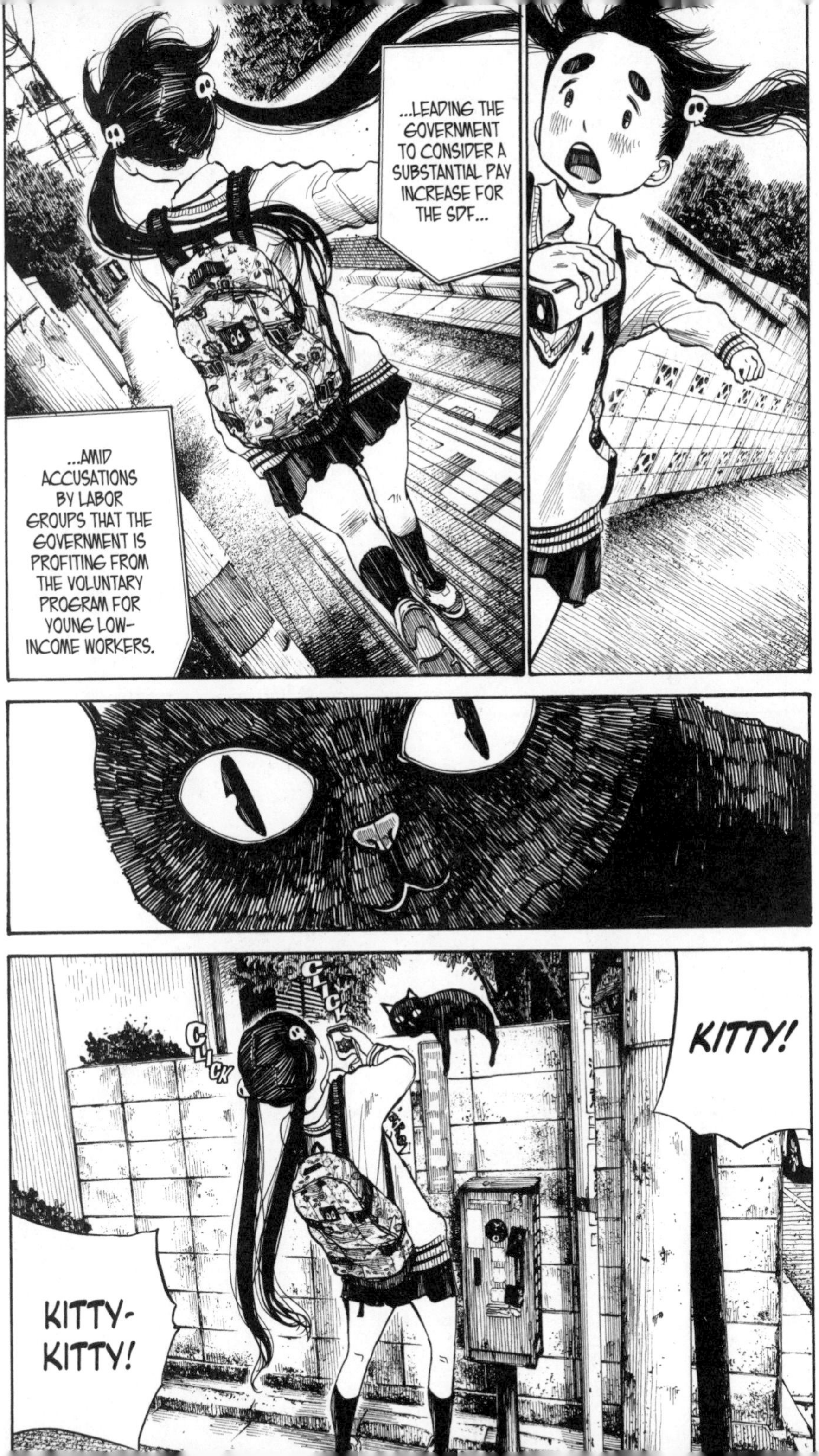
...LEADING THE GOVERNMENT TO CONSIDER A SUBSTANTIAL PAY INCREASE FOR THE SDF...
...AMID ACCUSATIONS BY LABOR GROUPS THAT THE GOVERNMENT IS PROFITING FROM THE VOLUNTARY PROGRAM FOR YOUNG LOW-INCOME WORKERS.
KITTY!
CLICK
CLICK
KITTY-KITTY!

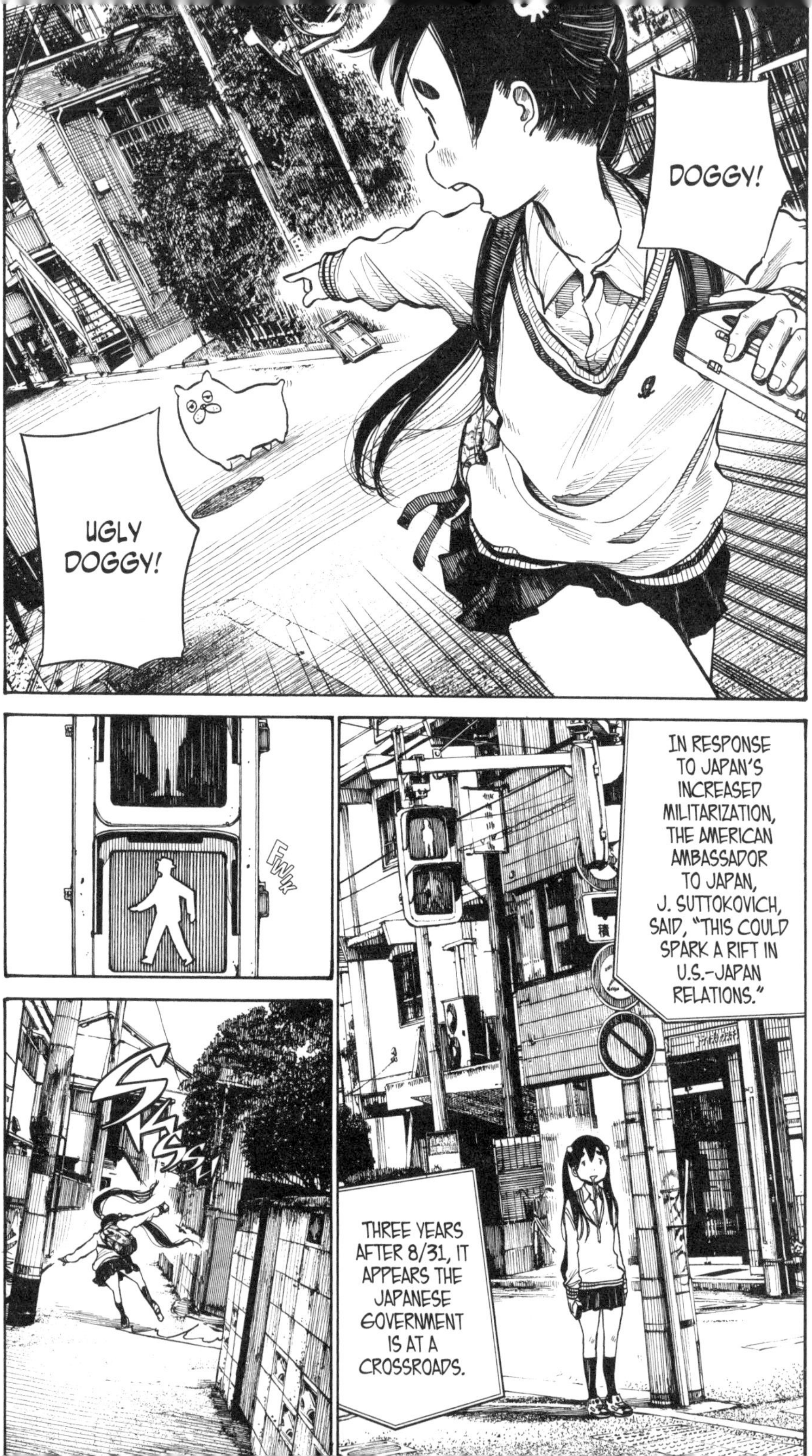
DOGGY!
UGLY DOGGY!
IN RESPONSE TO JAPAN'S INCREASED MILITARIZATION, THE AMERICAN AMBASSADOR TO JAPAN, J. SUTTOKOVICH, SAID, "THIS COULD SPARK A RIFT IN U.S.-JAPAN RELATIONS."
THREE YEARS AFTER 8/31, IT APPEARS THE JAPANESE GOVERNMENT IS AT A CROSSROADS.
FWIK

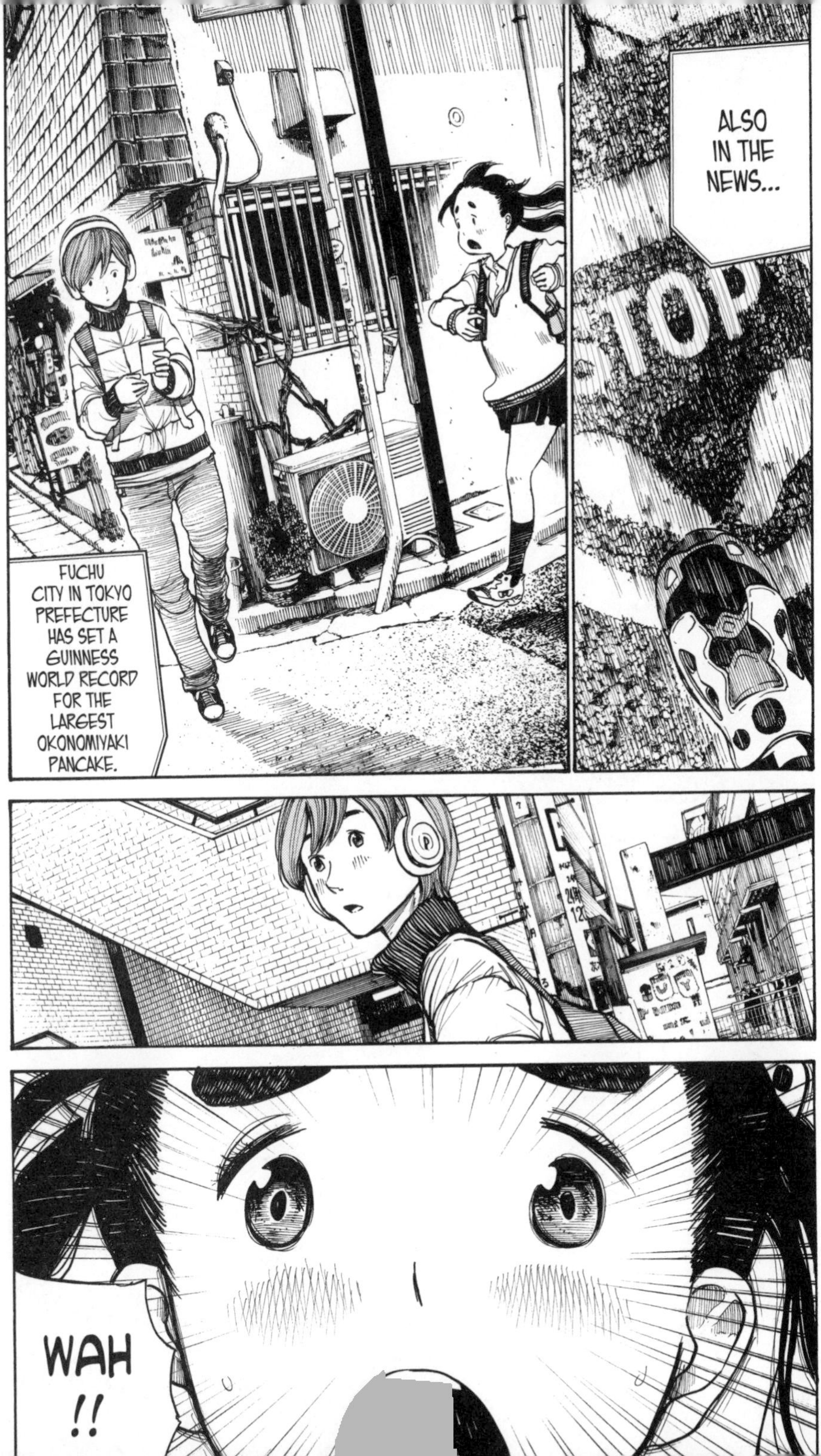
ALSO IN THE NEWS...
FUCHU CITY IN TOKYO PREFECTURE HAS SET A GUINNESS WORLD RECORD FOR THE LARGEST OKONOMIYAKI PANCAKE.
WAH !!

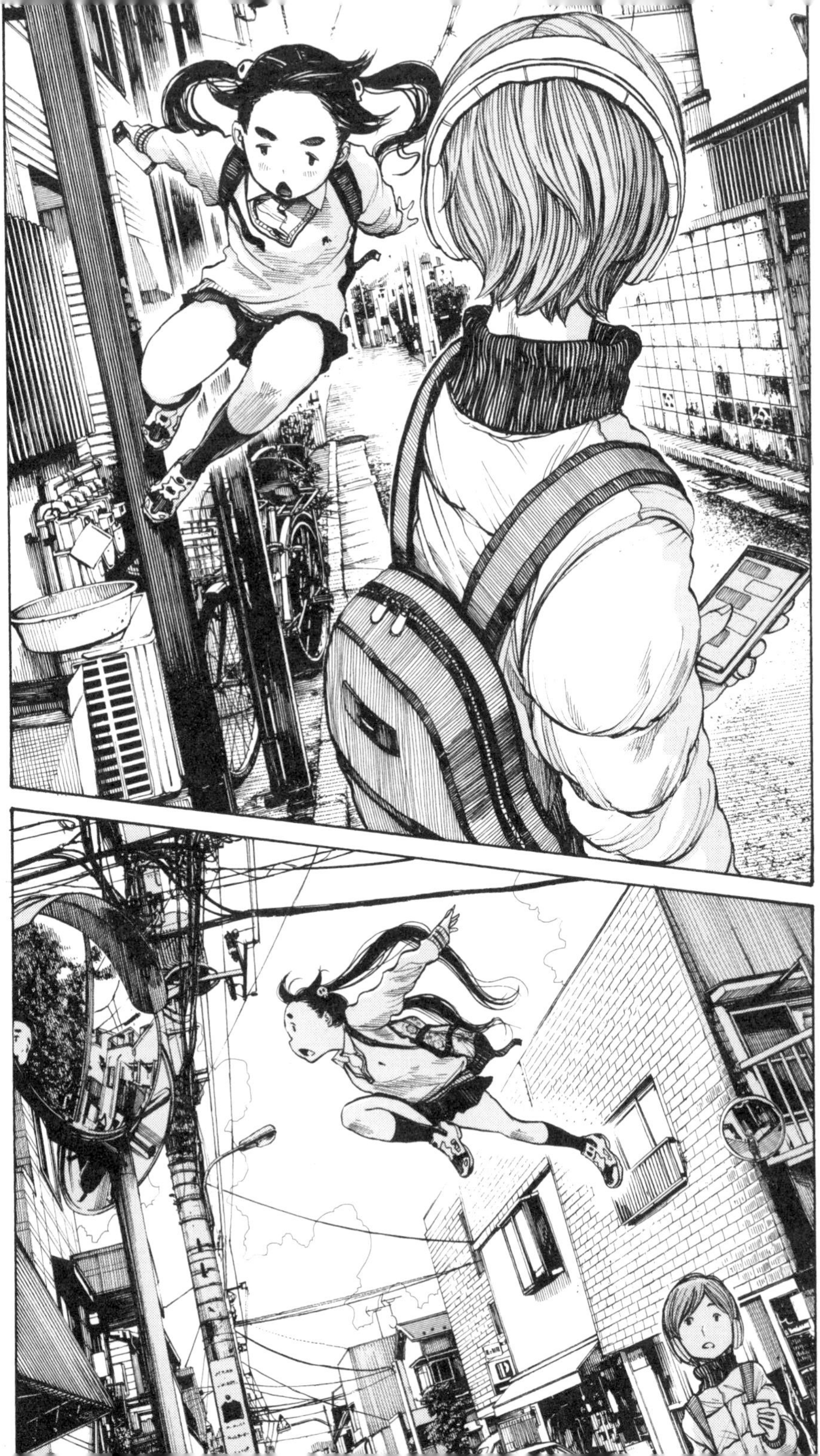

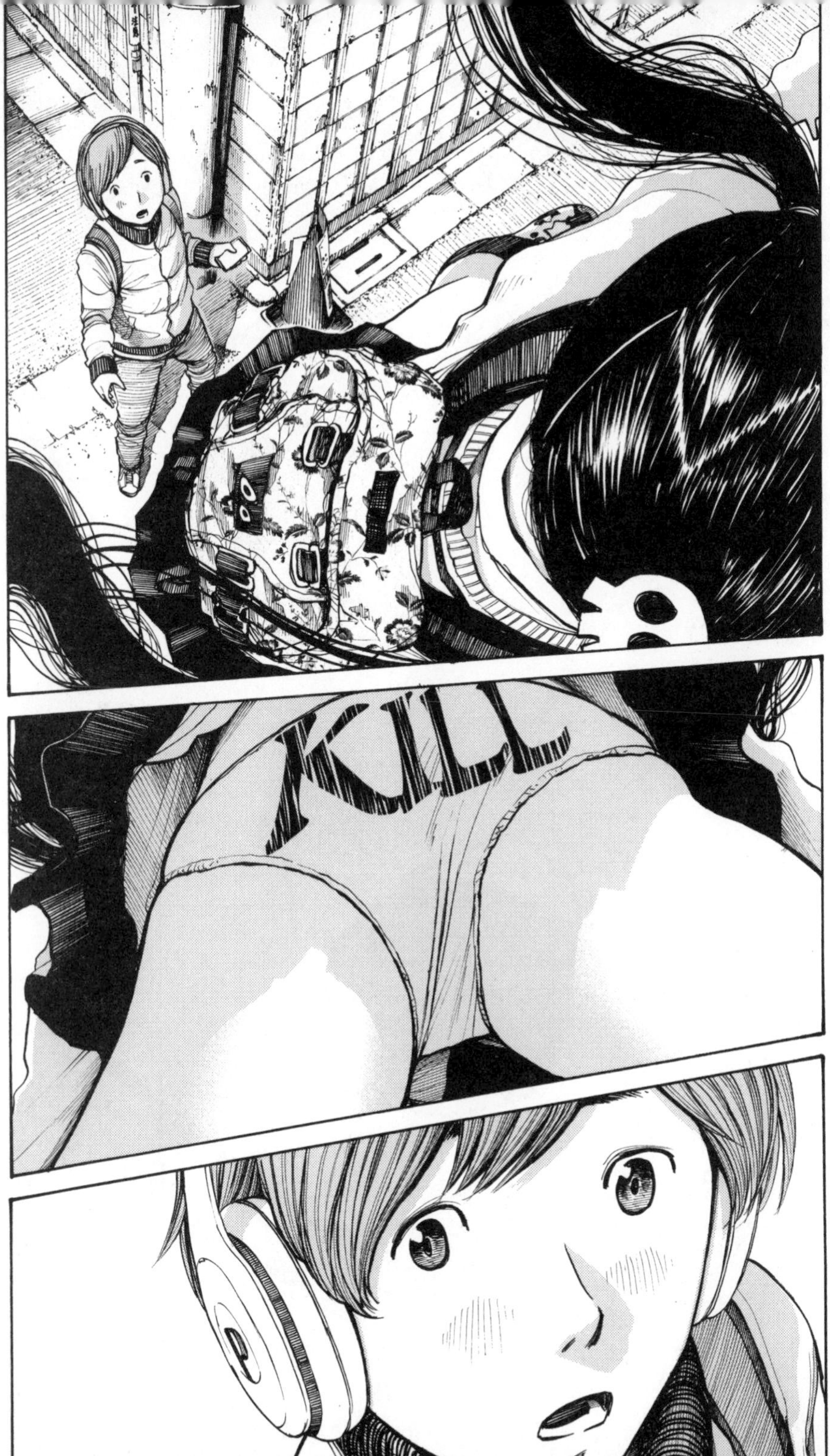
KILL

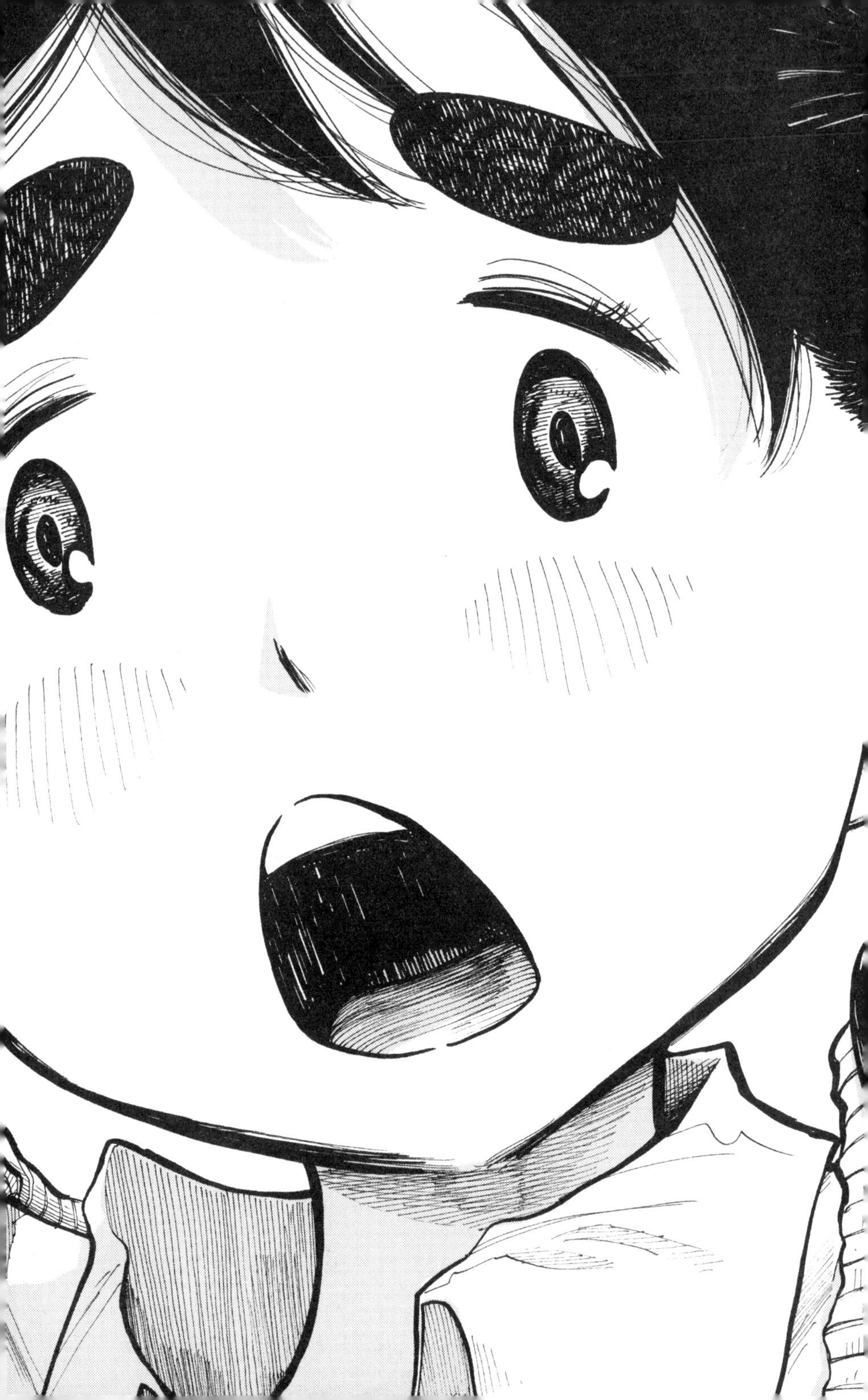

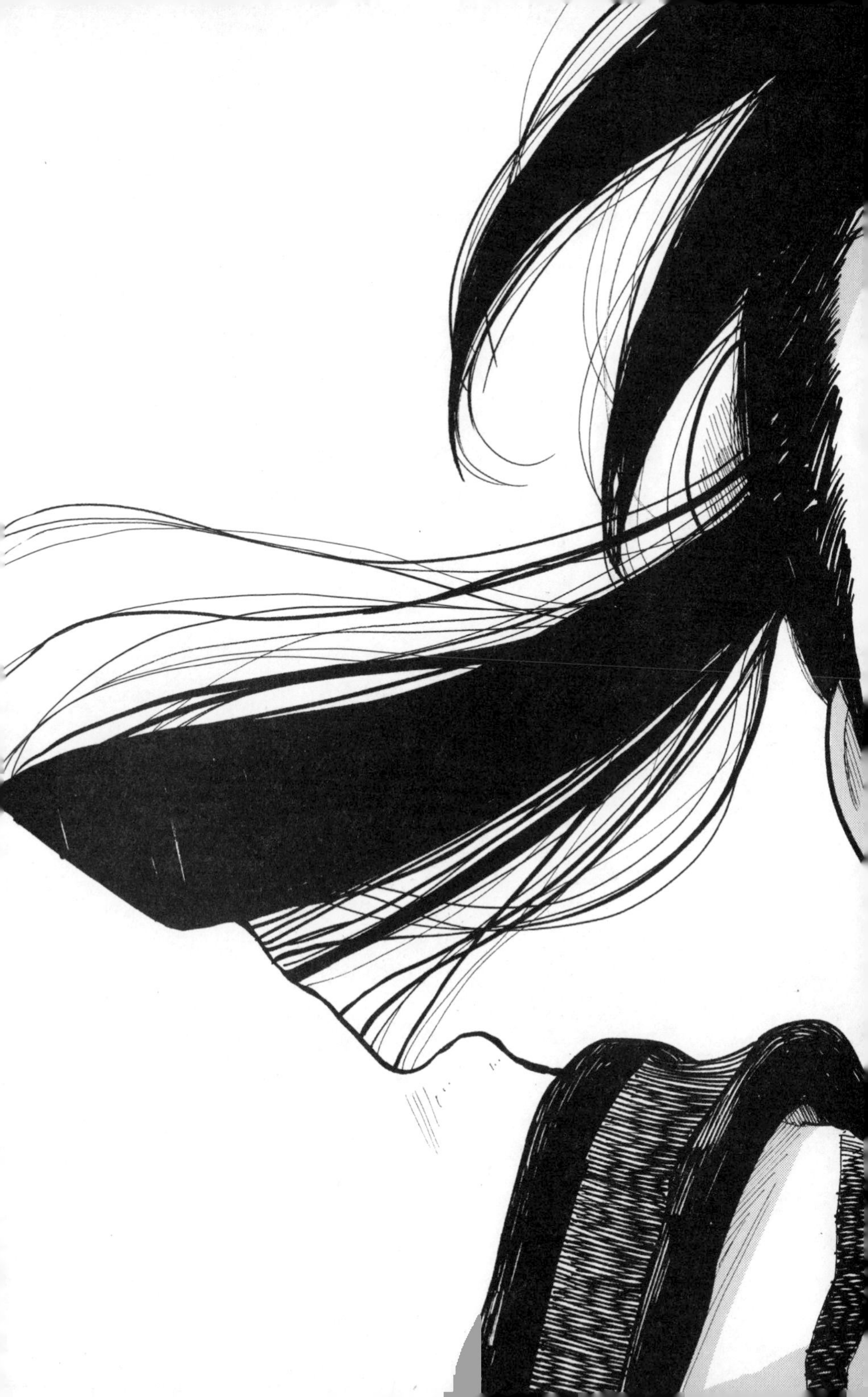

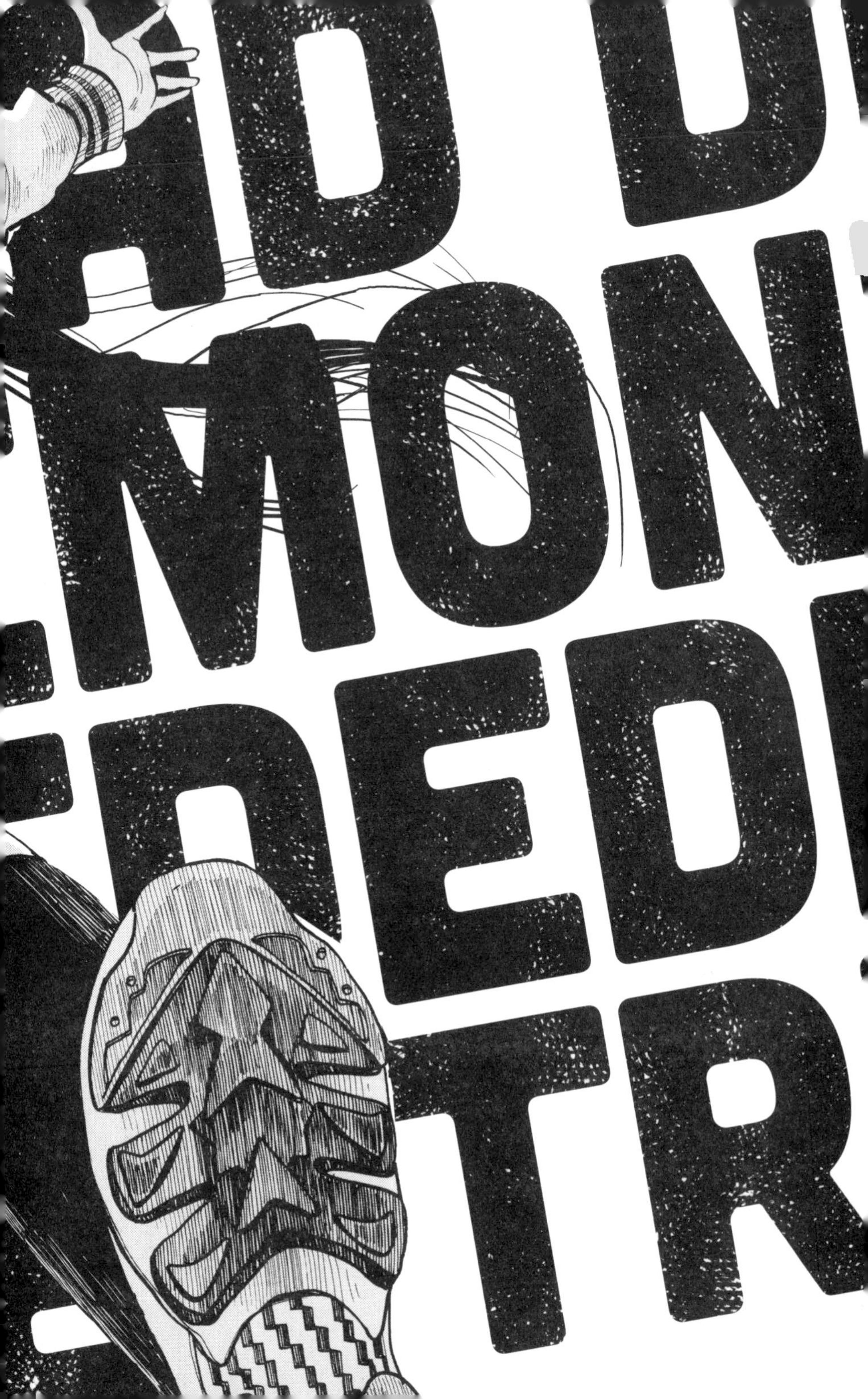

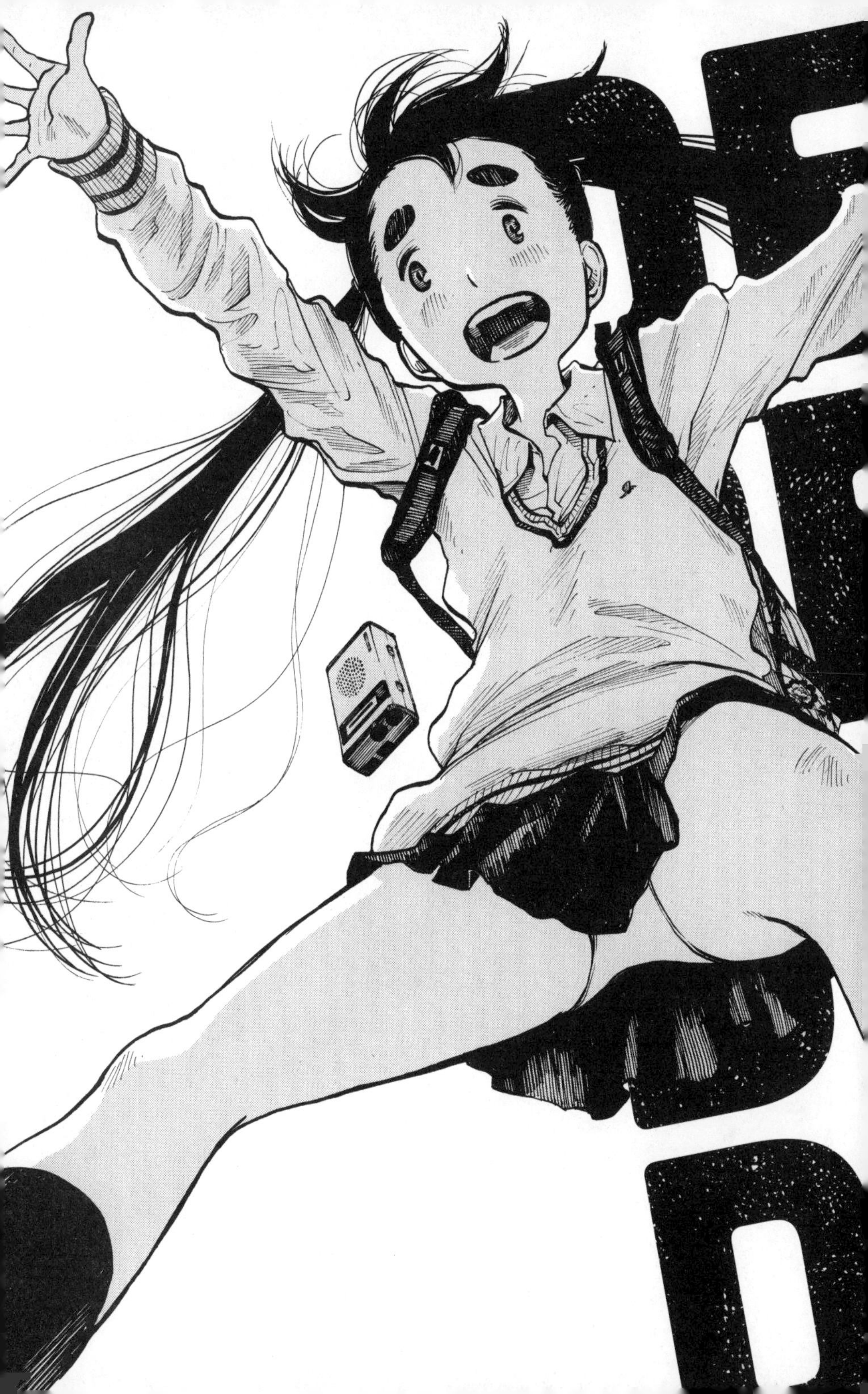

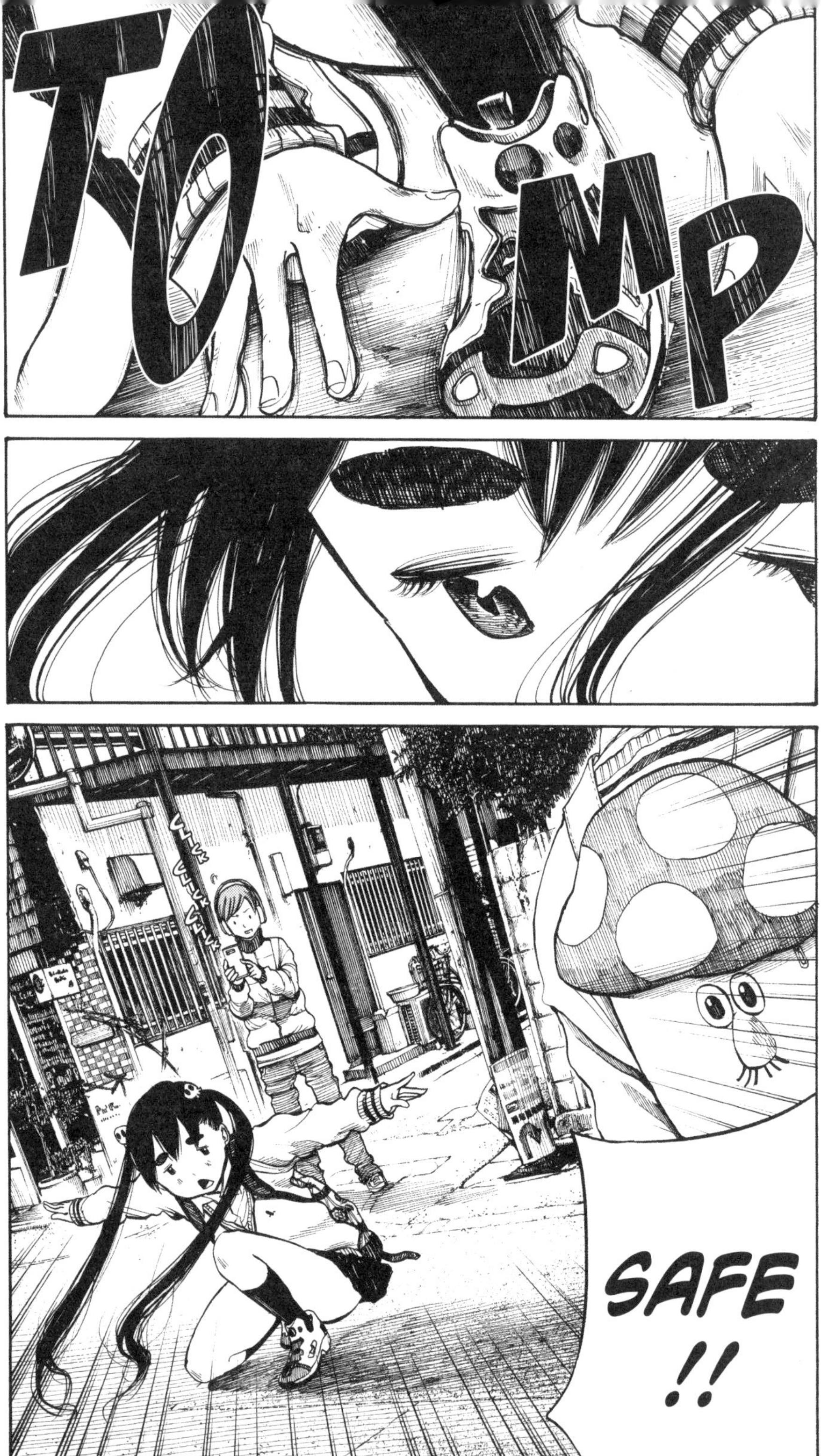
TOMP
CLICK CLICK CLICK
SAFE !!

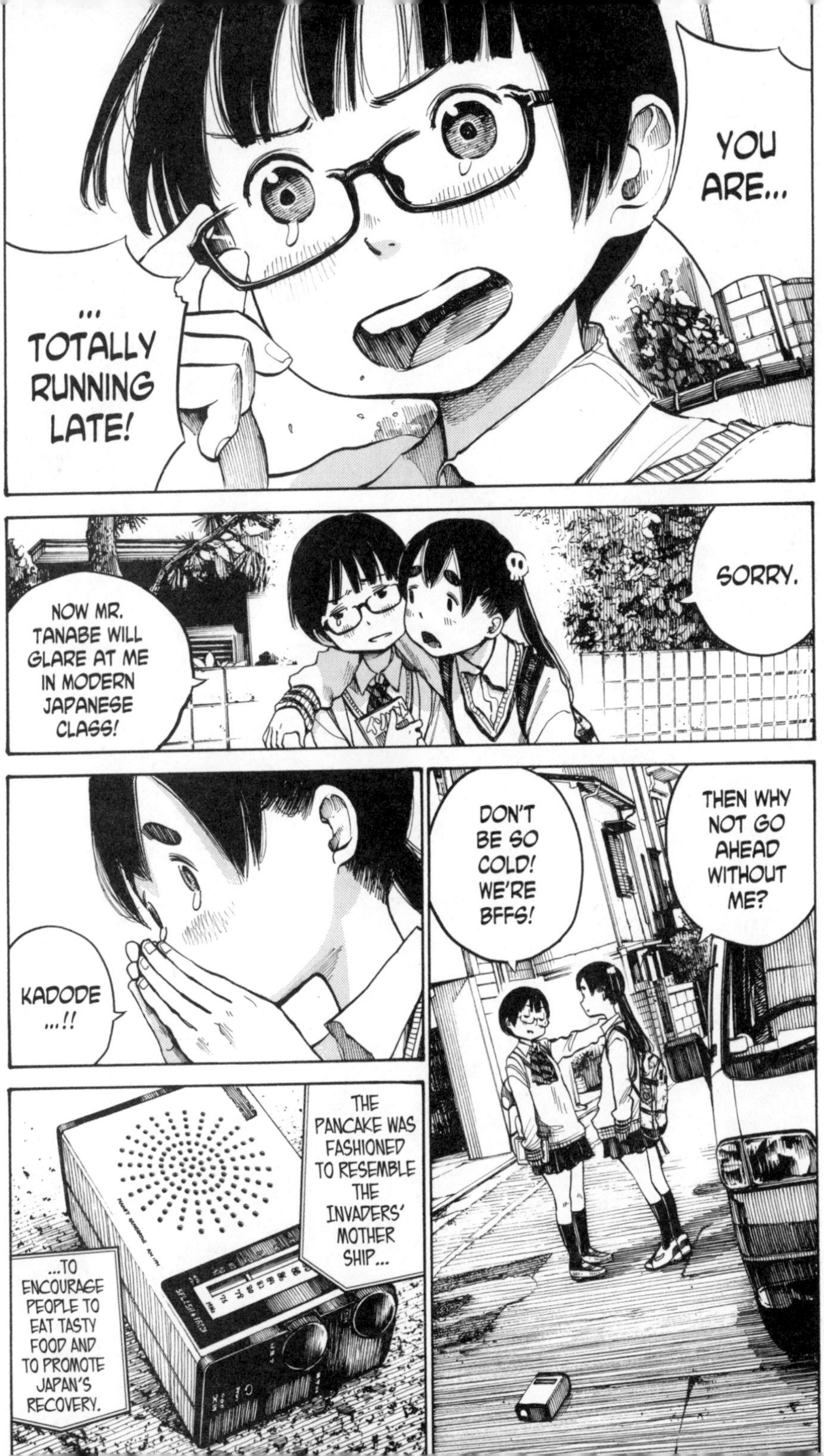
YOU ARE...
...TOTALLY RUNNING LATE!
SORRY.
NOW MR. TANABE WILL GLARE AT ME IN MODERN JAPANESE CLASS!
THEN WHY NOT GO AHEAD WITHOUT ME?
DON'T BE SO COLD! WE'RE BFFS!
KADODE ...!!
THE PANCAKE WAS FASHIONED TO RESEMBLE THE INVADERS' MOTHER SHIP...
...TO ENCOURAGE PEOPLE TO EAT TASTY FOOD AND TO PROMOTE JAPAN'S RECOVERY.

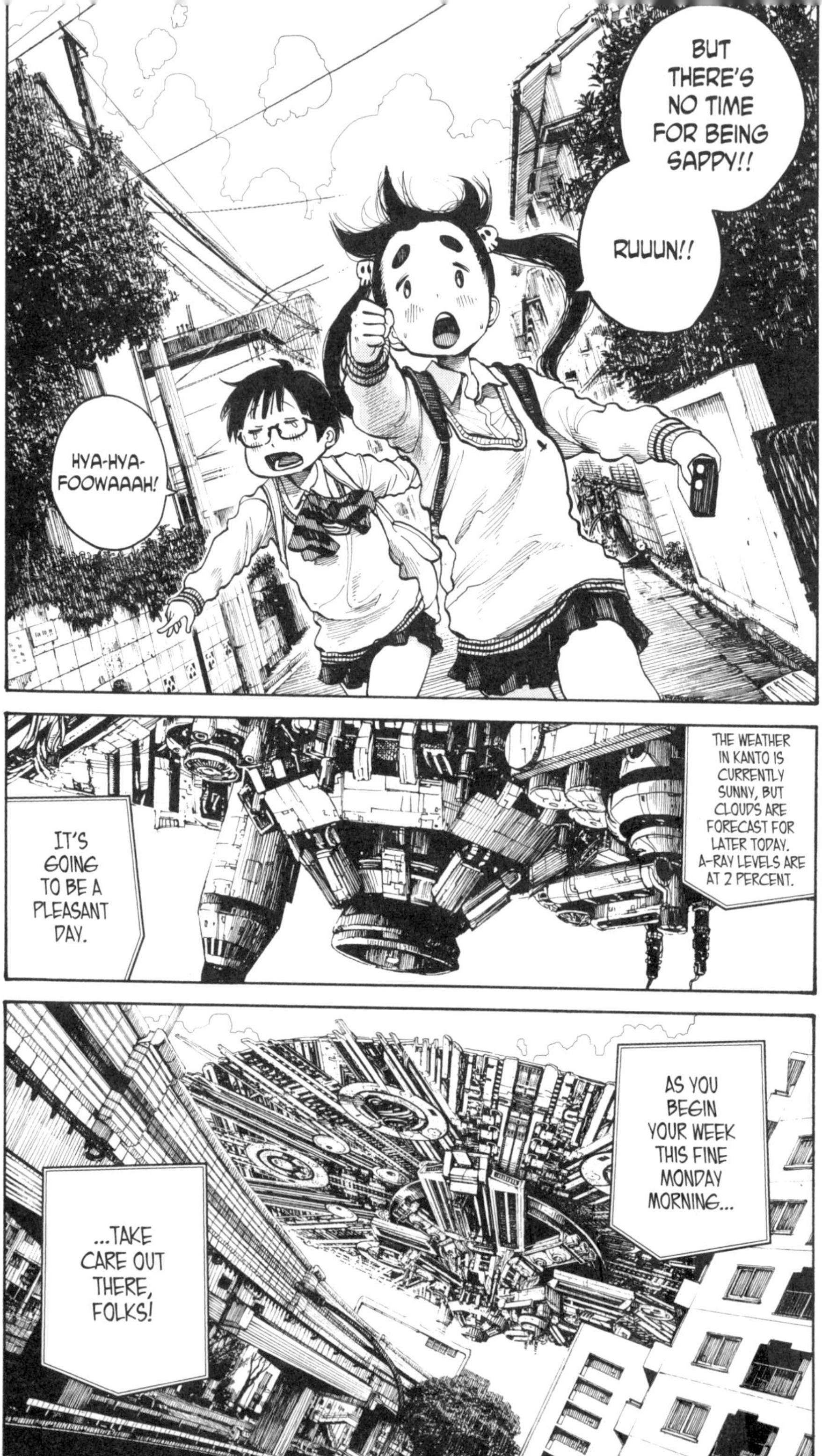
BUT THERE'S NO TIME FOR BEING SAPPY!!
RUUUN!!
HYA-HYA-FOOWAAAH!
THE WEATHER IN KANTO IS CURRENTLY SUNNY, BUT CLOUDS ARE FORECAST FOR LATER TODAY. A-RAY LEVELS ARE AT 2 PERCENT.
IT'S GOING TO BE A PLEASANT DAY.
AS YOU BEGIN YOUR WEEK THIS FINE MONDAY MORNING...
...TAKE CARE OUT THERE, FOLKS!

DEDE DE DE

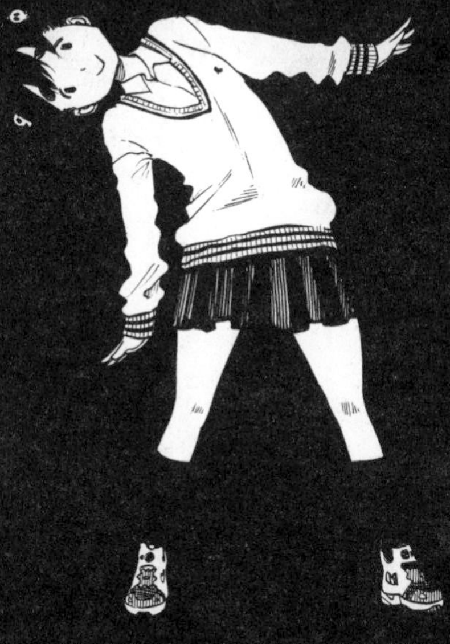

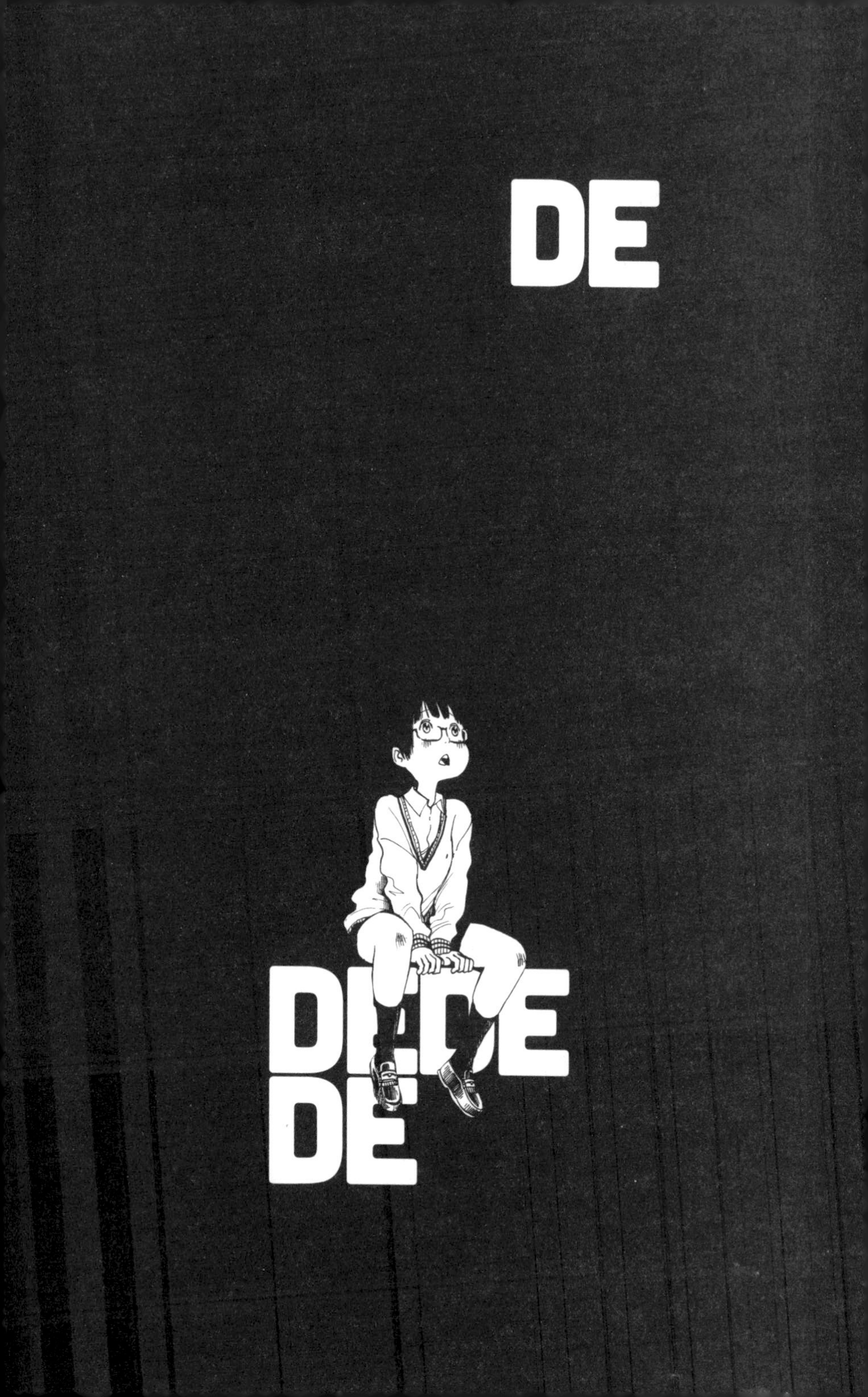
DE
DEDE
DE

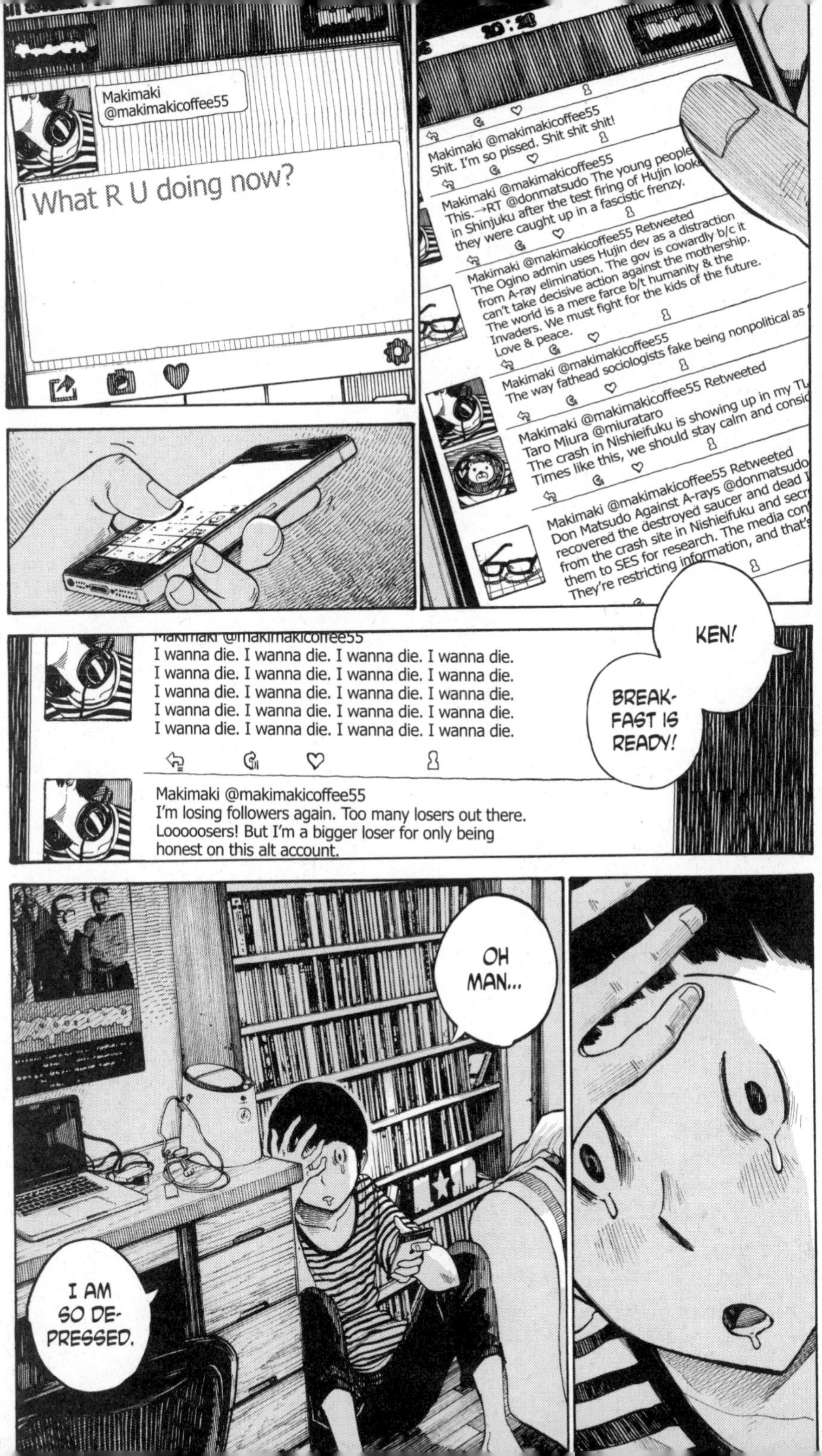
Makimaki @makimakicoffee55
Shit. I'm so pissed. Shit shit shit!
Makimaki @makimakicoffee55
This.→RT @donmatsudo The young people
in Shinjuku after the test firing of Hujin
they were caught up in a fascistic frenzy.
Makimaki @makimakicoffee55 Retweeted
The Ogino admin uses Hujin dev as a distraction
from A-ray elimination. The gov is cowardly b/c it
can't take decisive action against the mothership.
The world is a mere farce b/t humanity & the
Invaders. We must fight for the kids of the future.
Love & peace.
Makimaki @makimakicoffee55
The way fathead sociologists fake being nonpolitical as
Makimaki @makimakicoffee55 Retweeted
Taro Miura @miurataro
The crash in Nishieifuku is showing up in my
Times like this, we should stay calm and
Makimaki @makimakicoffee55 Retweeted
Don Matsudo Against A-rays @donmatsudo
recovered the destroyed saucer and dead
from the crash site in Nishieifuku and
them to SES for research. The media
They're restricting information, and
Makimaki
@makimakicoffee55
What R U doing now?
I wanna die. I wanna die. I wanna die. I wanna die.
I wanna die. I wanna die. I wanna die. I wanna die.
I wanna die. I wanna die. I wanna die. I wanna die.
I wanna die. I wanna die. I wanna die. I wanna die.
I wanna die. I wanna die. I wanna die. I wanna die.
Makimaki @makimakicoffee55
I'm losing followers again. Too many losers out there.
Loooooosers! But I'm a bigger loser for only being
honest on this alt account.
KEN!
BREAKFAST IS READY!
OH MAN...
I AM SO DEPRESSED.

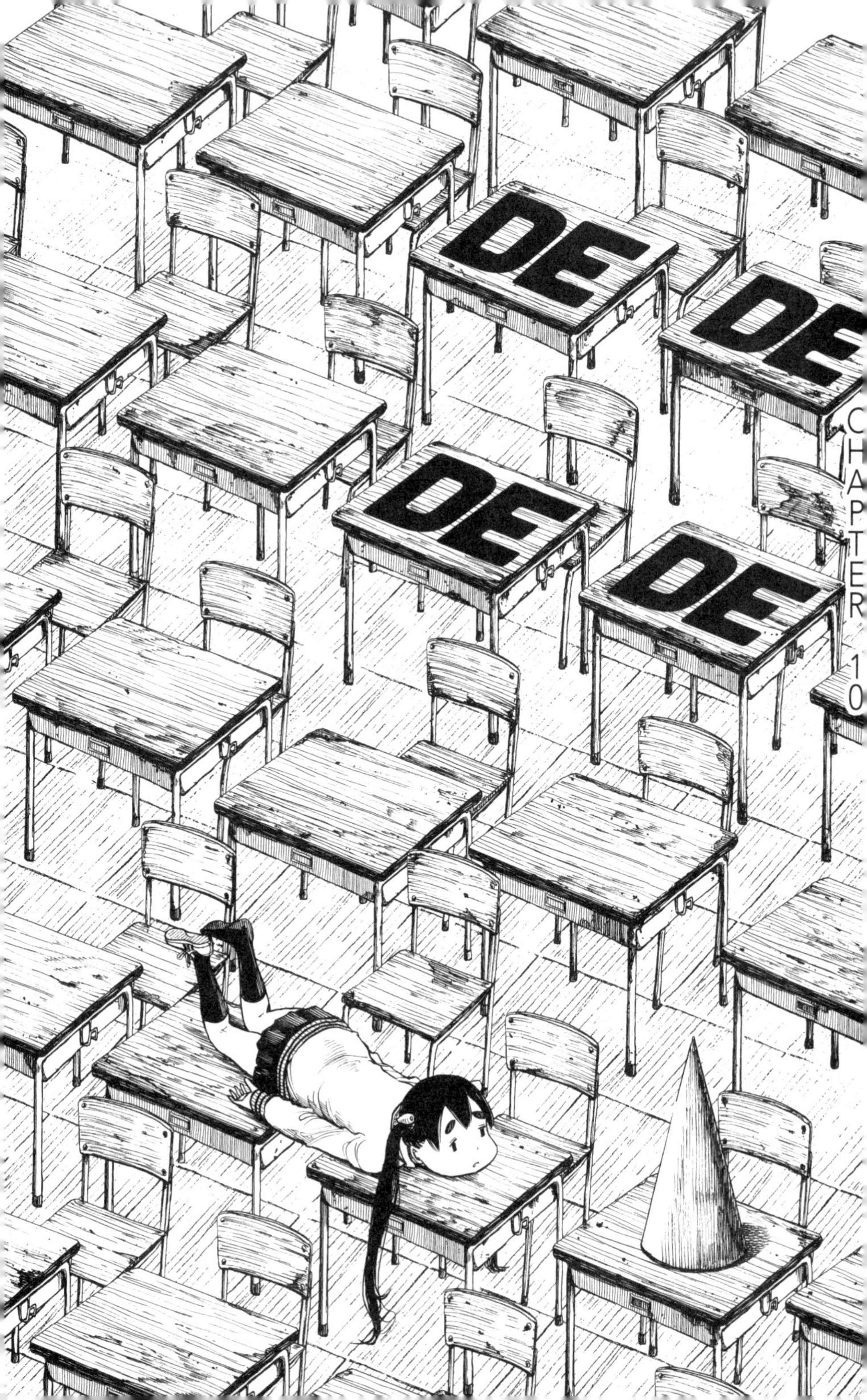
DE
DE
DE
DE
CHAPTER 10

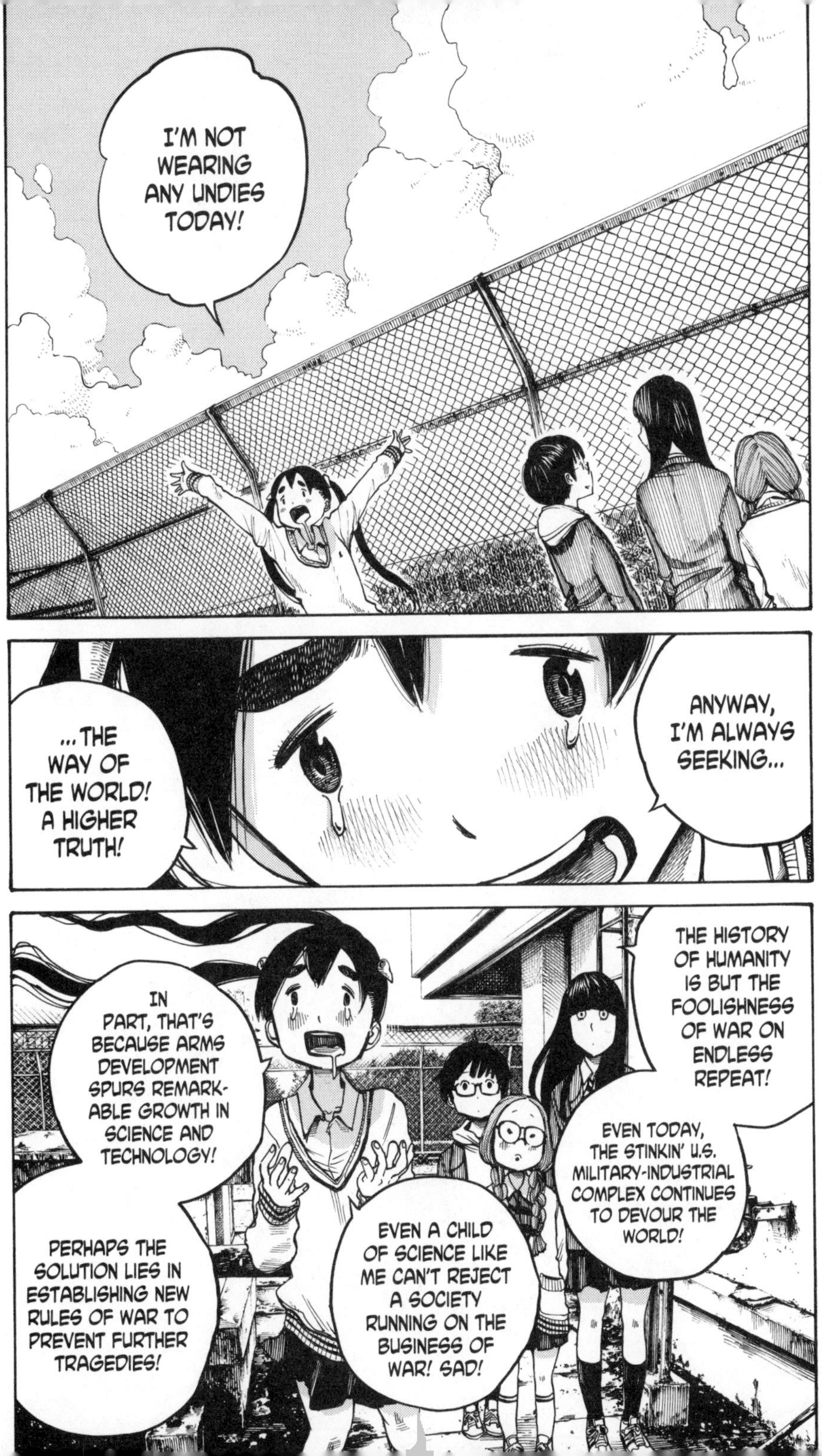
I'M NOT WEARING ANY UNDIES TODAY!
ANYWAY, I'M ALWAYS SEEKING...
...THE WAY OF THE WORLD! A HIGHER TRUTH!
THE HISTORY OF HUMANITY IS BUT THE FOOLISHNESS OF WAR ON ENDLESS REPEAT!
EVEN TODAY, THE STINKIN' U.S. MILITARY-INDUSTRIAL COMPLEX CONTINUES TO DEVOUR THE WORLD!
EVEN A CHILD OF SCIENCE LIKE ME CAN'T REJECT A SOCIETY RUNNING ON THE BUSINESS OF WAR! SAD!
IN PART, THAT'S BECAUSE ARMS DEVELOPMENT SPURS REMARK-ABLE GROWTH IN SCIENCE AND TECHNOLOGY!
PERHAPS THE SOLUTION LIES IN ESTABLISHING NEW RULES OF WAR TO PREVENT FURTHER TRAGEDIES!

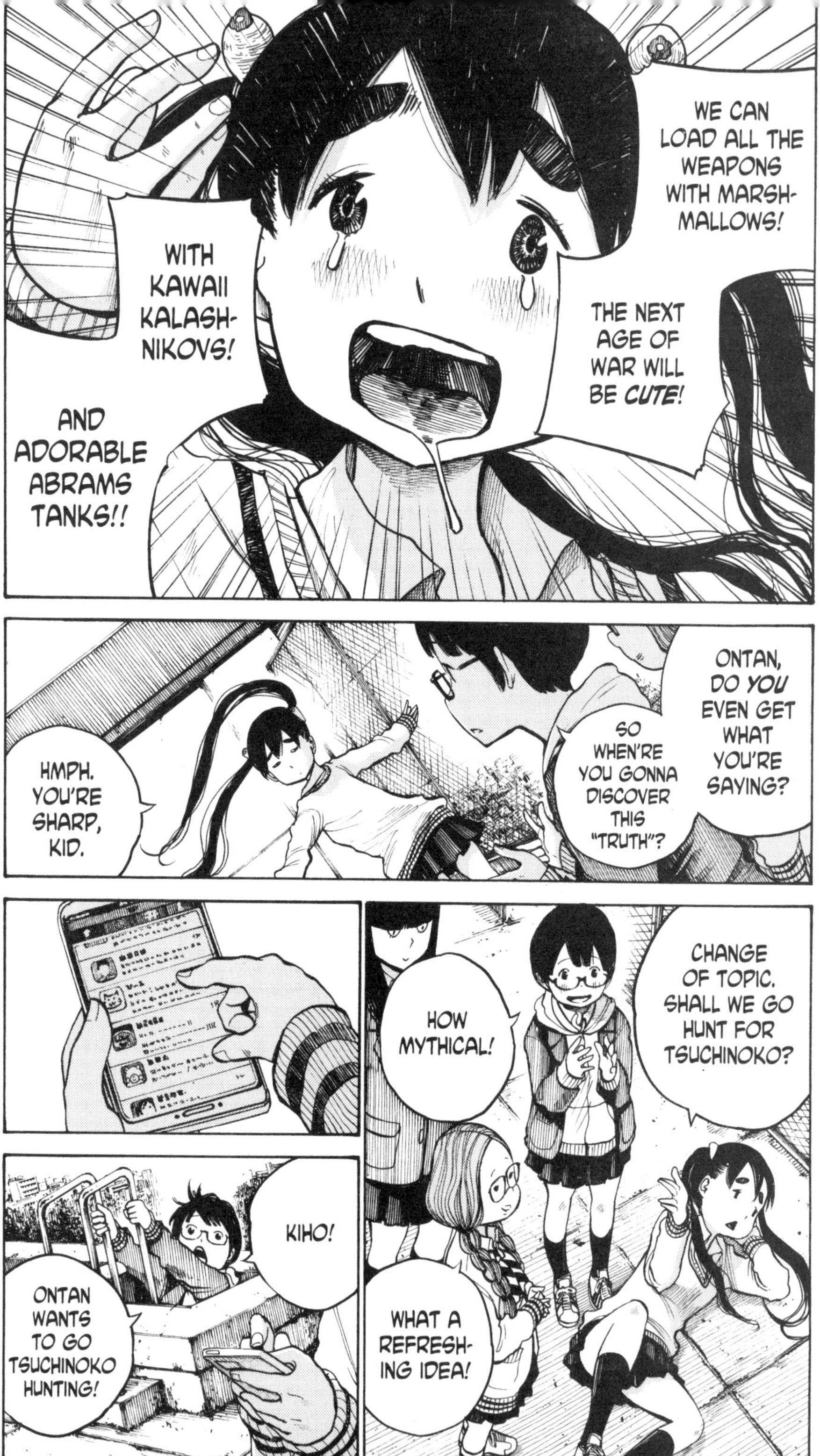
WE CAN LOAD ALL THE WEAPONS WITH MARSH-MALLOWS!
THE NEXT AGE OF WAR WILL BE *CUTE*!
WITH KAWAII KALASH-NIKOVS!
AND ADORABLE ABRAMS TANKS!!
ONTAN, DO *YOU* EVEN GET WHAT YOU'RE SAYING?
SO WHEN'RE YOU GONNA DISCOVER THIS "TRUTH"?
HMPH. YOU'RE SHARP, KID.
CHANGE OF TOPIC. SHALL WE GO HUNT FOR TSUCHINOKO?
HOW MYTHICAL!
WHAT A REFRESH-ING IDEA!
KIHO!
ONTAN WANTS TO GO TSUCHINOKO HUNTING!

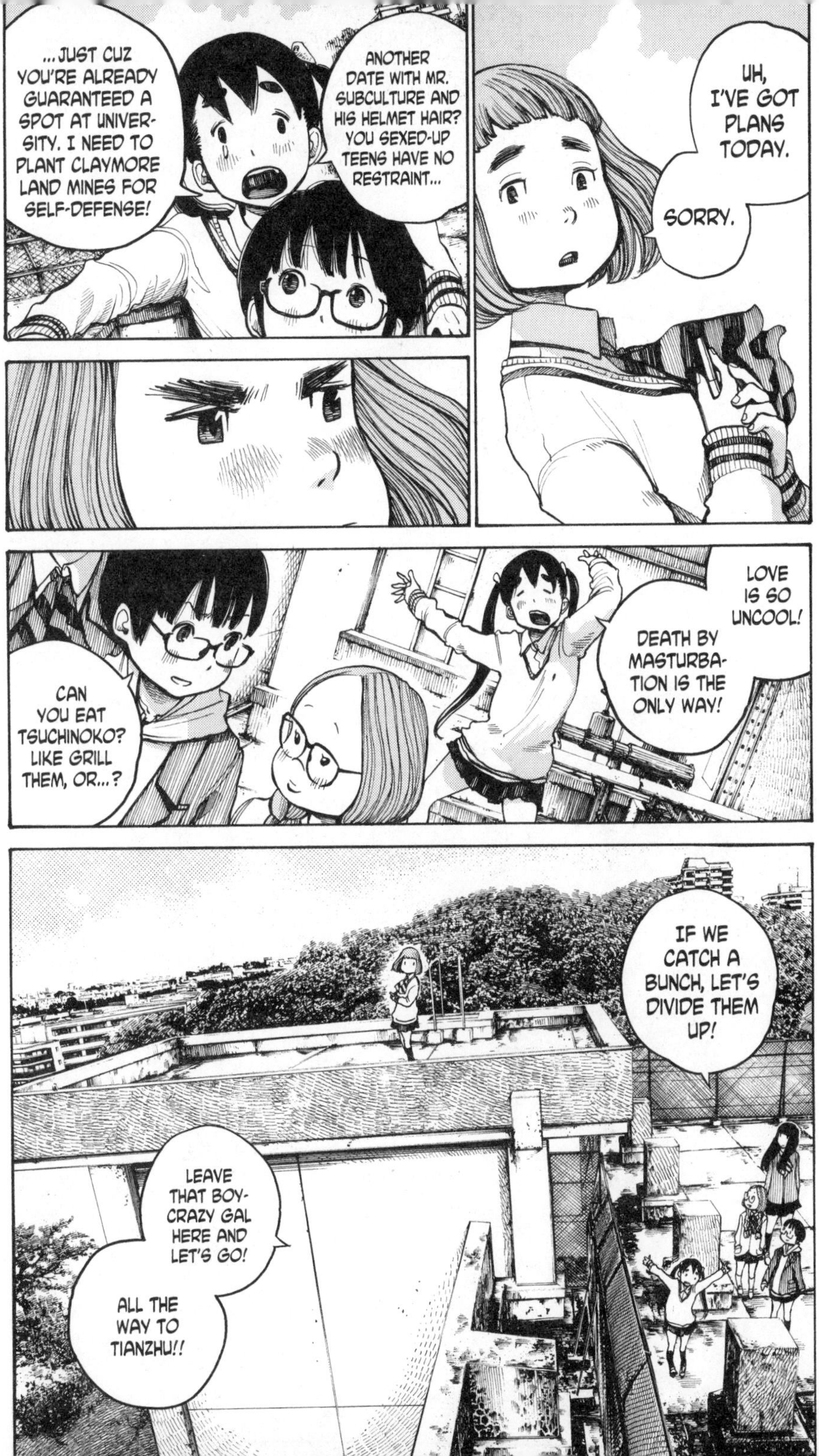
UH, I'VE GOT PLANS TODAY.
SORRY.
ANOTHER DATE WITH MR. SUBCULTURE AND HIS HELMET HAIR? YOU SEXED-UP TEENS HAVE NO RESTRAINT...
...JUST CUZ YOU'RE ALREADY GUARANTEED A SPOT AT UNIVERSITY. I NEED TO PLANT CLAYMORE LAND MINES FOR SELF-DEFENSE!
LOVE IS SO UNCOOL!
DEATH BY MASTURBATION IS THE ONLY WAY!
CAN YOU EAT TSUCHINOKO? LIKE GRILL THEM, OR...?
IF WE CATCH A BUNCH, LET'S DIVIDE THEM UP!
LEAVE THAT BOY-CRAZY GAL HERE AND LET'S GO!
ALL THE WAY TO TIANZHU!!

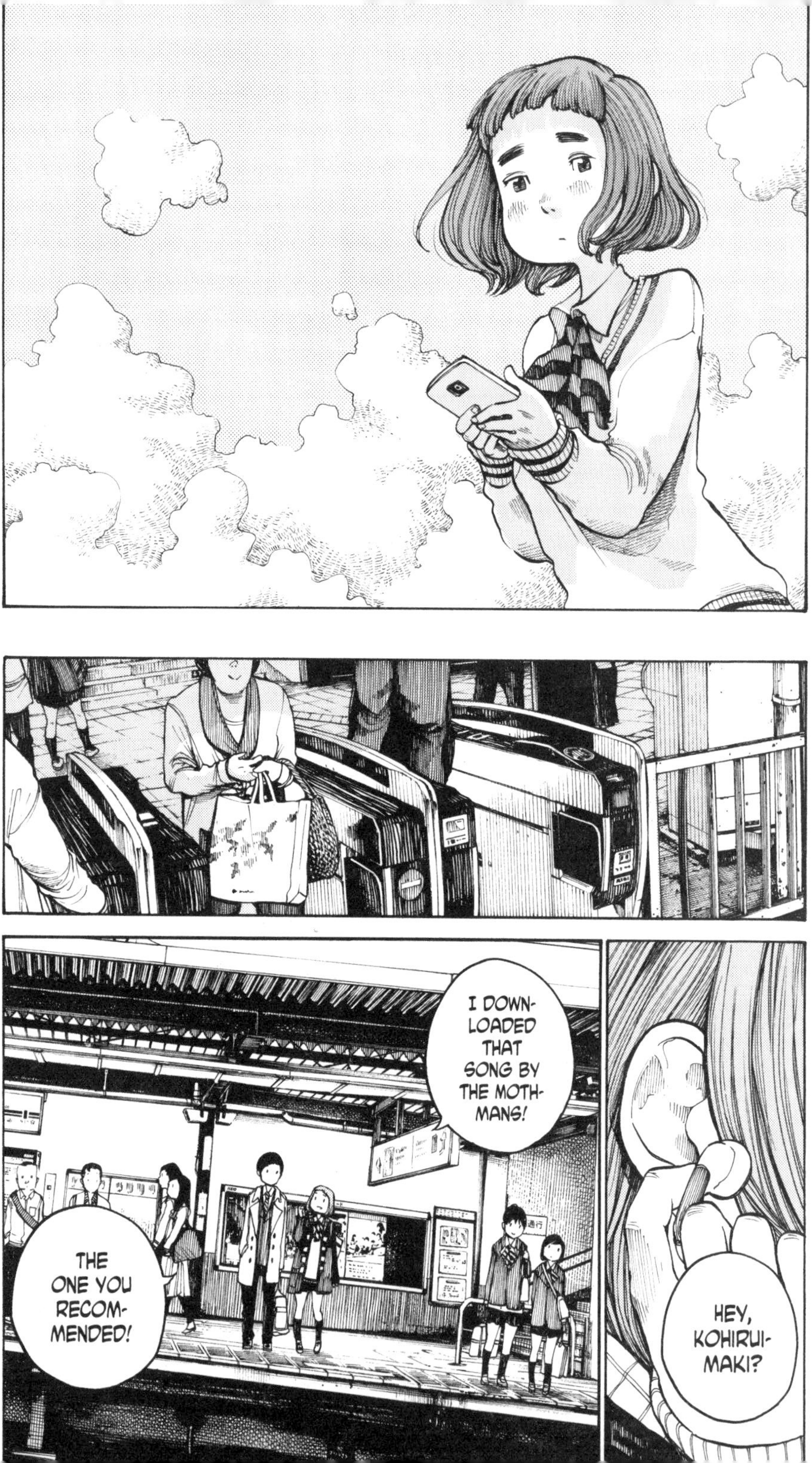
HEY, KOHIRUI-MAKI?
I DOWN-LOADED THAT SONG BY THE MOTH-MANS!
THE ONE YOU RECOM-MENDED!

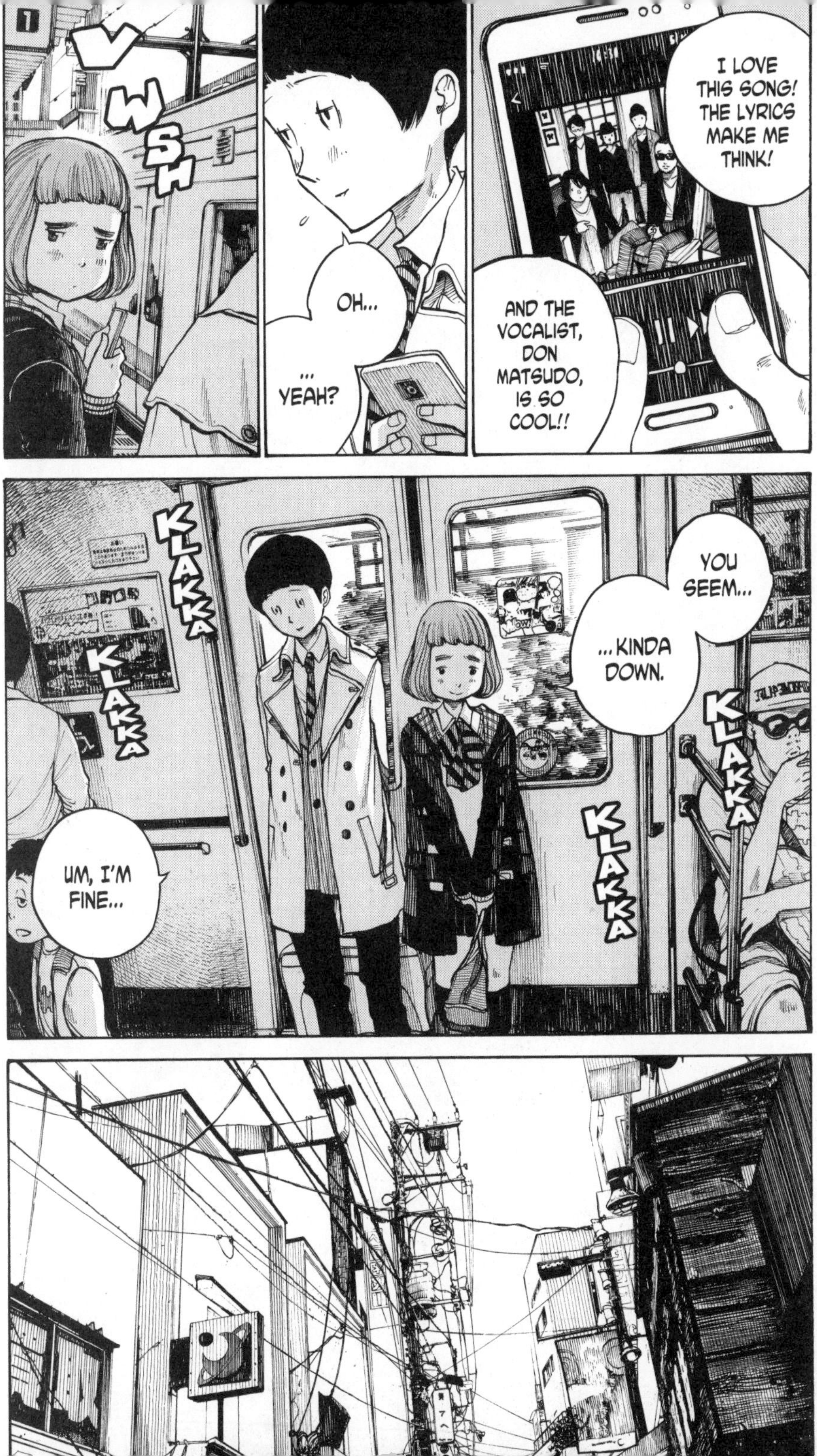
I LOVE THIS SONG! THE LYRICS MAKE ME THINK!
AND THE VOCALIST, DON MATSUDO, IS SO COOL!!
OH...
... YEAH?
VWSH
YOU SEEM...
...KINDA DOWN.
KLAKKA
KLAKKA
KLAKKA
KLAKKA
KLAKKA
UM, I'M FINE...

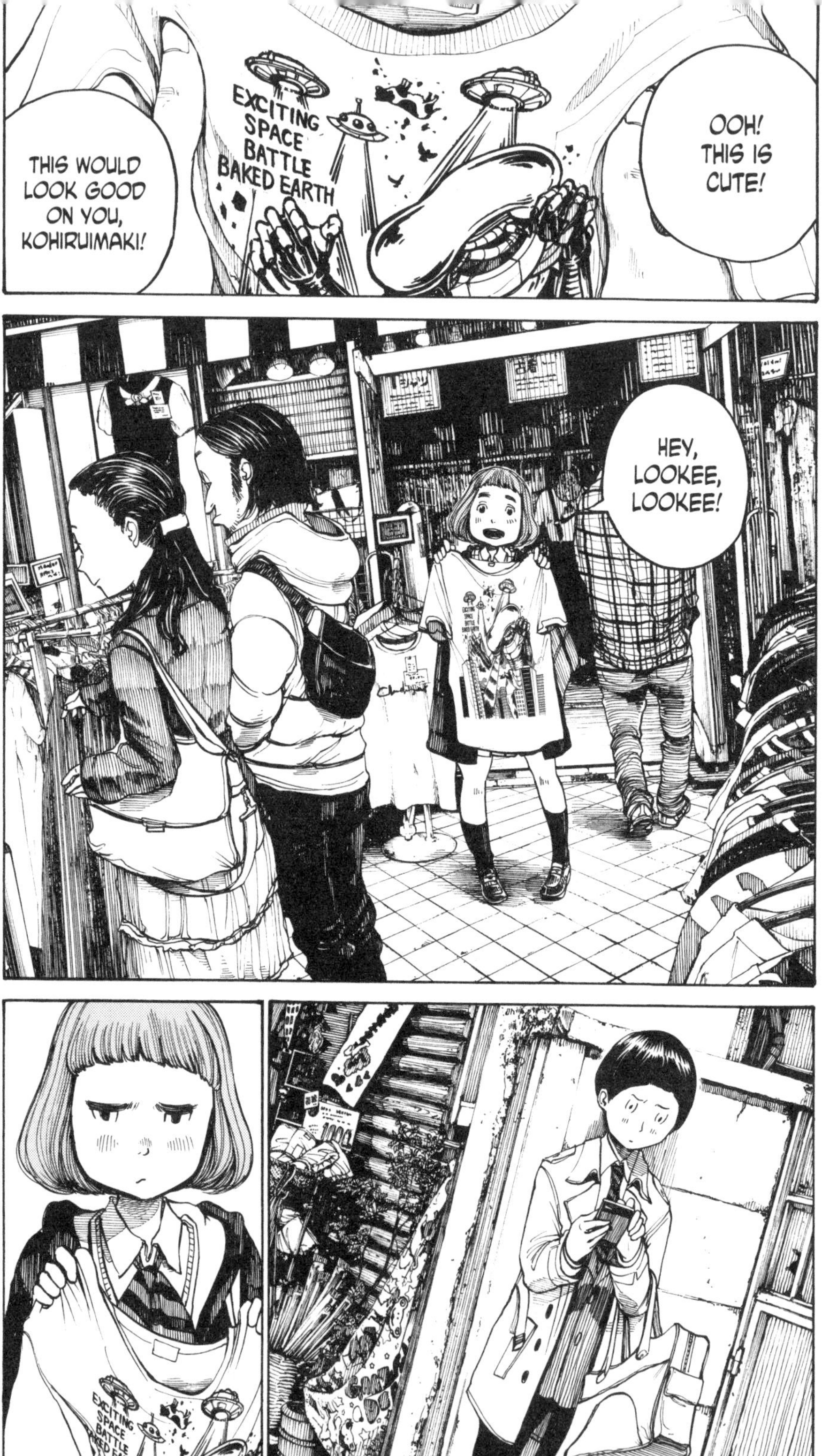
OOH! THIS IS CUTE!
EXCITING SPACE BATTLE BAKED EARTH
THIS WOULD LOOK GOOD ON YOU, KOHIRUIMAKI!
HEY, LOOKEE, LOOKEE!
EXCITING SPACE BATTLE BAKED EARTH

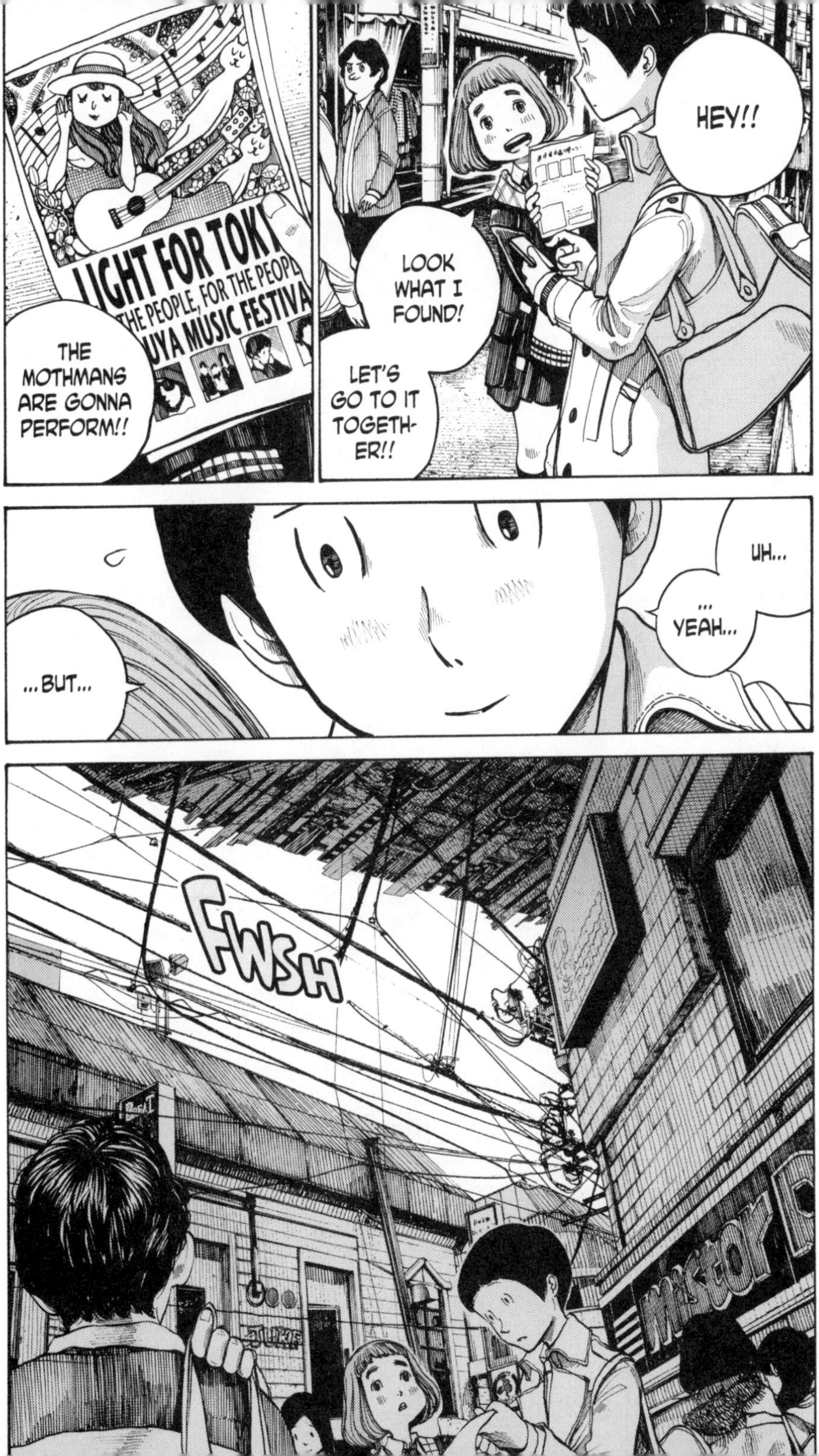
HEY!!
LOOK WHAT I FOUND!
LET'S GO TO IT TOGETH-ER!!
LIGHT FOR TOK
THE PEOPLE, FOR THE PEOPL
UYA MUSIC FESTIVA
THE MOTHMANS ARE GONNA PERFORM!!
UH...
... YEAH...
...BUT...
FWSH

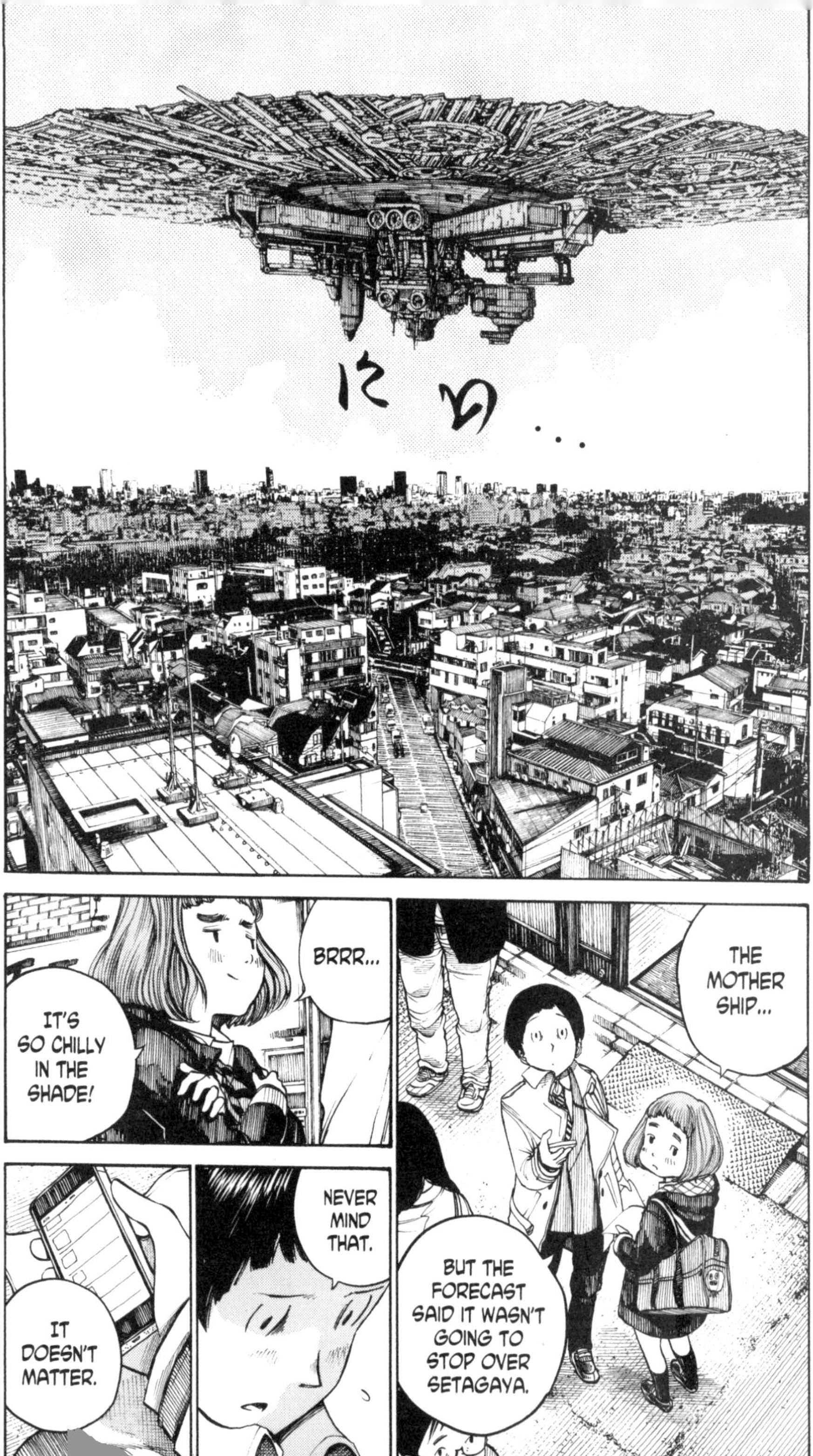
にめ…
THE MOTHER SHIP...
BUT THE FORECAST SAID IT WASN'T GOING TO STOP OVER SETAGAYA.
BRRR...
IT'S SO CHILLY IN THE SHADE!
NEVER MIND THAT.
IT DOESN'T MATTER.

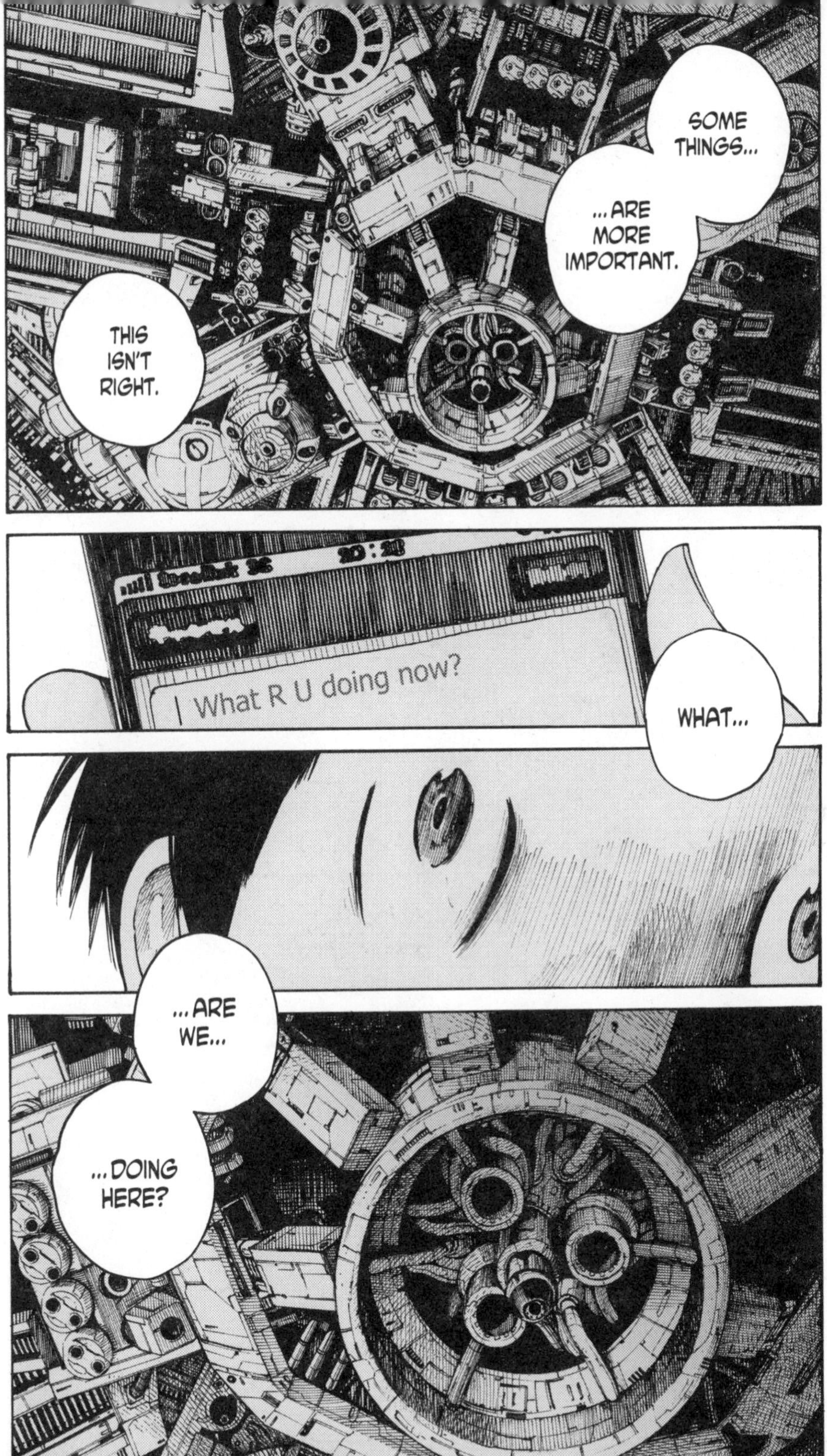
SOME THINGS...
...ARE MORE IMPORTANT.
THIS ISN'T RIGHT.
What R U doing now?
WHAT...
...ARE WE...
...DOING HERE?

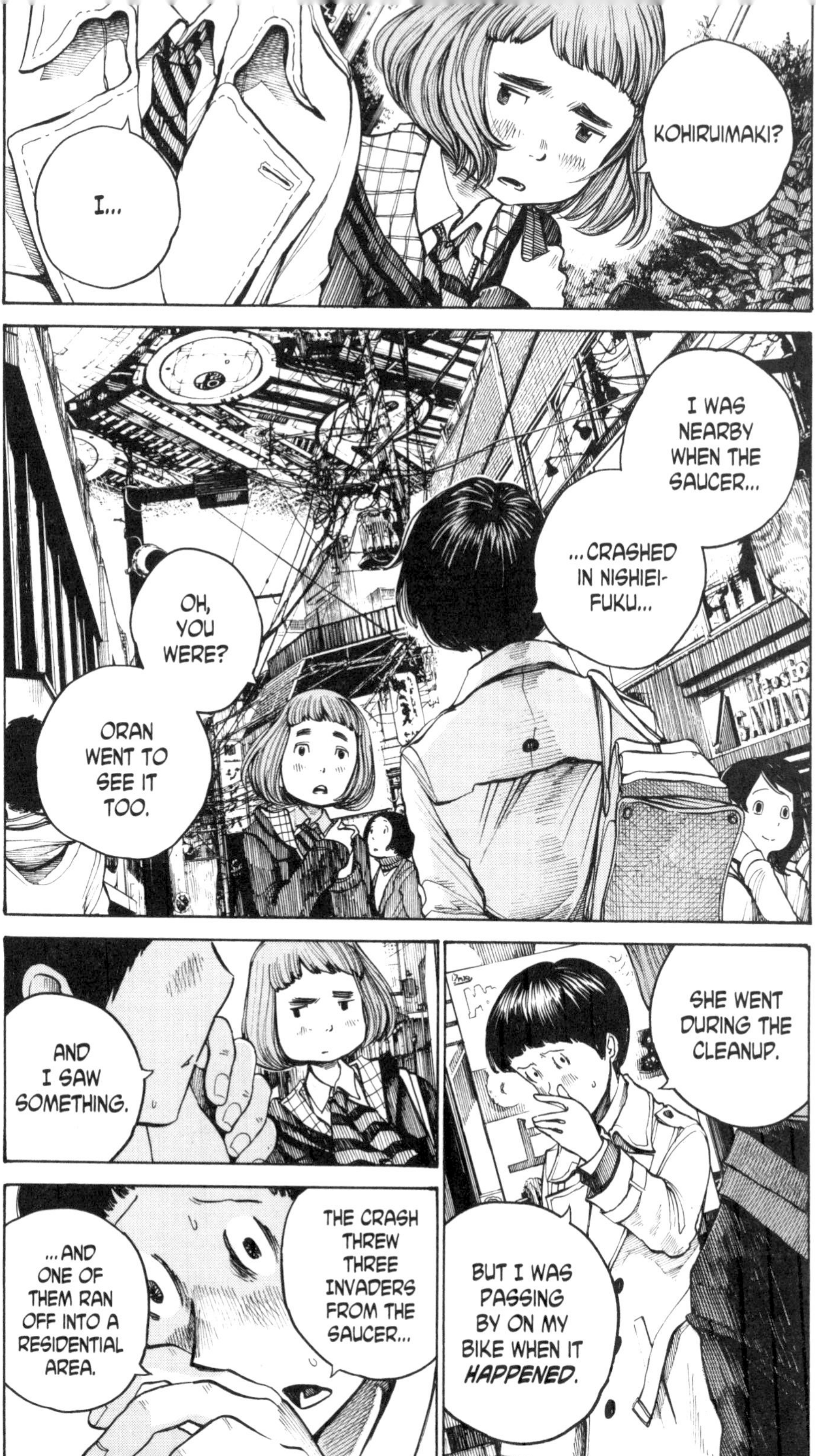
KOHIRUIMAKI?
I...
I WAS NEARBY WHEN THE SAUCER...
...CRASHED IN NISHIEI-FUKU...
OH, YOU WERE?
ORAN WENT TO SEE IT TOO.
SHE WENT DURING THE CLEANUP.
BUT I WAS PASSING BY ON MY BIKE WHEN IT *HAPPENED*.
AND I SAW SOMETHING.
THE CRASH THREW THREE INVADERS FROM THE SAUCER...
...AND ONE OF THEM RAN OFF INTO A RESIDENTIAL AREA.

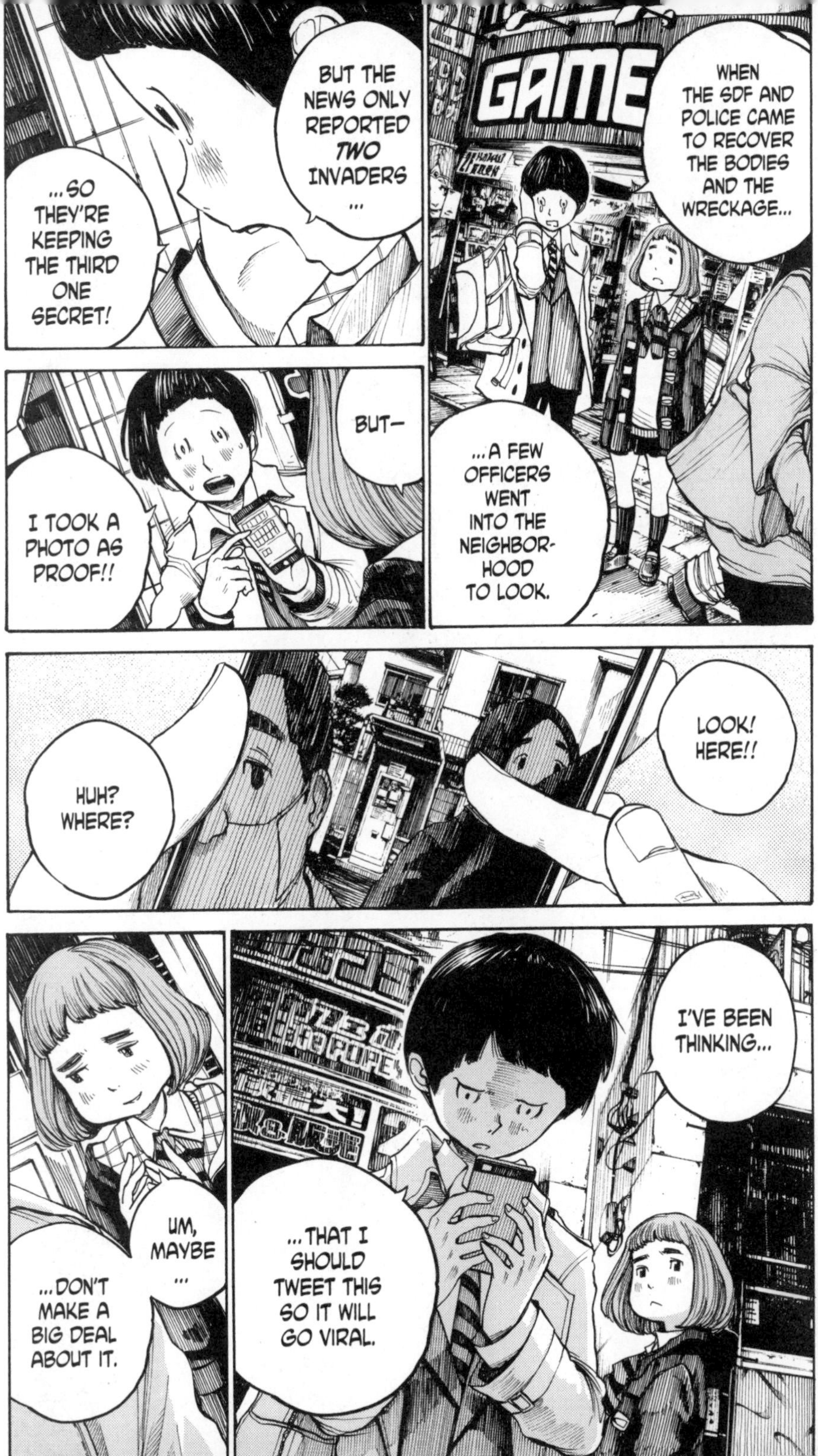
WHEN THE SDF AND POLICE CAME TO RECOVER THE BODIES AND THE WRECKAGE...
...A FEW OFFICERS WENT INTO THE NEIGHBOR-HOOD TO LOOK.
BUT THE NEWS ONLY REPORTED *TWO* INVADERS ...
...SO THEY'RE KEEPING THE THIRD ONE SECRET!
BUT—
I TOOK A PHOTO AS PROOF!!
LOOK! HERE!!
HUH? WHERE?
I'VE BEEN THINKING...
...THAT I SHOULD TWEET THIS SO IT WILL GO VIRAL.
UM, MAYBE ...
...DON'T MAKE A BIG DEAL ABOUT IT.

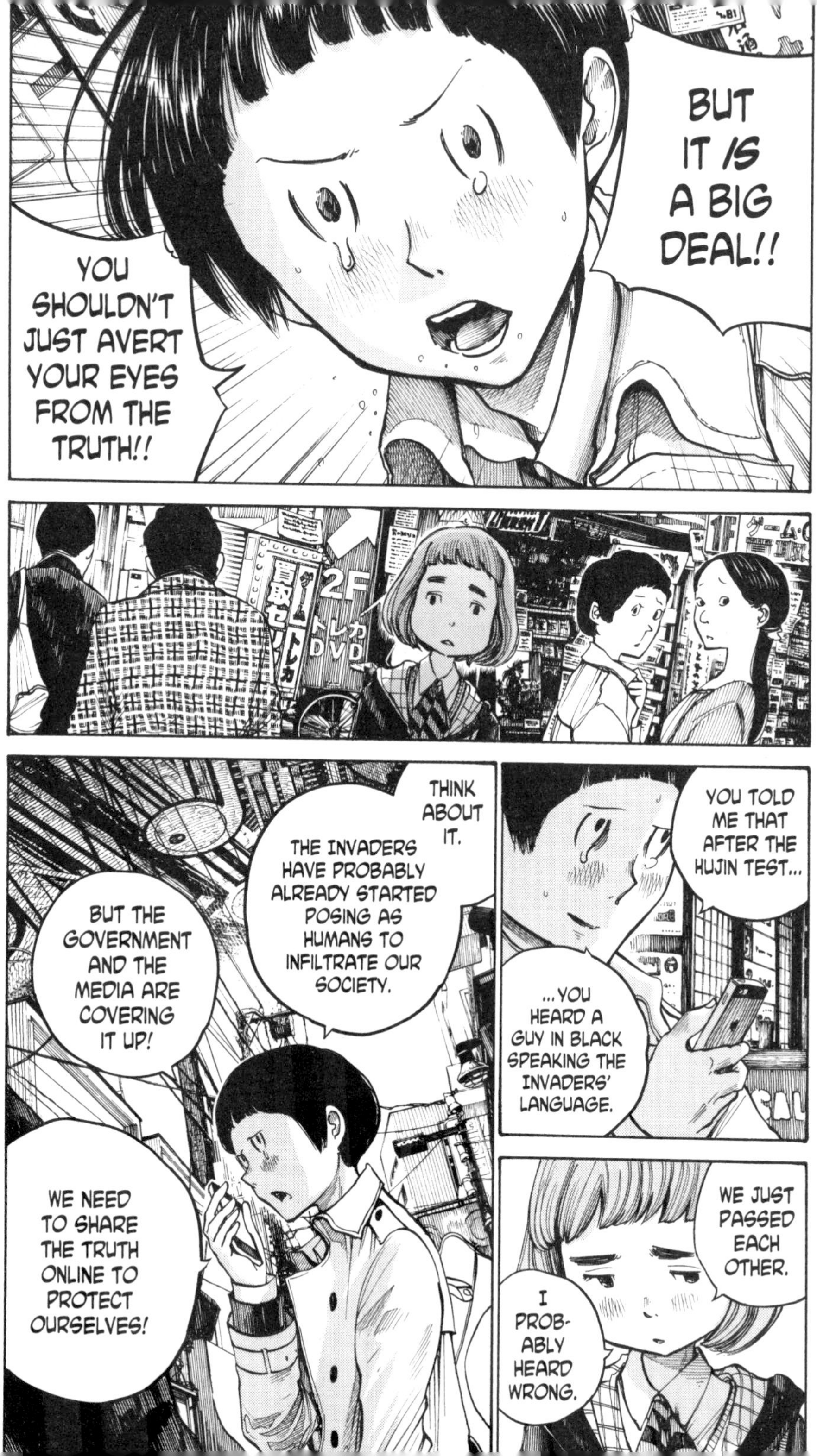
BUT IT IS A BIG DEAL!!
YOU SHOULDN'T JUST AVERT YOUR EYES FROM THE TRUTH!!
1F
2F
トレカ
DVD
YOU TOLD ME THAT AFTER THE HUJIN TEST...
...YOU HEARD A GUY IN BLACK SPEAKING THE INVADERS' LANGUAGE.
WE JUST PASSED EACH OTHER.
I PROB-ABLY HEARD WRONG.
THINK ABOUT IT.
THE INVADERS HAVE PROBABLY ALREADY STARTED POSING AS HUMANS TO INFILTRATE OUR SOCIETY.
BUT THE GOVERNMENT AND THE MEDIA ARE COVERING IT UP!
WE NEED TO SHARE THE TRUTH ONLINE TO PROTECT OURSELVES!

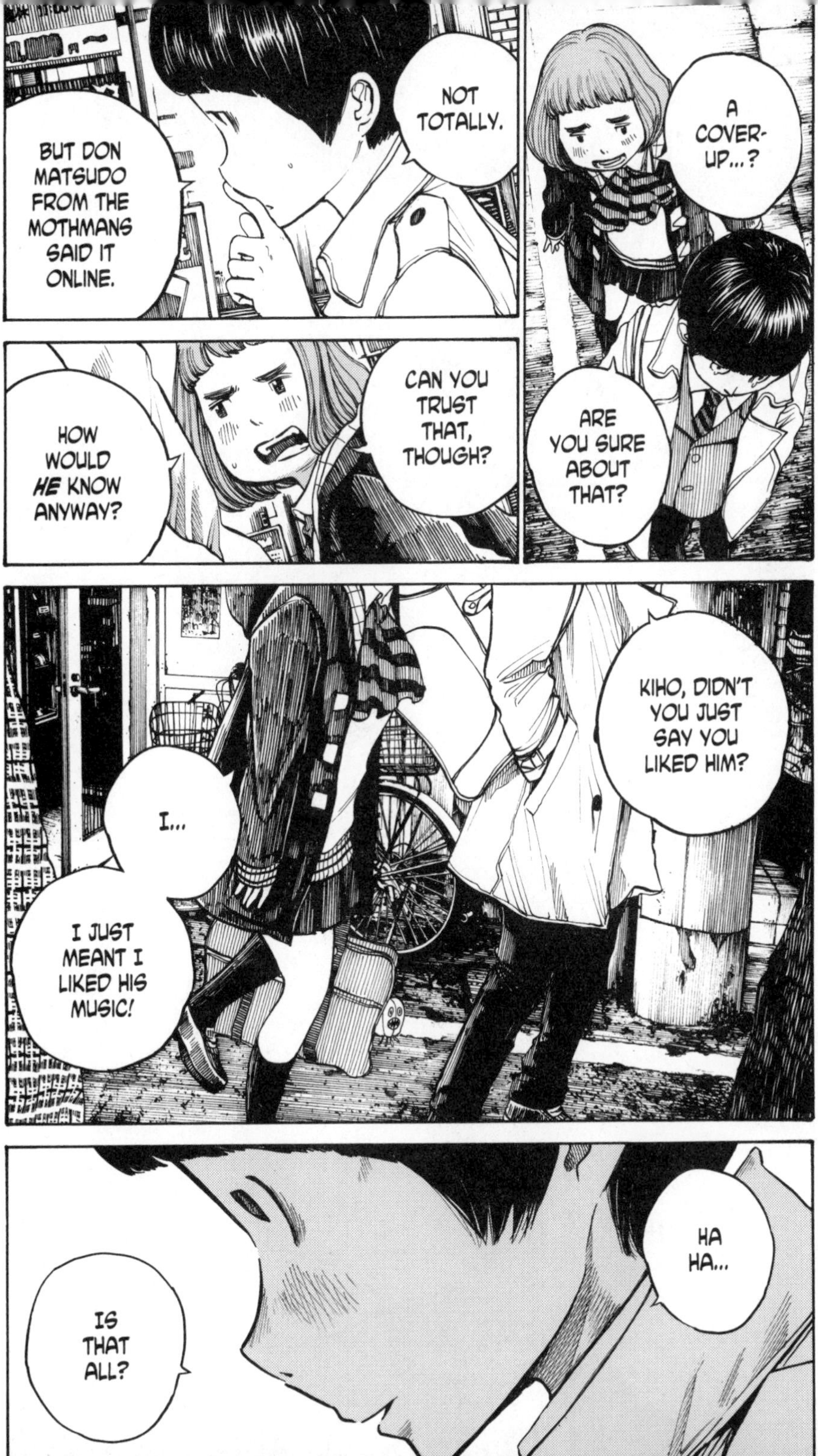
A COVER-UP...?
ARE YOU SURE ABOUT THAT?
NOT TOTALLY.
BUT DON MATSUDO FROM THE MOTHMANS SAID IT ONLINE.
CAN YOU TRUST THAT, THOUGH?
HOW WOULD *HE* KNOW ANYWAY?
KIHO, DIDN'T YOU JUST SAY YOU LIKED HIM?
I...
I JUST MEANT I LIKED HIS MUSIC!
HA HA...
IS THAT ALL?

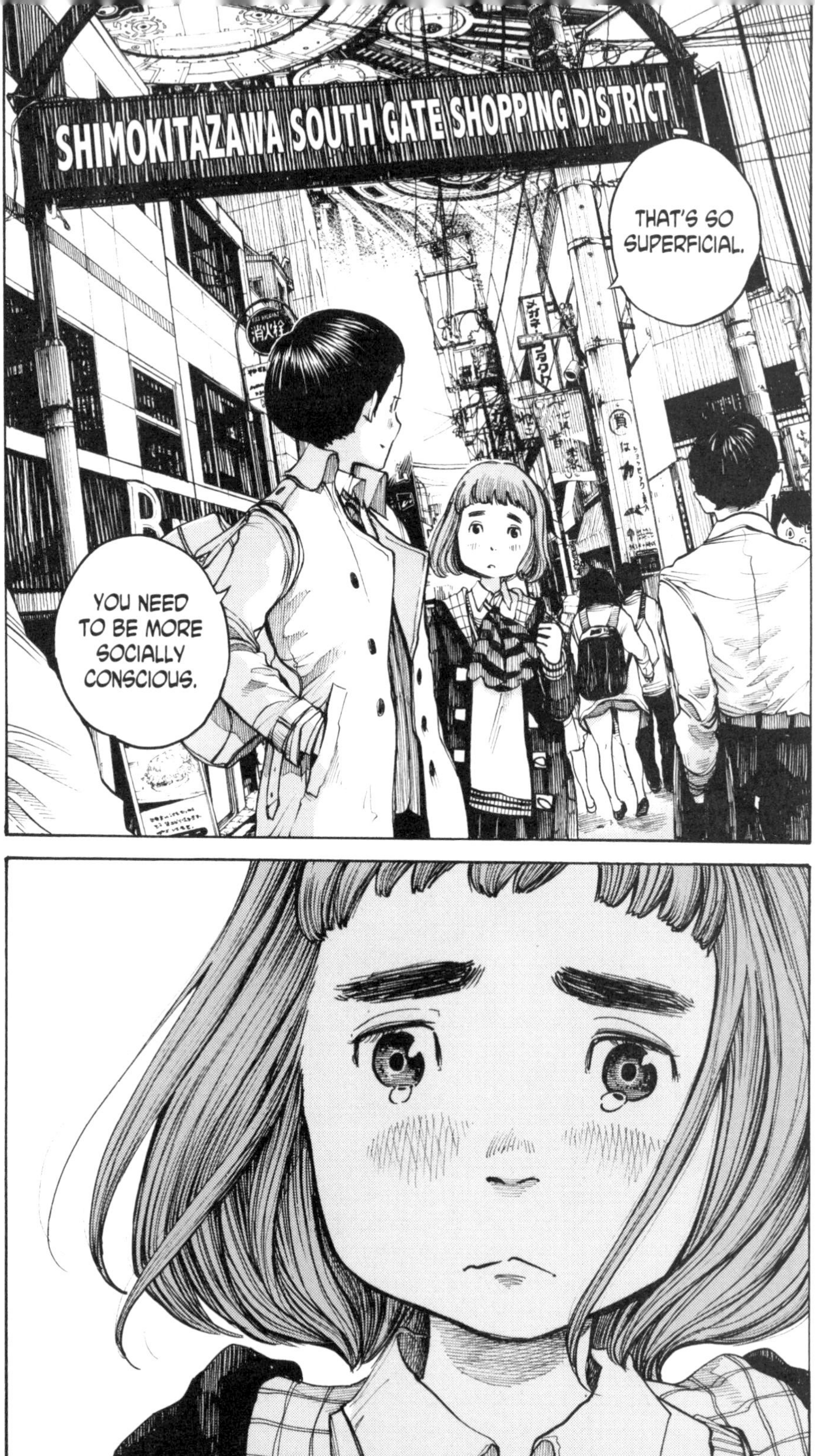
SHIMOKITAZAWA SOUTH GATE SHOPPING DISTRICT
THAT'S SO SUPERFICIAL.
YOU NEED TO BE MORE SOCIALLY CONSCIOUS.
消火栓

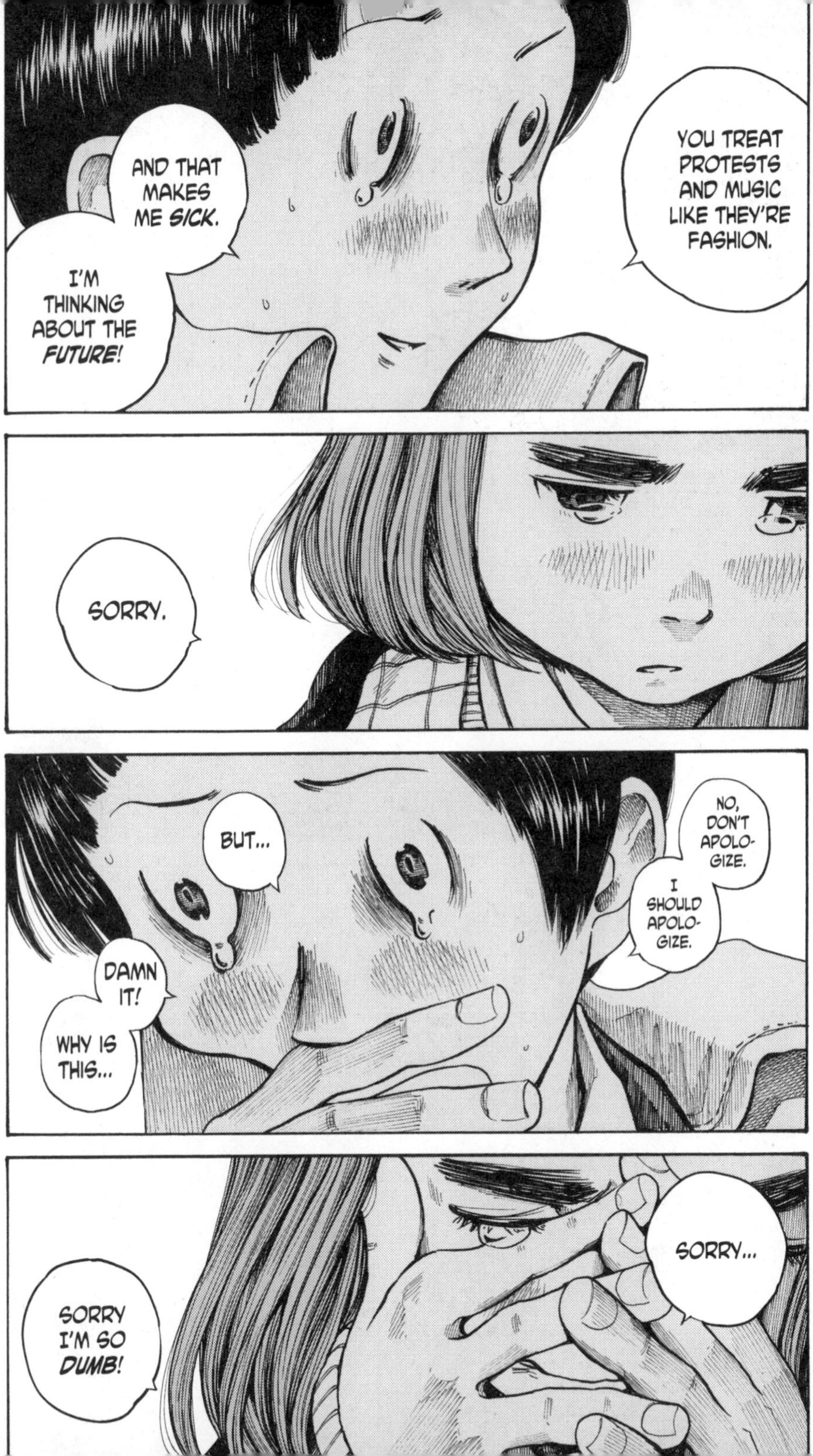
YOU TREAT PROTESTS AND MUSIC LIKE THEY'RE FASHION.
AND THAT MAKES ME *SICK*.
I'M THINKING ABOUT THE *FUTURE*!
SORRY.
NO, DON'T APOLOGIZE.
I SHOULD APOLOGIZE.
BUT...
DAMN IT!
WHY IS THIS...
SORRY...
SORRY I'M SO *DUMB*!

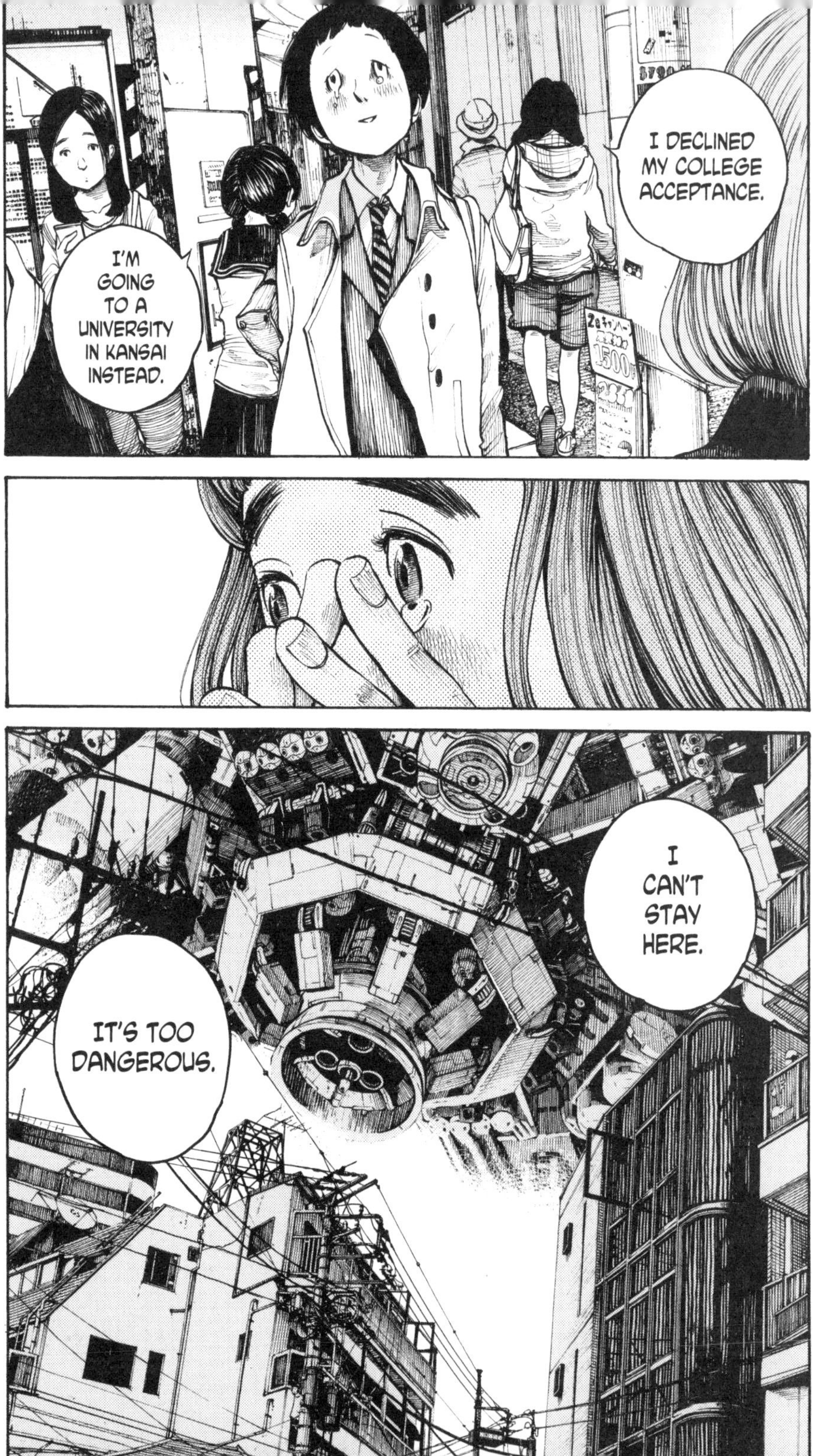
I DECLINED MY COLLEGE ACCEPTANCE.
I'M GOING TO A UNIVERSITY IN KANSAI INSTEAD.
I CAN'T STAY HERE.
IT'S TOO DANGEROUS.

CHAPTER 11

DEAD DEAD DEMON'S DEDEDEDE DESTRUCTION

COMMAND

▶TALK   SPELL

STATUS   ITEM

EQUIP   SEARCH

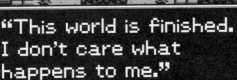

"This world is finished. I don't care what happens to me."

NEW GAME

CONTINUE

presented by INIO ASANO

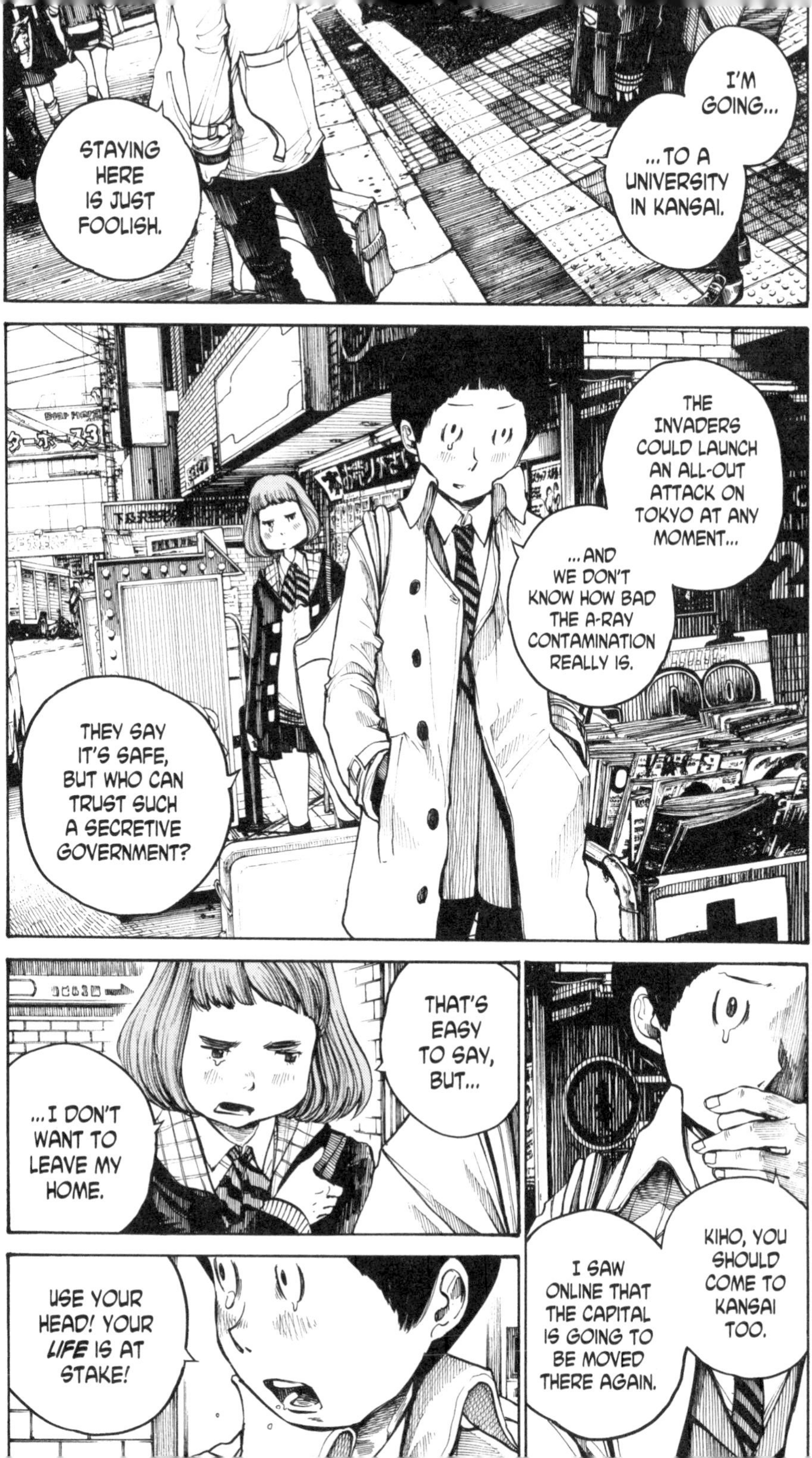
I'M GOING...
...TO A UNIVERSITY IN KANSAI.
STAYING HERE IS JUST FOOLISH.
THE INVADERS COULD LAUNCH AN ALL-OUT ATTACK ON TOKYO AT ANY MOMENT...
...AND WE DON'T KNOW HOW BAD THE A-RAY CONTAMINATION REALLY IS.
THEY SAY IT'S SAFE, BUT WHO CAN TRUST SUCH A SECRETIVE GOVERNMENT?
KIHO, YOU SHOULD COME TO KANSAI TOO.
I SAW ONLINE THAT THE CAPITAL IS GOING TO BE MOVED THERE AGAIN.
THAT'S EASY TO SAY, BUT...
...I DON'T WANT TO LEAVE MY HOME.
USE YOUR HEAD! YOUR *LIFE* IS AT STAKE!

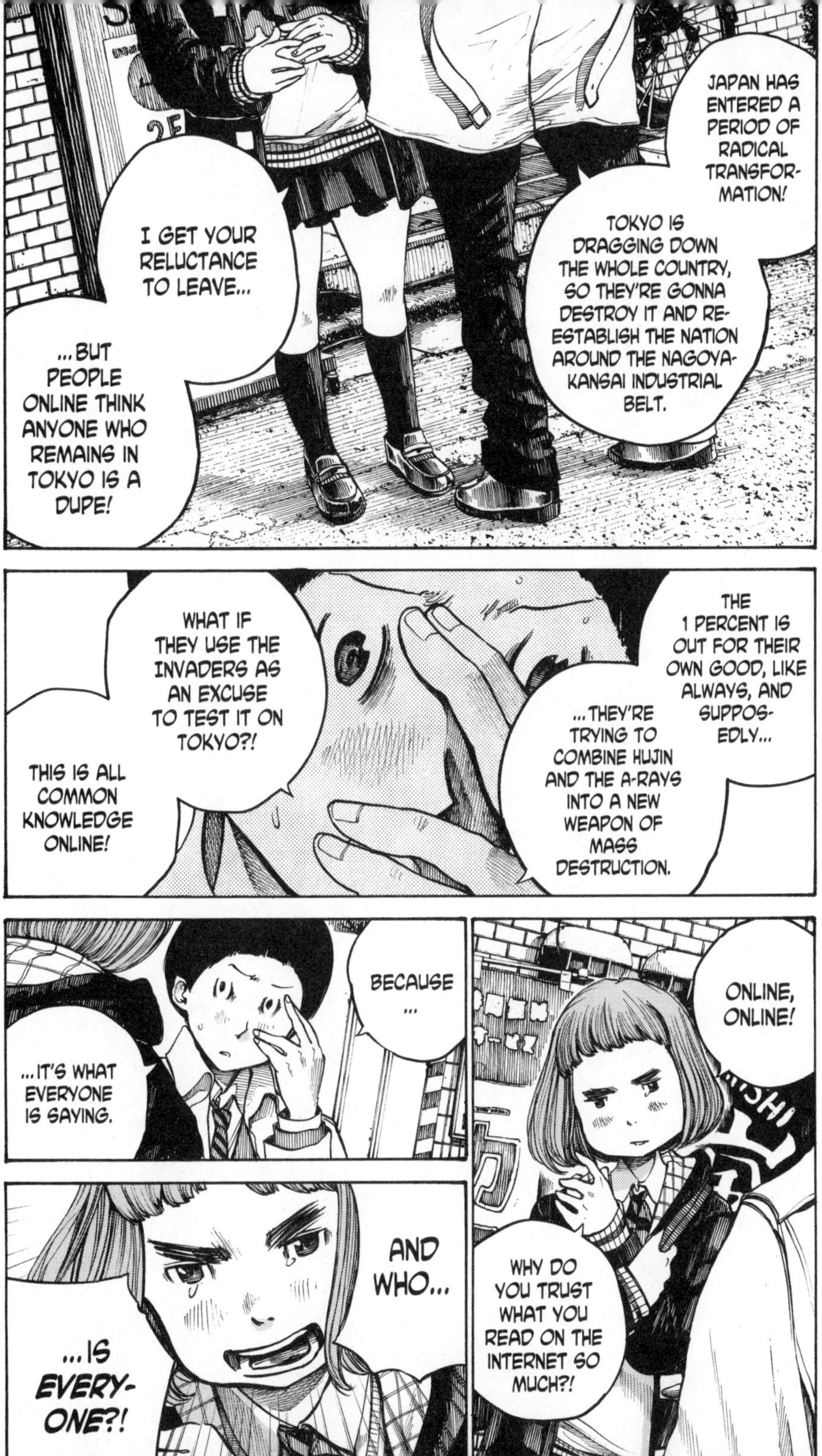

JAPAN HAS ENTERED A PERIOD OF RADICAL TRANSFORMATION!
TOKYO IS DRAGGING DOWN THE WHOLE COUNTRY, SO THEY'RE GONNA DESTROY IT AND RE-ESTABLISH THE NATION AROUND THE NAGOYA-KANSAI INDUSTRIAL BELT.
I GET YOUR RELUCTANCE TO LEAVE...
...BUT PEOPLE ONLINE THINK ANYONE WHO REMAINS IN TOKYO IS A DUPE!
THE 1 PERCENT IS OUT FOR THEIR OWN GOOD, LIKE ALWAYS, AND SUPPOSEDLY...
...THEY'RE TRYING TO COMBINE HUJIN AND THE A-RAYS INTO A NEW WEAPON OF MASS DESTRUCTION.
WHAT IF THEY USE THE INVADERS AS AN EXCUSE TO TEST IT ON TOKYO?!
THIS IS ALL COMMON KNOWLEDGE ONLINE!
ONLINE, ONLINE!
WHY DO YOU TRUST WHAT YOU READ ON THE INTERNET SO MUCH?!
BECAUSE...
...IT'S WHAT EVERYONE IS SAYING.
AND WHO...
...IS *EVERYONE*?!

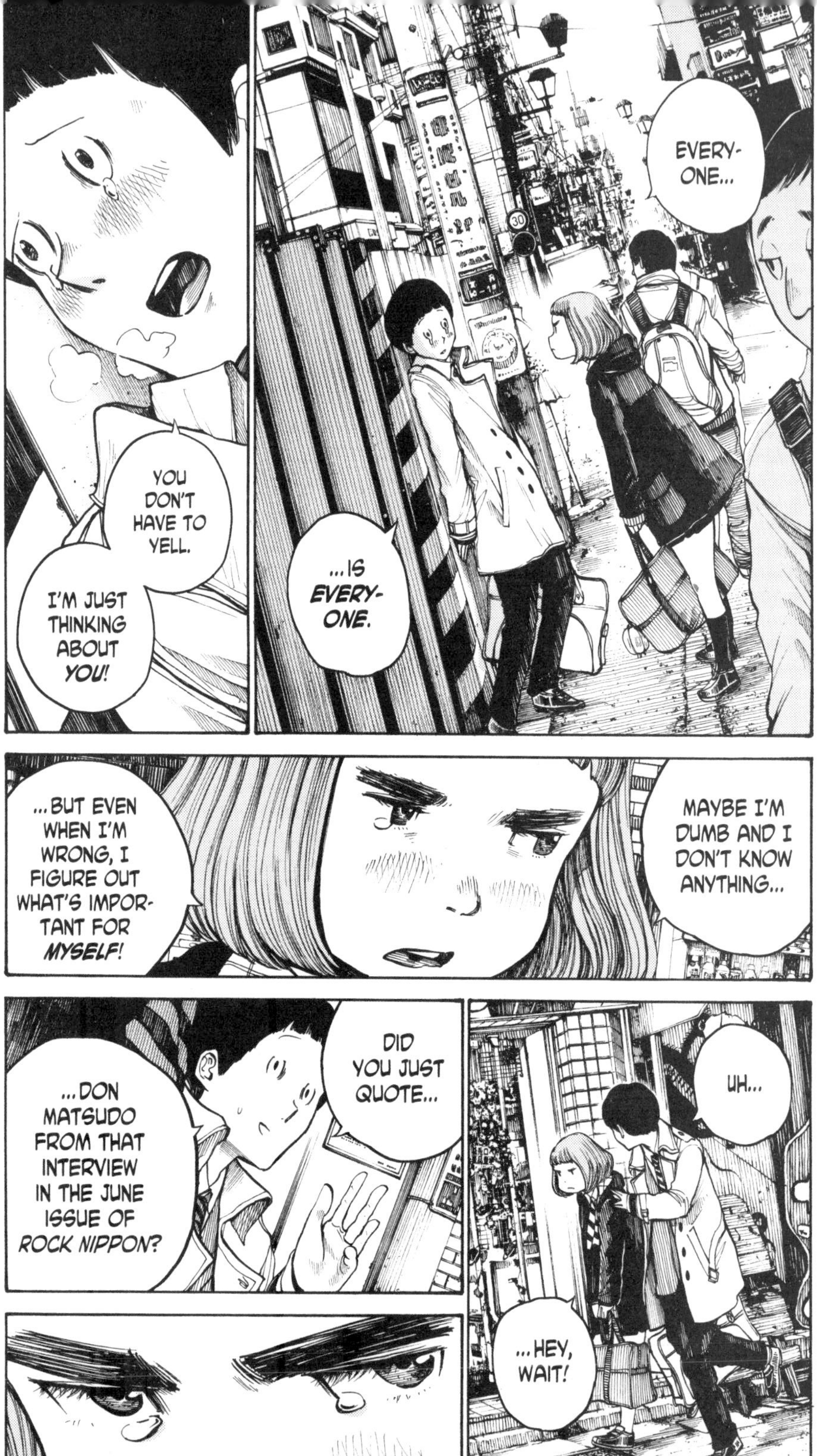
EVERY-ONE...
...IS *EVERY-ONE*.
YOU DON'T HAVE TO YELL.
I'M JUST THINKING ABOUT *YOU*!
MAYBE I'M DUMB AND I DON'T KNOW ANYTHING...
...BUT EVEN WHEN I'M WRONG, I FIGURE OUT WHAT'S IMPOR-TANT FOR *MYSELF*!
UH...
...HEY, WAIT!
DID YOU JUST QUOTE...
...DON MATSUDO FROM THAT INTERVIEW IN THE JUNE ISSUE OF *ROCK NIPPON*?

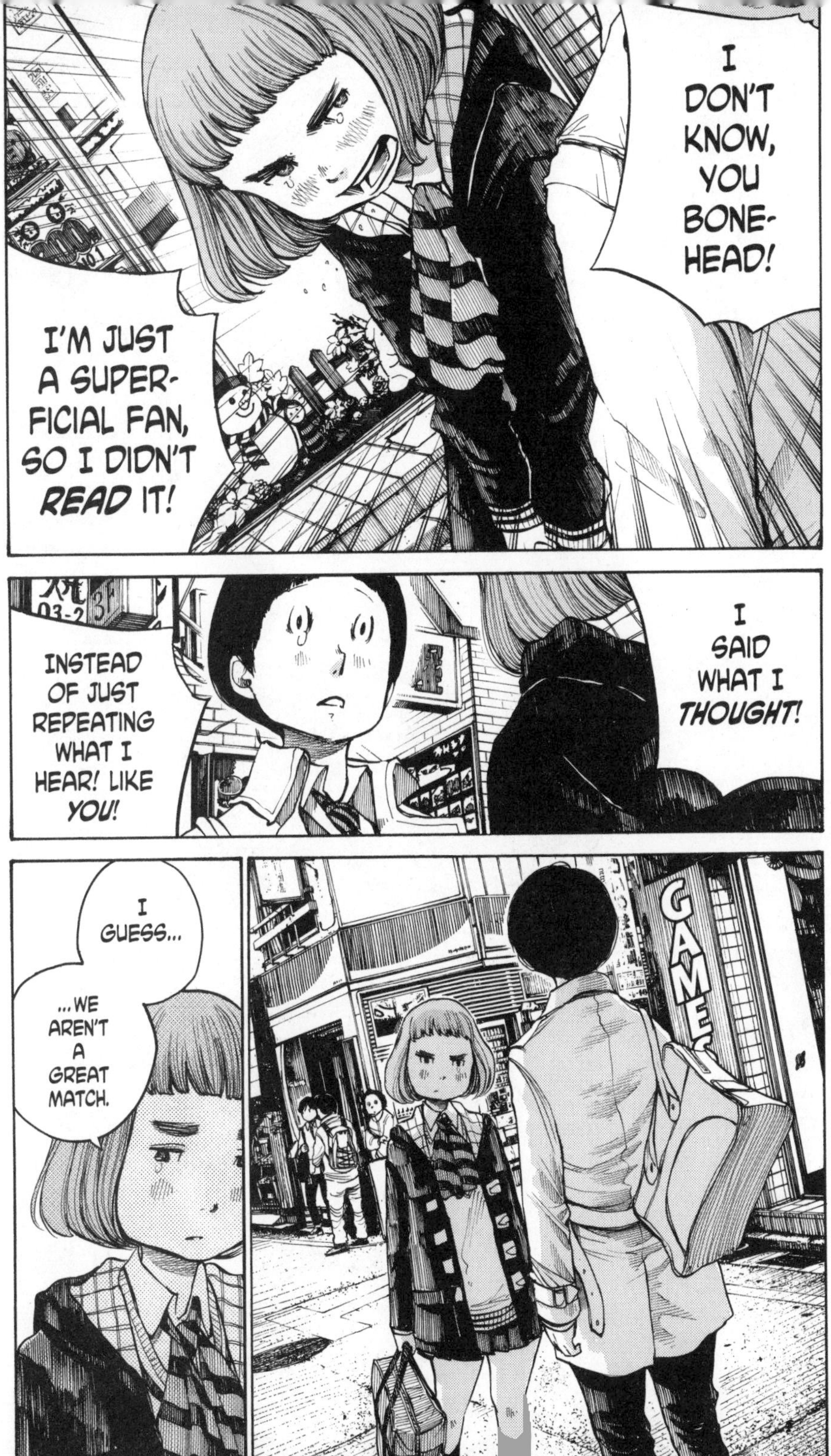
I DON'T KNOW, YOU BONE-HEAD!
I'M JUST A SUPER-FICIAL FAN, SO I DIDN'T *READ* IT!
I SAID WHAT I *THOUGHT*!
INSTEAD OF JUST REPEATING WHAT I HEAR! LIKE *YOU*!
GAMES
I GUESS...
...WE AREN'T A GREAT MATCH.

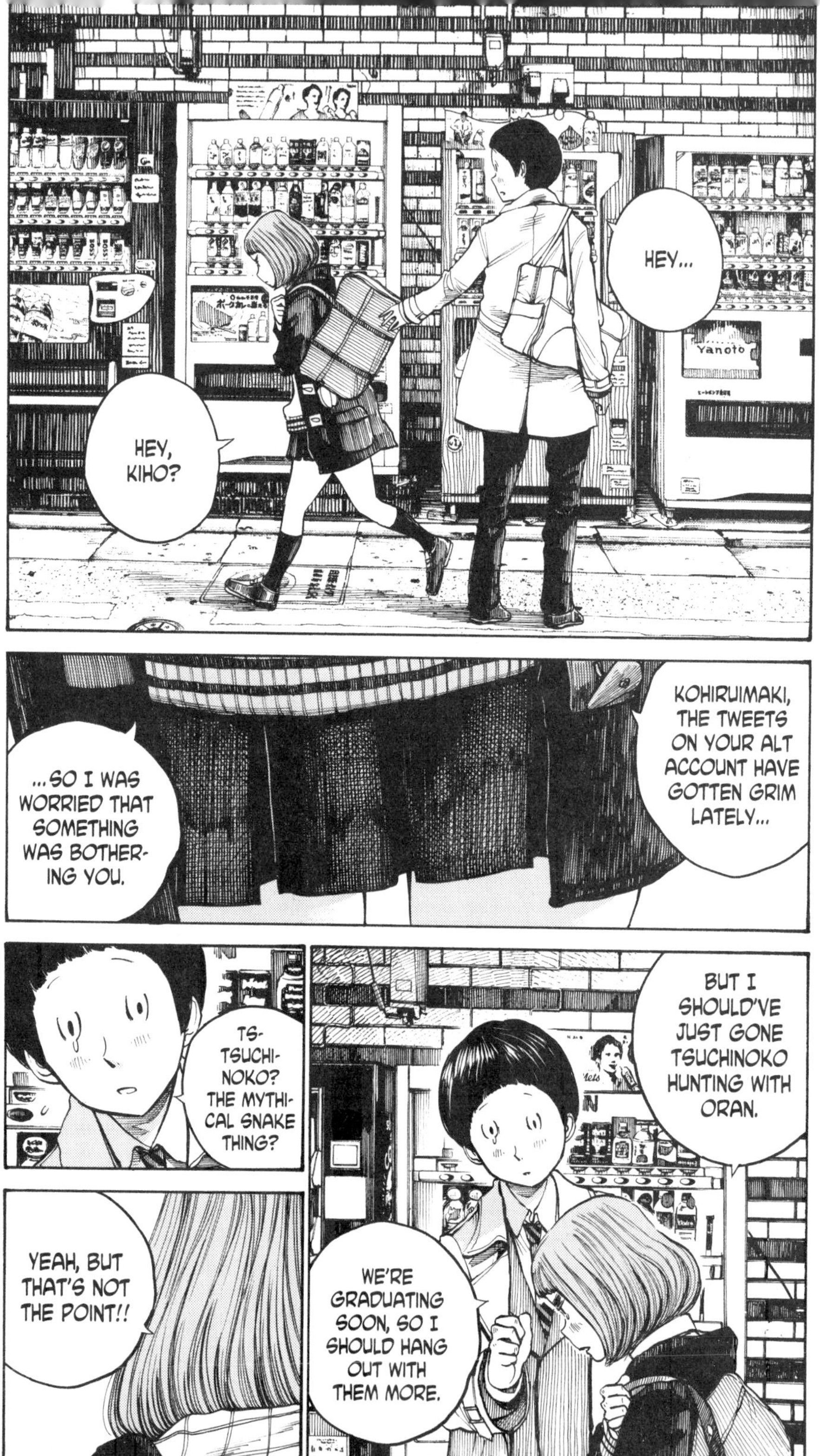
HEY...
HEY, KIHO?
KOHIRUIMAKI, THE TWEETS ON YOUR ALT ACCOUNT HAVE GOTTEN GRIM LATELY...
...SO I WAS WORRIED THAT SOMETHING WAS BOTHER-ING YOU.
BUT I SHOULD'VE JUST GONE TSUCHINOKO HUNTING WITH ORAN.
WE'RE GRADUATING SOON, SO I SHOULD HANG OUT WITH THEM MORE.
TS-TSUCHI-NOKO? THE MYTHI-CAL SNAKE THING?
YEAH, BUT THAT'S NOT THE POINT!!
Yanoto

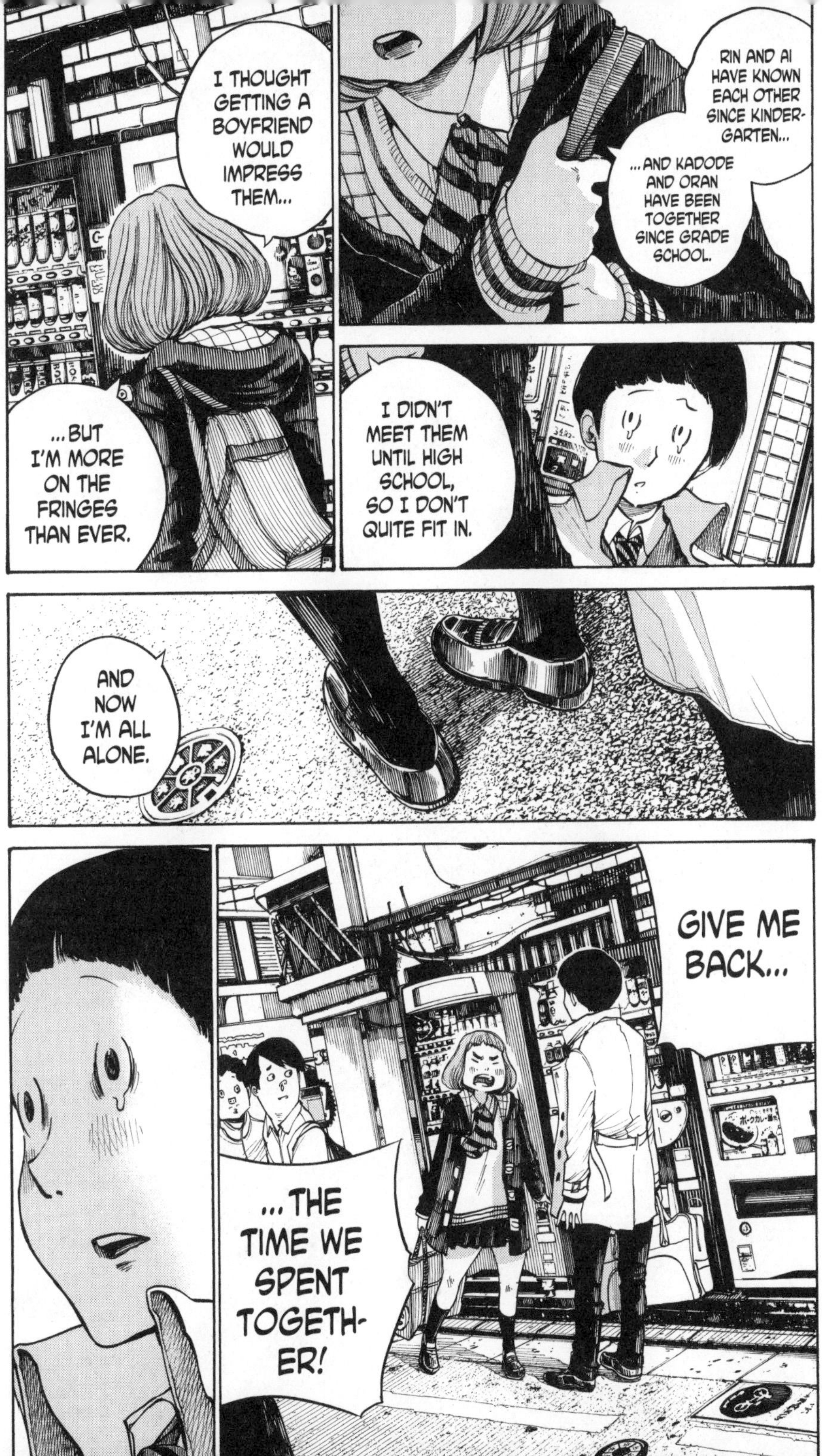
RIN AND AI HAVE KNOWN EACH OTHER SINCE KINDER-GARTEN...
...AND KADODE AND ORAN HAVE BEEN TOGETHER SINCE GRADE SCHOOL.
I THOUGHT GETTING A BOYFRIEND WOULD IMPRESS THEM...
I DIDN'T MEET THEM UNTIL HIGH SCHOOL, SO I DON'T QUITE FIT IN.
...BUT I'M MORE ON THE FRINGES THAN EVER.
AND NOW I'M ALL ALONE.
GIVE ME BACK...
...THE TIME WE SPENT TOGETH-ER!

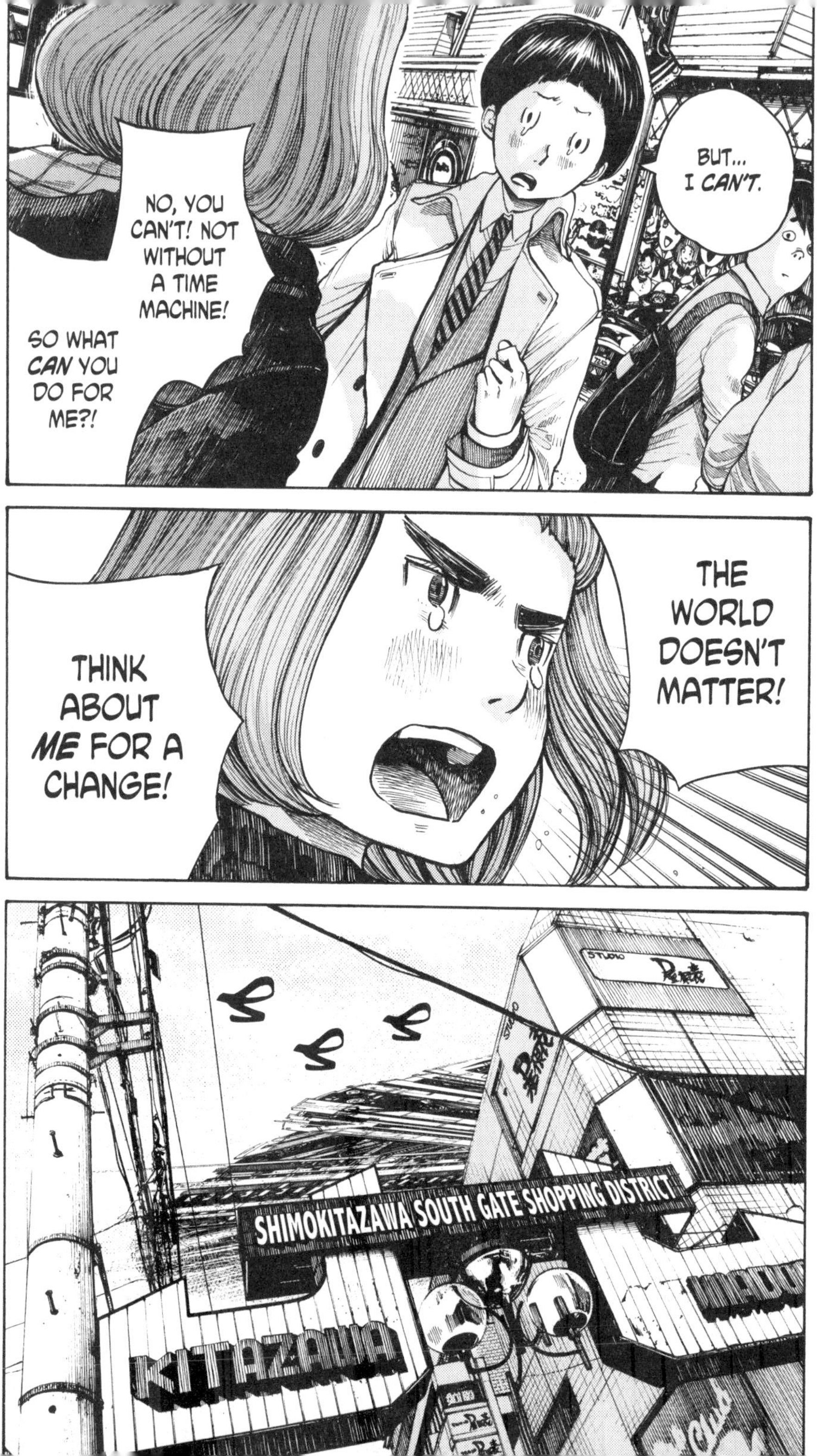
BUT... I *CAN'T*.
NO, YOU CAN'T! NOT WITHOUT A TIME MACHINE!
SO WHAT *CAN* YOU DO FOR ME?!
THE WORLD DOESN'T MATTER!
THINK ABOUT *ME* FOR A CHANGE!
SHIMOKITAZAWA SOUTH GATE SHOPPING DISTRICT
KITAZAWA

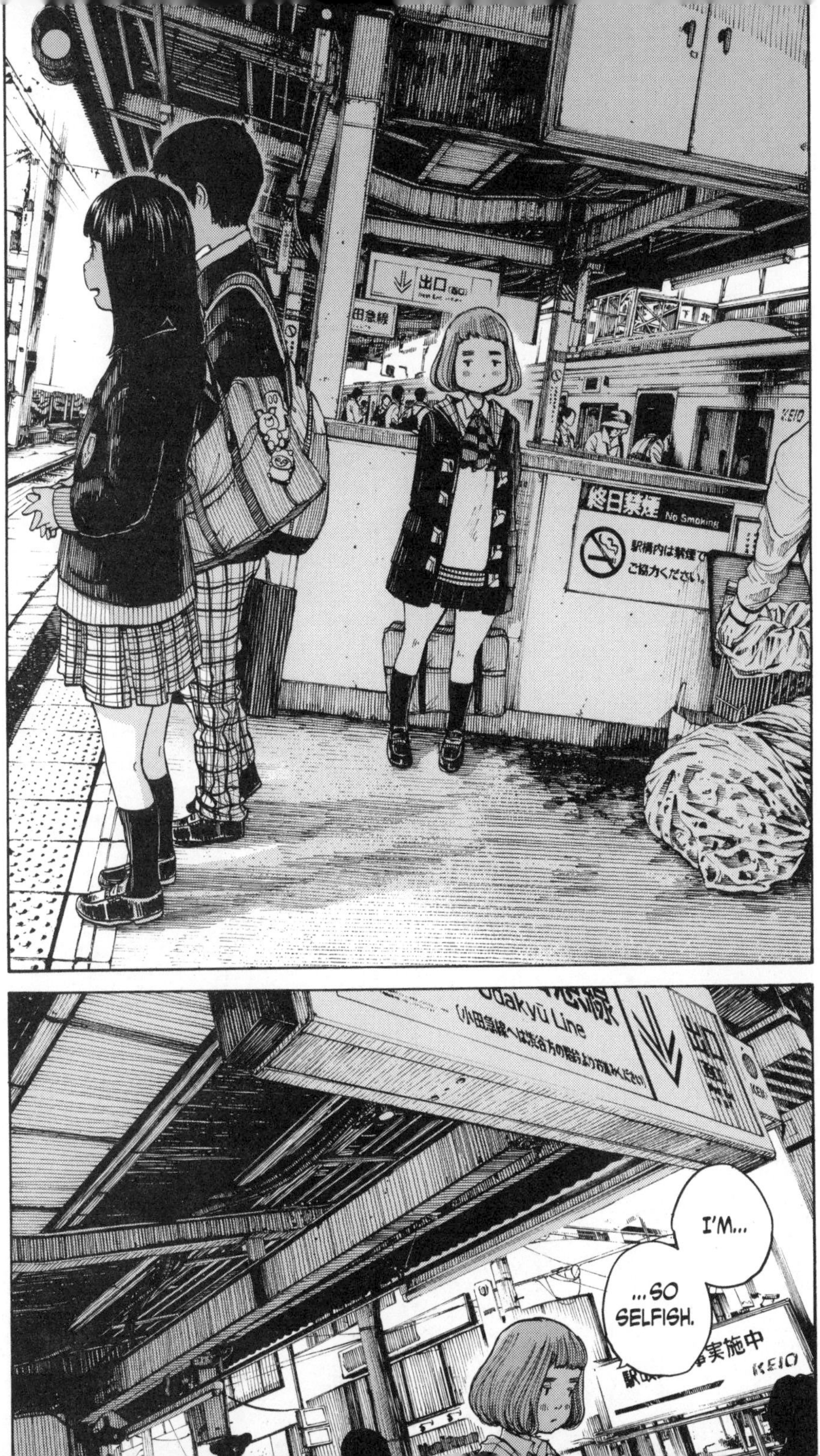
出口
終日禁煙 No Smoking
ご協力ください。
KEIO
Odakyū Line
I'M...
...SO SELFISH.
実施中
KEIO

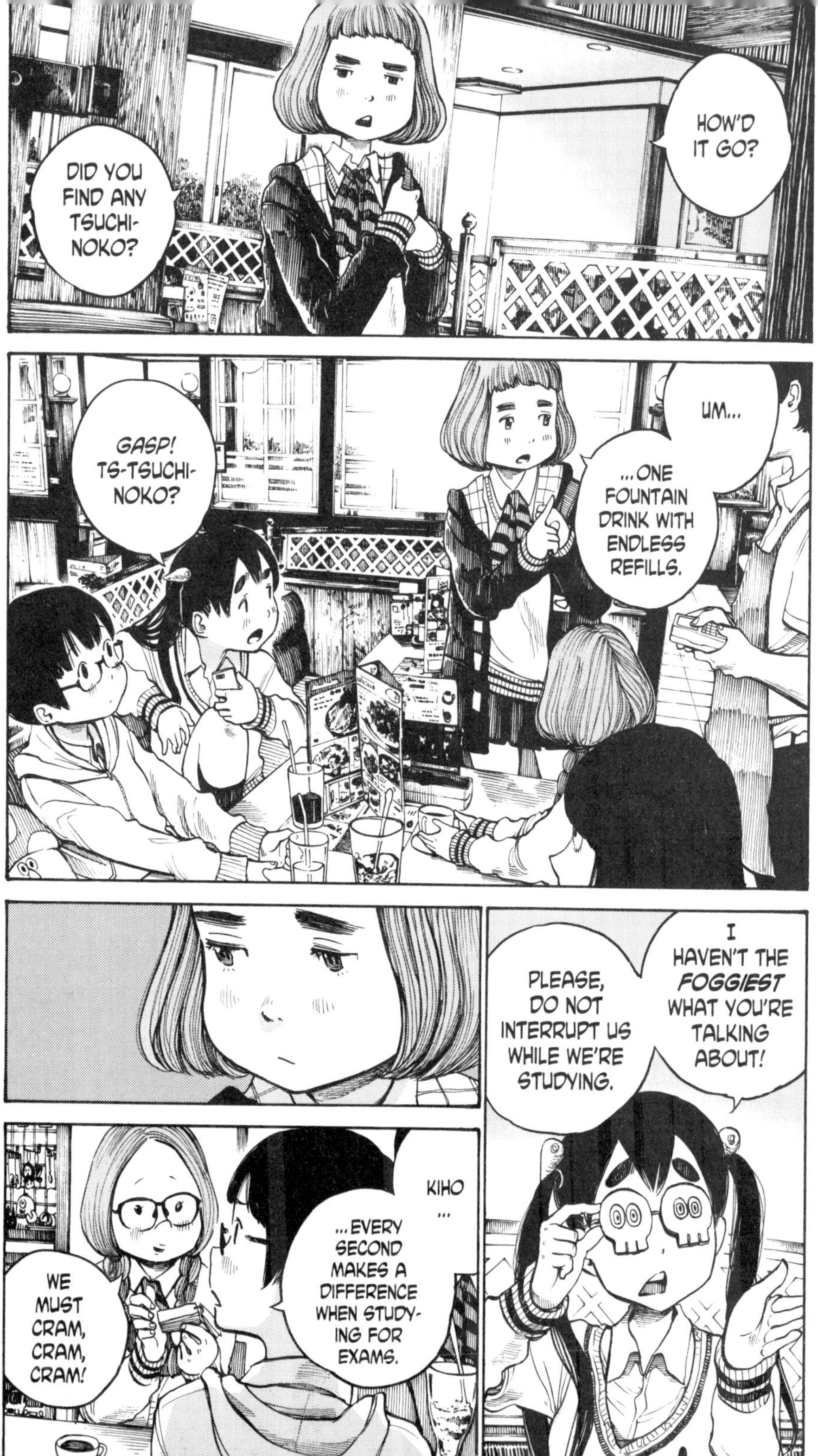
HOW'D IT GO?
DID YOU FIND ANY TSUCHI-NOKO?
UM...
...ONE FOUNTAIN DRINK WITH ENDLESS REFILLS.
GASP! TS-TSUCHI-NOKO?
I HAVEN'T THE *FOGGIEST* WHAT YOU'RE TALKING ABOUT!
PLEASE, DO NOT INTERRUPT US WHILE WE'RE STUDYING.
KIHO ...
...EVERY SECOND MAKES A DIFFERENCE WHEN STUDY-ING FOR EXAMS.
WE MUST CRAM, CRAM, CRAM!

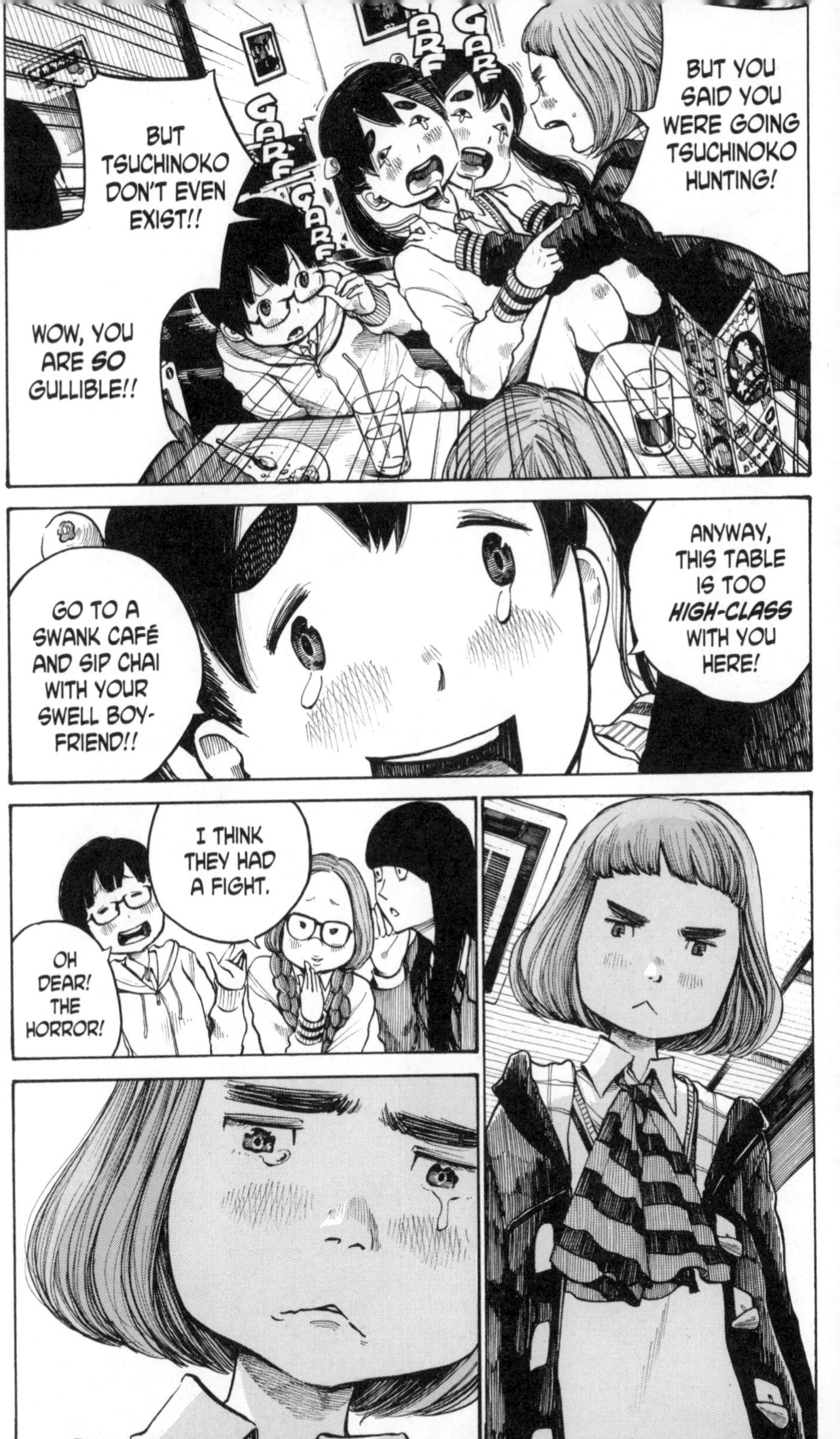
BUT YOU SAID YOU WERE GOING TSUCHINOKO HUNTING!
GARF
GARF
GARF
GARF
BUT TSUCHINOKO DON'T EVEN EXIST!!
WOW, YOU ARE *SO* GULLIBLE!!
ANYWAY, THIS TABLE IS TOO *HIGH-CLASS* WITH YOU HERE!
GO TO A SWANK CAFÉ AND SIP CHAI WITH YOUR SWELL BOY-FRIEND!!
I THINK THEY HAD A FIGHT.
OH DEAR! THE HORROR!

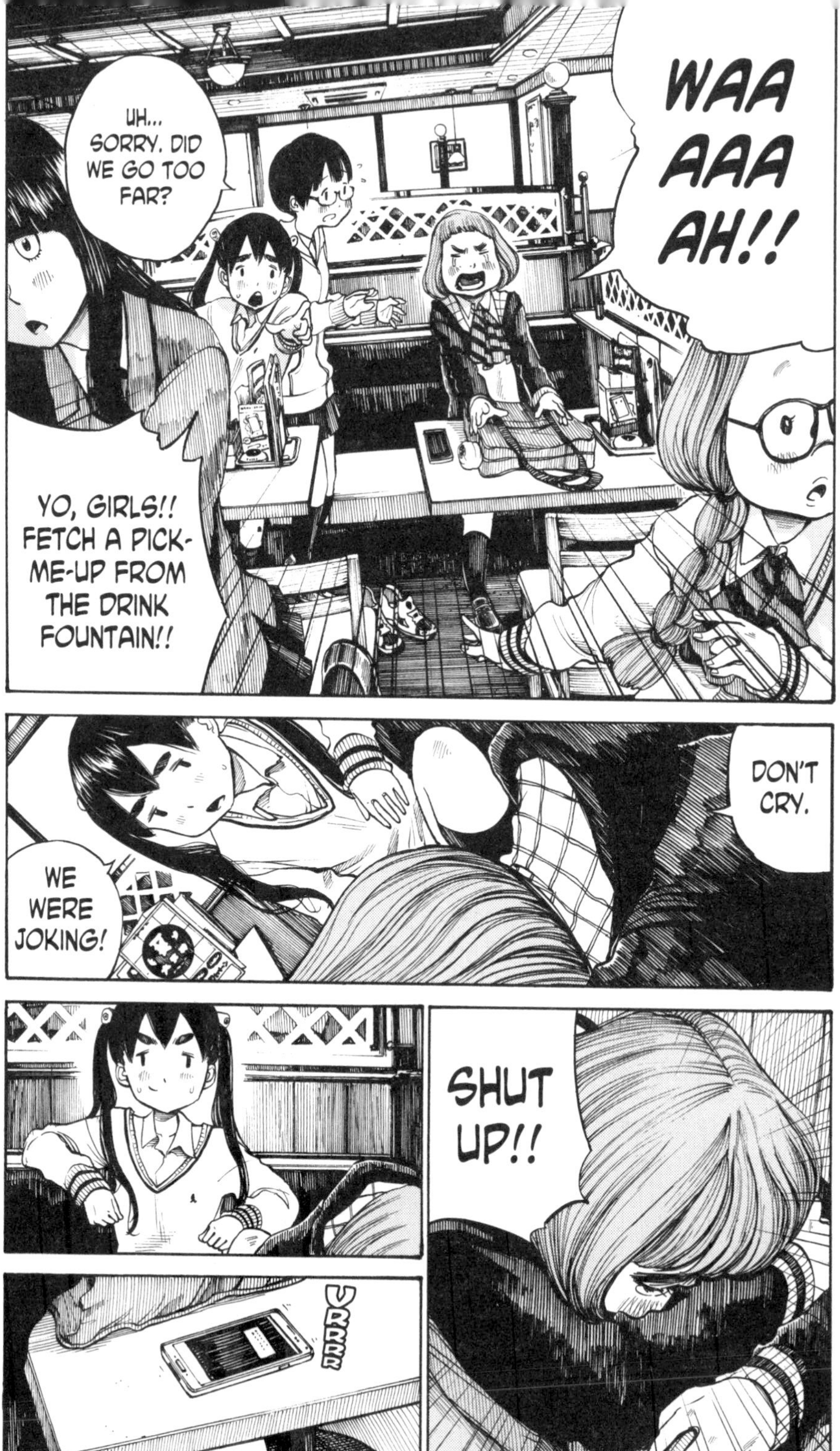
WAA AAA AH!!
UH... SORRY. DID WE GO TOO FAR?
YO, GIRLS!! FETCH A PICK-ME-UP FROM THE DRINK FOUNTAIN!!
DON'T CRY.
WE WERE JOKING!
SHUT UP!!
URRRR

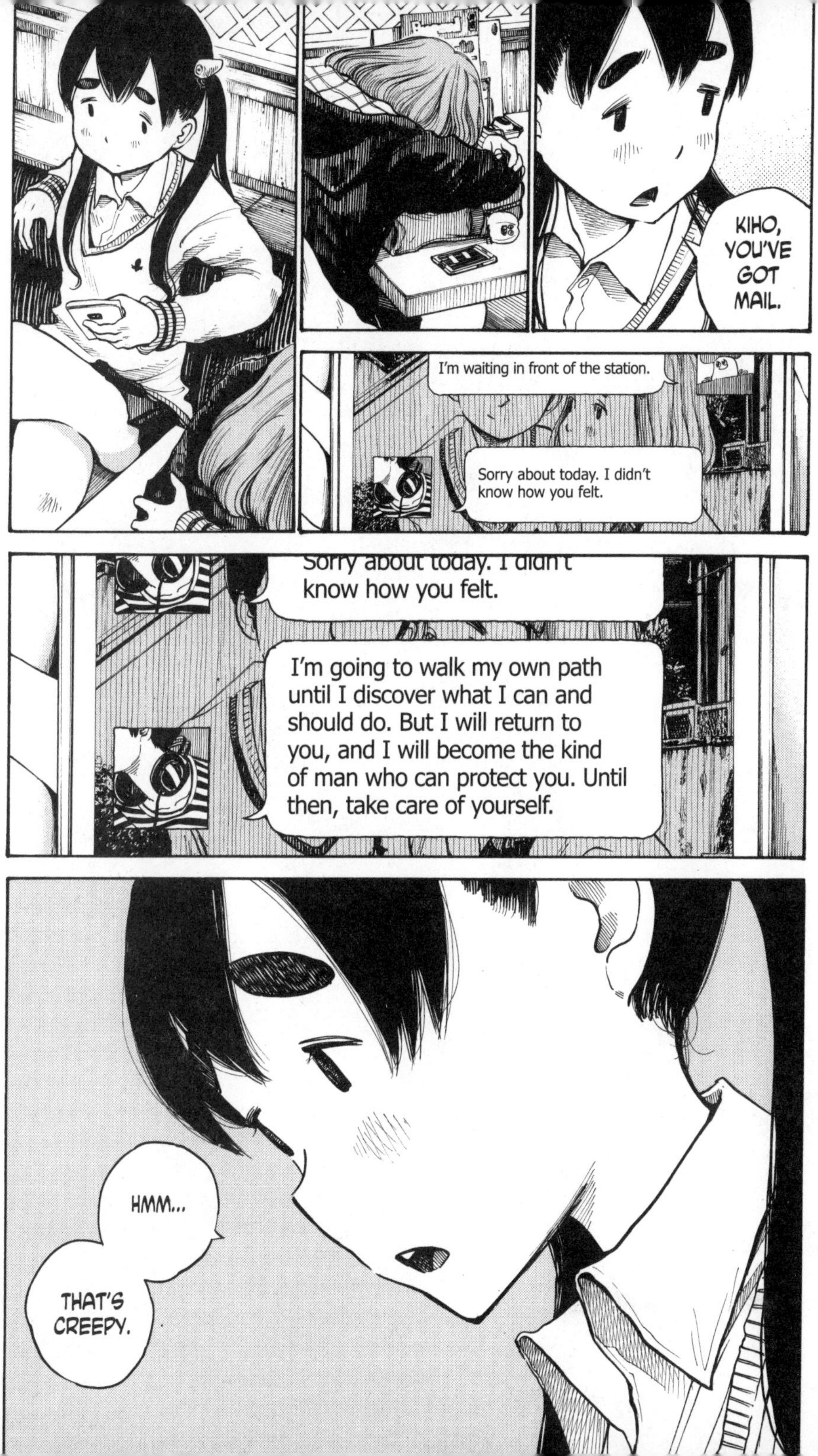
KIHO, YOU'VE GOT MAIL.
I'm waiting in front of the station.
Sorry about today. I didn't know how you felt.
Sorry about today. I didn't know how you felt.
I'm going to walk my own path until I discover what I can and should do. But I will return to you, and I will become the kind of man who can protect you. Until then, take care of yourself.
HMM...
THAT'S CREEPY.

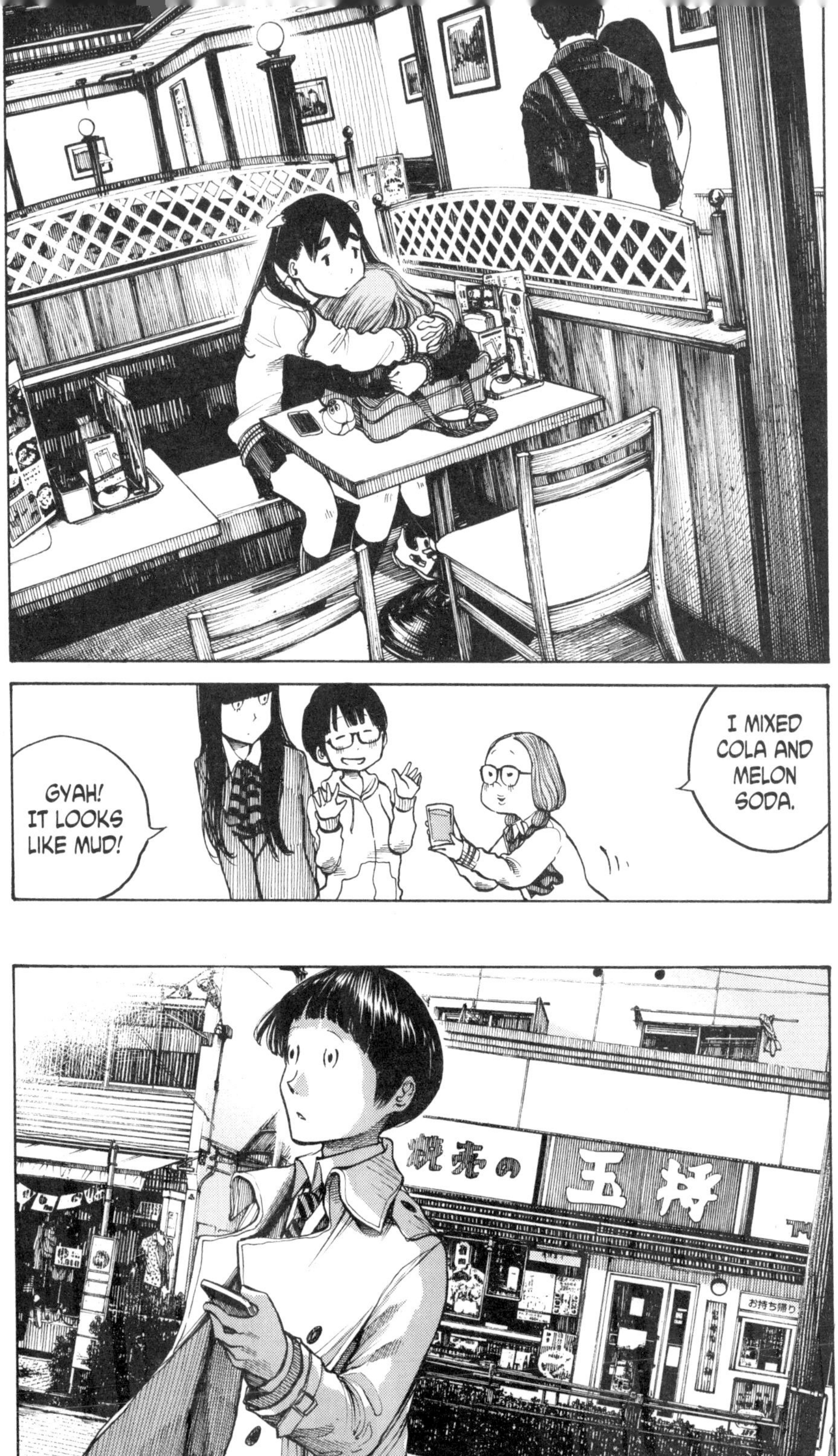
I MIXED COLA AND MELON SODA.
GYAH! IT LOOKS LIKE MUD!
お持ち帰り

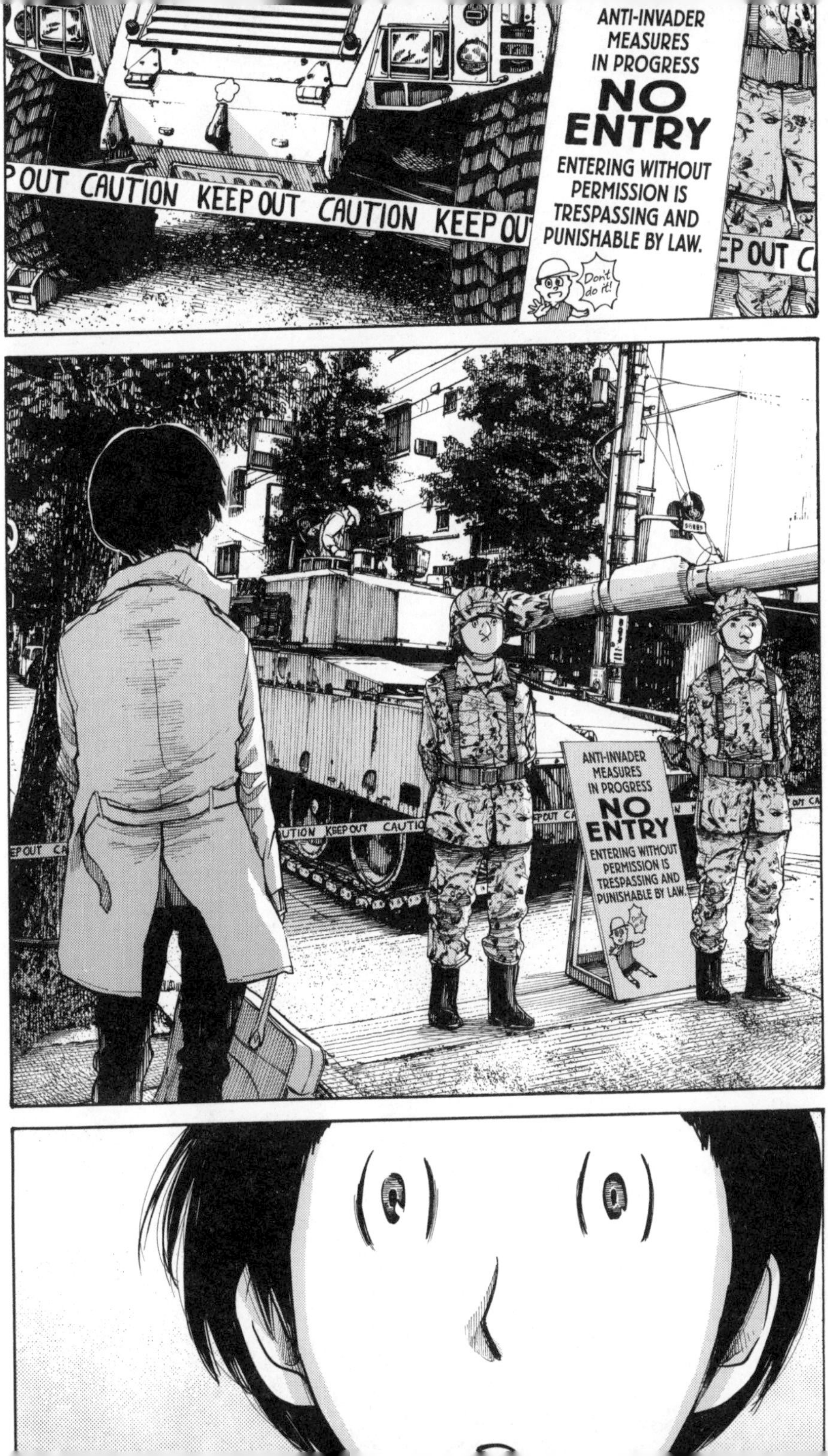
ANTI-INVADER MEASURES IN PROGRESS
NO ENTRY
ENTERING WITHOUT PERMISSION IS TRESPASSING AND PUNISHABLE BY LAW.
Don't do it!
EP OUT CAUTION KEEP OUT CAUTION KEEP OUT
EP OUT C
ANTI-INVADER MEASURES IN PROGRESS
NO ENTRY
ENTERING WITHOUT PERMISSION IS TRESPASSING AND PUNISHABLE BY LAW.
CAUTION KEEP OUT CAUTION
EP OUT CA

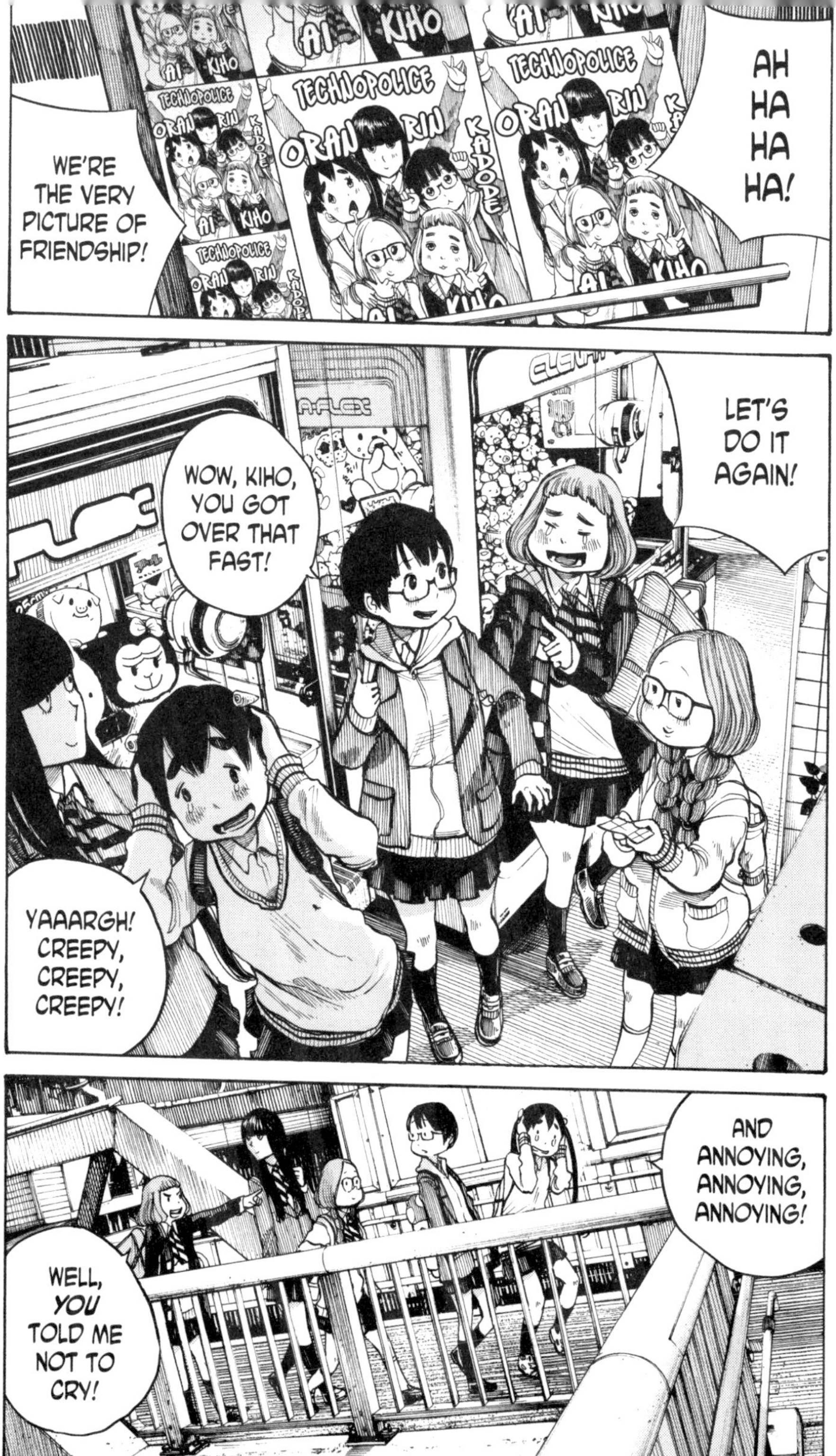
AH HA HA HA!
WE'RE THE VERY PICTURE OF FRIENDSHIP!
TECHNOPOLICE
ORAN
RIN
KADODE
AI
KIHO
LET'S DO IT AGAIN!
WOW, KIHO, YOU GOT OVER THAT FAST!
YAAARGH! CREEPY, CREEPY, CREEPY!
AND ANNOYING, ANNOYING, ANNOYING!
WELL, *YOU* TOLD ME NOT TO CRY!

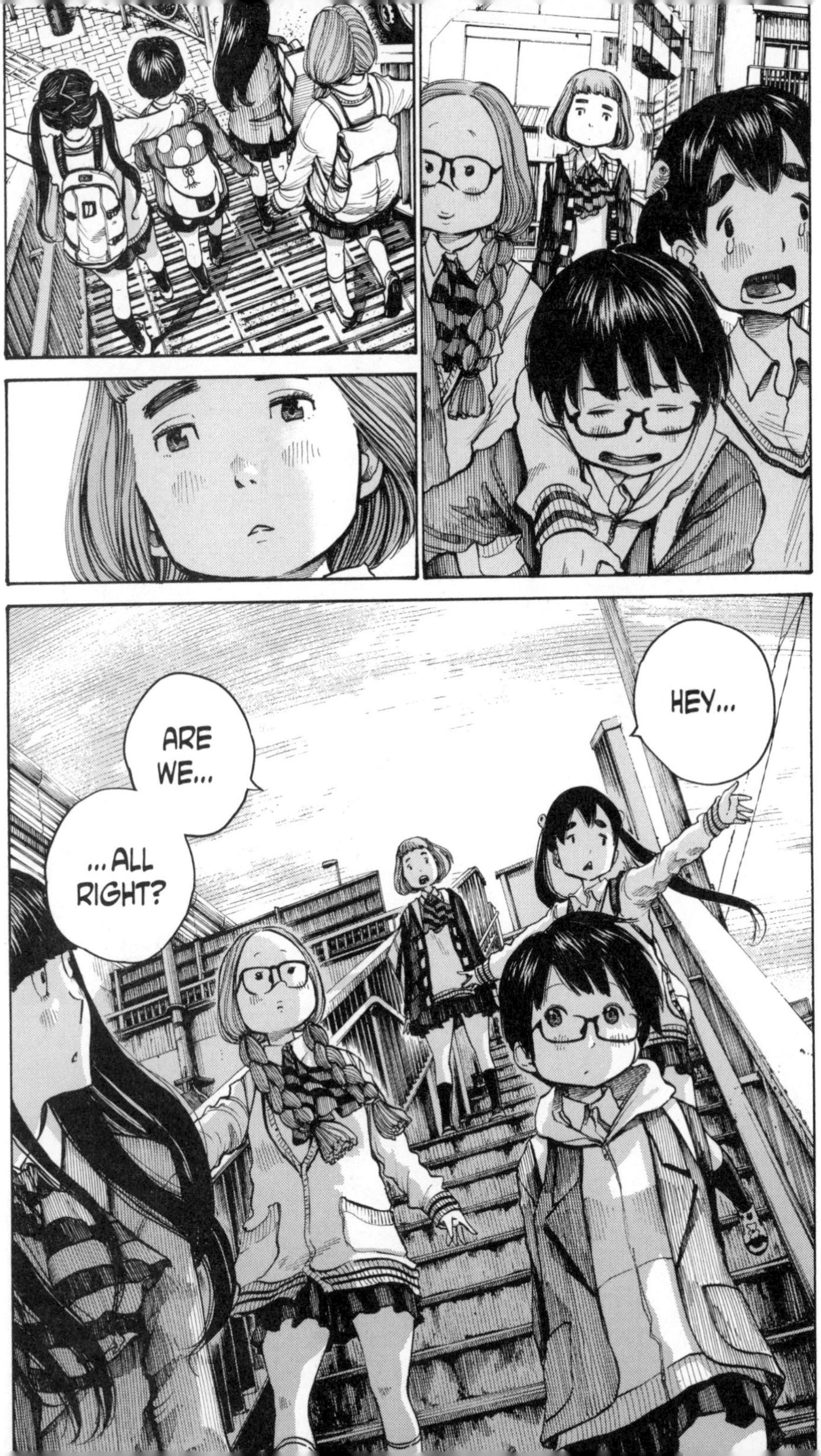
HEY...
ARE WE...
...ALL RIGHT?

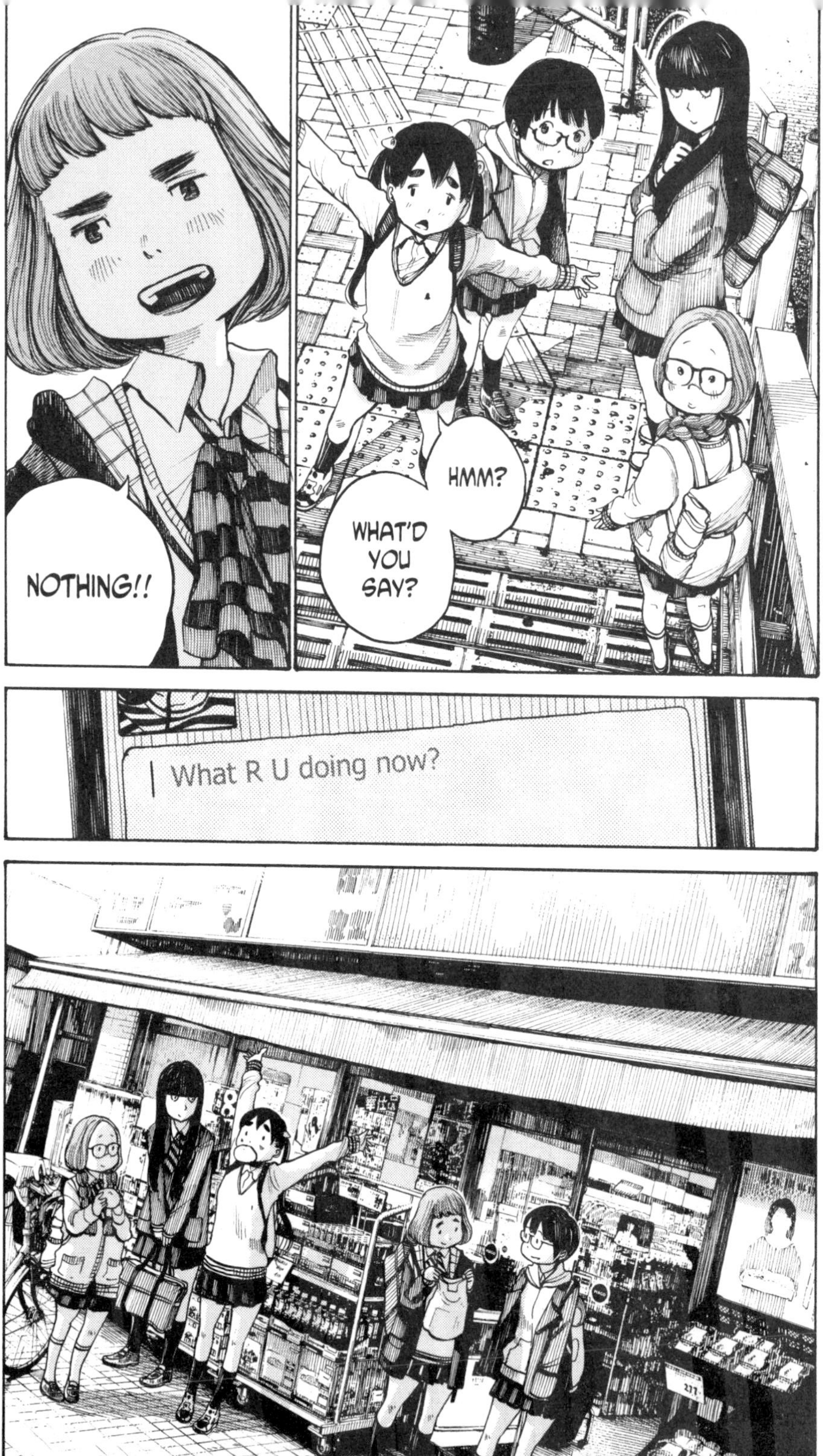
HMM?
WHAT'D YOU SAY?
NOTHING!!
What R U doing now?

DE
DE
DEDE

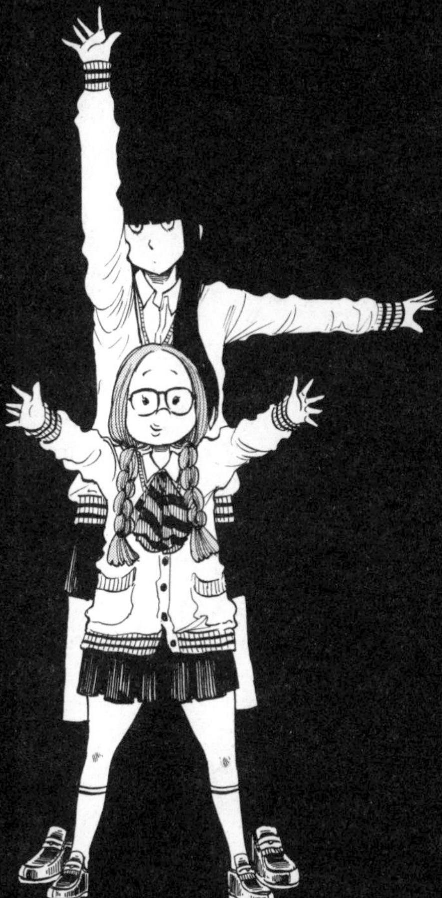

DE DE DE DE

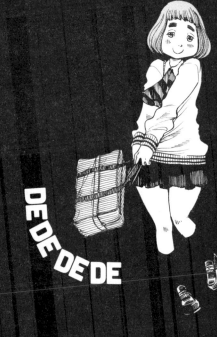

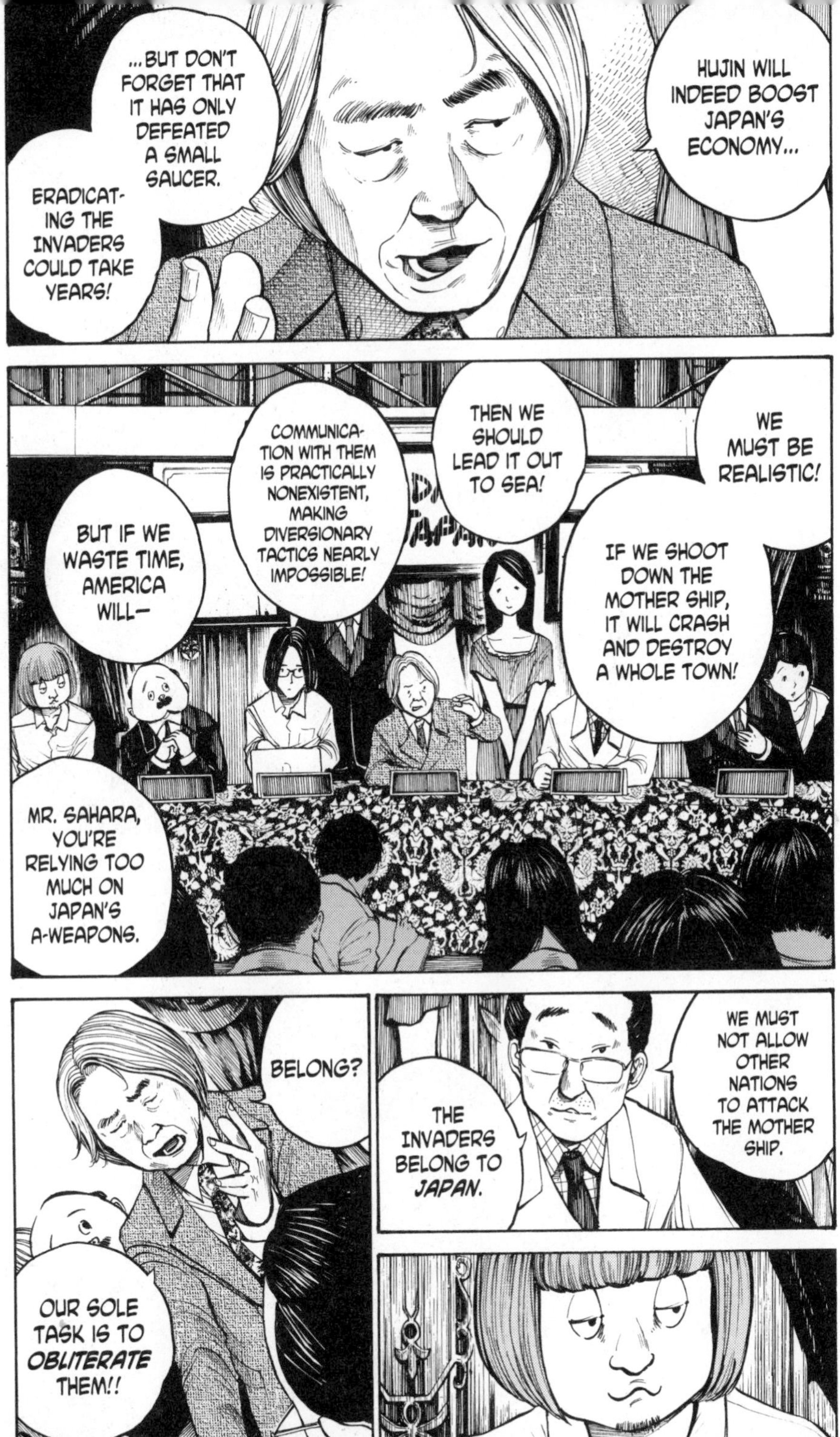
HUJIN WILL INDEED BOOST JAPAN'S ECONOMY...
...BUT DON'T FORGET THAT IT HAS ONLY DEFEATED A SMALL SAUCER.
ERADICATING THE INVADERS COULD TAKE YEARS!
WE MUST BE REALISTIC!
IF WE SHOOT DOWN THE MOTHER SHIP, IT WILL CRASH AND DESTROY A WHOLE TOWN!
THEN WE SHOULD LEAD IT OUT TO SEA!
COMMUNICATION WITH THEM IS PRACTICALLY NONEXISTENT, MAKING DIVERSIONARY TACTICS NEARLY IMPOSSIBLE!
BUT IF WE WASTE TIME, AMERICA WILL—
MR. SAHARA, YOU'RE RELYING TOO MUCH ON JAPAN'S A-WEAPONS.
WE MUST NOT ALLOW OTHER NATIONS TO ATTACK THE MOTHER SHIP.
THE INVADERS BELONG TO *JAPAN*.
BELONG?
OUR SOLE TASK IS TO *OBLITERATE* THEM!!

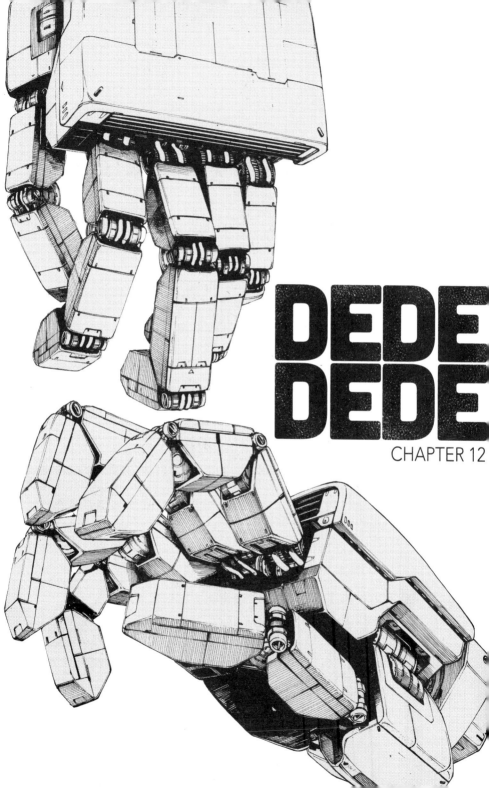

DEDE
DEDE

CHAPTER 12

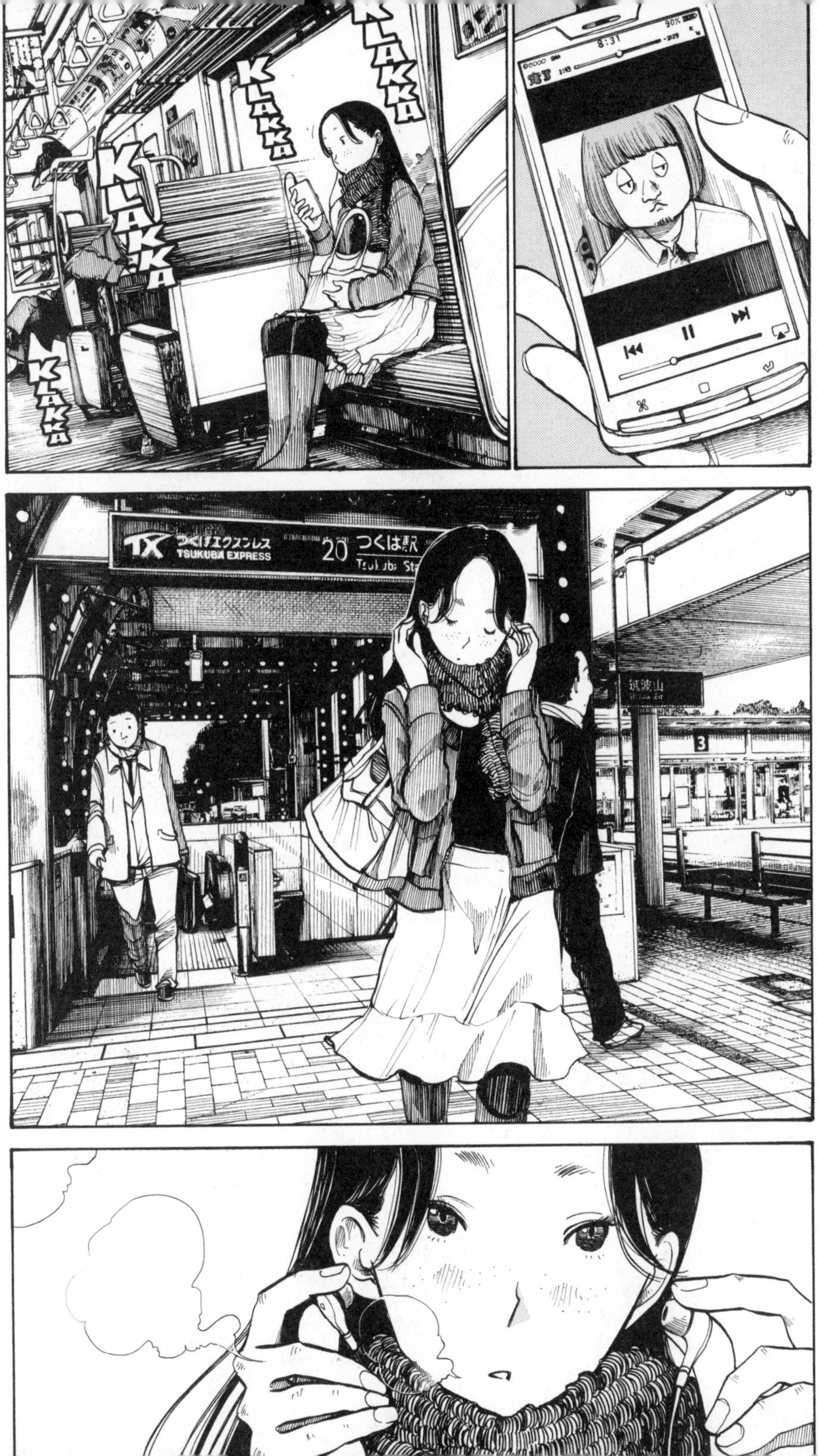
8:31
90%
KLAKKA
KLAKKA
KLAKKA
KLAKKA
TX
つくばエクスプレス
TSUKUBA EXPRESS
20
つくば駅
筑波山
3

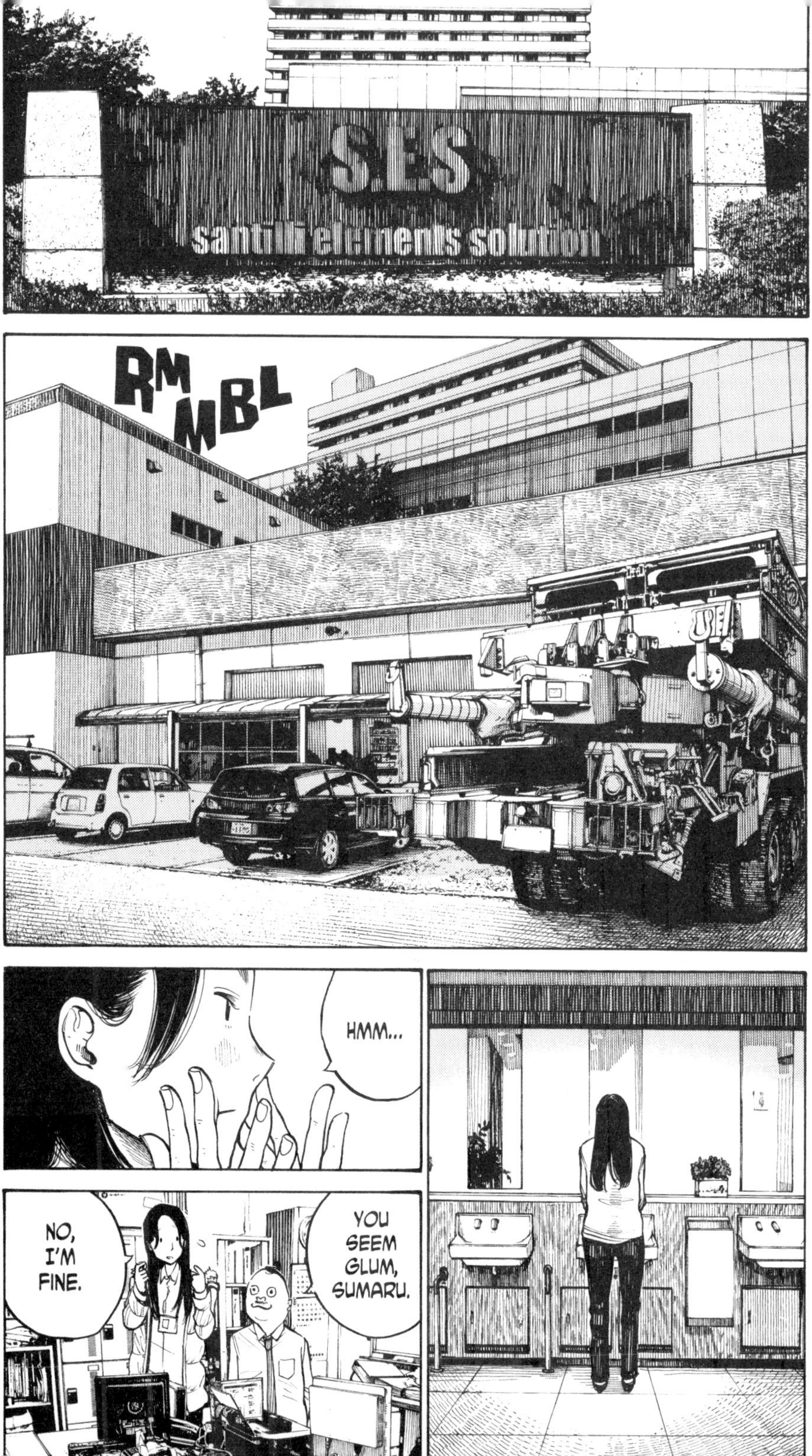
S.E.S
RMMBL
HMM...
YOU SEEM GLUM, SUMARU.
NO, I'M FINE.

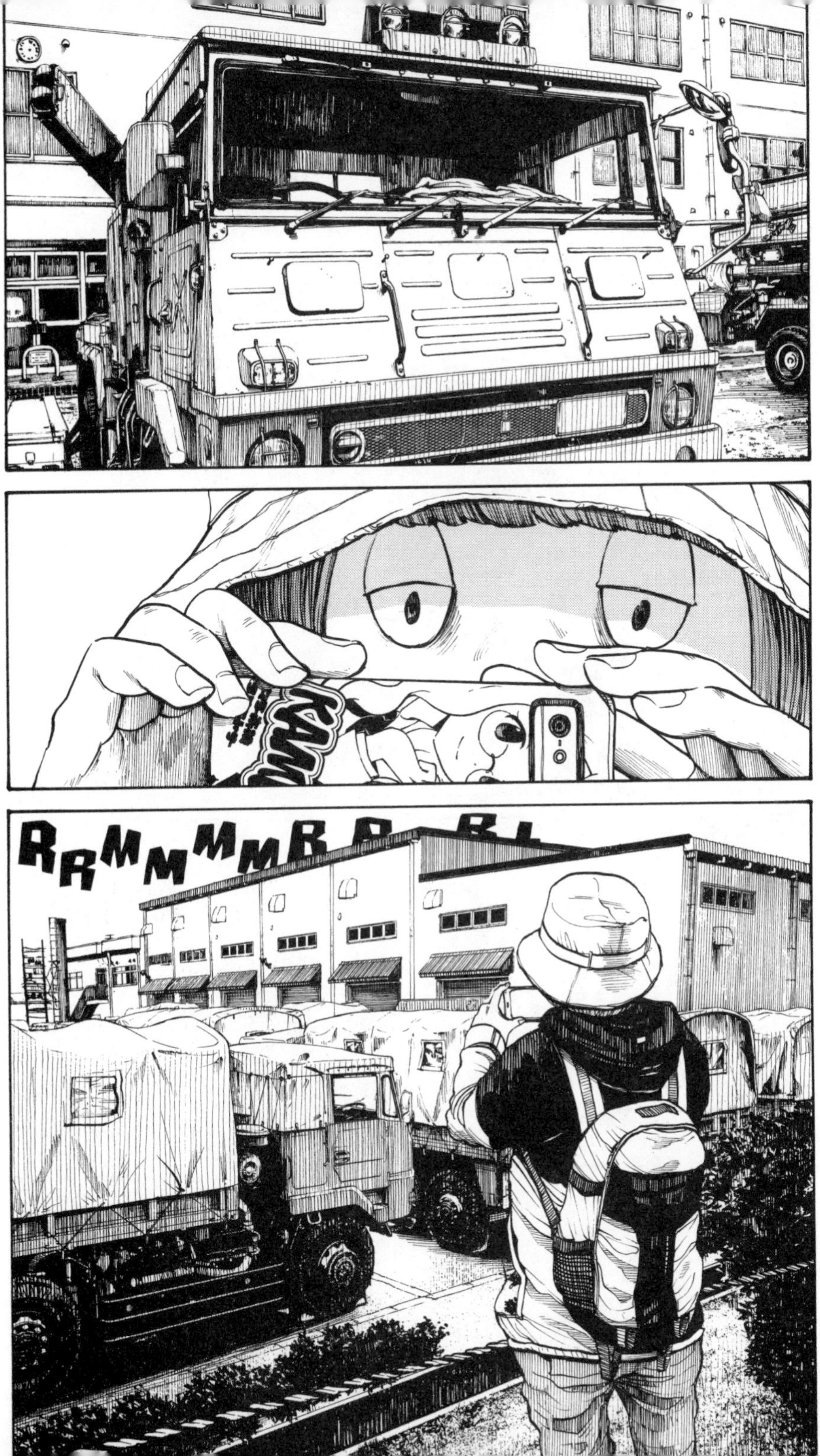
RRMMMMB

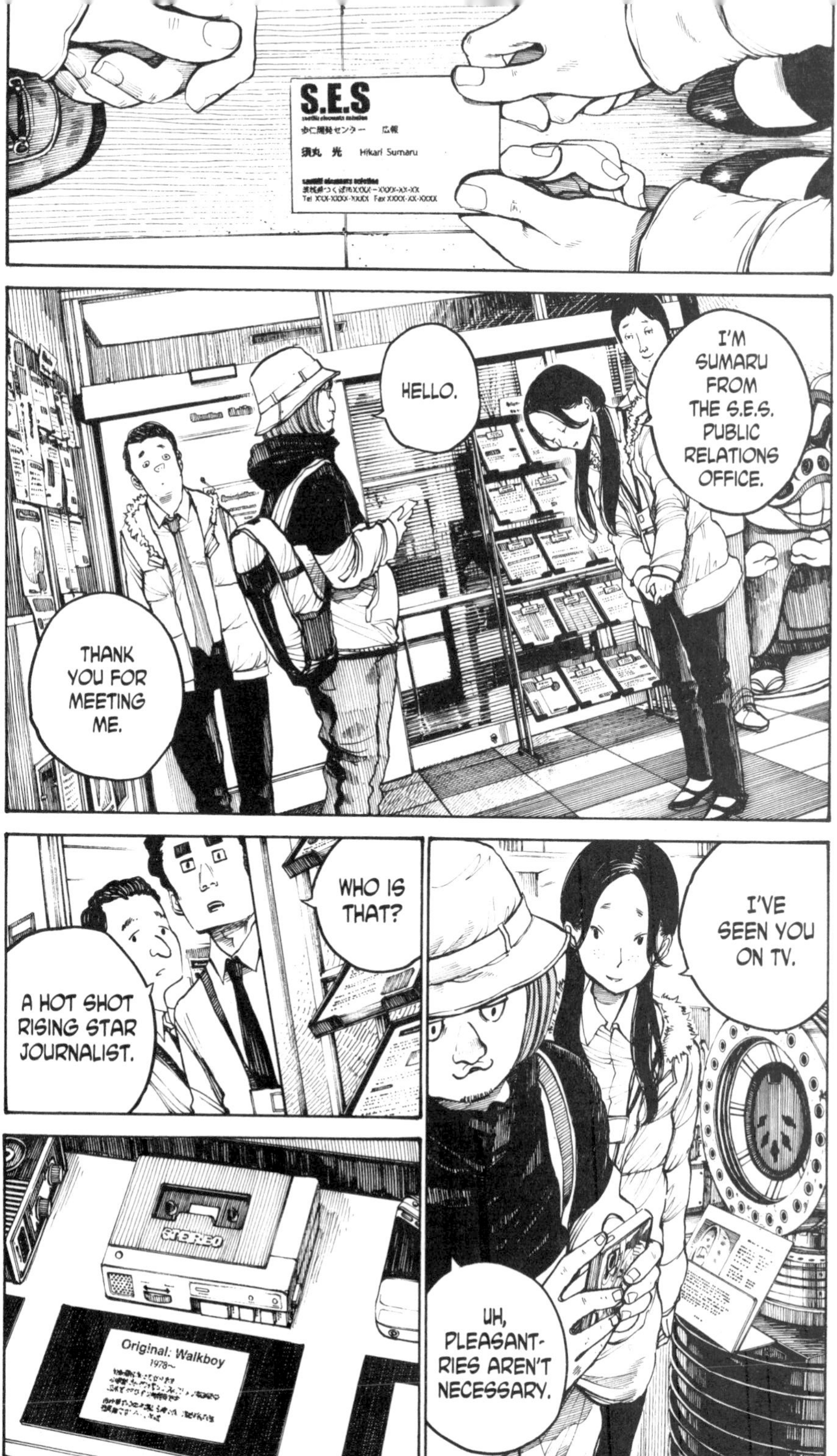

S.E.S
少仁開発センター 広報
須丸 光 Hikari Sumaru
I'M SUMARU FROM THE S.E.S. PUBLIC RELATIONS OFFICE.
HELLO.
THANK YOU FOR MEETING ME.
I'VE SEEN YOU ON TV.
UH, PLEASANTRIES AREN'T NECESSARY.
WHO IS THAT?
A HOT SHOT RISING STAR JOURNALIST.
STEREO
Original: Walkboy
1978~

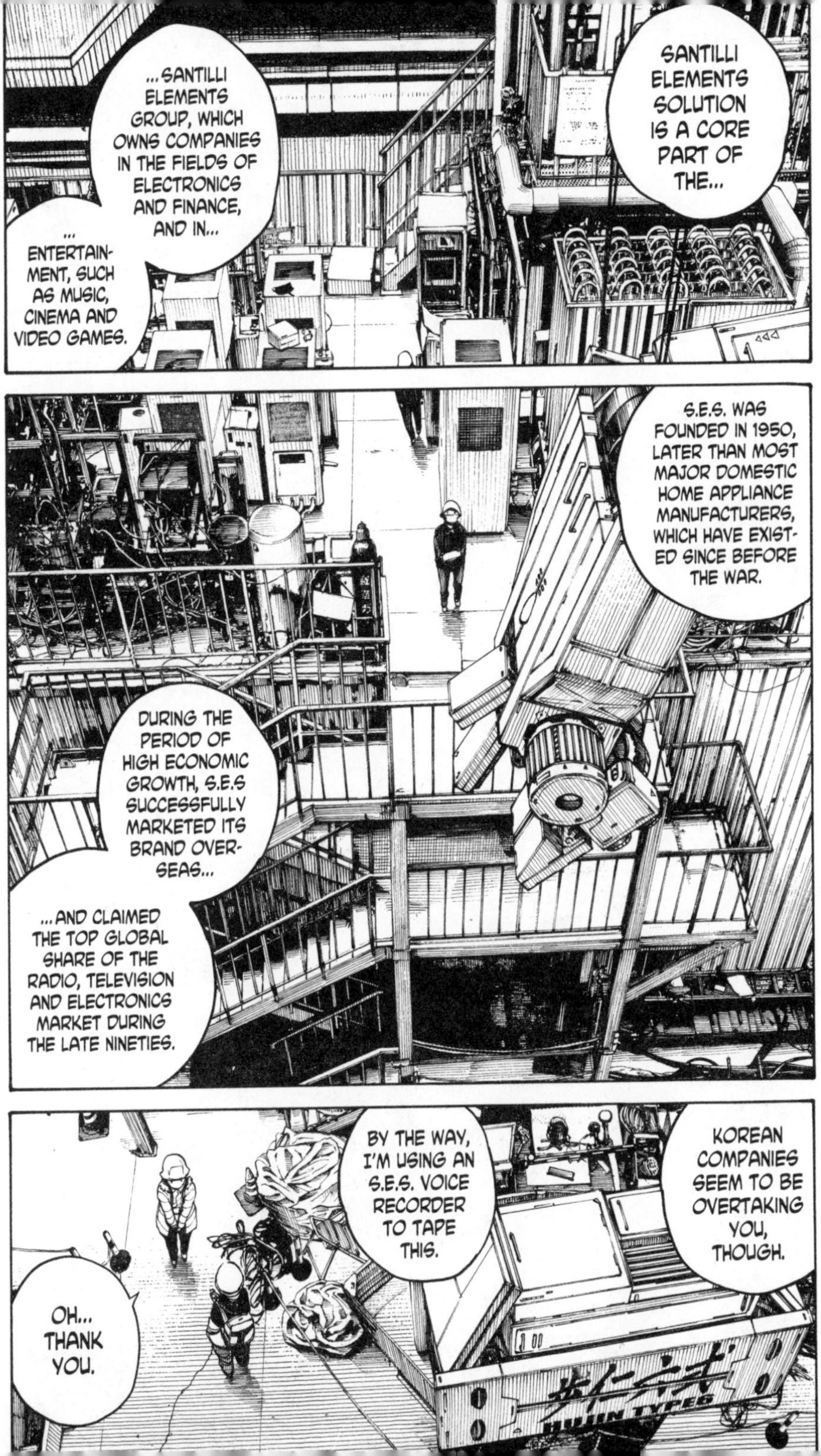
SANTILLI ELEMENTS SOLUTION IS A CORE PART OF THE...
...SANTILLI ELEMENTS GROUP, WHICH OWNS COMPANIES IN THE FIELDS OF ELECTRONICS AND FINANCE, AND IN...
...ENTERTAINMENT, SUCH AS MUSIC, CINEMA AND VIDEO GAMES.
S.E.S. WAS FOUNDED IN 1950, LATER THAN MOST MAJOR DOMESTIC HOME APPLIANCE MANUFACTURERS, WHICH HAVE EXISTED SINCE BEFORE THE WAR.
DURING THE PERIOD OF HIGH ECONOMIC GROWTH, S.E.S SUCCESSFULLY MARKETED ITS BRAND OVERSEAS...
...AND CLAIMED THE TOP GLOBAL SHARE OF THE RADIO, TELEVISION AND ELECTRONICS MARKET DURING THE LATE NINETIES.
KOREAN COMPANIES SEEM TO BE OVERTAKING YOU, THOUGH.
BY THE WAY, I'M USING AN S.E.S. VOICE RECORDER TO TAPE THIS.
OH... THANK YOU.

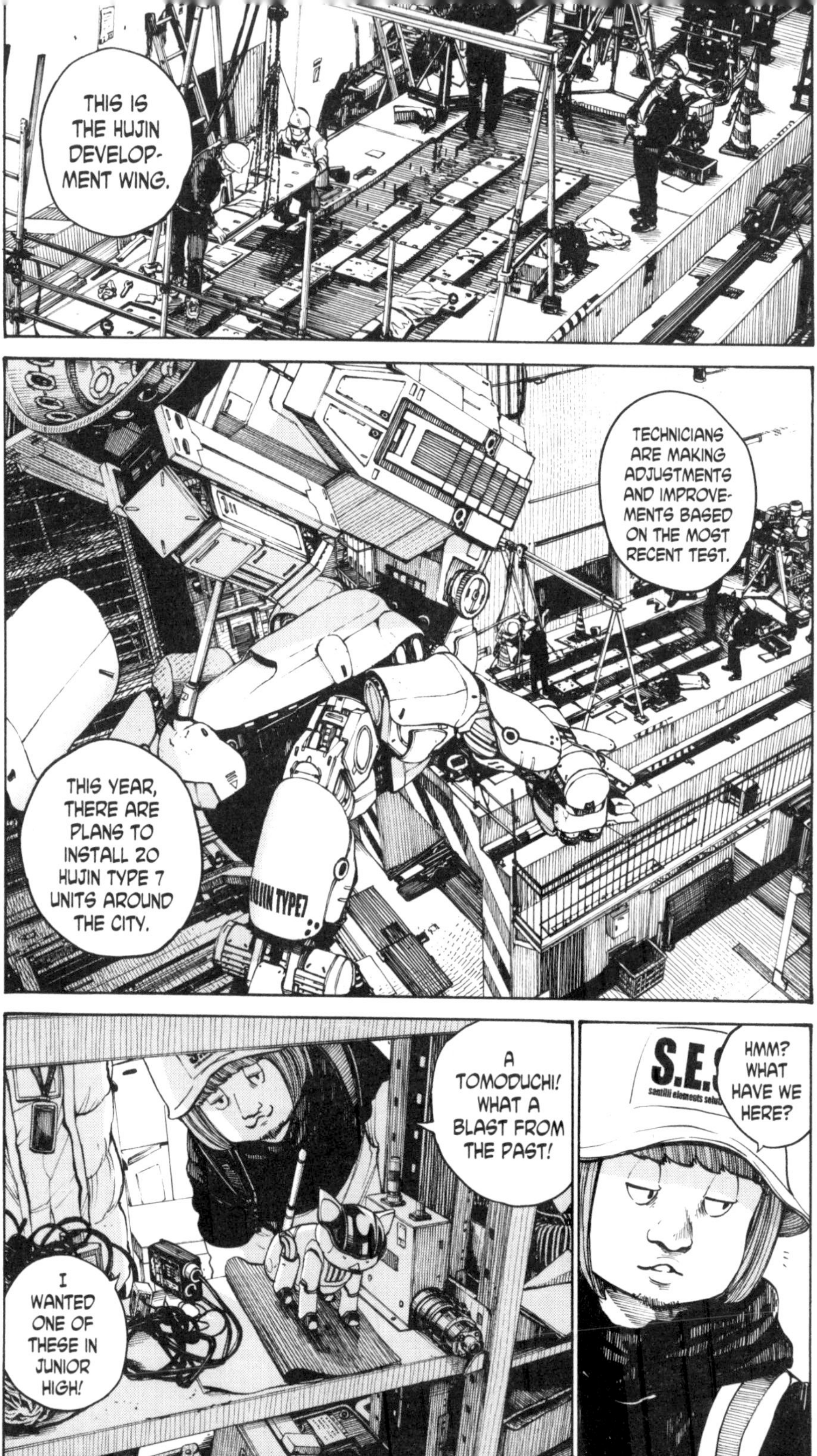
THIS IS THE HUJIN DEVELOPMENT WING.
TECHNICIANS ARE MAKING ADJUSTMENTS AND IMPROVEMENTS BASED ON THE MOST RECENT TEST.
THIS YEAR, THERE ARE PLANS TO INSTALL 20 HUJIN TYPE 7 UNITS AROUND THE CITY.
HMM? WHAT HAVE WE HERE?
A TOMODUCHI! WHAT A BLAST FROM THE PAST!
I WANTED ONE OF THESE IN JUNIOR HIGH!

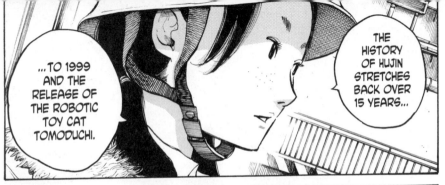

THE HISTORY OF HUJIN STRETCHES BACK OVER 15 YEARS...
...TO 1999 AND THE RELEASE OF THE ROBOTIC TOY CAT TOMODUCHI.
S.E.S. MARKETED TOMODUCHI AS AN AUTONOMOUS ROBOTIC PET FOR $250.
AT THE TIME, THAT WAS THE SAME PRICE AS A LARGE TV, SO IT BECAME A SOCIAL PHENOMENON.
BUT WE FROZE TOMODUCHI PRODUCTION IN 2005, AFTER THE BOOM ENDED.
LATER, WE COLLABORATED WITH NANAHOSHI HEAVY INDUSTRIES TO DESIGN LARGE AGRICULTURAL ROBOTS, WHICH WERE IN HIGH DEMAND DUE TO THE AGING FARMER POPULATION.
DURING THAT SAME PERIOD, A DIFFERENT TEAM WAS DEVELOPING A LASER INTERCEPT SYSTEM, WHICH THEY REDESIGNED AS A GREEN-RAY DEVICE.
IN JUST THREE YEARS, THE WORLD'S LEADING TECHNOLOGIES WERE COMBINED TO CREATE A CUTTING-EDGE PRODUCT AT THE FOREFRONT OF INDUSTRY—HUJIN.

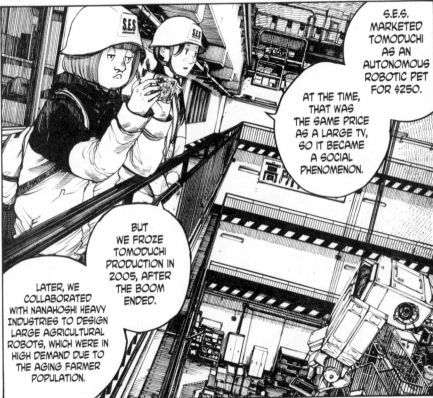

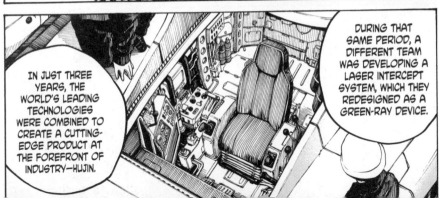

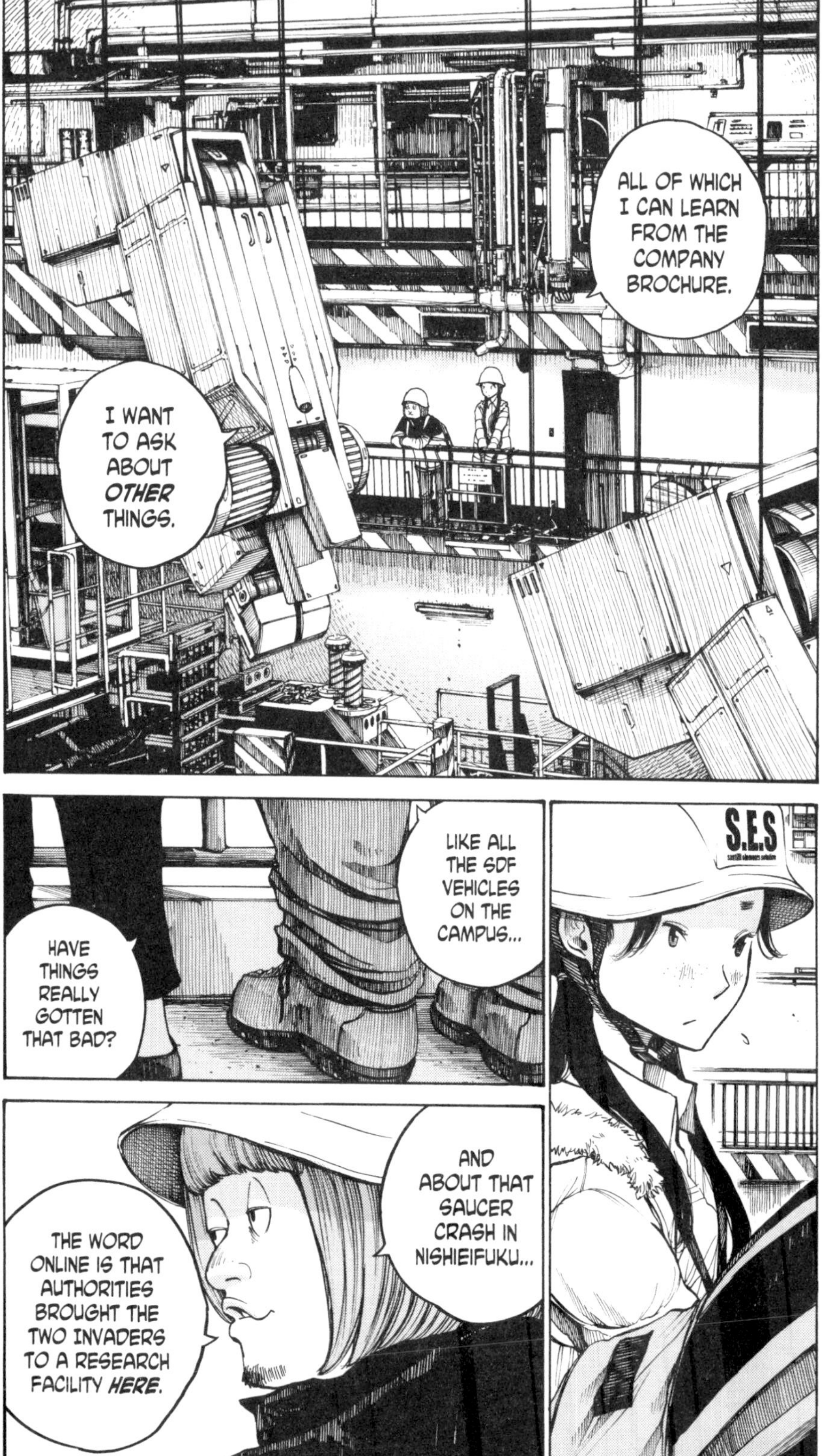
ALL OF WHICH I CAN LEARN FROM THE COMPANY BROCHURE.
I WANT TO ASK ABOUT *OTHER* THINGS.
S.E.S
LIKE ALL THE SDF VEHICLES ON THE CAMPUS...
HAVE THINGS REALLY GOTTEN THAT BAD?
AND ABOUT THAT SAUCER CRASH IN NISHIEIFUKU...
THE WORD ONLINE IS THAT AUTHORITIES BROUGHT THE TWO INVADERS TO A RESEARCH FACILITY *HERE*.

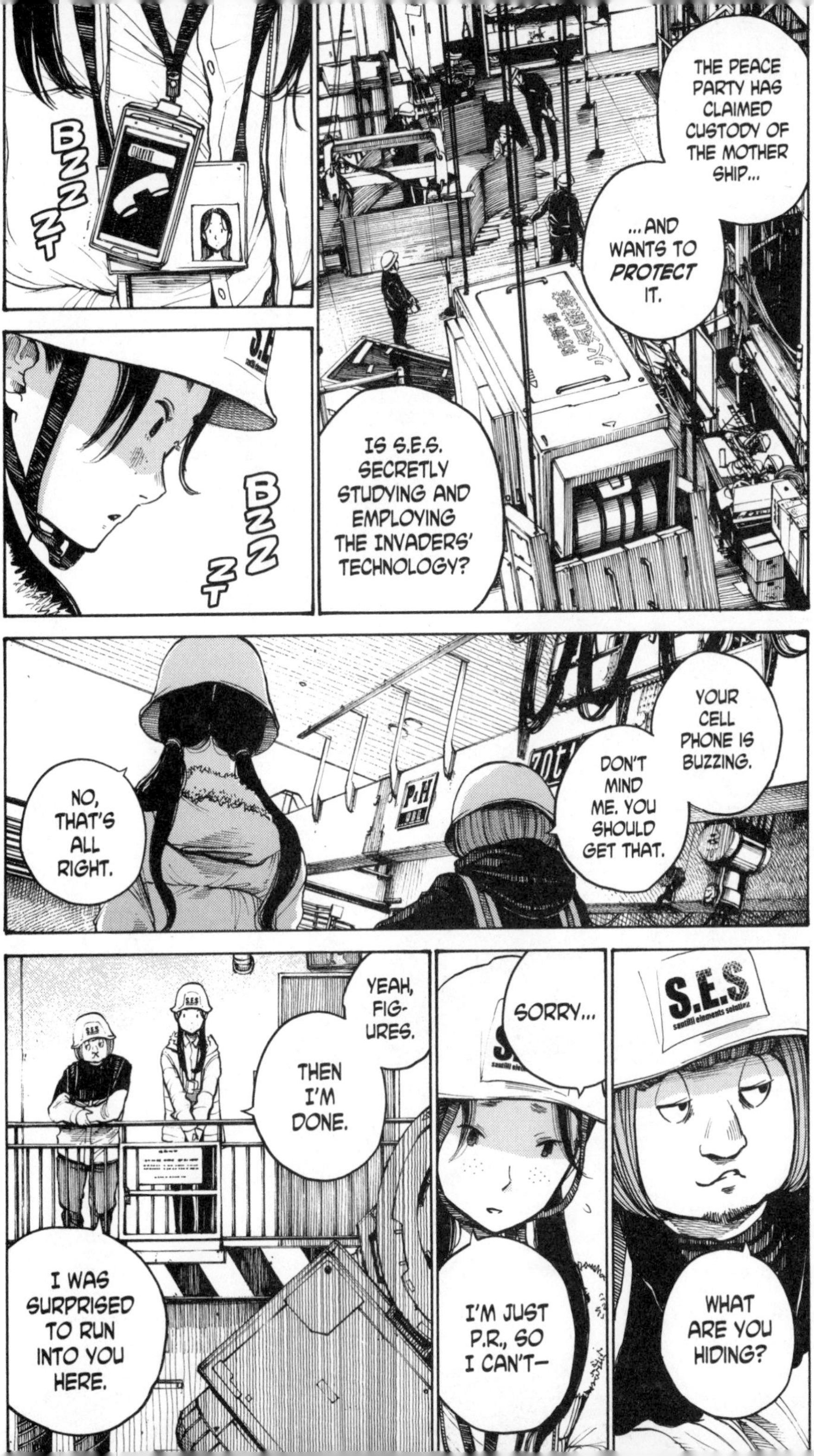
THE PEACE PARTY HAS CLAIMED CUSTODY OF THE MOTHER SHIP...
...AND WANTS TO *PROTECT* IT.
IS S.E.S. SECRETLY STUDYING AND EMPLOYING THE INVADERS' TECHNOLOGY?
BZZZT
BZZZT
YOUR CELL PHONE IS BUZZING.
DON'T MIND ME. YOU SHOULD GET THAT.
NO, THAT'S ALL RIGHT.
S.E.S
WHAT ARE YOU HIDING?
SORRY...
I'M JUST P.R., SO I CAN'T—
YEAH, FIGURES.
THEN I'M DONE.
I WAS SURPRISED TO RUN INTO YOU HERE.

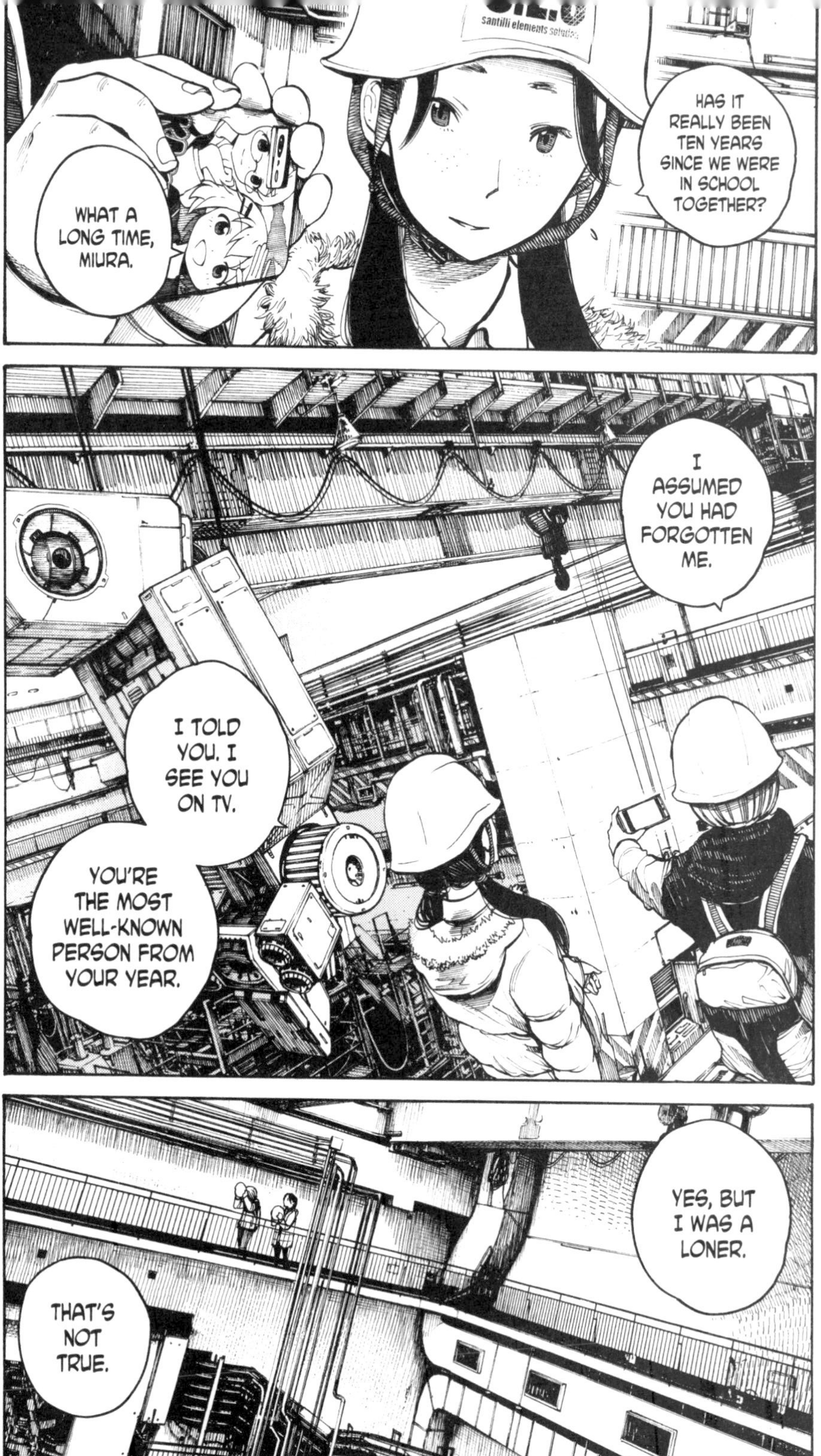
HAS IT REALLY BEEN TEN YEARS SINCE WE WERE IN SCHOOL TOGETHER?
WHAT A LONG TIME, MIURA.
I ASSUMED YOU HAD FORGOTTEN ME.
I TOLD YOU. I SEE YOU ON TV.
YOU'RE THE MOST WELL-KNOWN PERSON FROM YOUR YEAR.
YES, BUT I WAS A LONER.
THAT'S NOT TRUE.

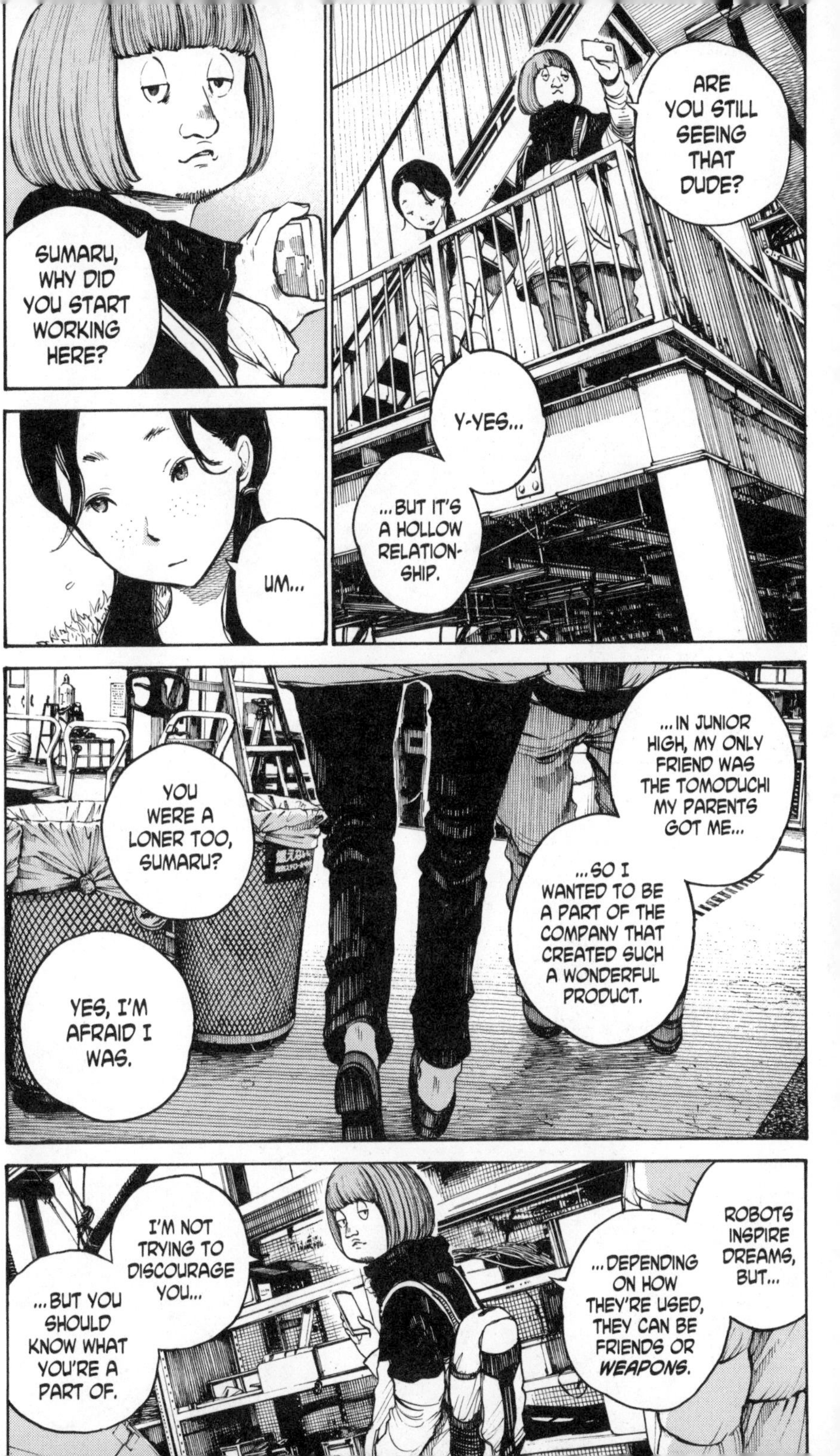
ARE YOU STILL SEEING THAT DUDE?
Y-YES...
...BUT IT'S A HOLLOW RELATION-SHIP.
SUMARU, WHY DID YOU START WORKING HERE?
UM...
...IN JUNIOR HIGH, MY ONLY FRIEND WAS THE TOMODUCHI MY PARENTS GOT ME...
...SO I WANTED TO BE A PART OF THE COMPANY THAT CREATED SUCH A WONDERFUL PRODUCT.
YOU WERE A LONER TOO, SUMARU?
YES, I'M AFRAID I WAS.
ROBOTS INSPIRE DREAMS, BUT...
...DEPENDING ON HOW THEY'RE USED, THEY CAN BE FRIENDS OR *WEAPONS*.
I'M NOT TRYING TO DISCOURAGE YOU...
...BUT YOU SHOULD KNOW WHAT YOU'RE A PART OF.

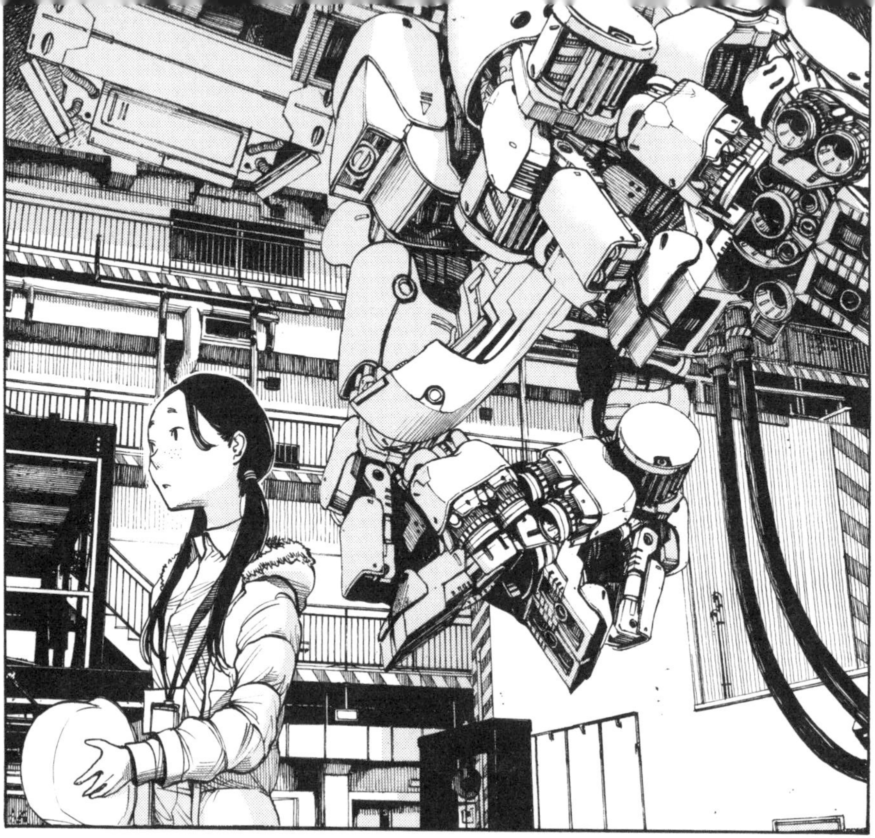

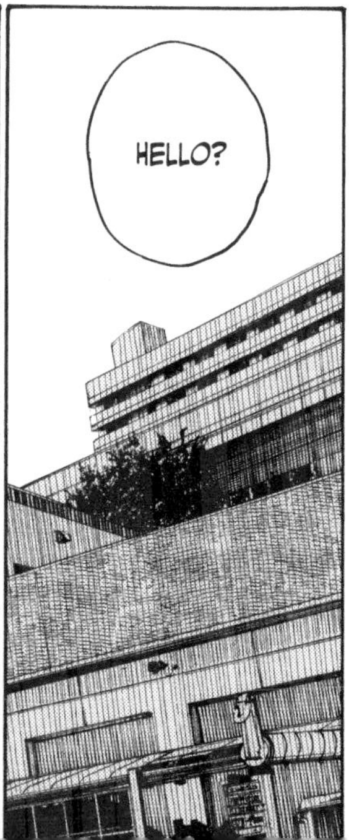
HELLO?

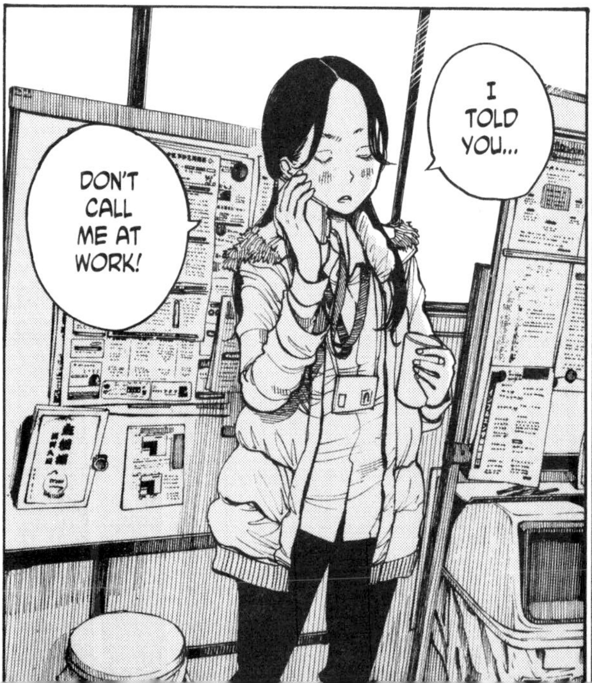
I TOLD YOU...
DON'T CALL ME AT WORK!

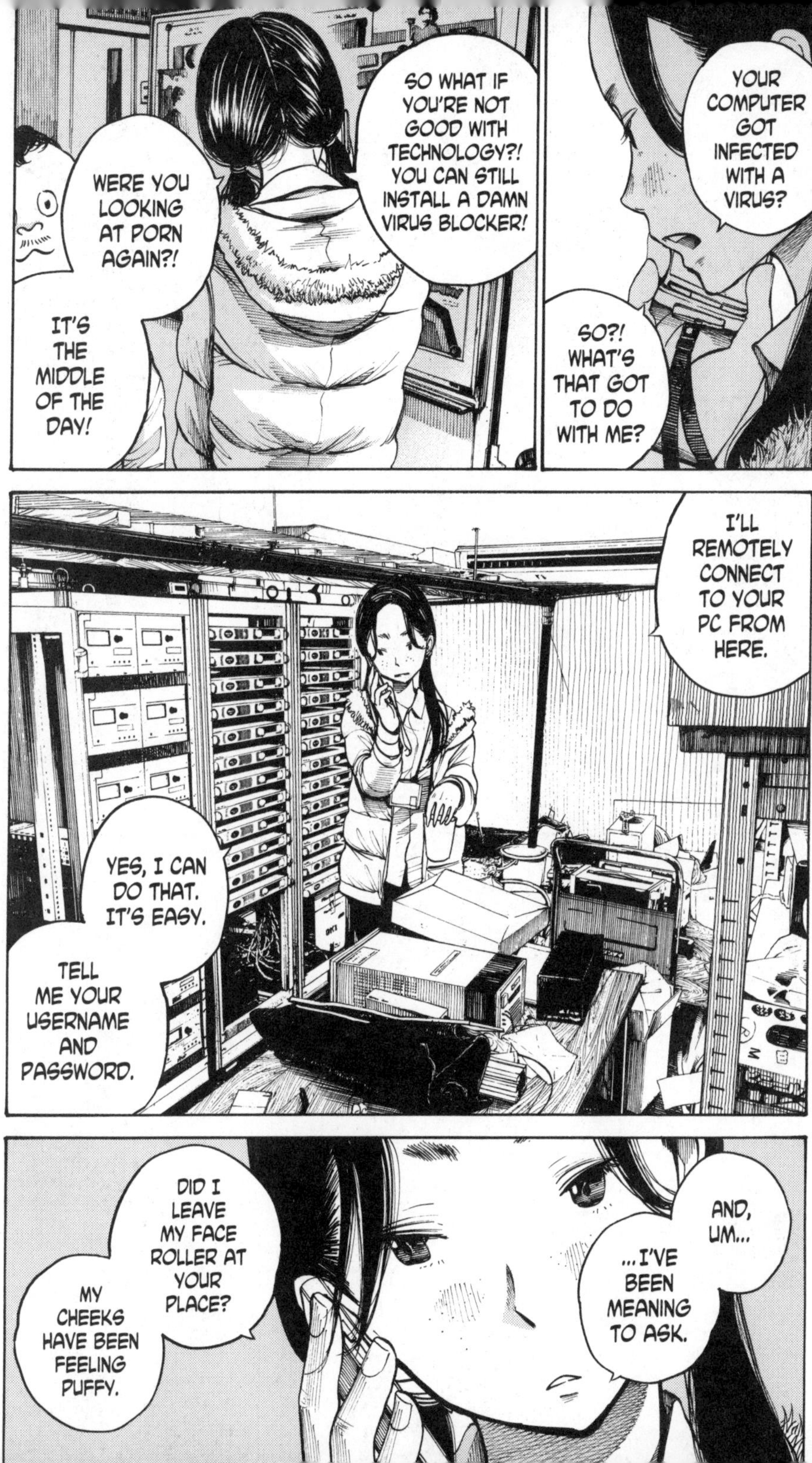
YOUR COMPUTER GOT INFECTED WITH A VIRUS?
SO?! WHAT'S THAT GOT TO DO WITH ME?
SO WHAT IF YOU'RE NOT GOOD WITH TECHNOLOGY?! YOU CAN STILL INSTALL A DAMN VIRUS BLOCKER!
WERE YOU LOOKING AT PORN AGAIN?!
IT'S THE MIDDLE OF THE DAY!
I'LL REMOTELY CONNECT TO YOUR PC FROM HERE.
YES, I CAN DO THAT. IT'S EASY.
TELL ME YOUR USERNAME AND PASSWORD.
AND, UM...
...I'VE BEEN MEANING TO ASK.
DID I LEAVE MY FACE ROLLER AT YOUR PLACE?
MY CHEEKS HAVE BEEN FEELING PUFFY.

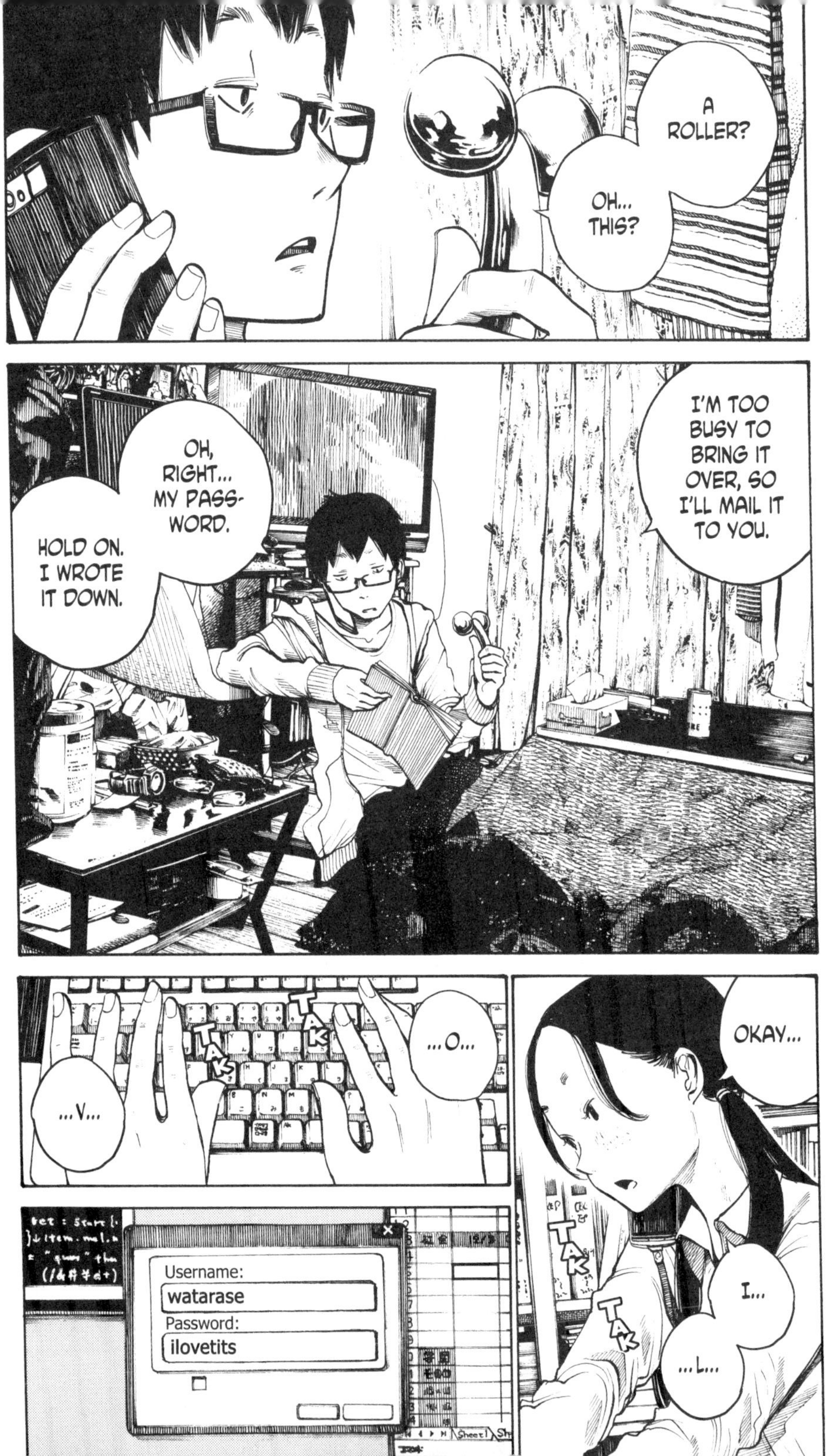
A ROLLER?
OH... THIS?
I'M TOO BUSY TO BRING IT OVER, SO I'LL MAIL IT TO YOU.
OH, RIGHT... MY PASS-WORD.
HOLD ON. I WROTE IT DOWN.
OKAY...
TAK
TAK
I...
...L...
...O...
TAK
TAK
...V...
Username:
watarase
Password:
ilovetits
Sheet1

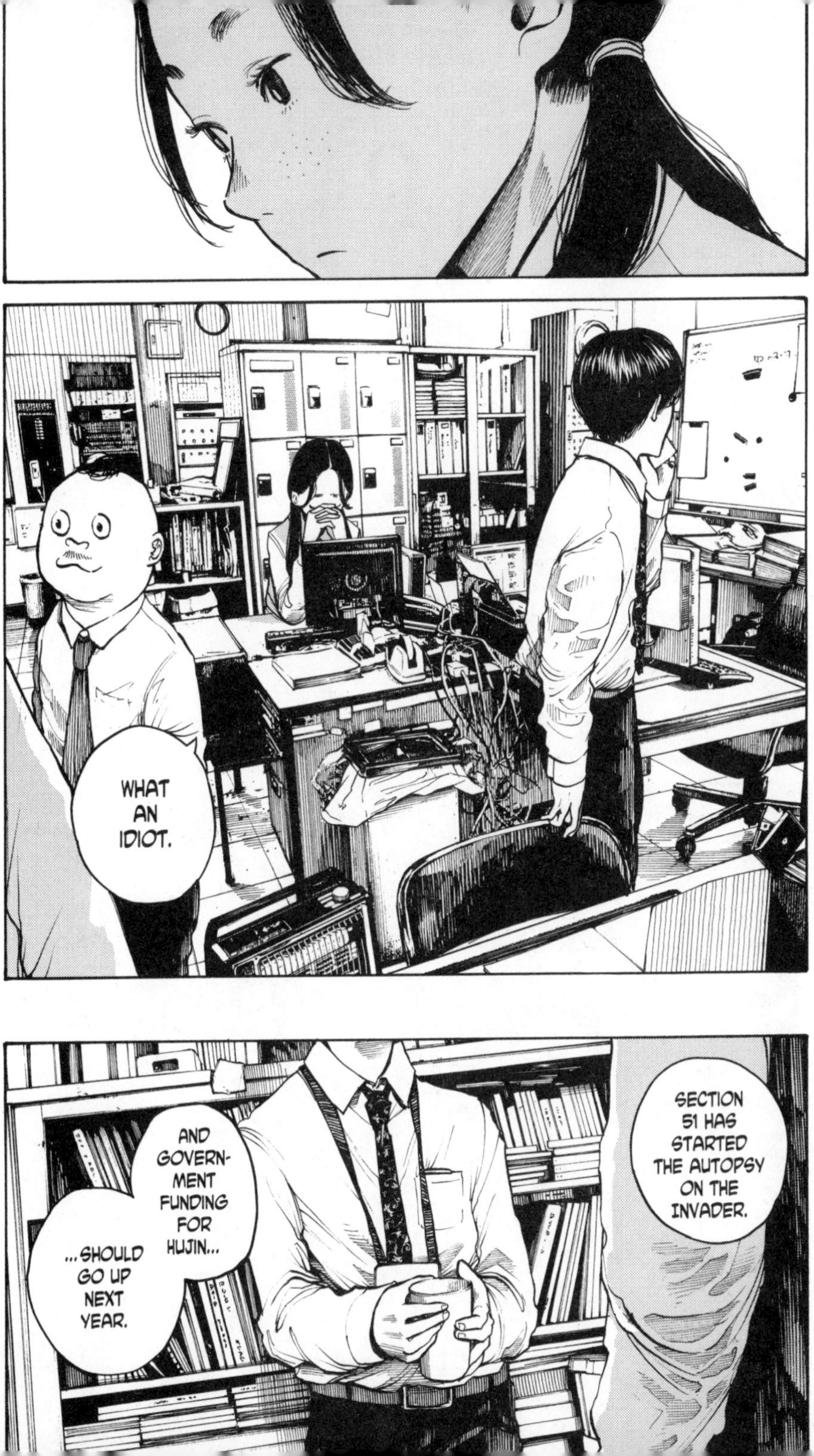
WHAT AN IDIOT.
SECTION 51 HAS STARTED THE AUTOPSY ON THE INVADER.
AND GOVERN-MENT FUNDING FOR HUJIN...
...SHOULD GO UP NEXT YEAR.

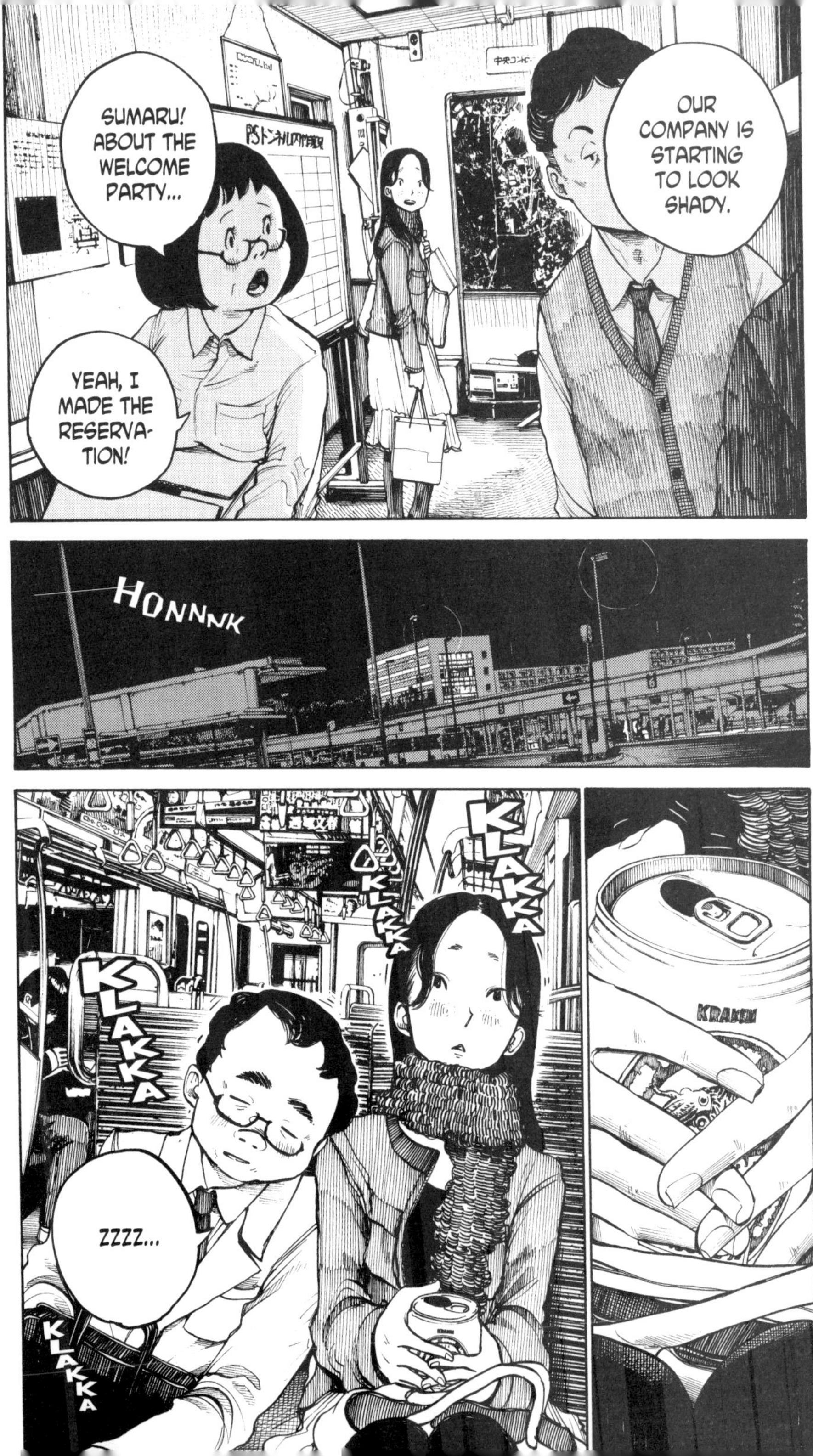
OUR COMPANY IS STARTING TO LOOK SHADY.
SUMARU! ABOUT THE WELCOME PARTY...
YEAH, I MADE THE RESERVA-TION!
HONNNK
KRAKEN
KLAKKA
KLAKKA
KLAKKA
ZZZZ...
KLAKKA

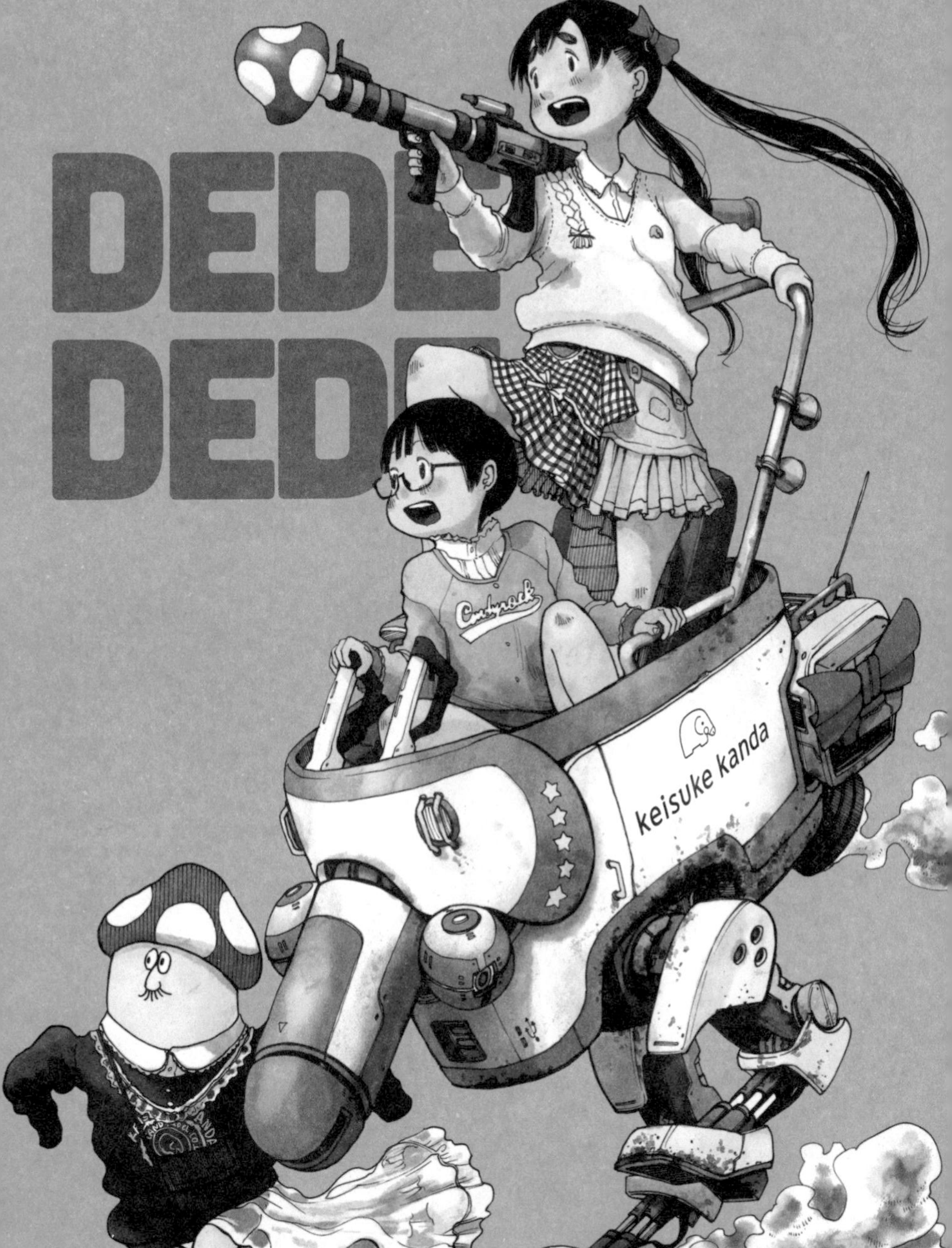
DEDE
keisuke kanda

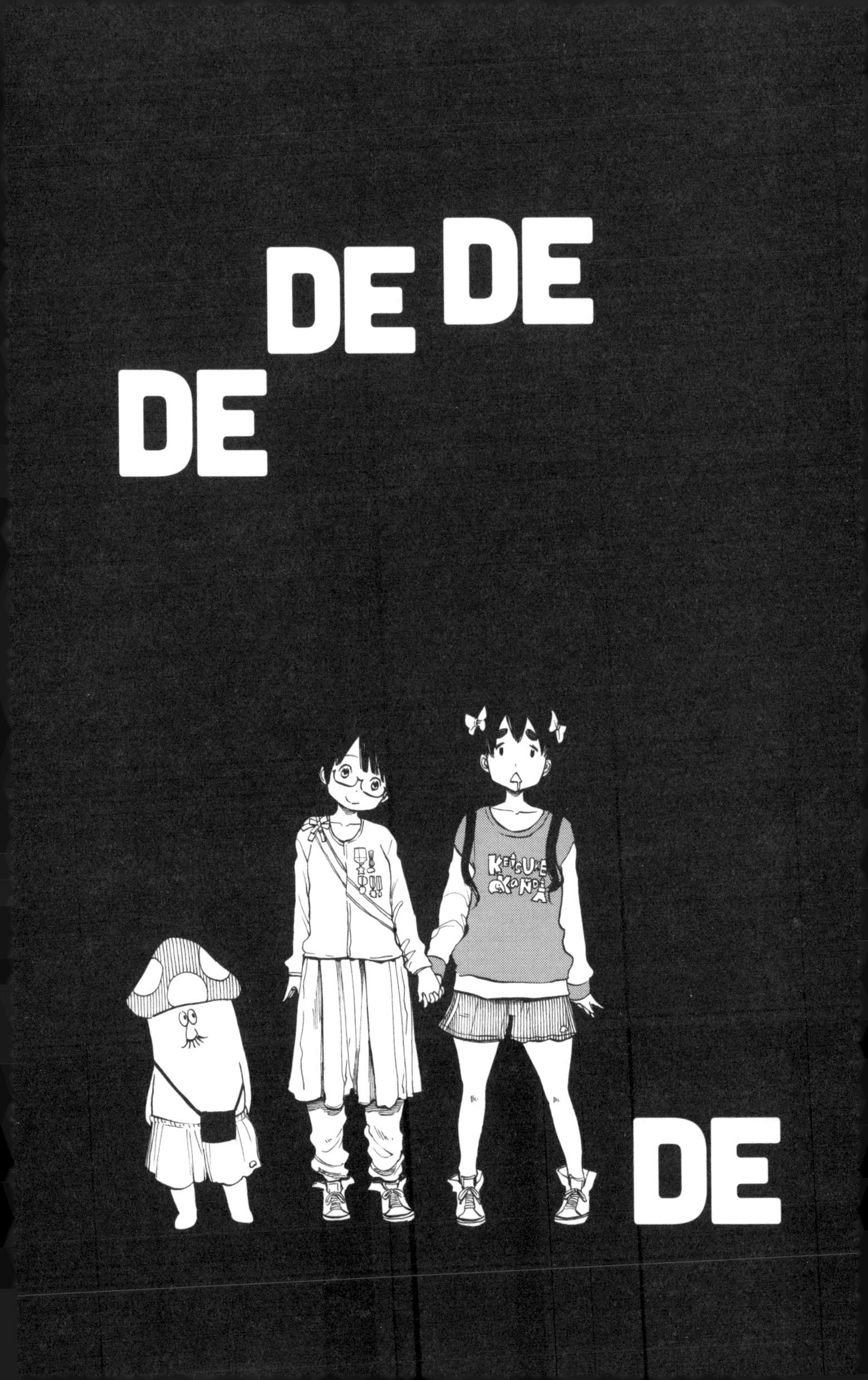
DE
DE
DE
DE

CHAPTER 13

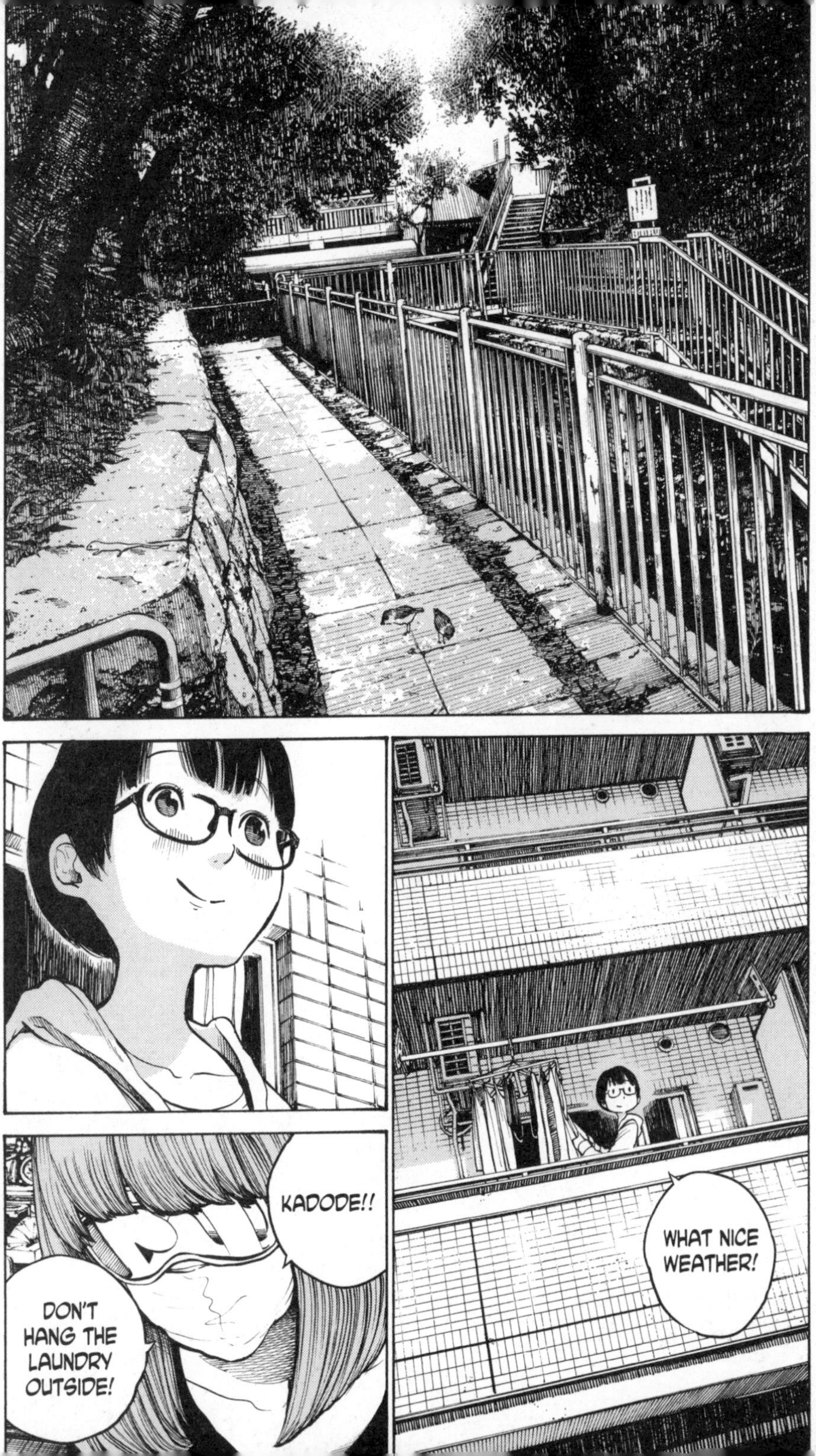
WHAT NICE WEATHER!
KADODE!!
DON'T HANG THE LAUNDRY OUTSIDE!

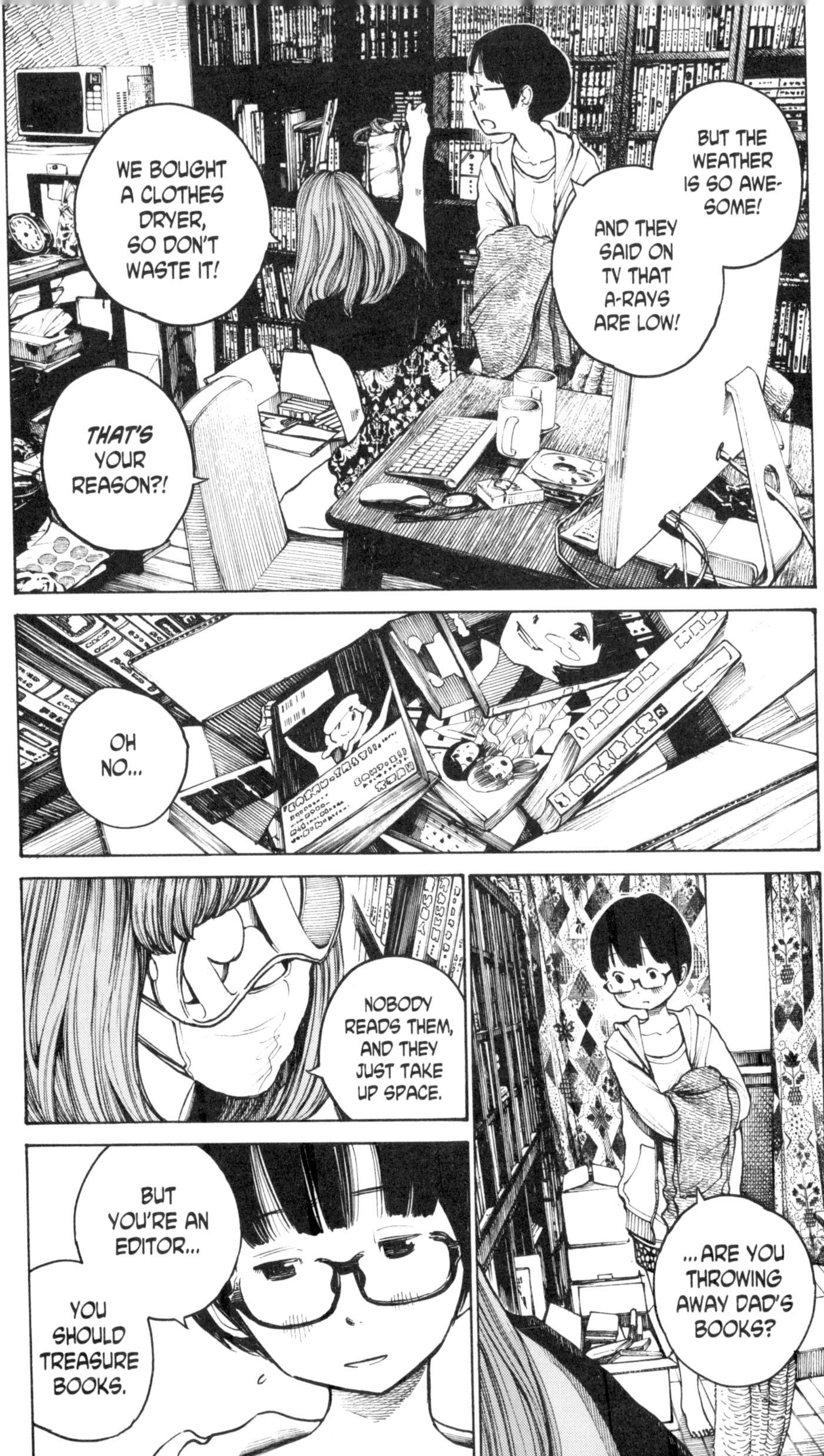
BUT THE WEATHER IS SO AWE-SOME!
AND THEY SAID ON TV THAT A-RAYS ARE LOW!
WE BOUGHT A CLOTHES DRYER, SO DON'T WASTE IT!
THAT'S YOUR REASON?!
OH NO...
...ARE YOU THROWING AWAY DAD'S BOOKS?
NOBODY READS THEM, AND THEY JUST TAKE UP SPACE.
BUT YOU'RE AN EDITOR...
YOU SHOULD TREASURE BOOKS.

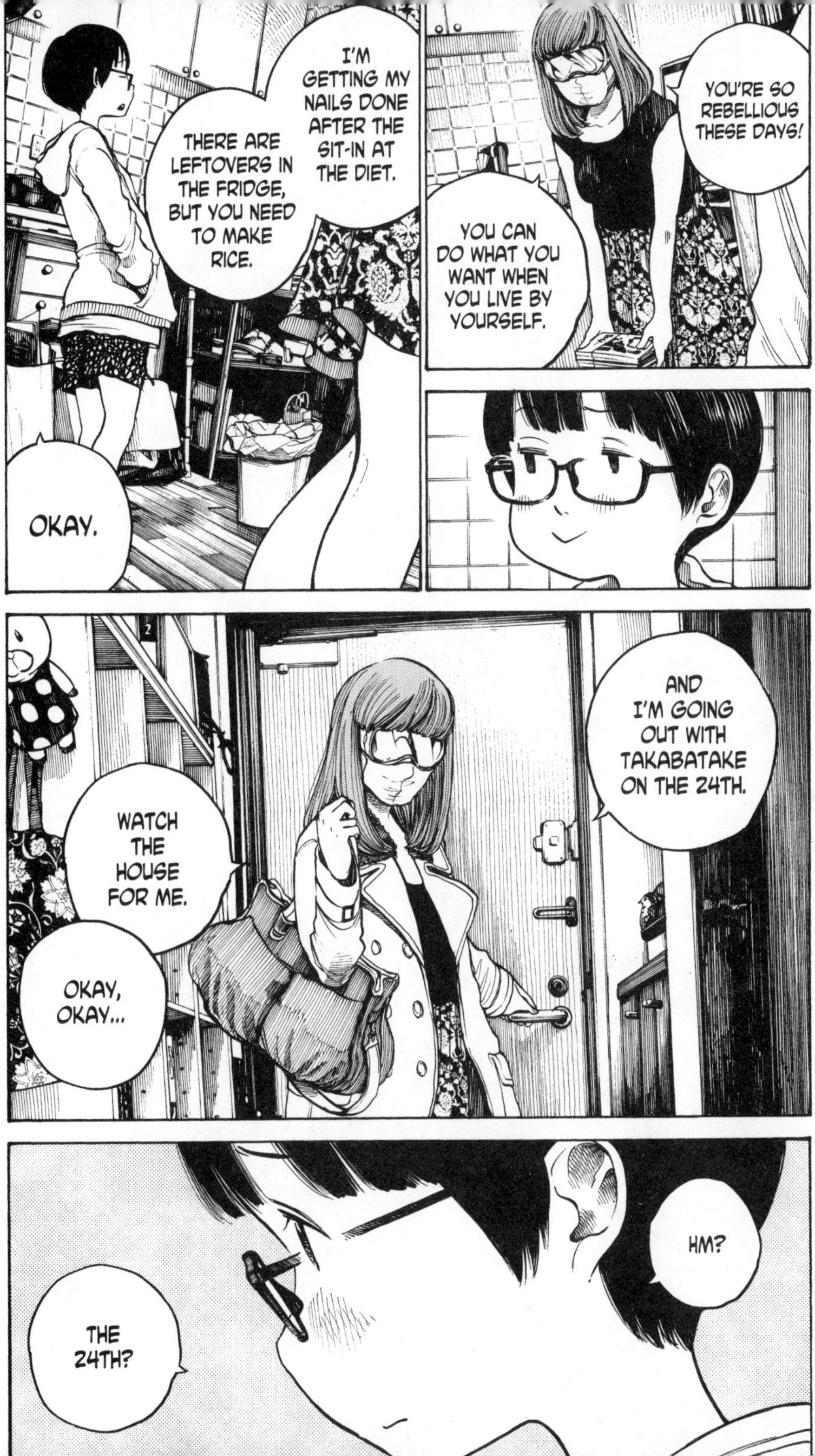
YOU'RE SO REBELLIOUS THESE DAYS!
YOU CAN DO WHAT YOU WANT WHEN YOU LIVE BY YOURSELF.
I'M GETTING MY NAILS DONE AFTER THE SIT-IN AT THE DIET.
THERE ARE LEFTOVERS IN THE FRIDGE, BUT YOU NEED TO MAKE RICE.
OKAY.
AND I'M GOING OUT WITH TAKABATAKE ON THE 24TH.
WATCH THE HOUSE FOR ME.
OKAY, OKAY...
HM?
THE 24TH?

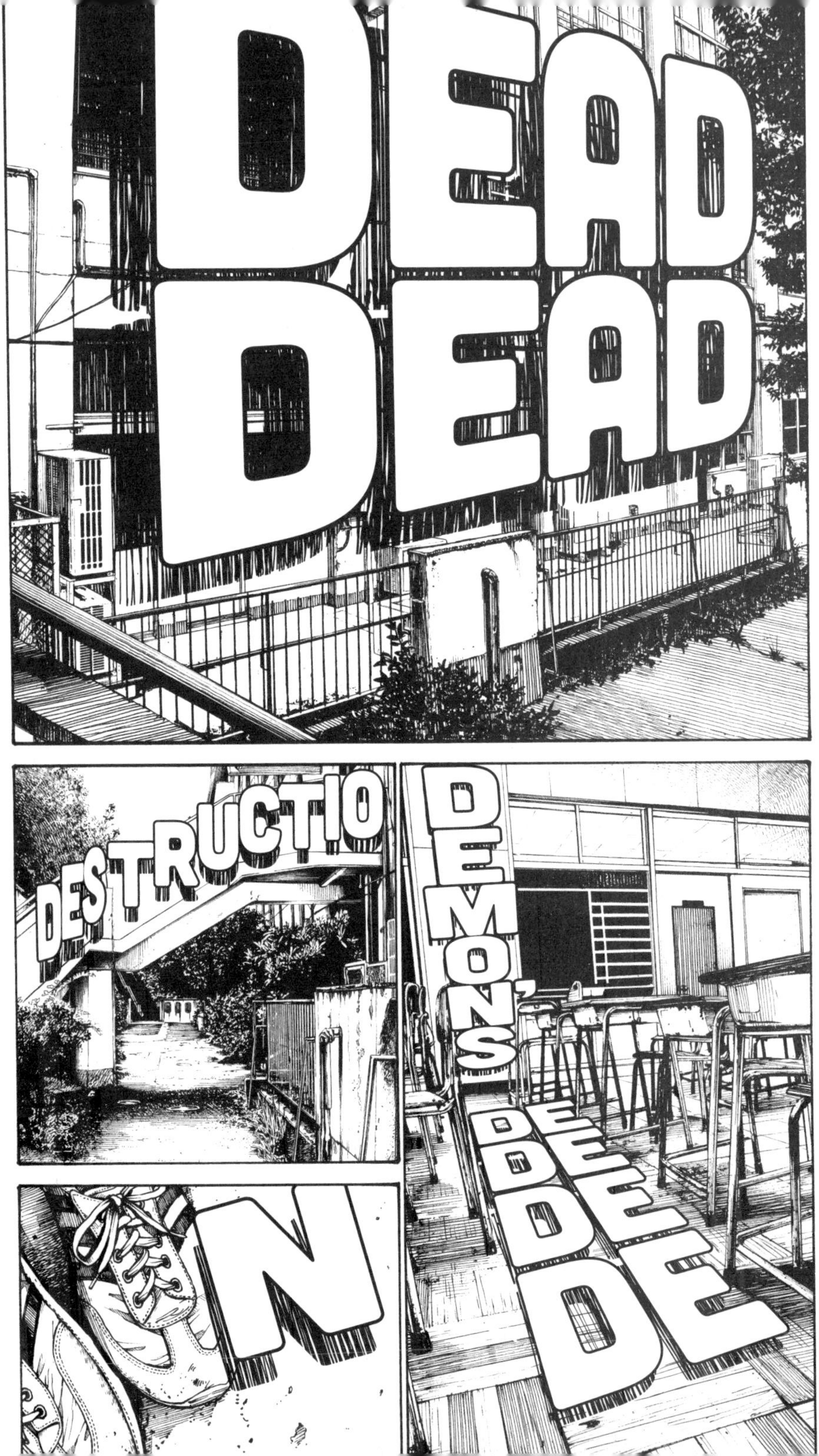
DEAD
DEAD
DEMON'S
DE
DE
DE
DE
DESTRUCTIO
N

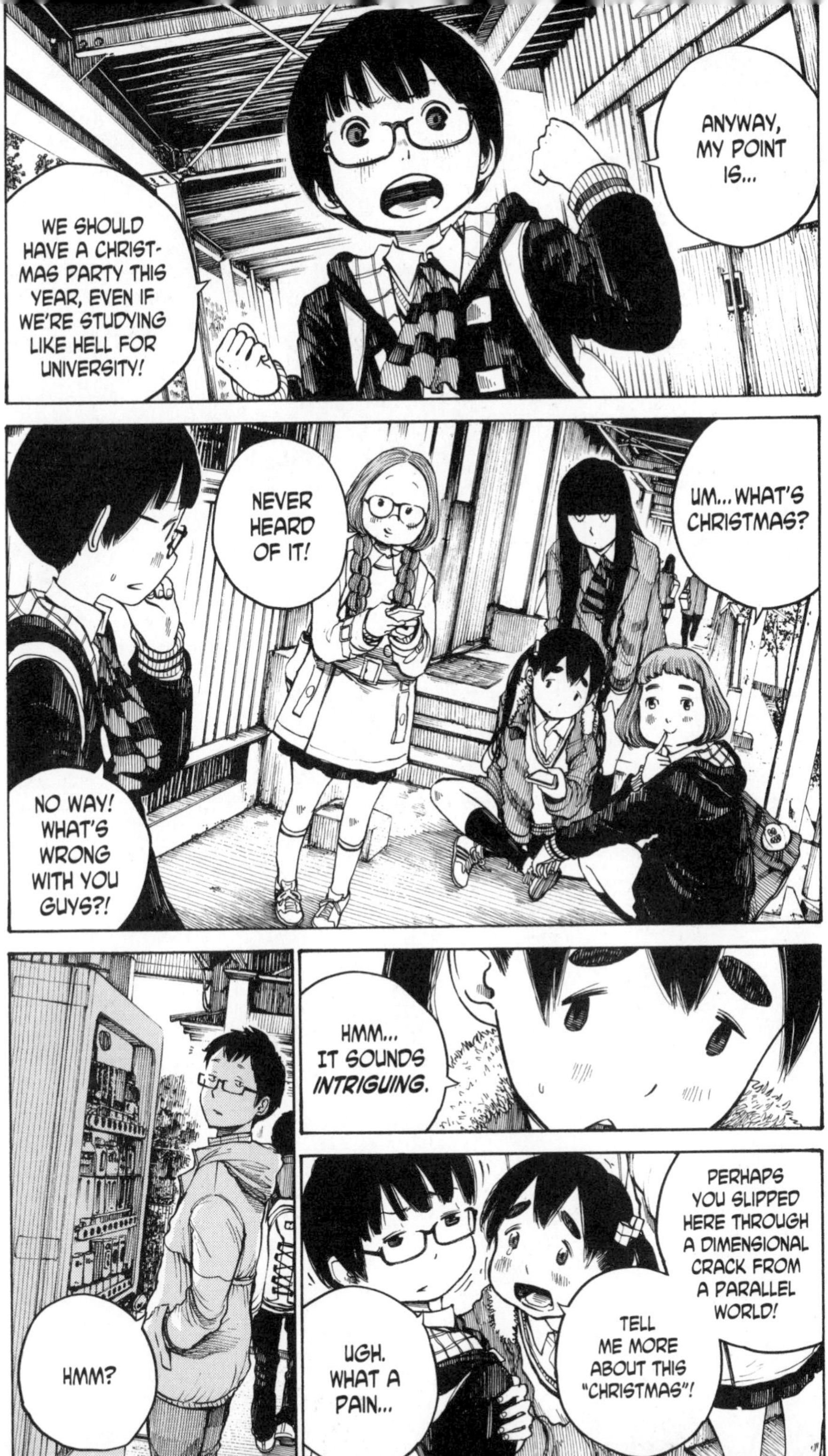
ANYWAY, MY POINT IS...
WE SHOULD HAVE A CHRIST-MAS PARTY THIS YEAR, EVEN IF WE'RE STUDYING LIKE HELL FOR UNIVERSITY!
UM... WHAT'S CHRISTMAS?
NEVER HEARD OF IT!
NO WAY! WHAT'S WRONG WITH YOU GUYS?!
HMM... IT SOUNDS *INTRIGUING.*
PERHAPS YOU SLIPPED HERE THROUGH A DIMENSIONAL CRACK FROM A PARALLEL WORLD!
TELL ME MORE ABOUT THIS "CHRISTMAS"!
UGH. WHAT A PAIN...
HMM?

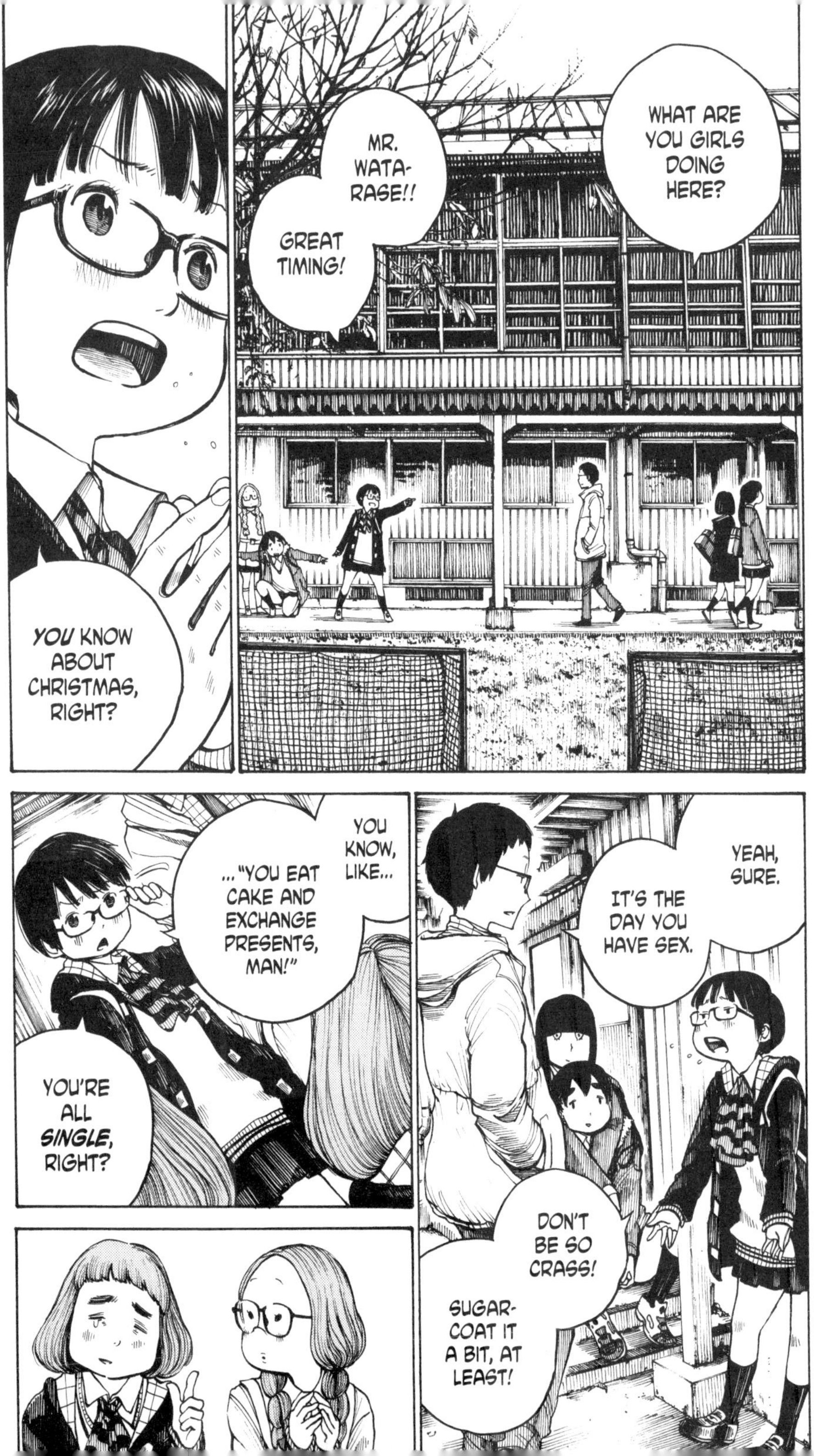
WHAT ARE YOU GIRLS DOING HERE?
MR. WATA-RASE!!
GREAT TIMING!
YOU KNOW ABOUT CHRISTMAS, RIGHT?
YEAH, SURE.
IT'S THE DAY YOU HAVE SEX.
DON'T BE SO CRASS!
SUGAR-COAT IT A BIT, AT LEAST!
YOU KNOW, LIKE...
..."YOU EAT CAKE AND EXCHANGE PRESENTS, MAN!"
YOU'RE ALL *SINGLE*, RIGHT?

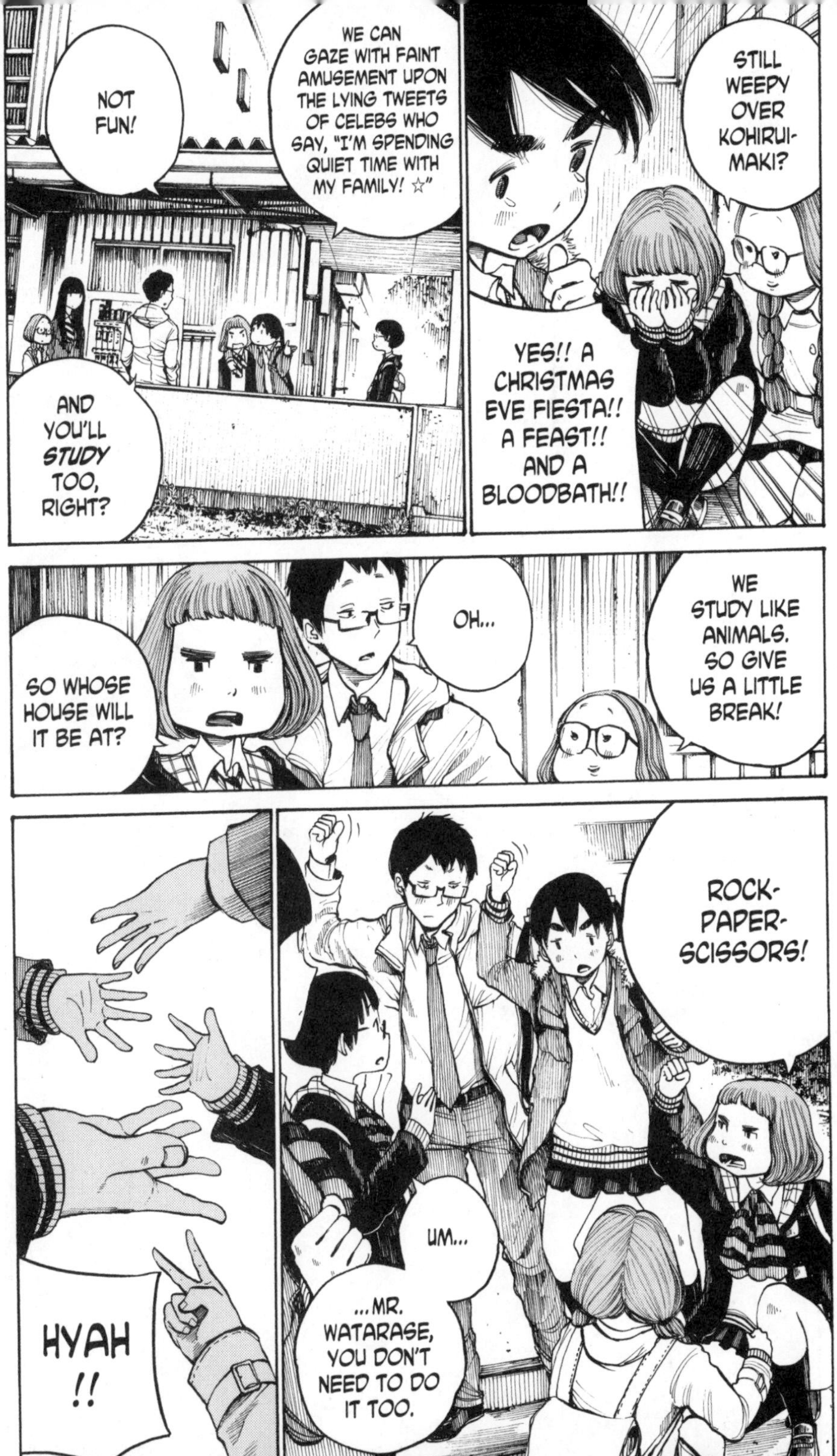
STILL WEEPY OVER KOHIRUI-MAKI?
YES!! A CHRISTMAS EVE FIESTA!! A FEAST!! AND A BLOODBATH!!
WE CAN GAZE WITH FAINT AMUSEMENT UPON THE LYING TWEETS OF CELEBS WHO SAY, "I'M SPENDING QUIET TIME WITH MY FAMILY! ☆"
NOT FUN!
AND YOU'LL *STUDY* TOO, RIGHT?
WE STUDY LIKE ANIMALS. SO GIVE US A LITTLE BREAK!
OH...
SO WHOSE HOUSE WILL IT BE AT?
ROCK-PAPER-SCISSORS!
UM...
...MR. WATARASE, YOU DON'T NEED TO DO IT TOO.
HYAH!!

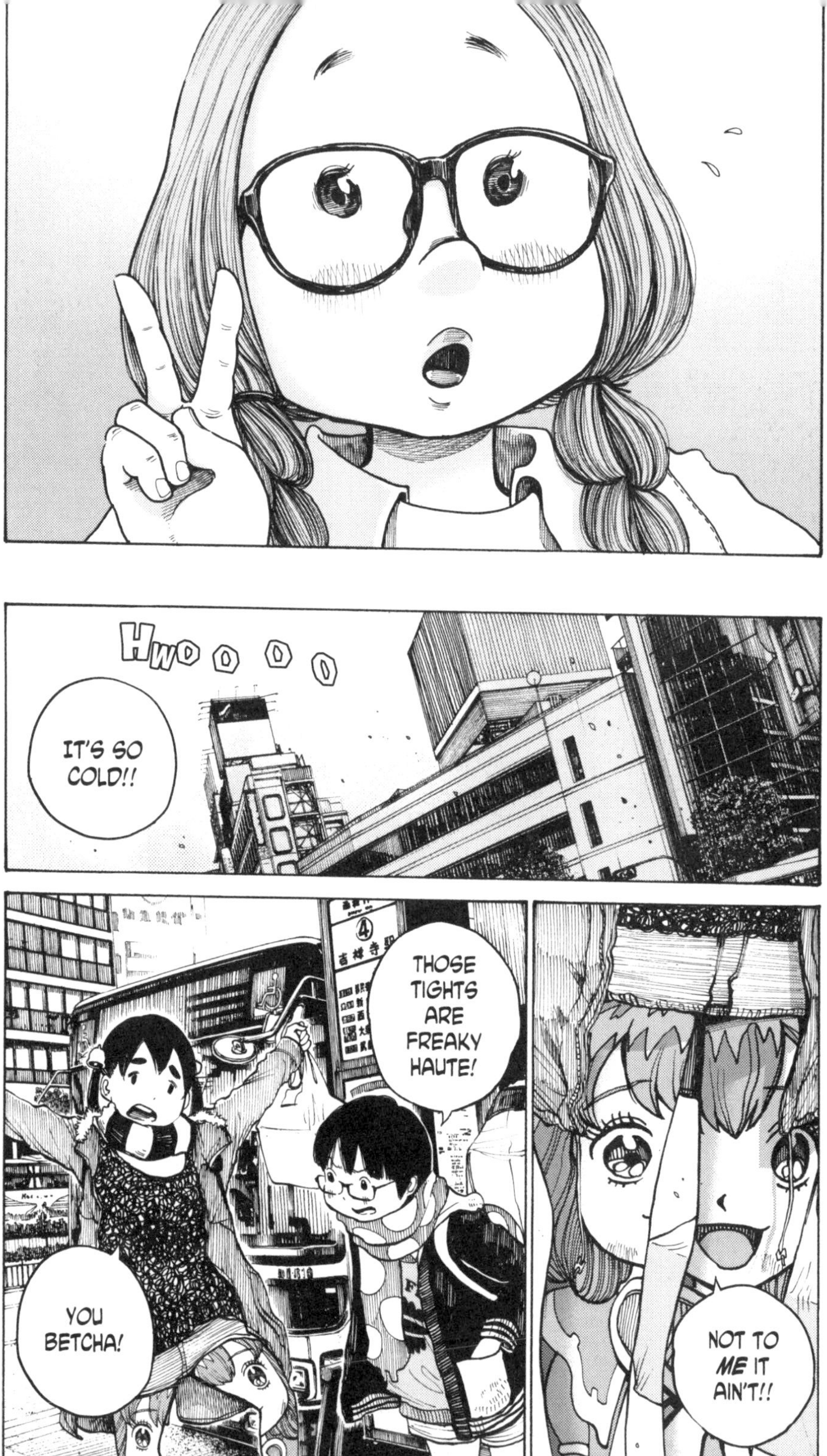
HWOOOOO
IT'S SO COLD!!
NOT TO *ME* IT AIN'T!!
THOSE TIGHTS ARE FREAKY HAUTE!
YOU BETCHA!

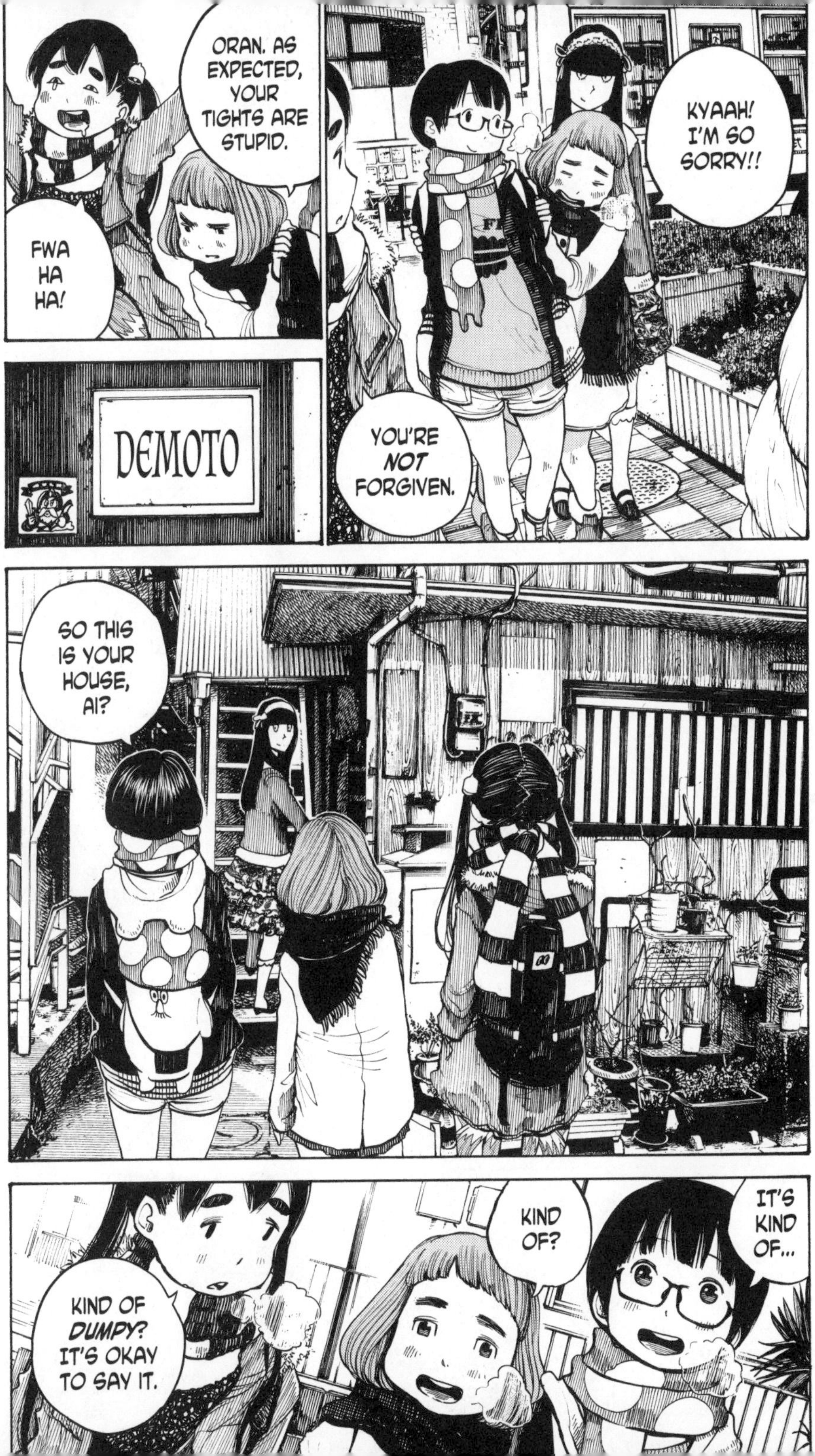
KYAAH! I'M SO SORRY!!
YOU'RE *NOT* FORGIVEN.
ORAN. AS EXPECTED, YOUR TIGHTS ARE STUPID.
FWA HA HA!
DEMOTO
SO THIS IS YOUR HOUSE, AI?
IT'S KIND OF...
KIND OF?
KIND OF ***DUMPY***? IT'S OKAY TO SAY IT.

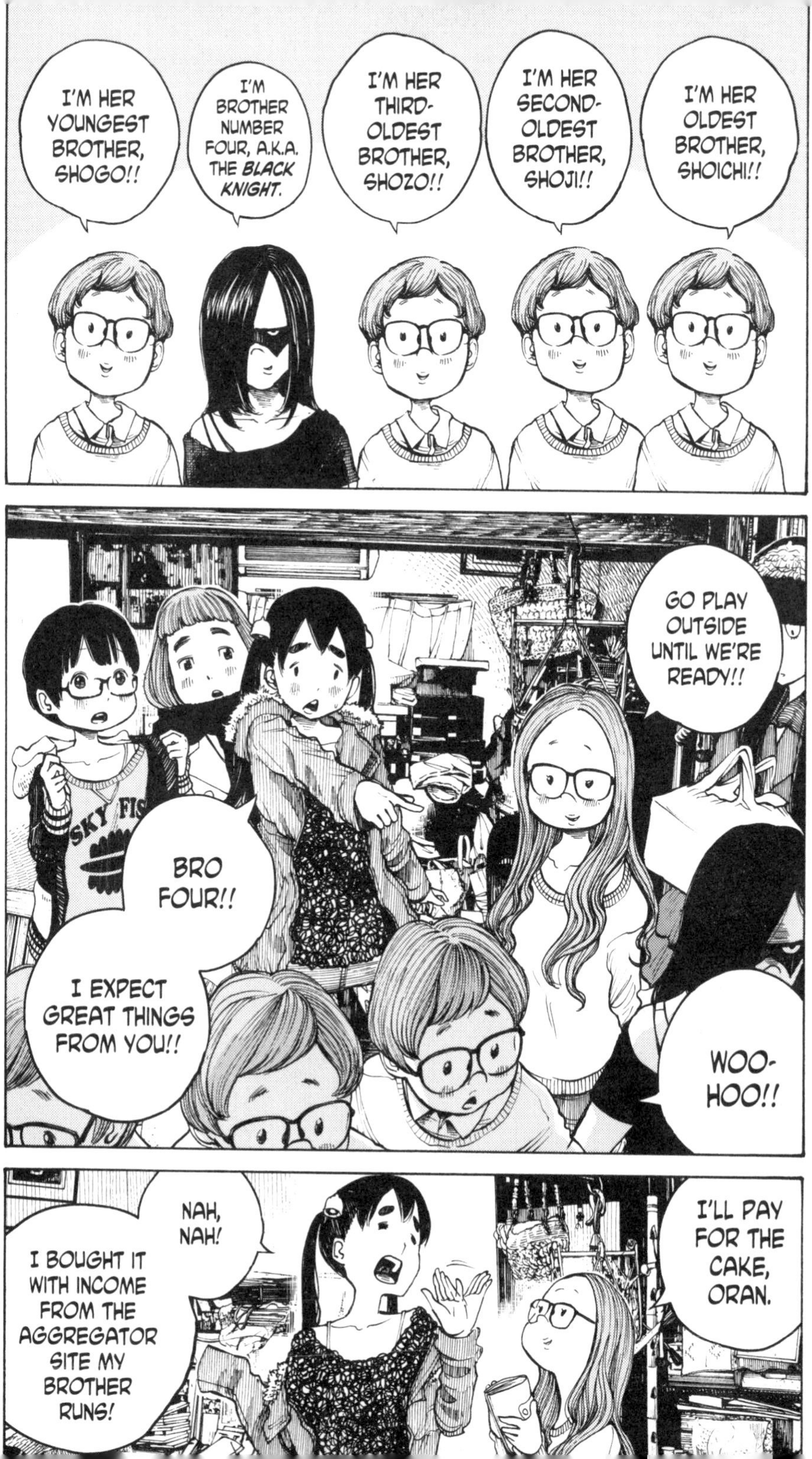
I'M HER OLDEST BROTHER, SHOICHI!!
I'M HER SECOND-OLDEST BROTHER, SHOJI!!
I'M HER THIRD-OLDEST BROTHER, SHOZO!!
I'M BROTHER NUMBER FOUR, A.K.A. THE *BLACK KNIGHT*.
I'M HER YOUNGEST BROTHER, SHOGO!!
GO PLAY OUTSIDE UNTIL WE'RE READY!!
WOO-HOO!!
BRO FOUR!!
I EXPECT GREAT THINGS FROM YOU!!
SKY FIS
I'LL PAY FOR THE CAKE, ORAN.
NAH, NAH!
I BOUGHT IT WITH INCOME FROM THE AGGREGATOR SITE MY BROTHER RUNS!

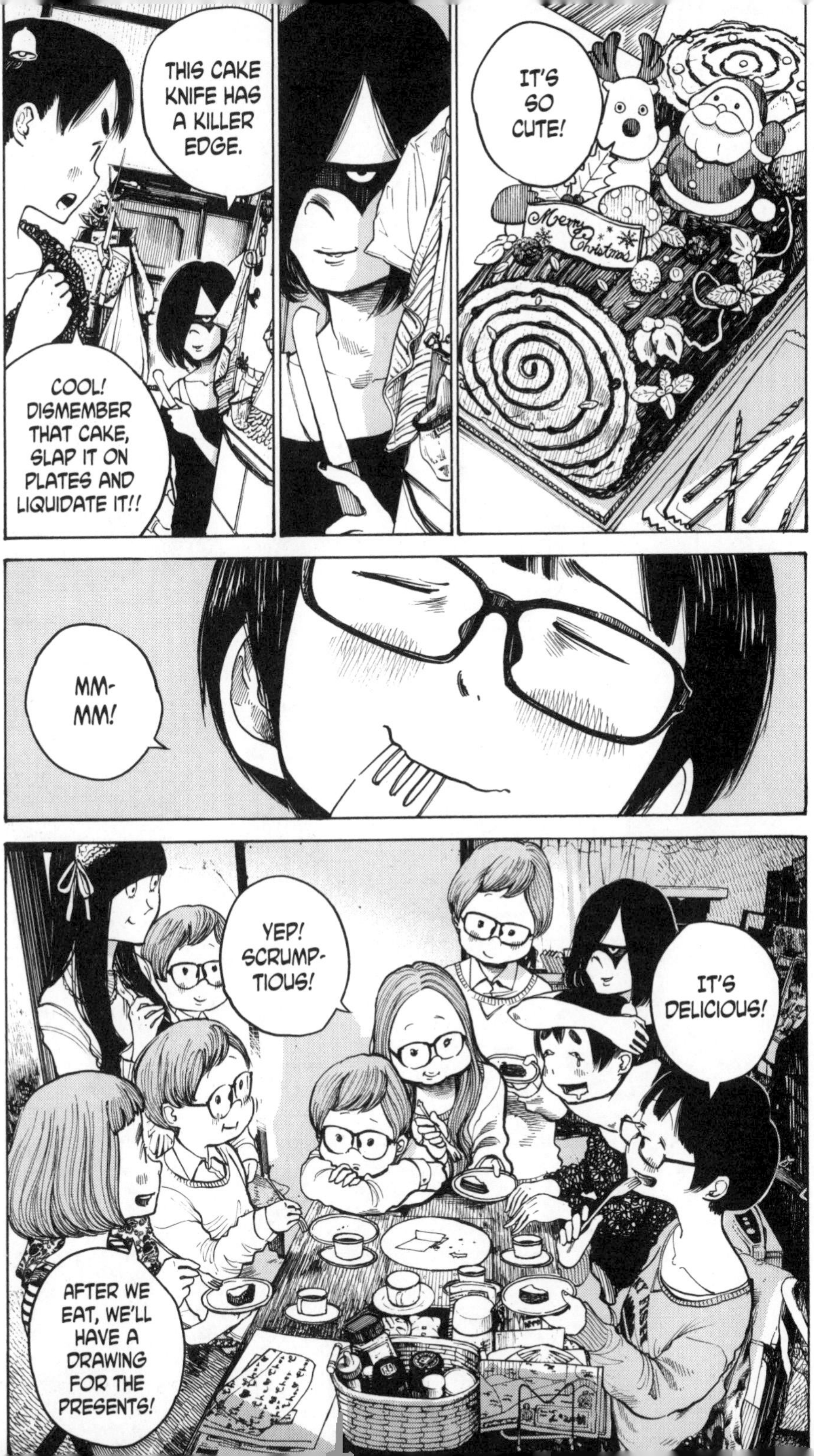
IT'S SO CUTE!
THIS CAKE KNIFE HAS A KILLER EDGE.
COOL! DISMEMBER THAT CAKE, SLAP IT ON PLATES AND LIQUIDATE IT!!
MM-MM!
IT'S DELICIOUS!
YEP! SCRUMP-TIOUS!
AFTER WE EAT, WE'LL HAVE A DRAWING FOR THE PRESENTS!

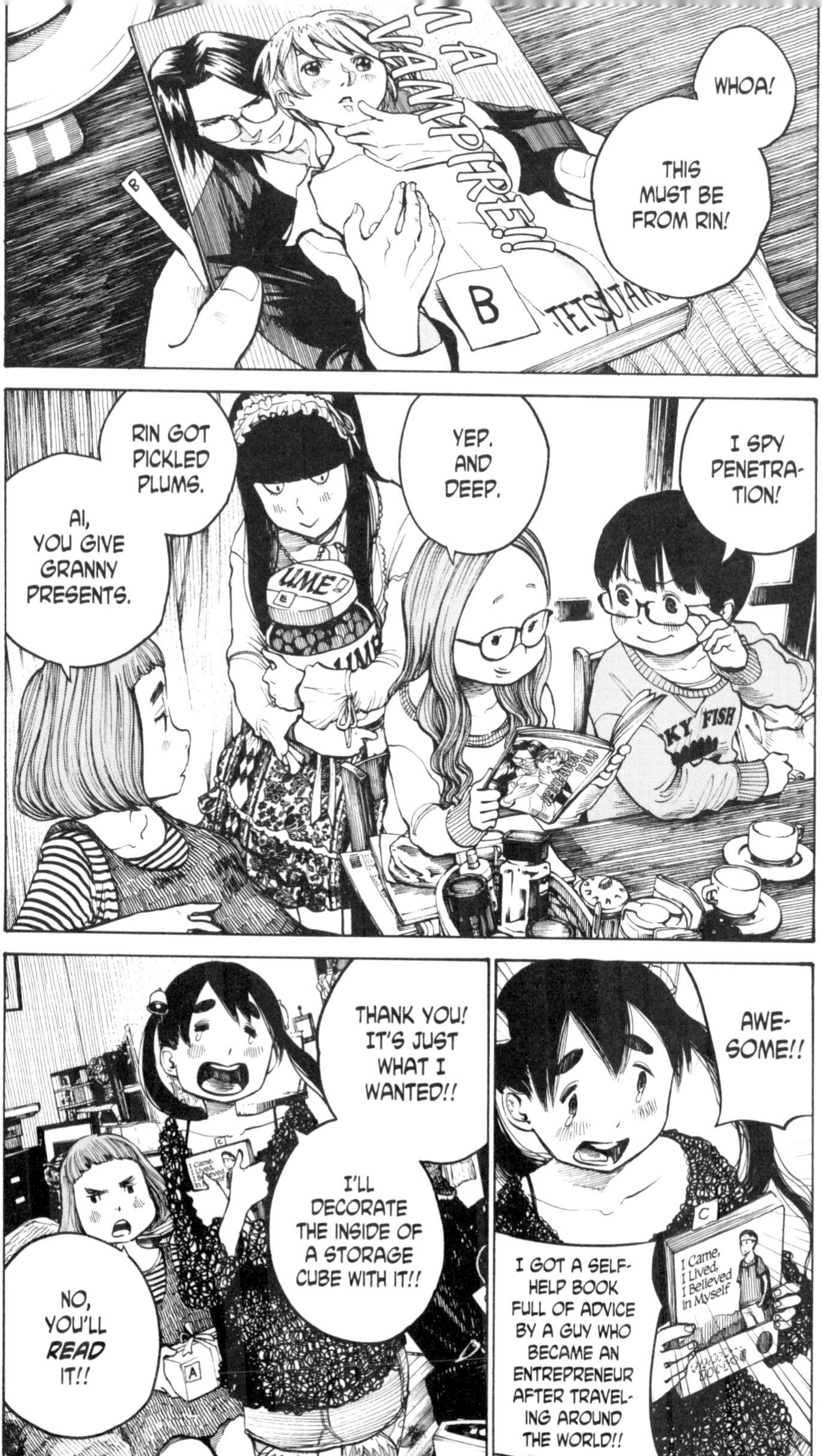
A VAMPIRE!!
WHOA!
THIS MUST BE FROM RIN!
I SPY PENETRATION!
YEP. AND DEEP.
RIN GOT PICKLED PLUMS.
AI, YOU GIVE GRANNY PRESENTS.
AWESOME!!
I GOT A SELF-HELP BOOK FULL OF ADVICE BY A GUY WHO BECAME AN ENTREPRENEUR AFTER TRAVELING AROUND THE WORLD!!
I Came, I Lived, I Believed in Myself
THANK YOU! IT'S JUST WHAT I WANTED!!
I'LL DECORATE THE INSIDE OF A STORAGE CUBE WITH IT!!
NO, YOU'LL *READ* IT!!

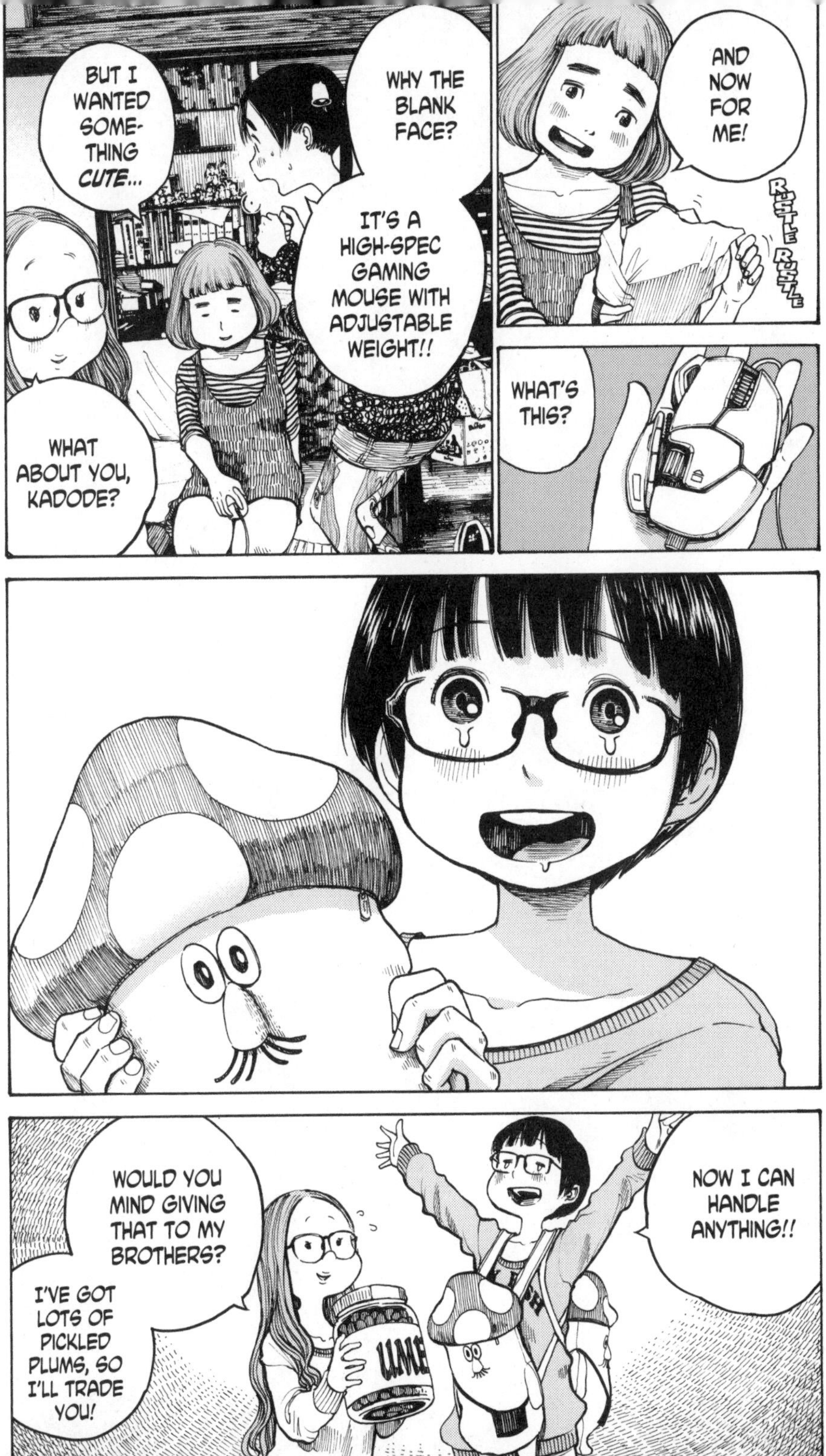
AND NOW FOR ME!
RUSTLE RUSTLE
WHAT'S THIS?
WHY THE BLANK FACE?
IT'S A HIGH-SPEC GAMING MOUSE WITH ADJUSTABLE WEIGHT!!
BUT I WANTED SOME-THING *CUTE*...
WHAT ABOUT YOU, KADODE?
NOW I CAN HANDLE ANYTHING!!
WOULD YOU MIND GIVING THAT TO MY BROTHERS?
I'VE GOT LOTS OF PICKLED PLUMS, SO I'LL TRADE YOU!
UME

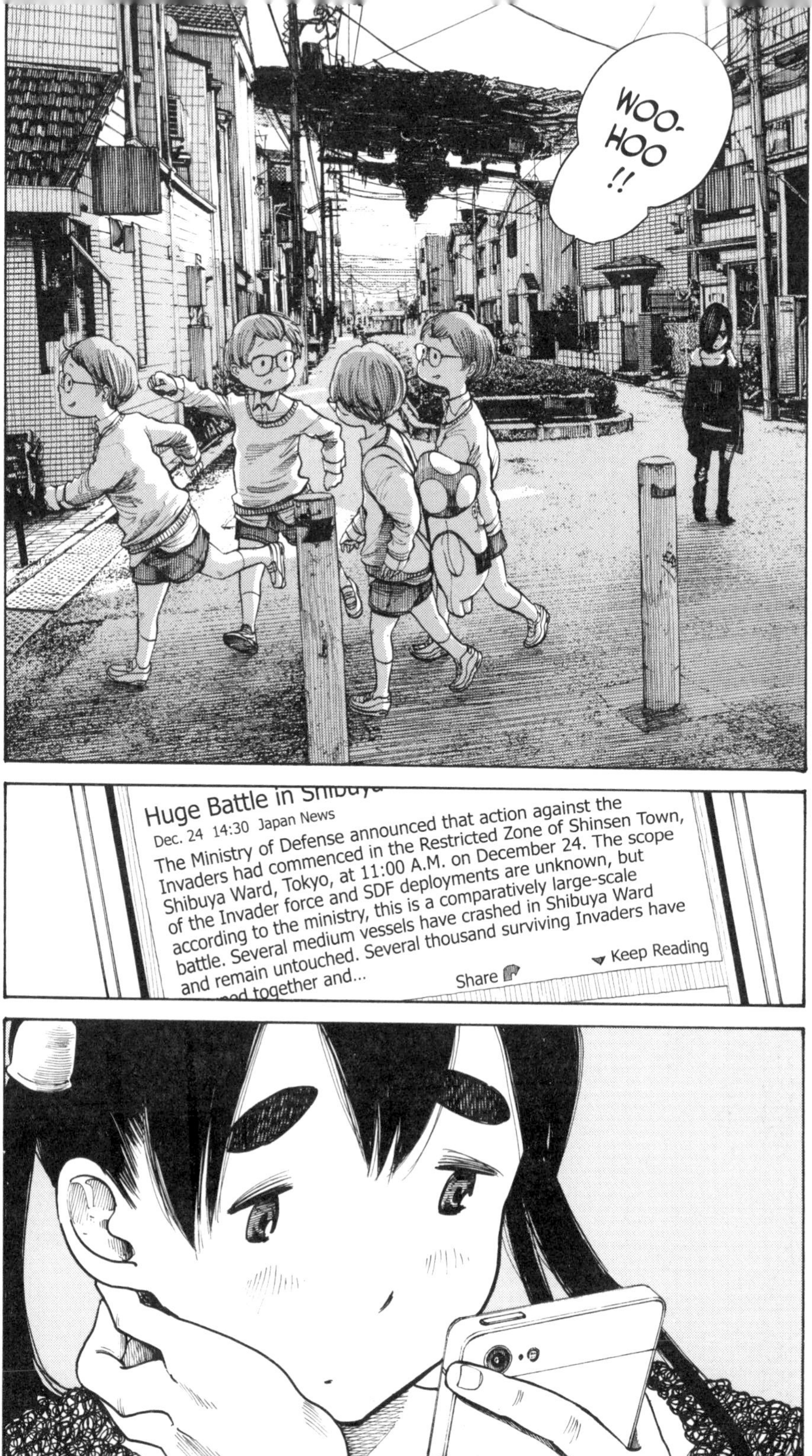
WOO-HOO !!
Huge Battle in Shibuya
Dec. 24 14:30 Japan News
The Ministry of Defense announced that action against the Invaders had commenced in the Restricted Zone of Shinsen Town, Shibuya Ward, Tokyo, at 11:00 A.M. on December 24. The scope of the Invader force and SDF deployments are unknown, but according to the ministry, this is a comparatively large-scale battle. Several medium vessels have crashed in Shibuya Ward and remain untouched. Several thousand surviving Invaders have ...ed together and...
Share
Keep Reading

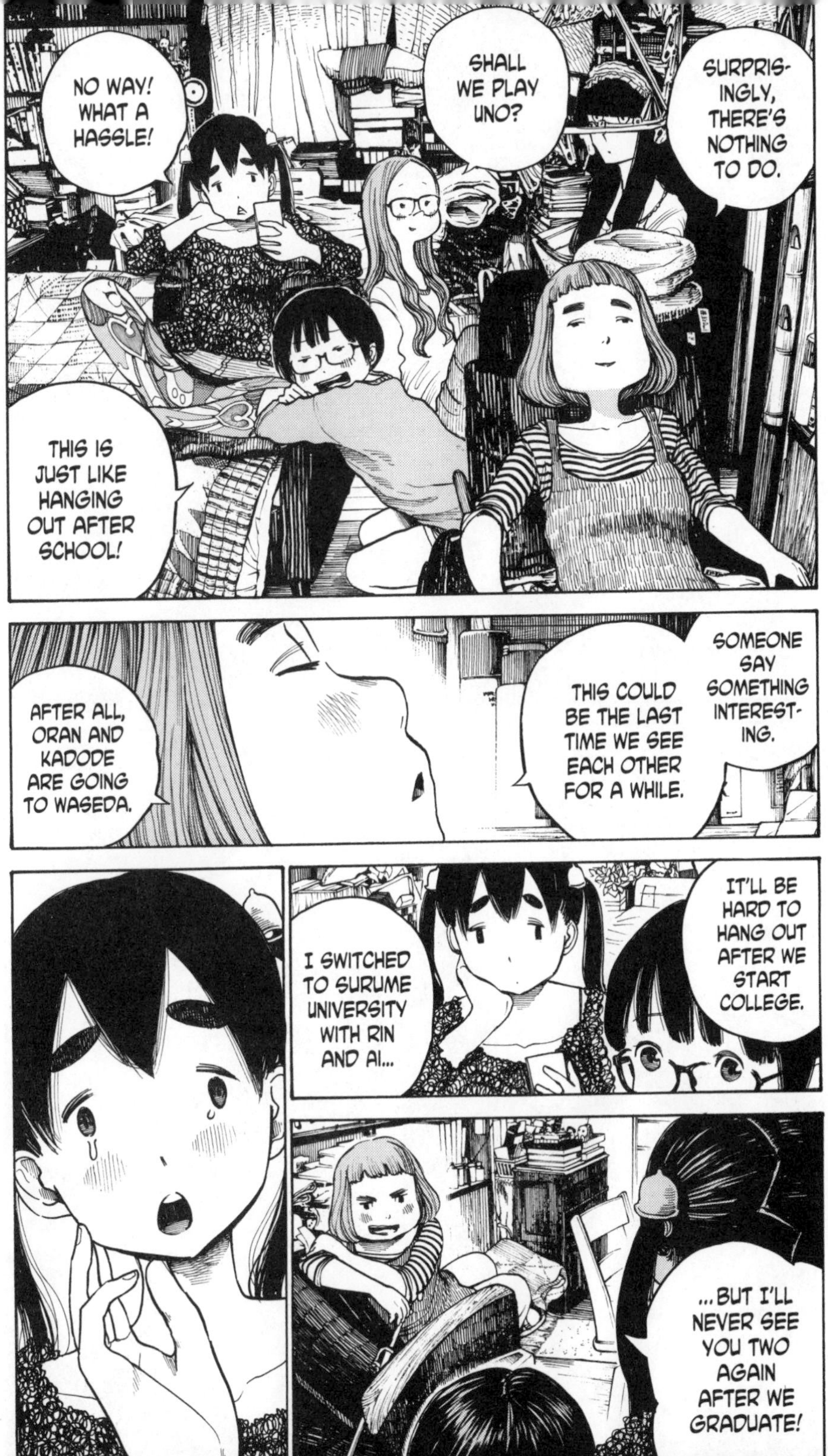
SURPRISINGLY, THERE'S NOTHING TO DO.
SHALL WE PLAY UNO?
NO WAY! WHAT A HASSLE!
THIS IS JUST LIKE HANGING OUT AFTER SCHOOL!
SOMEONE SAY SOMETHING INTERESTING.
THIS COULD BE THE LAST TIME WE SEE EACH OTHER FOR A WHILE.
AFTER ALL, ORAN AND KADODE ARE GOING TO WASEDA.
IT'LL BE HARD TO HANG OUT AFTER WE START COLLEGE.
I SWITCHED TO SURUME UNIVERSITY WITH RIN AND AI...
...BUT I'LL NEVER SEE YOU TWO AGAIN AFTER WE GRADUATE!

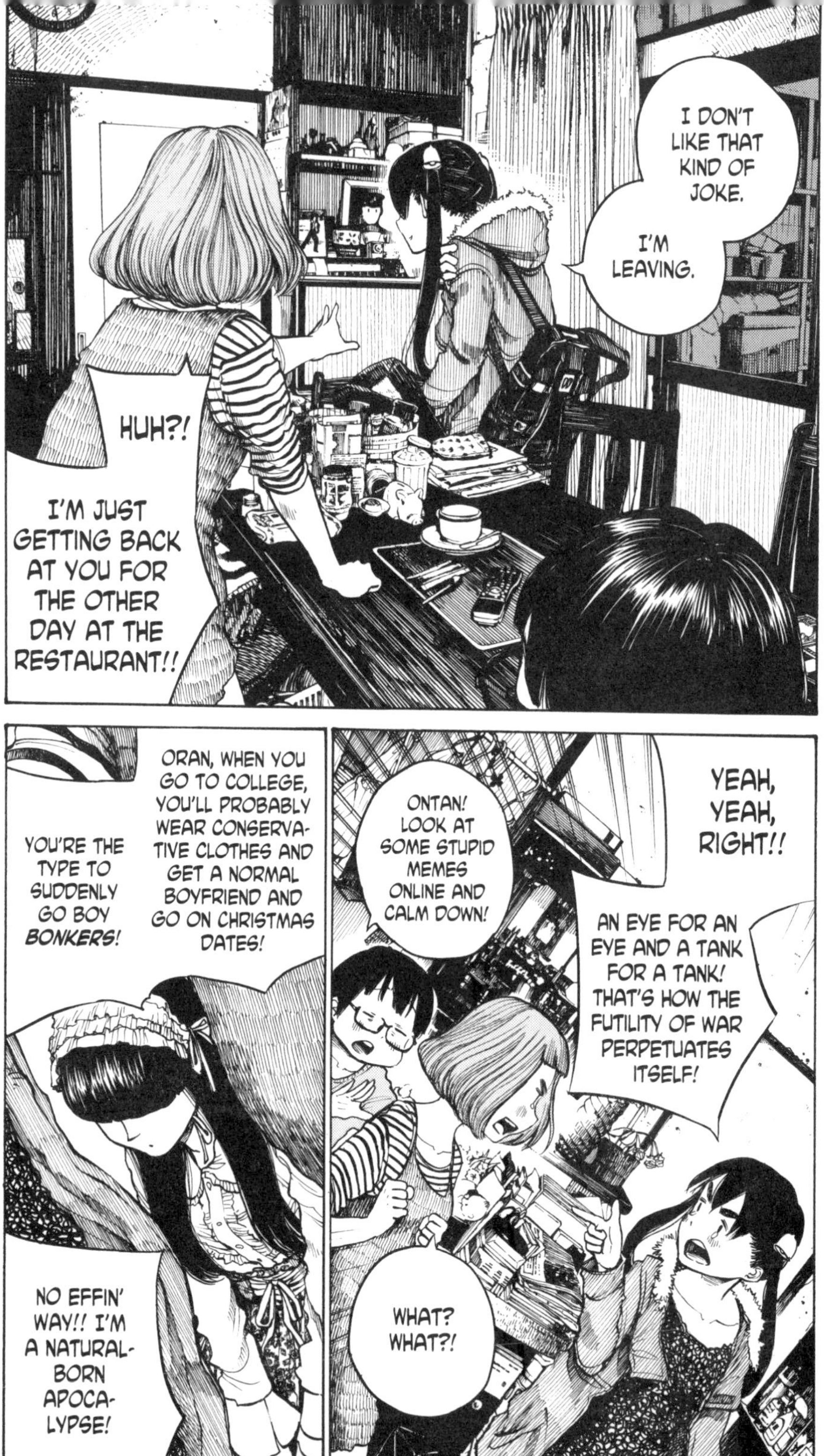
I DON'T LIKE THAT KIND OF JOKE.
I'M LEAVING.
HUH?!
I'M JUST GETTING BACK AT YOU FOR THE OTHER DAY AT THE RESTAURANT!!
YEAH, YEAH, RIGHT!!
AN EYE FOR AN EYE AND A TANK FOR A TANK! THAT'S HOW THE FUTILITY OF WAR PERPETUATES ITSELF!
ONTAN! LOOK AT SOME STUPID MEMES ONLINE AND CALM DOWN!
WHAT? WHAT?!
ORAN, WHEN YOU GO TO COLLEGE, YOU'LL PROBABLY WEAR CONSERVA-TIVE CLOTHES AND GET A NORMAL BOYFRIEND AND GO ON CHRISTMAS DATES!
YOU'RE THE TYPE TO SUDDENLY GO BOY *BONKERS*!
NO EFFIN' WAY!! I'M A NATURAL-BORN APOCA-LYPSE!

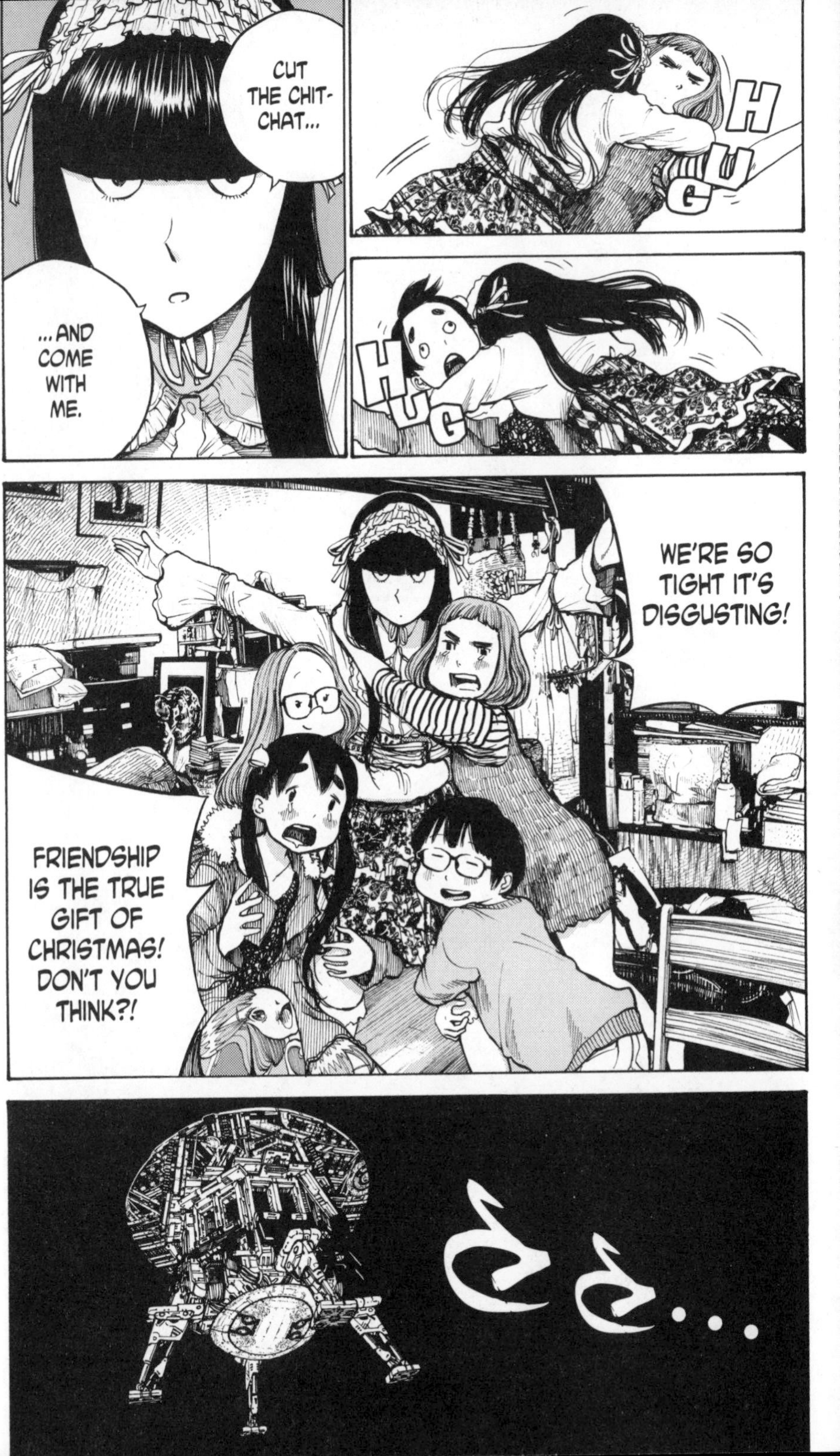
HUG
HUG
CUT THE CHIT-CHAT...
...AND COME WITH ME.
WE'RE SO TIGHT IT'S DISGUSTING!
FRIENDSHIP IS THE TRUE GIFT OF CHRISTMAS! DON'T YOU THINK?!

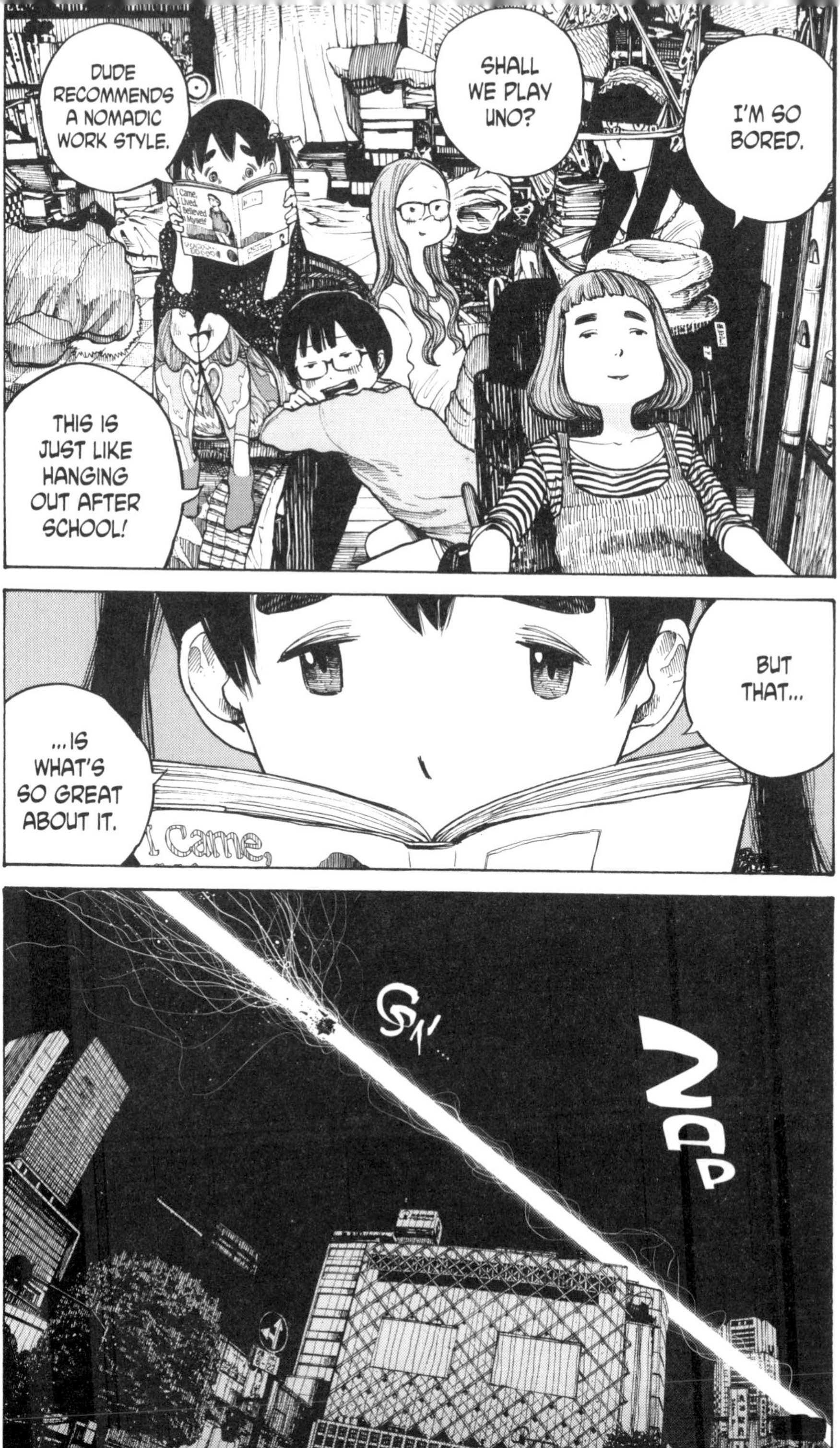
I'M SO BORED.
SHALL WE PLAY UNO?
DUDE RECOMMENDS A NOMADIC WORK STYLE.
THIS IS JUST LIKE HANGING OUT AFTER SCHOOL!
BUT THAT...
...IS WHAT'S SO GREAT ABOUT IT.
I Came,
ZAP

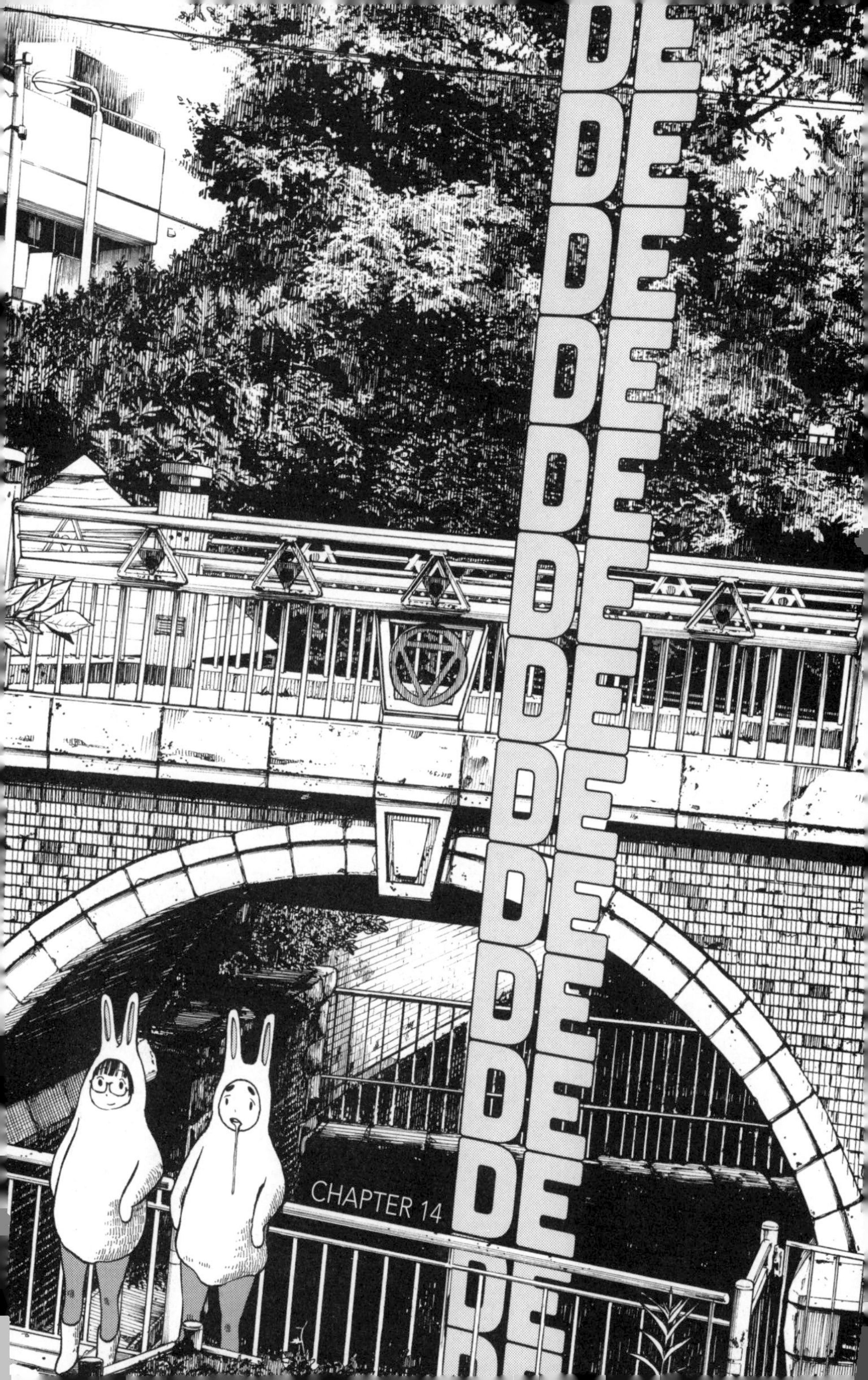
DEDEDEDEDEDEDEDEDEDEDEDE
DEDEDEDEDEDEDEDEDEDEDEDEDE
CHAPTER 14

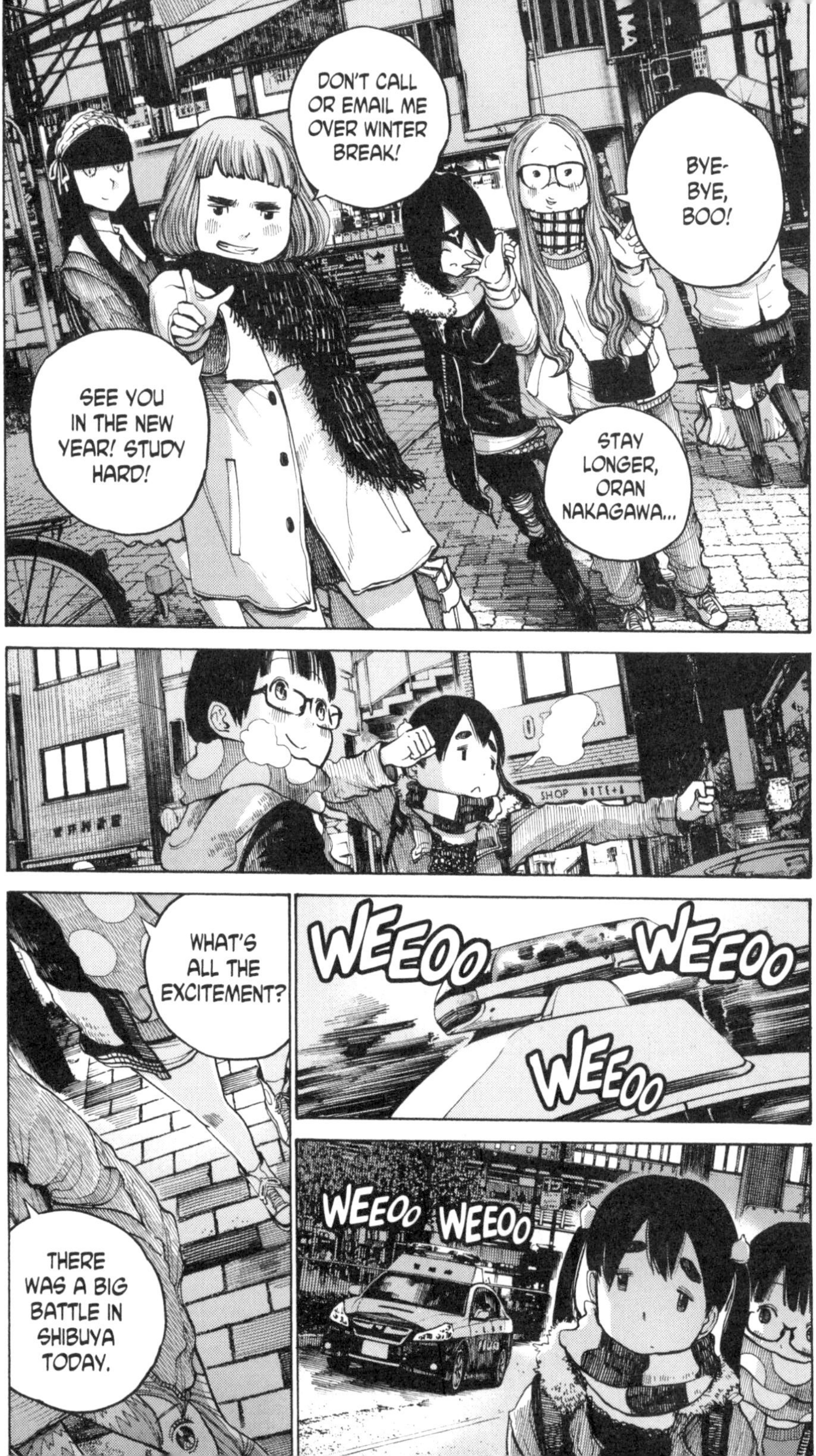
BYE-BYE, BOO!
DON'T CALL OR EMAIL ME OVER WINTER BREAK!
STAY LONGER, ORAN NAKAGAWA...
SEE YOU IN THE NEW YEAR! STUDY HARD!
WEEOO WEEOO
WEEOO
WEEOO WEEOO
WHAT'S ALL THE EXCITEMENT?
THERE WAS A BIG BATTLE IN SHIBUYA TODAY.

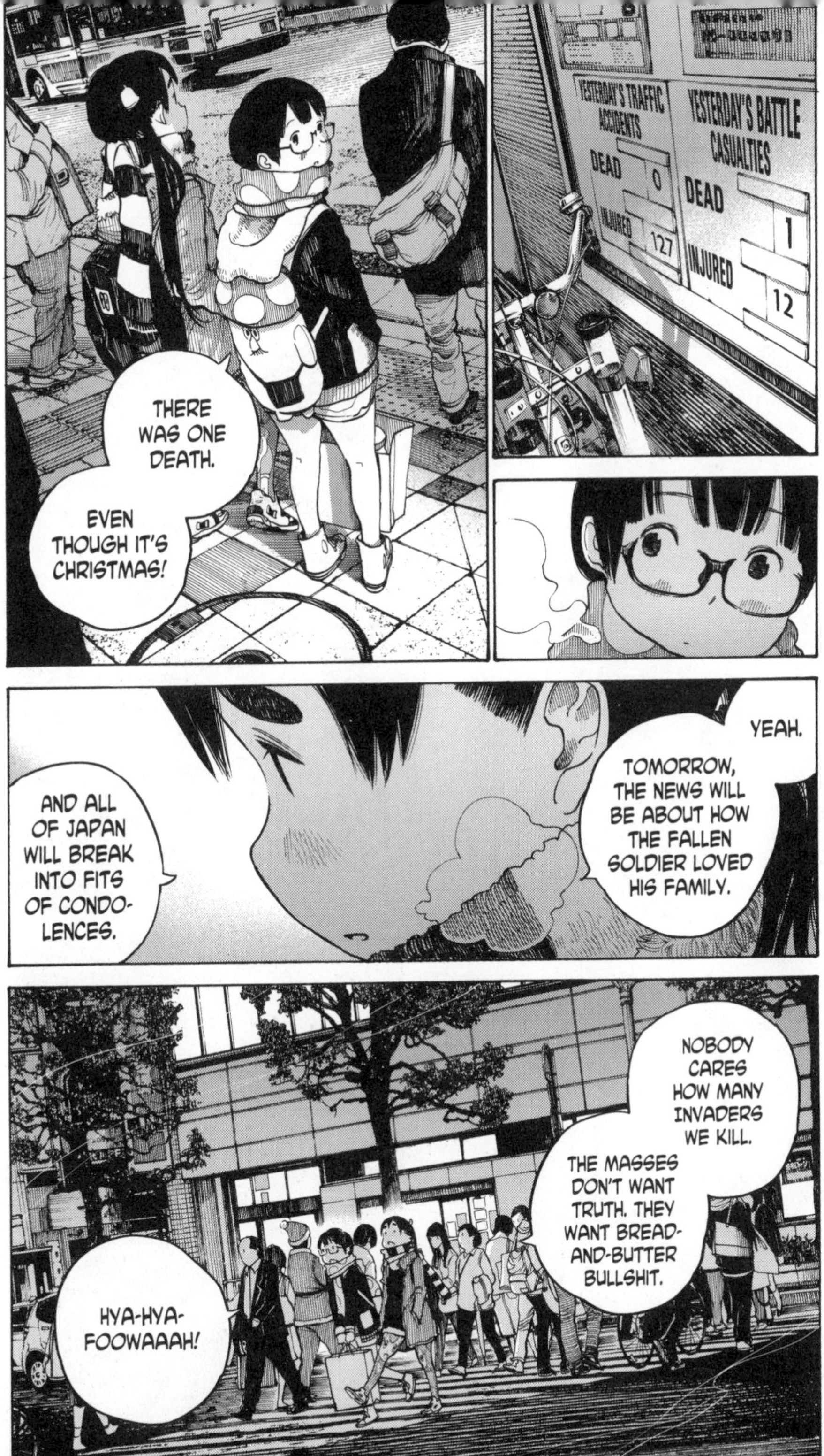
YESTERDAY'S BATTLE CASUALTIES
DEAD 1
INJURED 12
YESTERDAY'S TRAFFIC ACCIDENTS
DEAD 0
INJURED 127
THERE WAS ONE DEATH.
EVEN THOUGH IT'S CHRISTMAS!
YEAH.
TOMORROW, THE NEWS WILL BE ABOUT HOW THE FALLEN SOLDIER LOVED HIS FAMILY.
AND ALL OF JAPAN WILL BREAK INTO FITS OF CONDO-LENCES.
NOBODY CARES HOW MANY INVADERS WE KILL.
THE MASSES DON'T WANT TRUTH. THEY WANT BREAD-AND-BUTTER BULLSHIT.
HYA-HYA-FOOWAAAH!

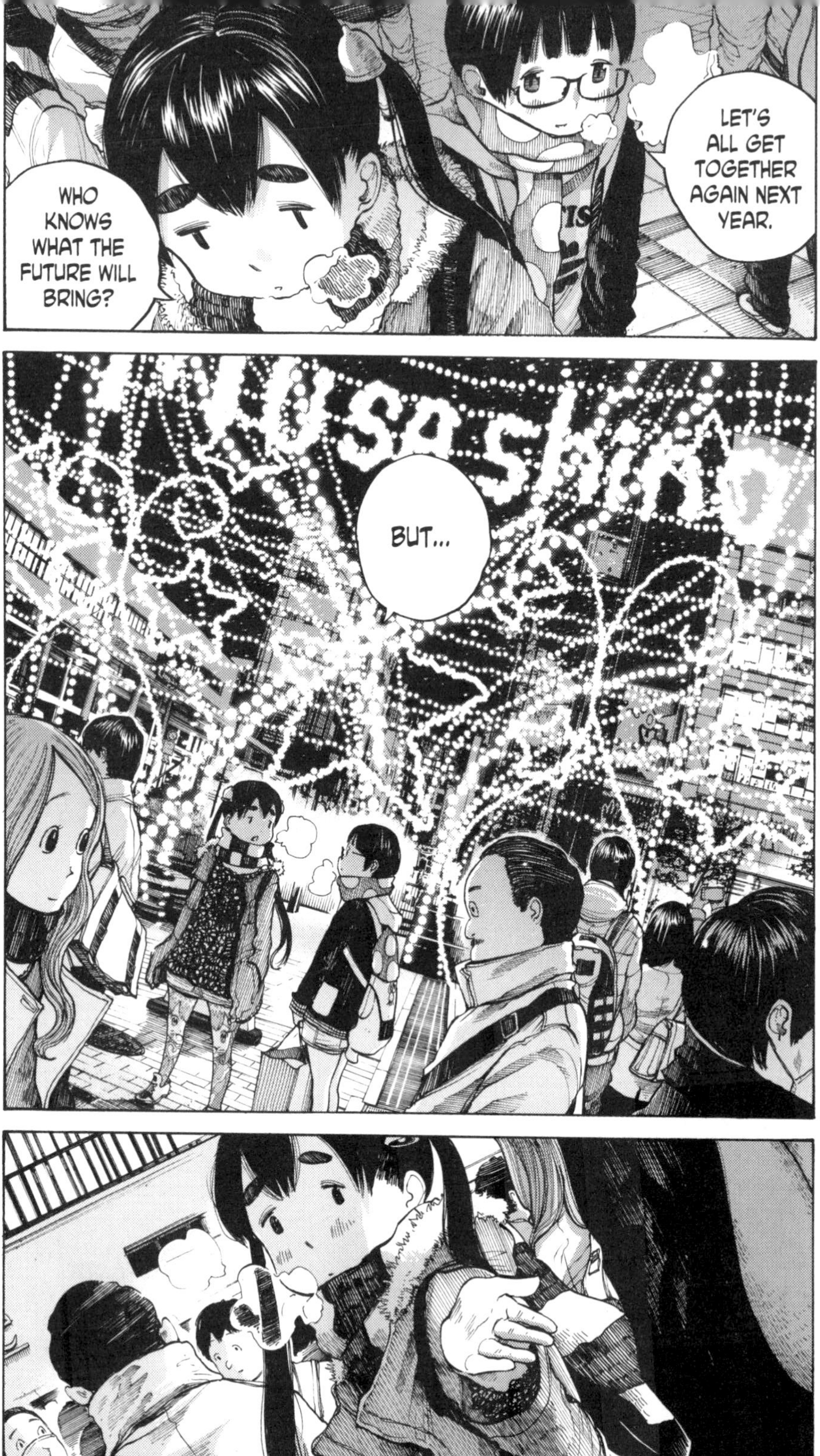
LET'S ALL GET TOGETHER AGAIN NEXT YEAR.
WHO KNOWS WHAT THE FUTURE WILL BRING?
BUT...

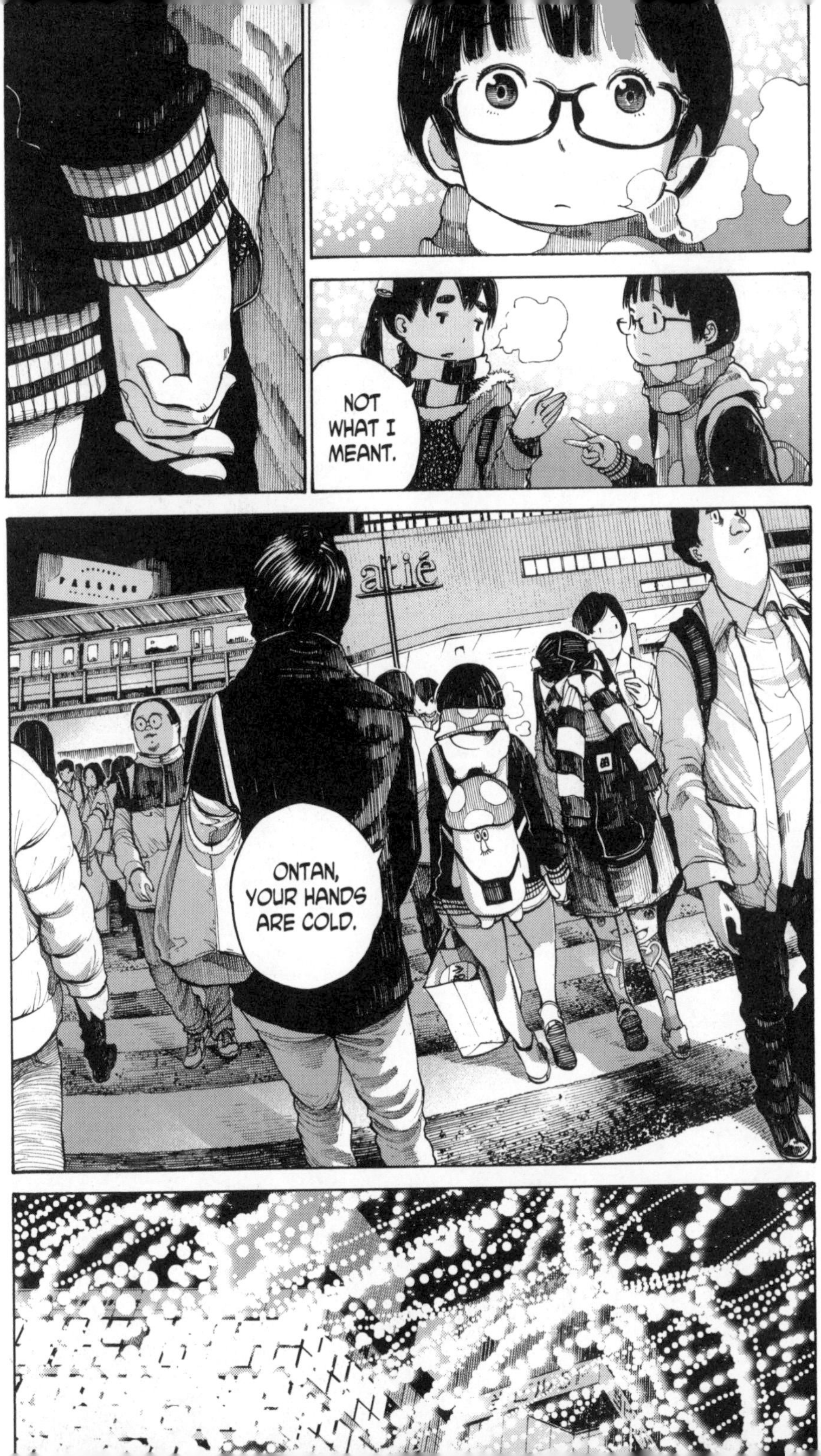
NOT WHAT I MEANT.
atié
ONTAN, YOUR HANDS ARE COLD.

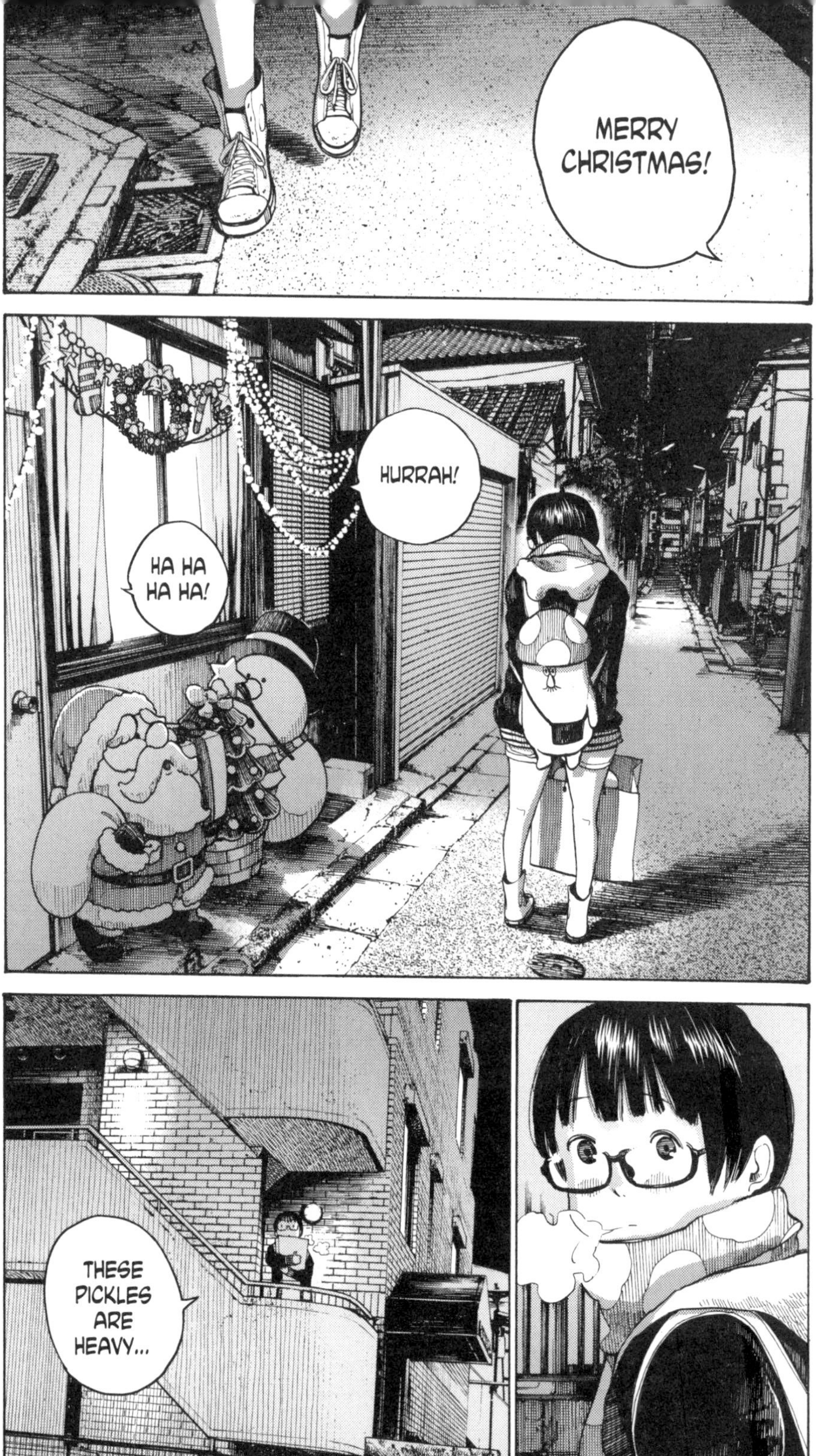
MERRY CHRISTMAS!
HURRAH!
HA HA HA HA!
THESE PICKLES ARE HEAVY...

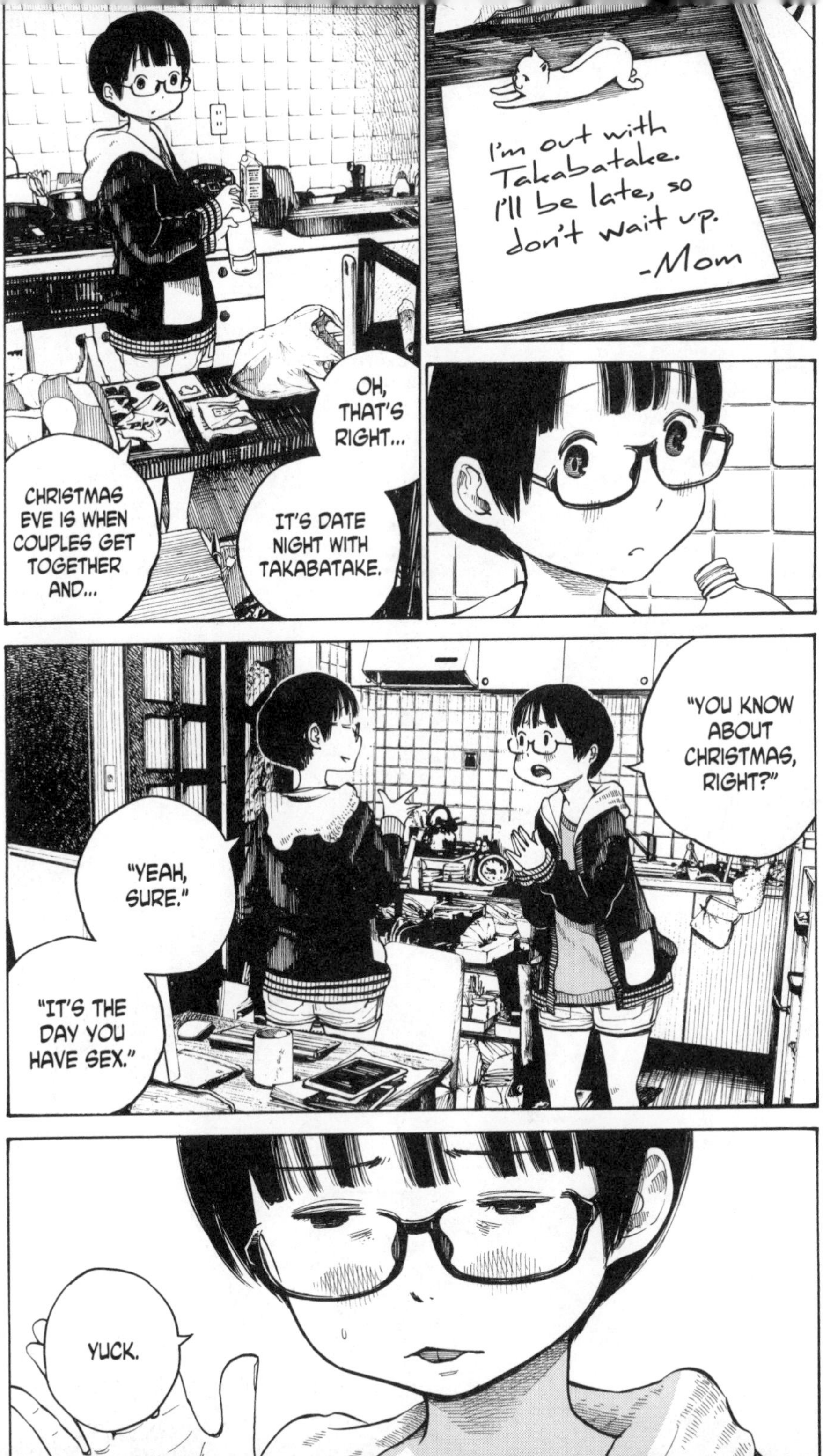

I'm out with Takabatake. I'll be late, so don't wait up. -Mom
OH, THAT'S RIGHT...
IT'S DATE NIGHT WITH TAKABATAKE.
CHRISTMAS EVE IS WHEN COUPLES GET TOGETHER AND...
"YOU KNOW ABOUT CHRISTMAS, RIGHT?"
"YEAH, SURE."
"IT'S THE DAY YOU HAVE SEX."
YUCK.

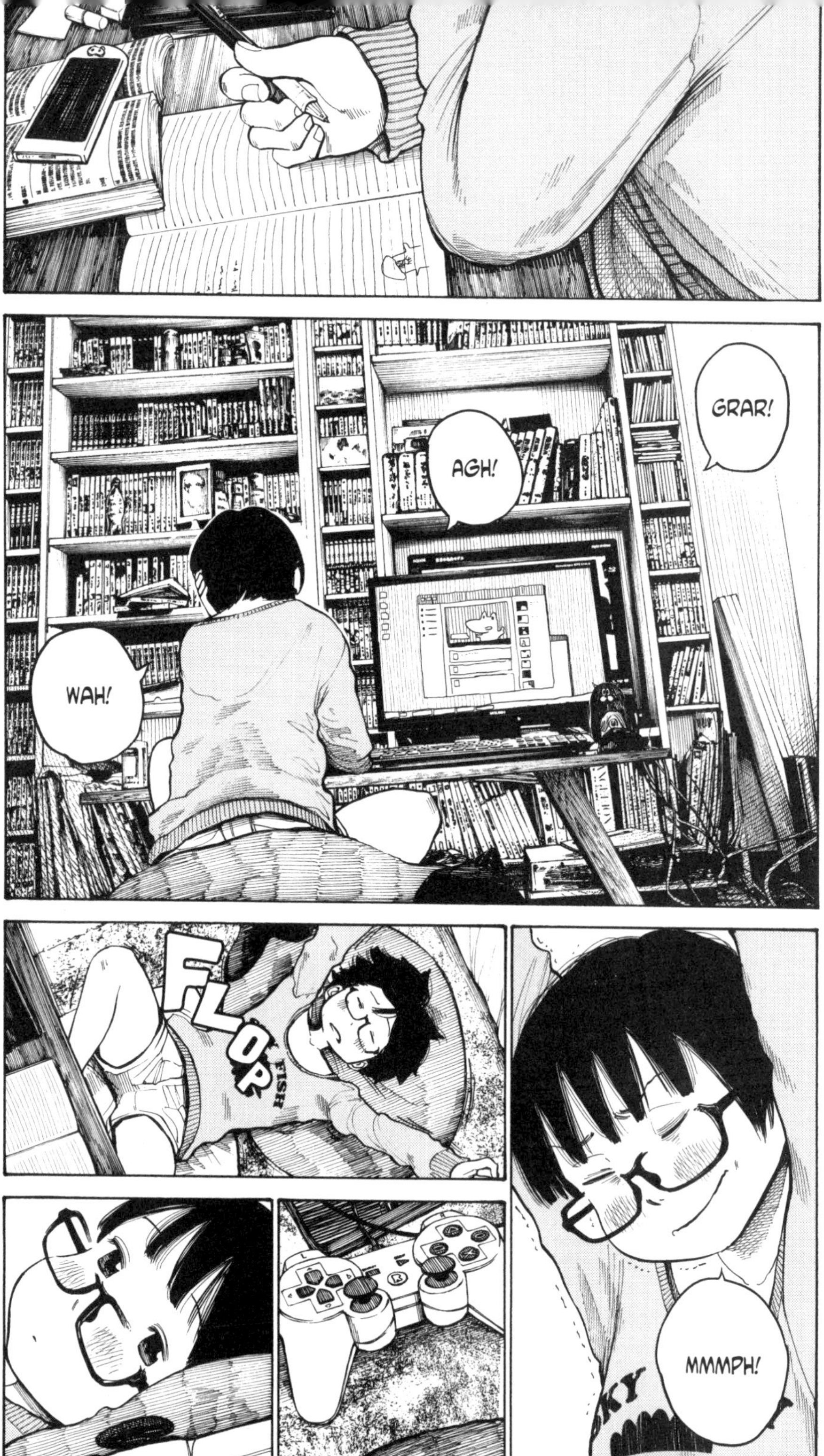
GRAR!
AGH!
WAH!
MMMPH!
FLOP
FISH

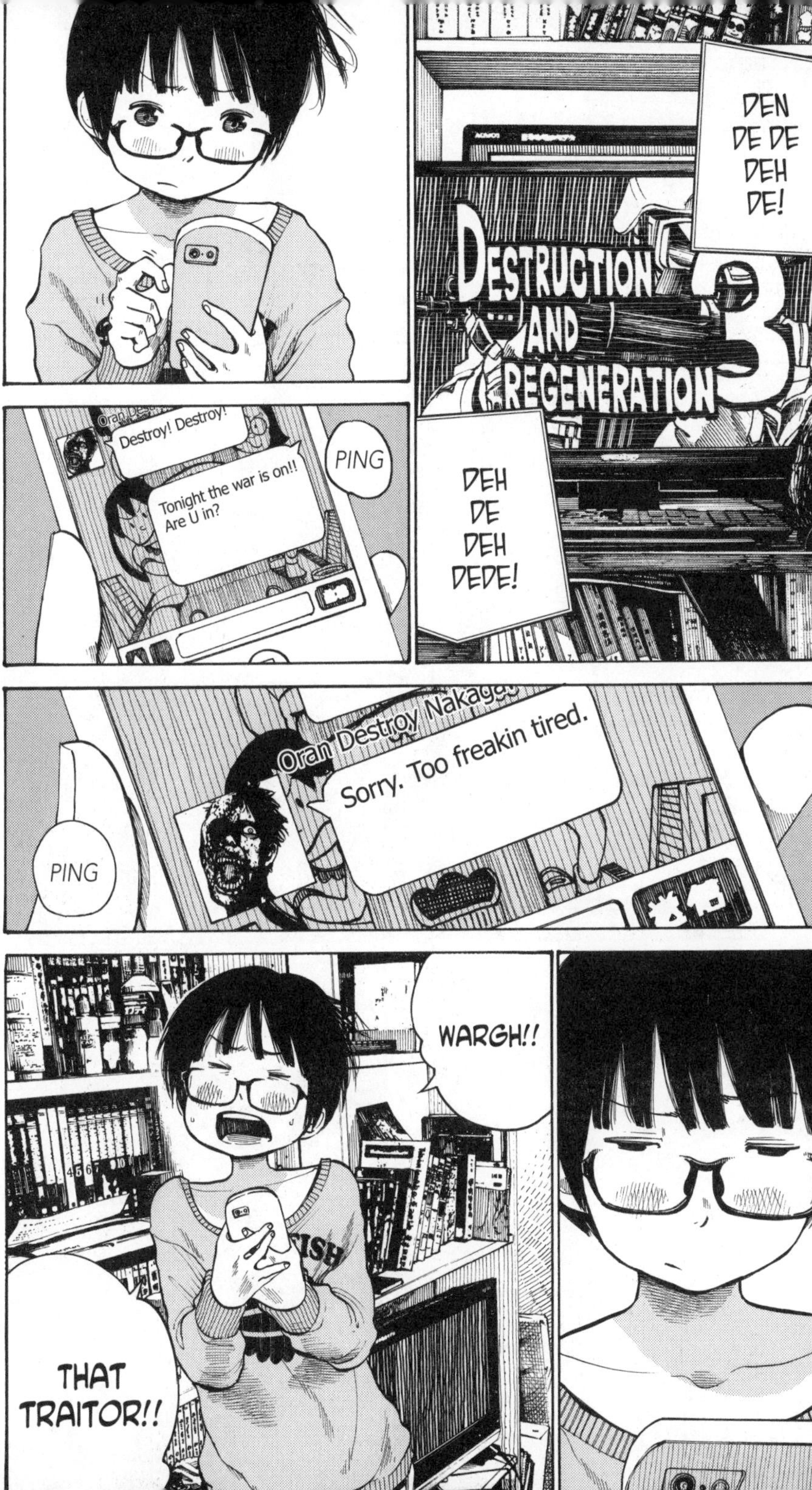

DEN DE DE DEH DE!
DESTRUCTION AND REGENERATION 3
DEH DE DEH DEDE!
Oran Destroy Nakagawa
Destroy! Destroy!
Tonight the war is on!! Are U in?
PING
Oran Destroy Nakagawa
Sorry. Too freakin tired.
PING
WARGH!!
THAT TRAITOR!!

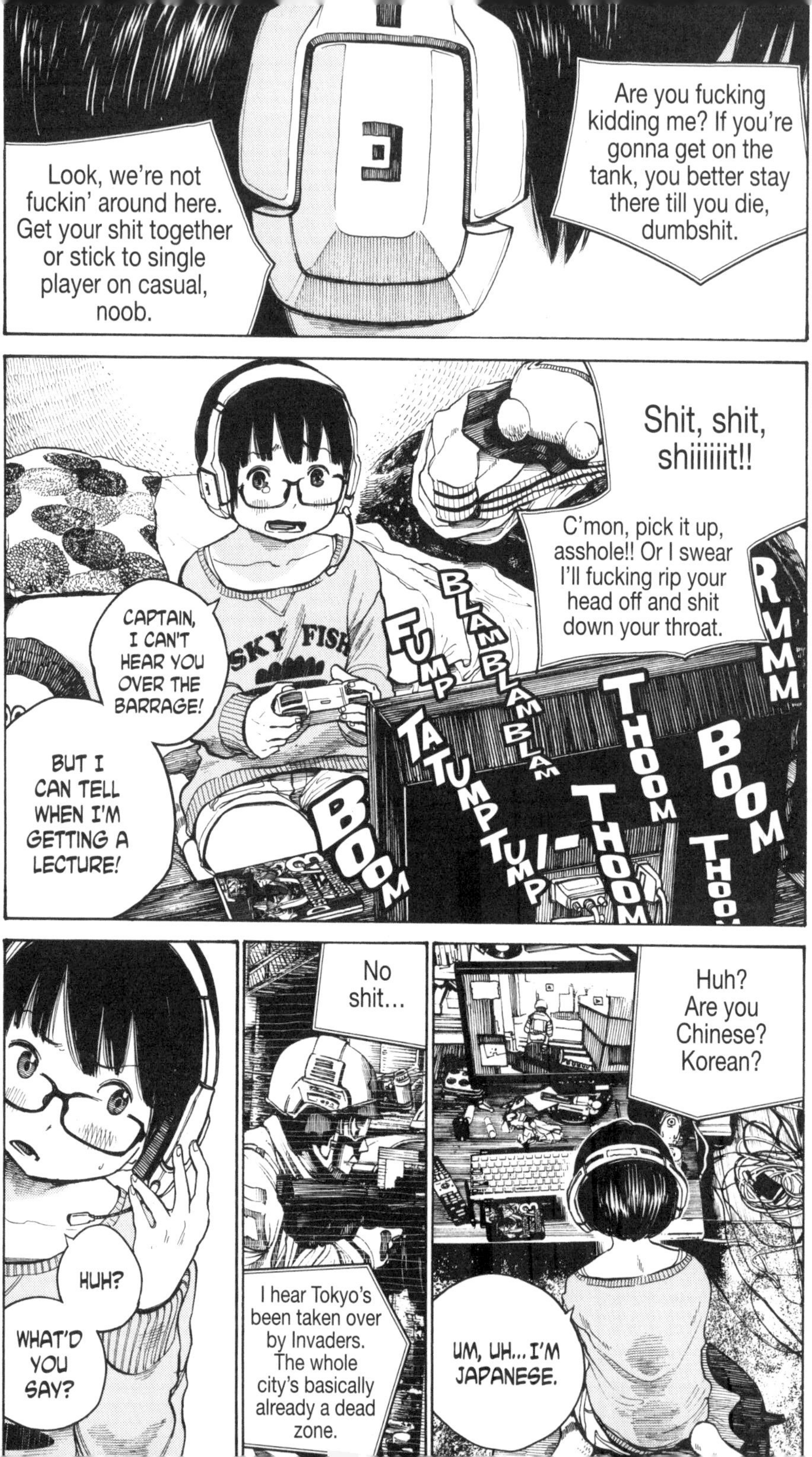
Are you fucking kidding me? If you're gonna get on the tank, you better stay there till you die, dumbshit.
Look, we're not fuckin' around here. Get your shit together or stick to single player on casual, noob.
Shit, shit, shiiiiiit!!
C'mon, pick it up, asshole!! Or I swear I'll fucking rip your head off and shit down your throat.
RMMM
BOOM
THOOM
THOOM
THOOM-THOOM
BLAMBLAMBLAM
FUMP
TATUMPTUMP
BOOM
CAPTAIN, I CAN'T HEAR YOU OVER THE BARRAGE!
BUT I CAN TELL WHEN I'M GETTING A LECTURE!
Huh? Are you Chinese? Korean?
UM, UH... I'M JAPANESE.
No shit...
I hear Tokyo's been taken over by Invaders. The whole city's basically already a dead zone.
HUH?
WHAT'D YOU SAY?

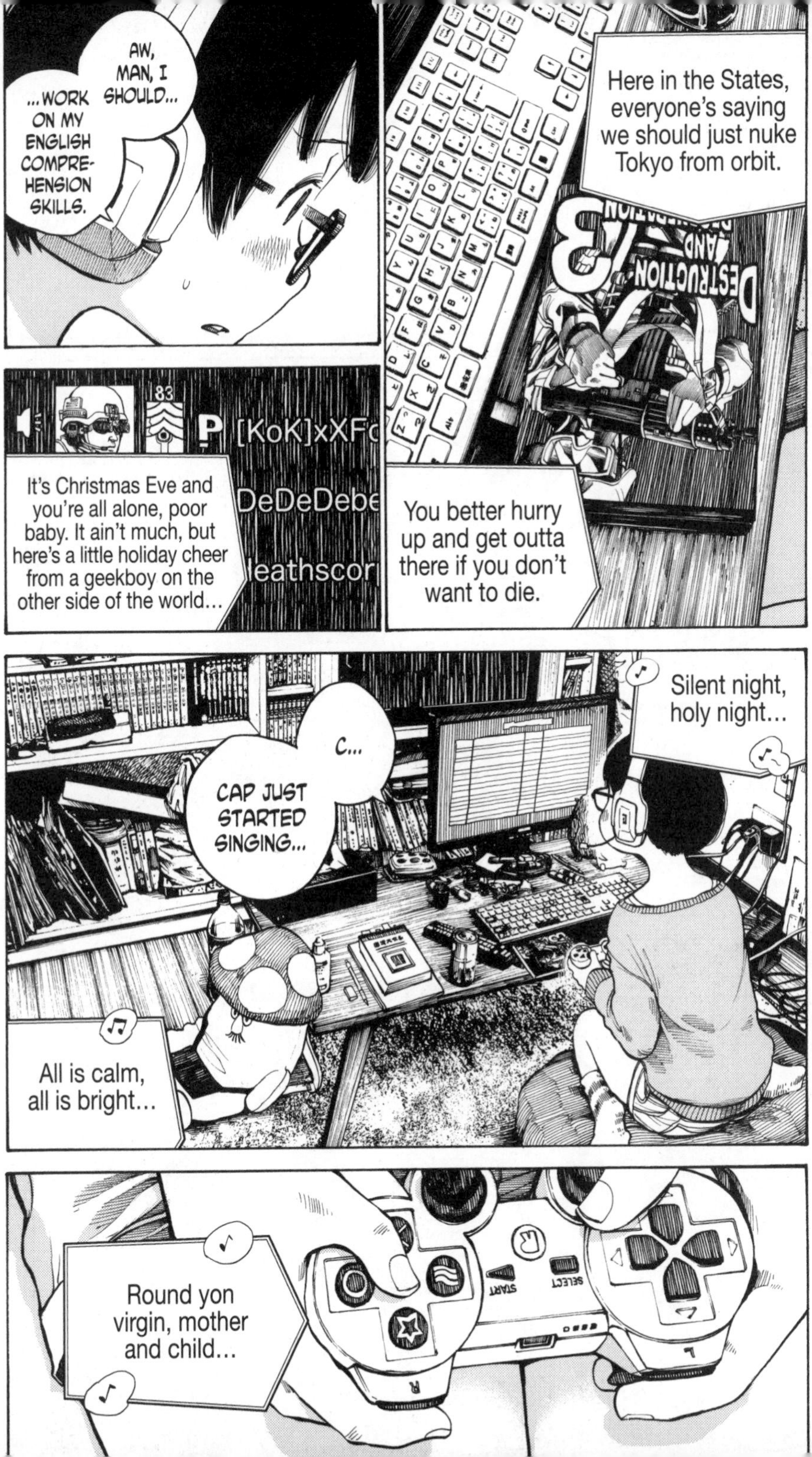

Here in the States, everyone's saying we should just nuke Tokyo from orbit.
You better hurry up and get outta there if you don't want to die.
AW, MAN, I SHOULD...
...WORK ON MY ENGLISH COMPREHENSION SKILLS.
It's Christmas Eve and you're all alone, poor baby. It ain't much, but here's a little holiday cheer from a geekboy on the other side of the world...
Silent night, holy night...
C...
CAP JUST STARTED SINGING...
All is calm, all is bright...
Round yon virgin, mother and child...

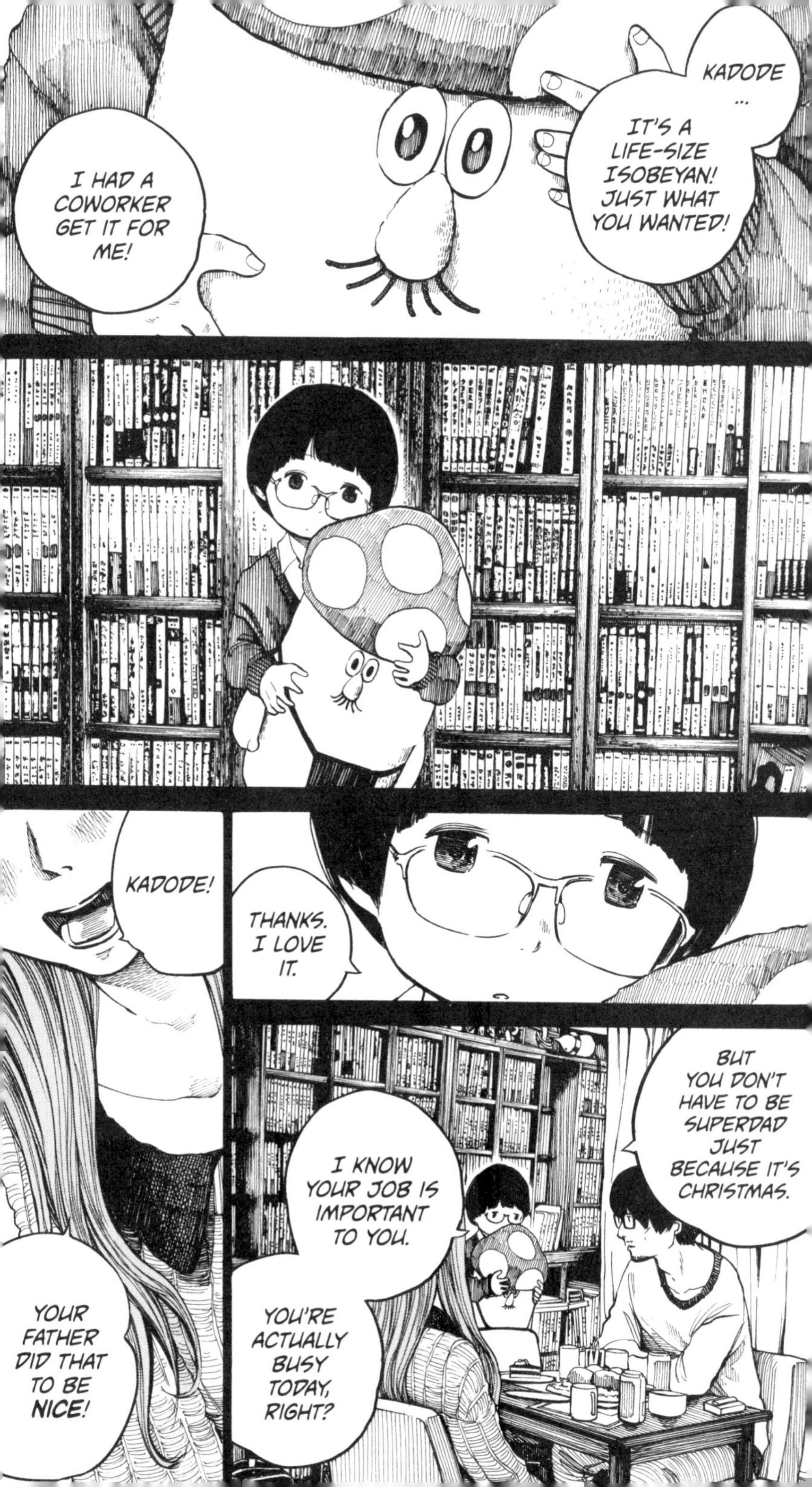
KADODE ...
IT'S A LIFE-SIZE ISOBEYAN! JUST WHAT YOU WANTED!
I HAD A COWORKER GET IT FOR ME!
THANKS. I LOVE IT.
BUT YOU DON'T HAVE TO BE SUPERDAD JUST BECAUSE IT'S CHRISTMAS.
I KNOW YOUR JOB IS IMPORTANT TO YOU.
YOU'RE ACTUALLY BUSY TODAY, RIGHT?
KADODE!
YOUR FATHER DID THAT TO BE **NICE**!

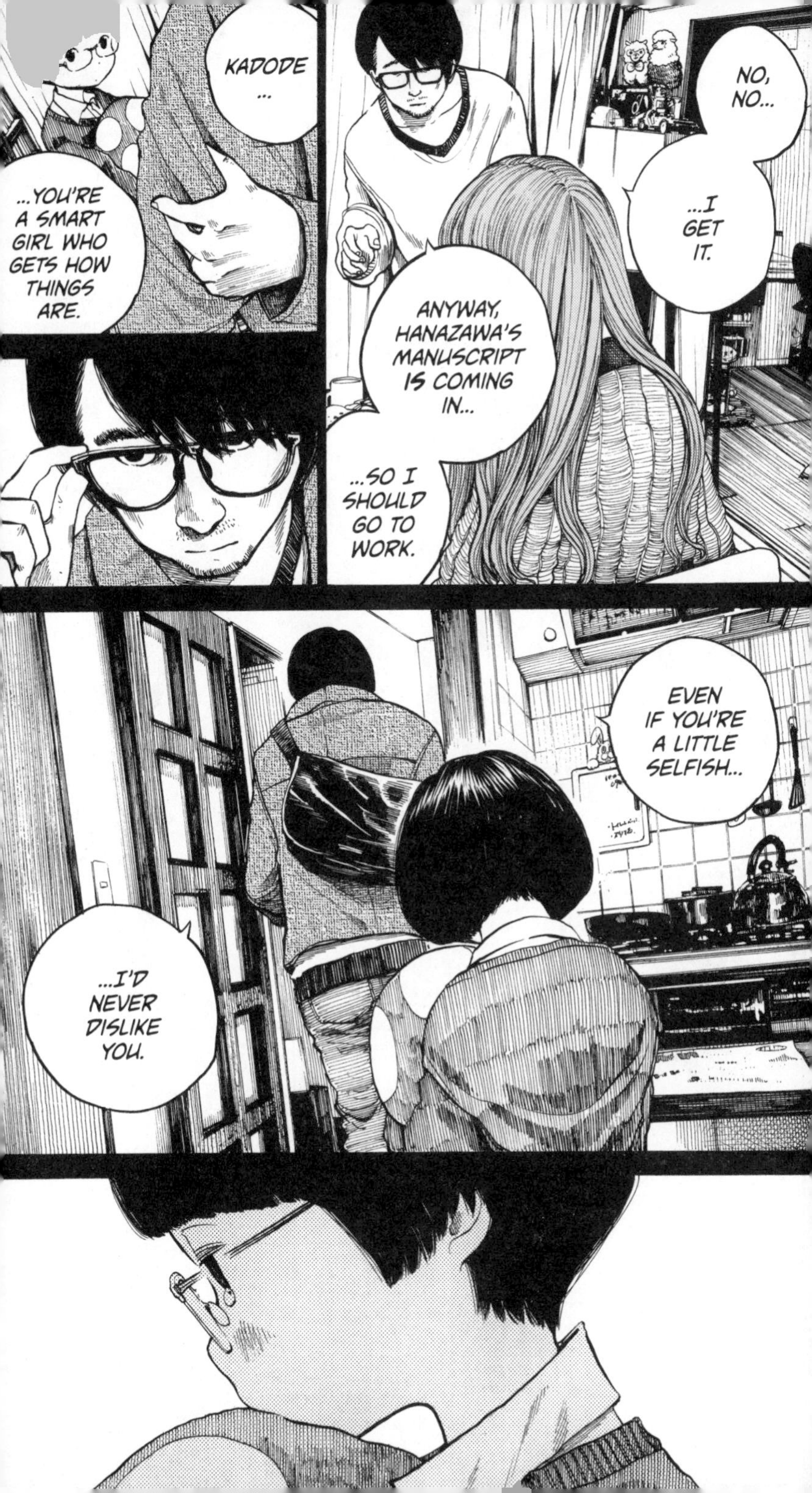
NO, NO...
...I GET IT.
ANYWAY, HANAZAWA'S MANUSCRIPT IS COMING IN...
...SO I SHOULD GO TO WORK.
KADODE...
...YOU'RE A SMART GIRL WHO GETS HOW THINGS ARE.
EVEN IF YOU'RE A LITTLE SELFISH...
...I'D NEVER DISLIKE YOU.

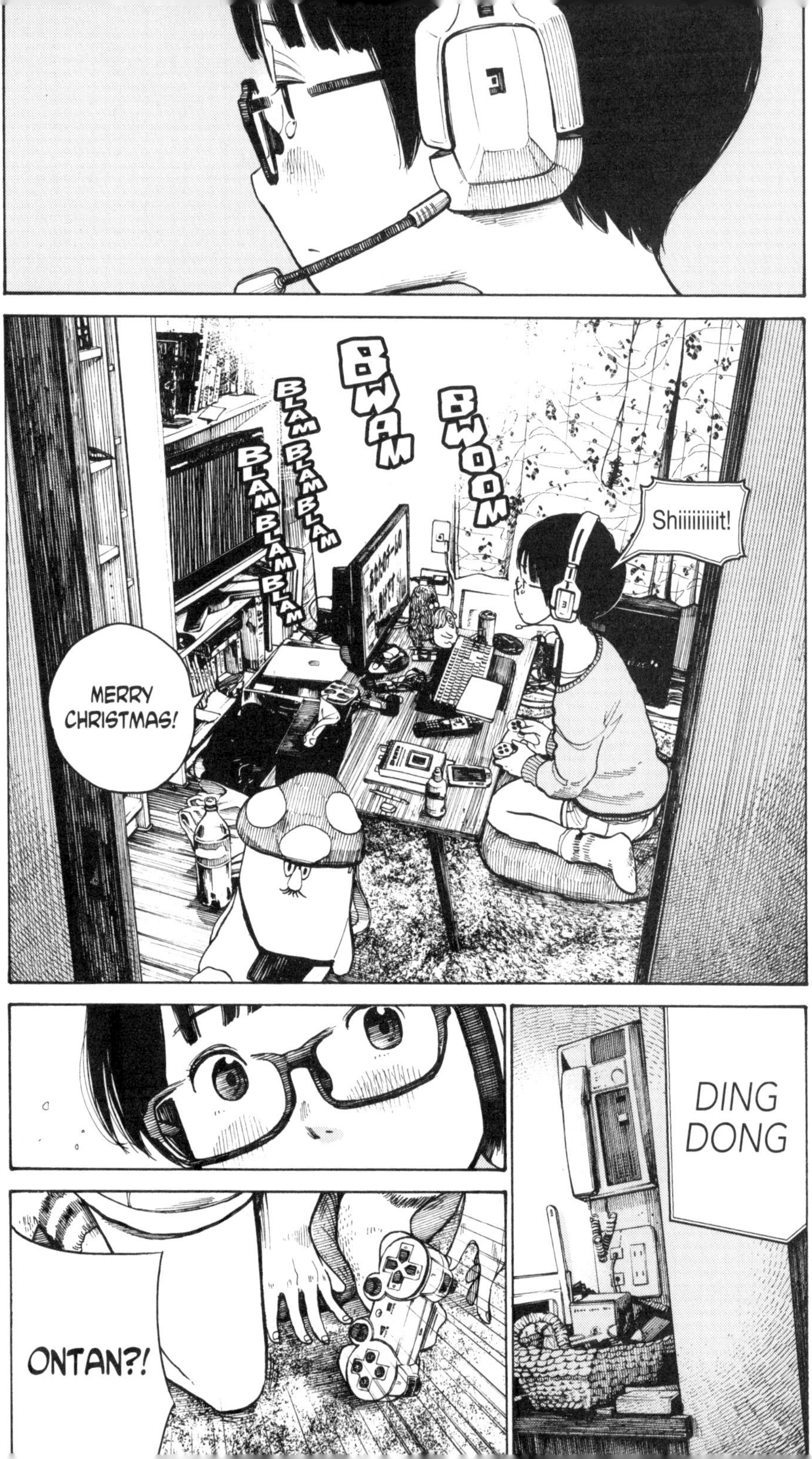
Shiiiiiiiit!
BWOOM
BWAM
BLAM BLAM BLAM
BLAM BLAM BLAM
MERRY CHRISTMAS!
DING DONG
ONTAN?!

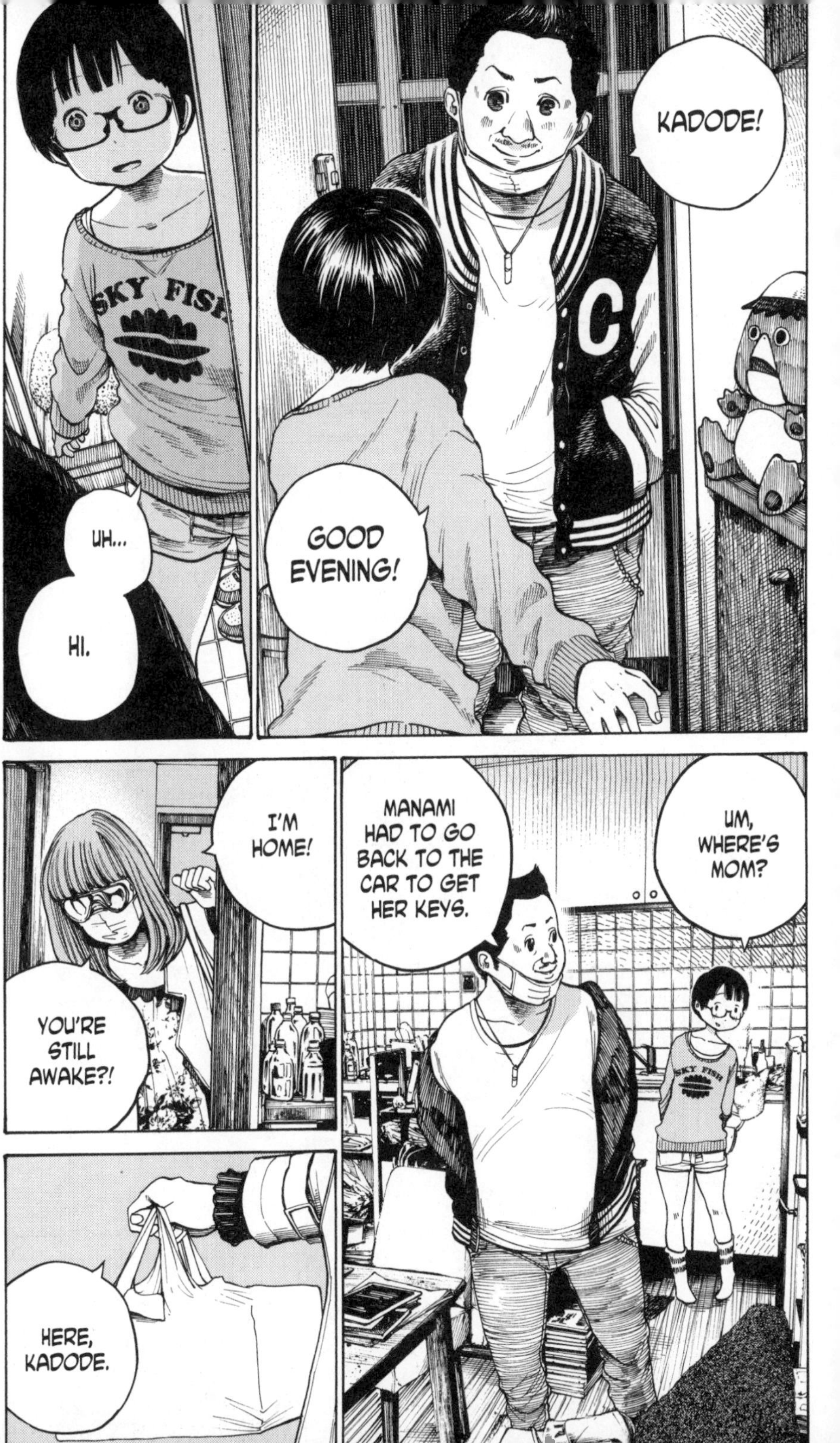
KADODE!
GOOD EVENING!
UH...
HI.
UM, WHERE'S MOM?
MANAMI HAD TO GO BACK TO THE CAR TO GET HER KEYS.
I'M HOME!
YOU'RE STILL AWAKE?!
HERE, KADODE.

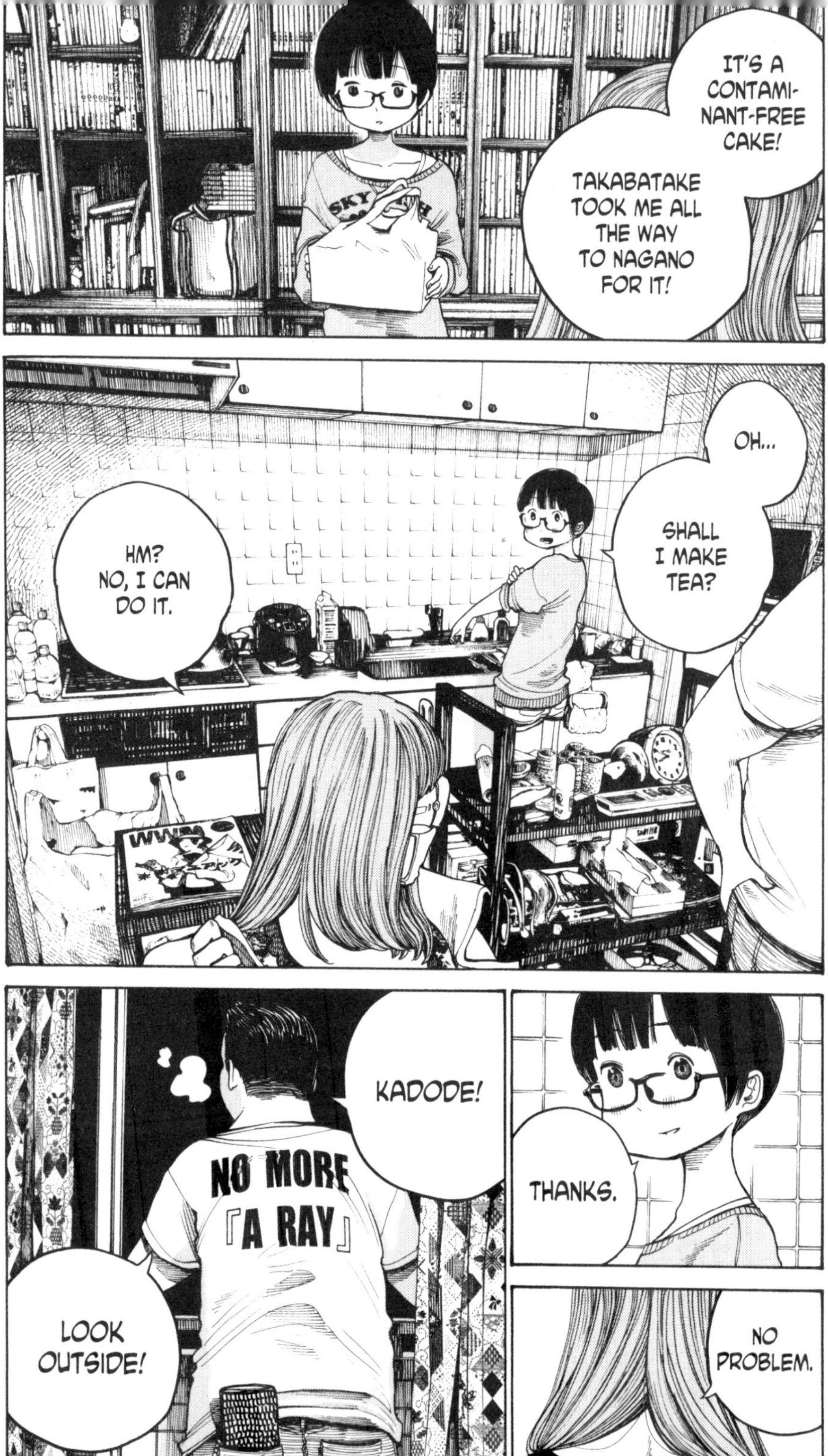
IT'S A CONTAMI-NANT-FREE CAKE!
TAKABATAKE TOOK ME ALL THE WAY TO NAGANO FOR IT!
OH...
SHALL I MAKE TEA?
HM? NO, I CAN DO IT.
THANKS.
NO PROBLEM.
KADODE!
NO MORE 『A RAY』
LOOK OUTSIDE!

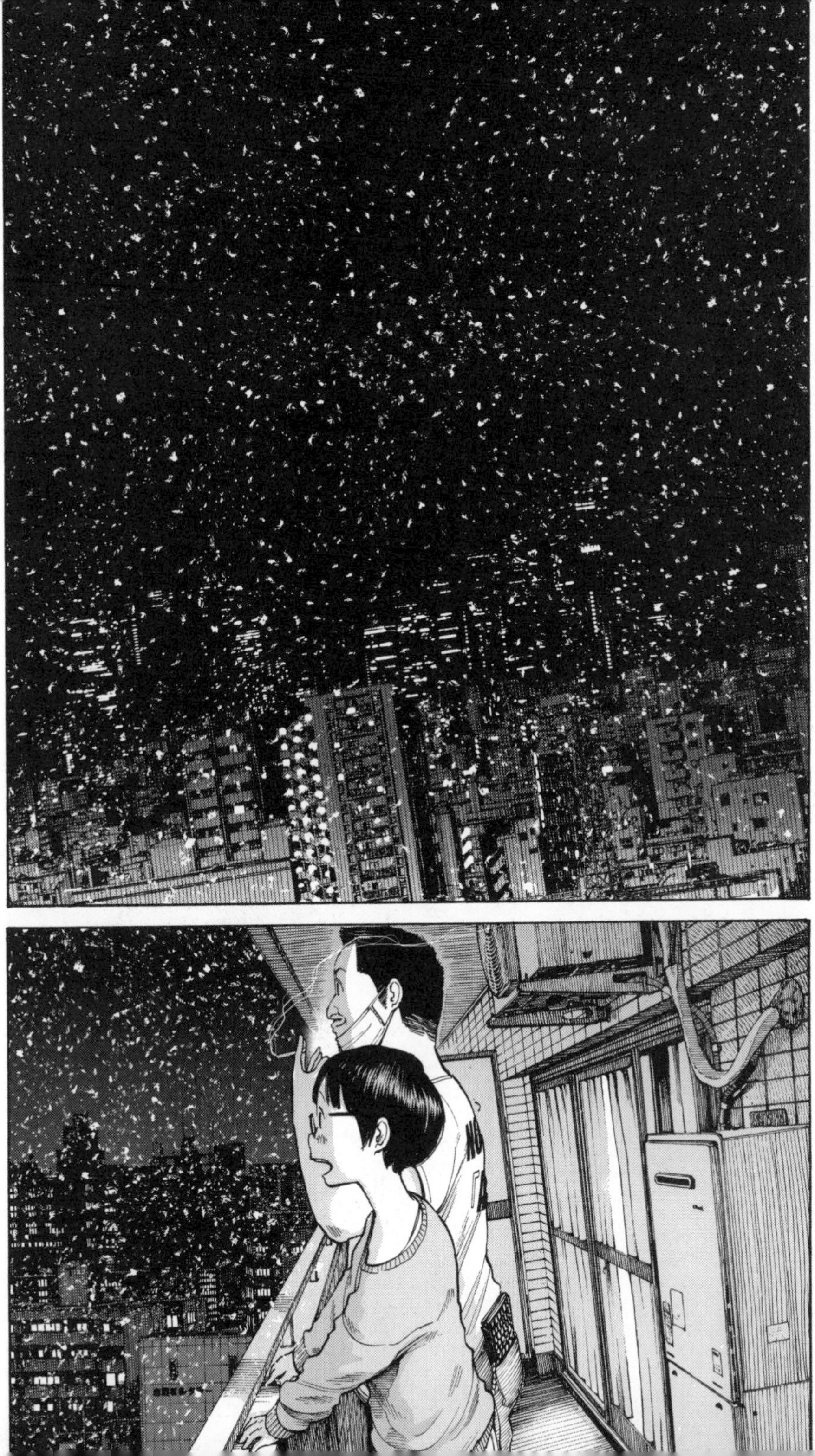

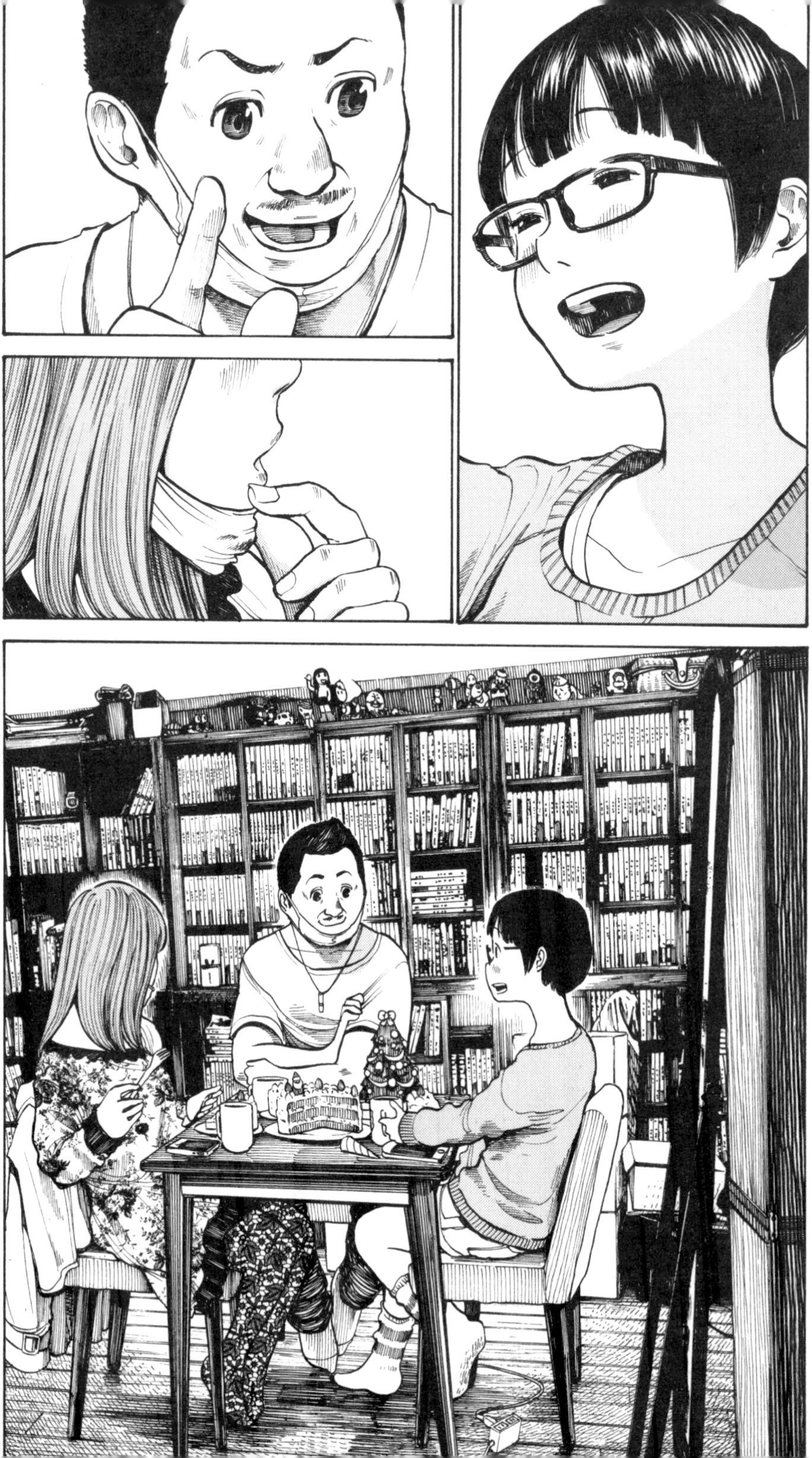

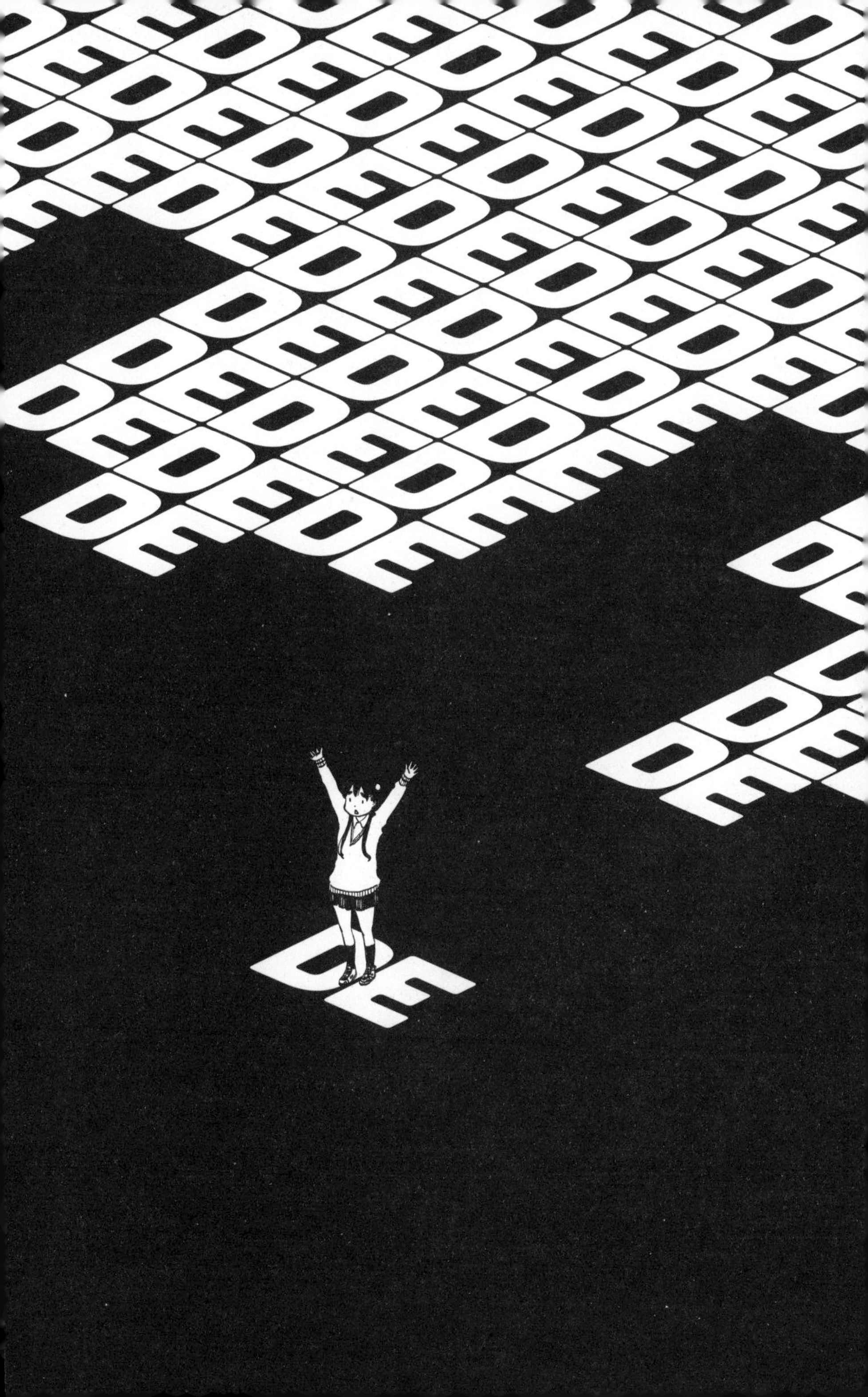

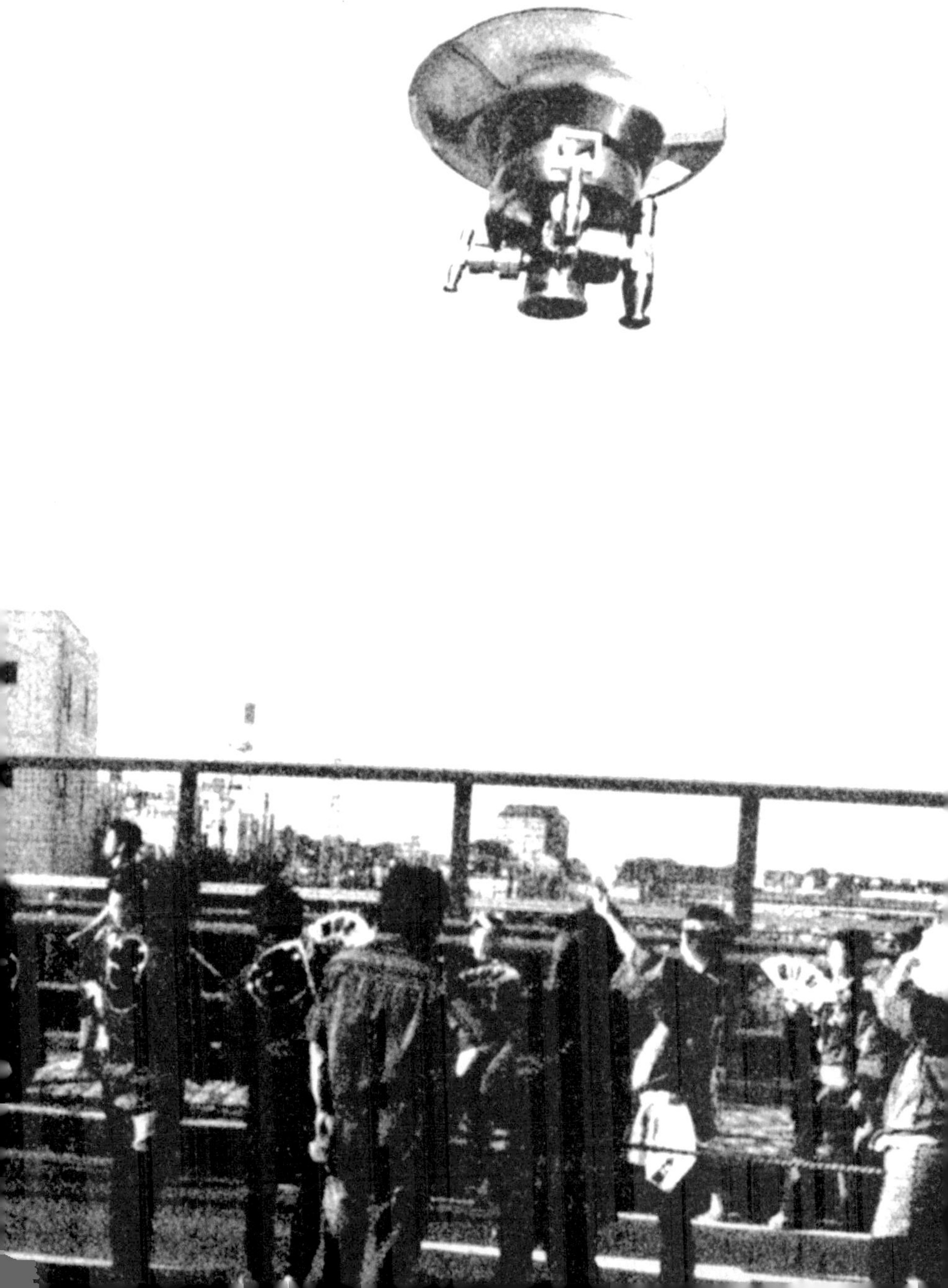

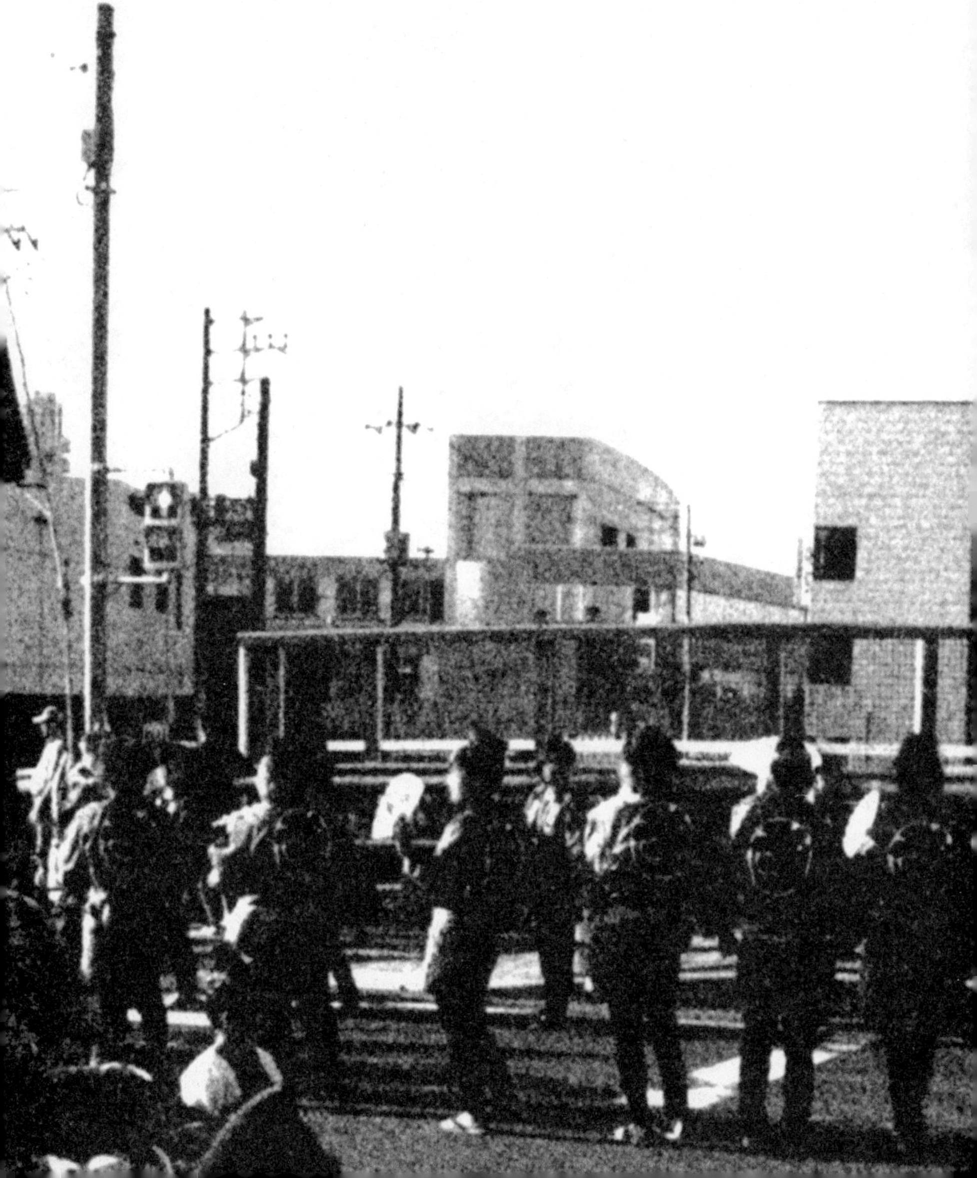

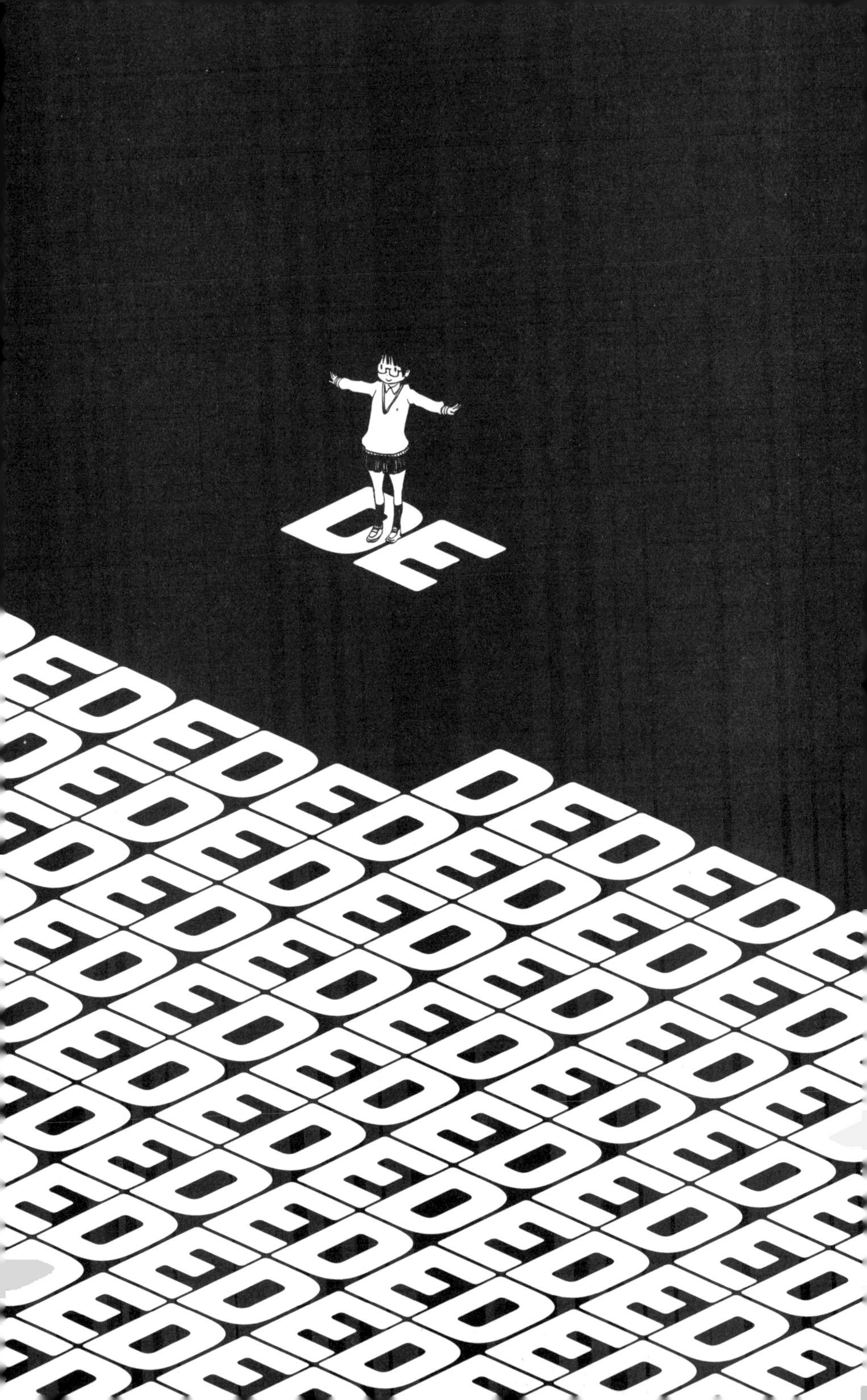

CHAPTER 15

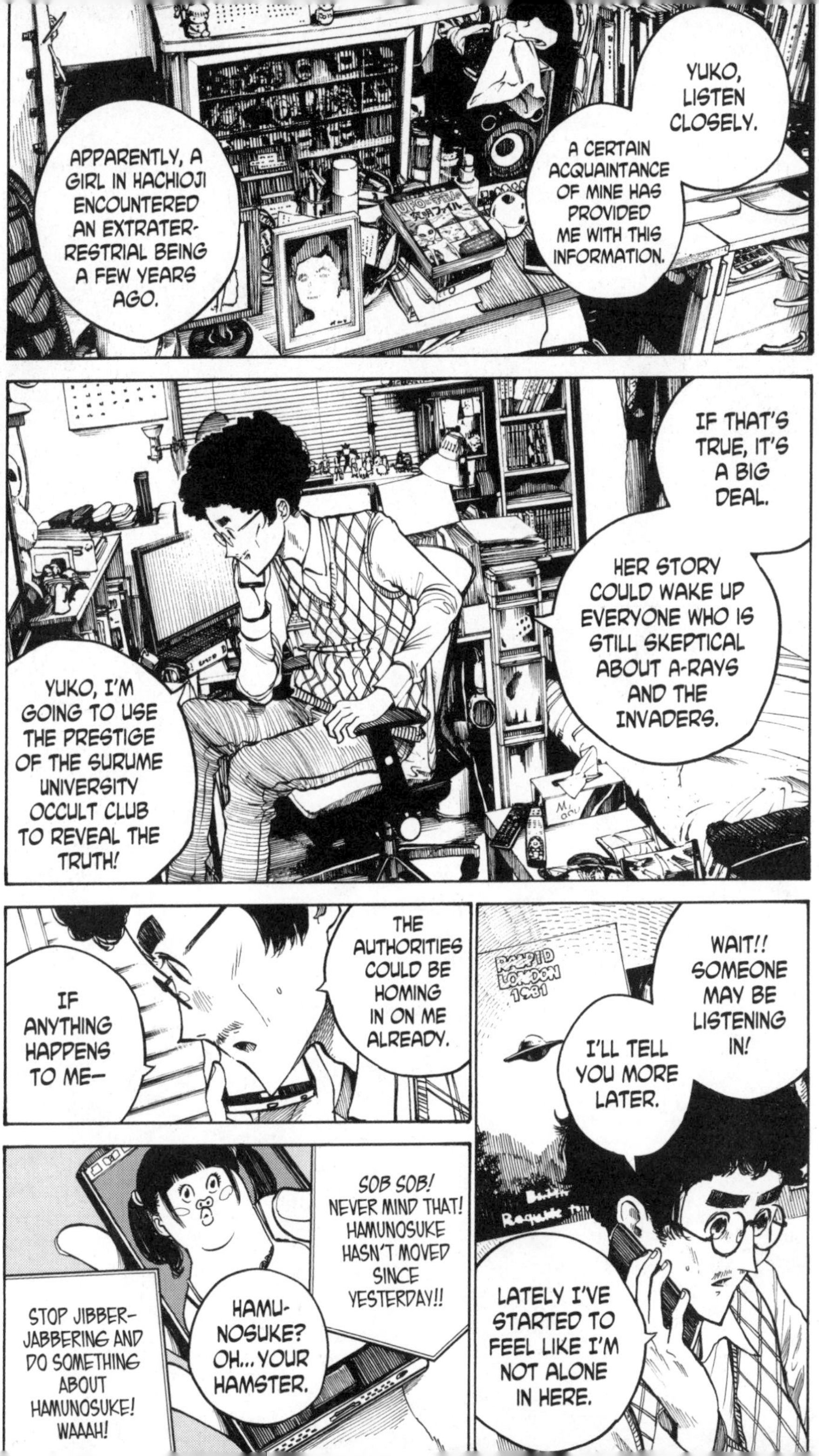
YUKO, LISTEN CLOSELY.
A CERTAIN ACQUAINTANCE OF MINE HAS PROVIDED ME WITH THIS INFORMATION.
APPARENTLY, A GIRL IN HACHIOJI ENCOUNTERED AN EXTRATER-RESTRIAL BEING A FEW YEARS AGO.
IF THAT'S TRUE, IT'S A BIG DEAL.
HER STORY COULD WAKE UP EVERYONE WHO IS STILL SKEPTICAL ABOUT A-RAYS AND THE INVADERS.
YUKO, I'M GOING TO USE THE PRESTIGE OF THE SURUME UNIVERSITY OCCULT CLUB TO REVEAL THE TRUTH!
RAPID LONDON 1981
WAIT!! SOMEONE MAY BE LISTENING IN!
I'LL TELL YOU MORE LATER.
LATELY I'VE STARTED TO FEEL LIKE I'M NOT ALONE IN HERE.
THE AUTHORITIES COULD BE HOMING IN ON ME ALREADY.
IF ANYTHING HAPPENS TO ME—
SOB SOB! NEVER MIND THAT! HAMUNOSUKE HASN'T MOVED SINCE YESTERDAY!!
HAMU-NOSUKE? OH... YOUR HAMSTER.
STOP JIBBER-JABBERING AND DO SOMETHING ABOUT HAMUNOSUKE! WAAAH!

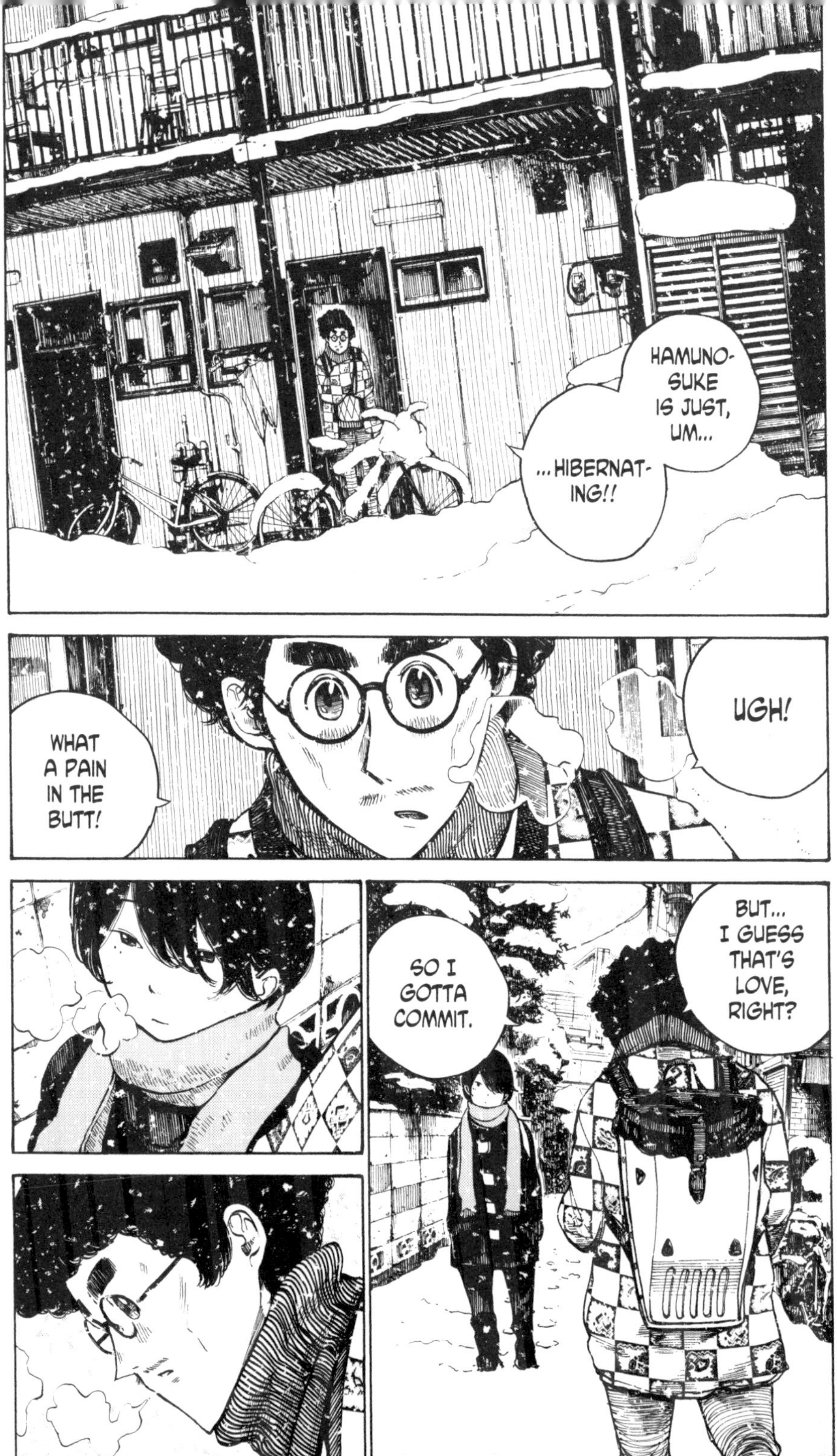
HAMUNO-SUKE IS JUST, UM...
...HIBERNAT-ING!!
UGH!
WHAT A PAIN IN THE BUTT!
BUT... I GUESS THAT'S LOVE, RIGHT?
SO I GOTTA COMMIT.

ALL CLEAR!

NO, I'M NOT *CRAZY*, PRETTY BOY!

LET'S GO!

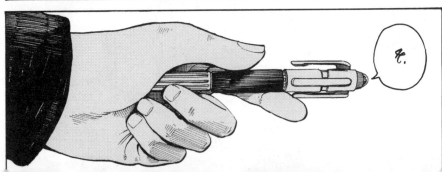

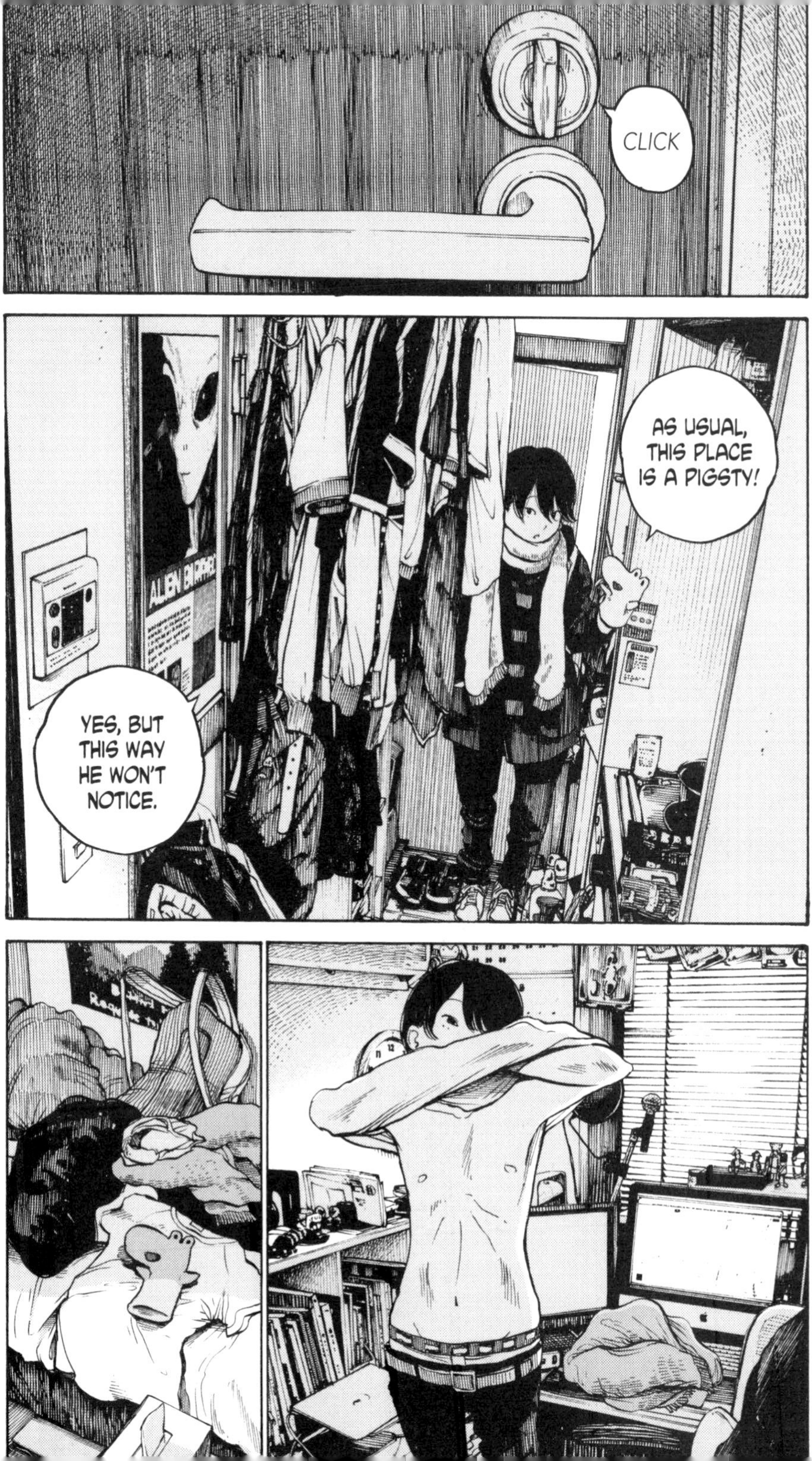
CLICK
AS USUAL, THIS PLACE IS A PIGSTY!
YES, BUT THIS WAY HE WON'T NOTICE.

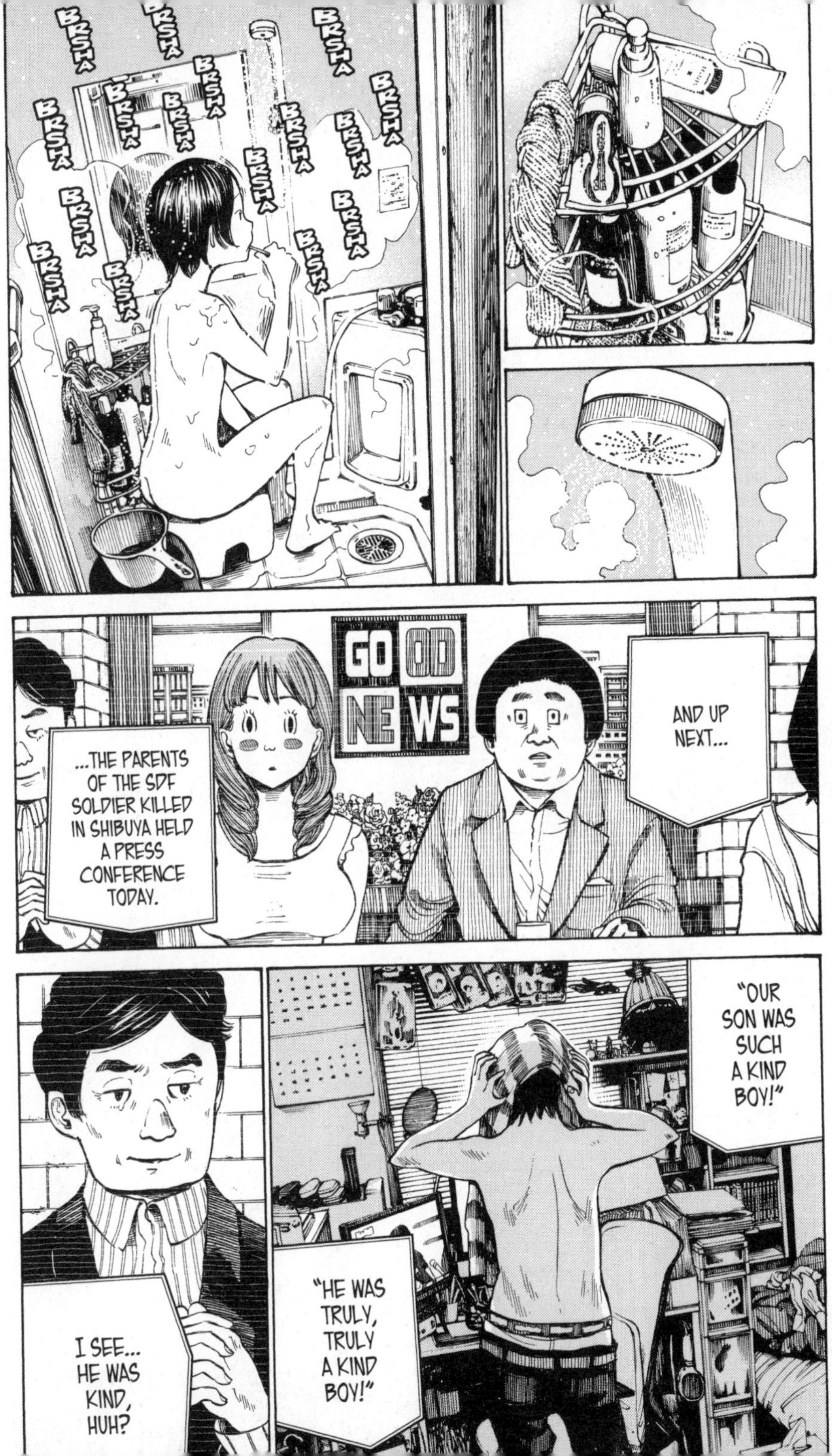
BRSHA
BRSHA
BRSHA
BRSHA
BRSHA
BRSHA
BRSHA
BRSHA
BRSHA
BRSHA
BRSHA
BRSHA
BRSHA
BRSHA
BRSHA
BRSHA
AND UP NEXT...
GOOD NEWS
...THE PARENTS OF THE SDF SOLDIER KILLED IN SHIBUYA HELD A PRESS CONFERENCE TODAY.
"OUR SON WAS SUCH A KIND BOY!"
"HE WAS TRULY, TRULY A KIND BOY!"
I SEE... HE WAS KIND, HUH?

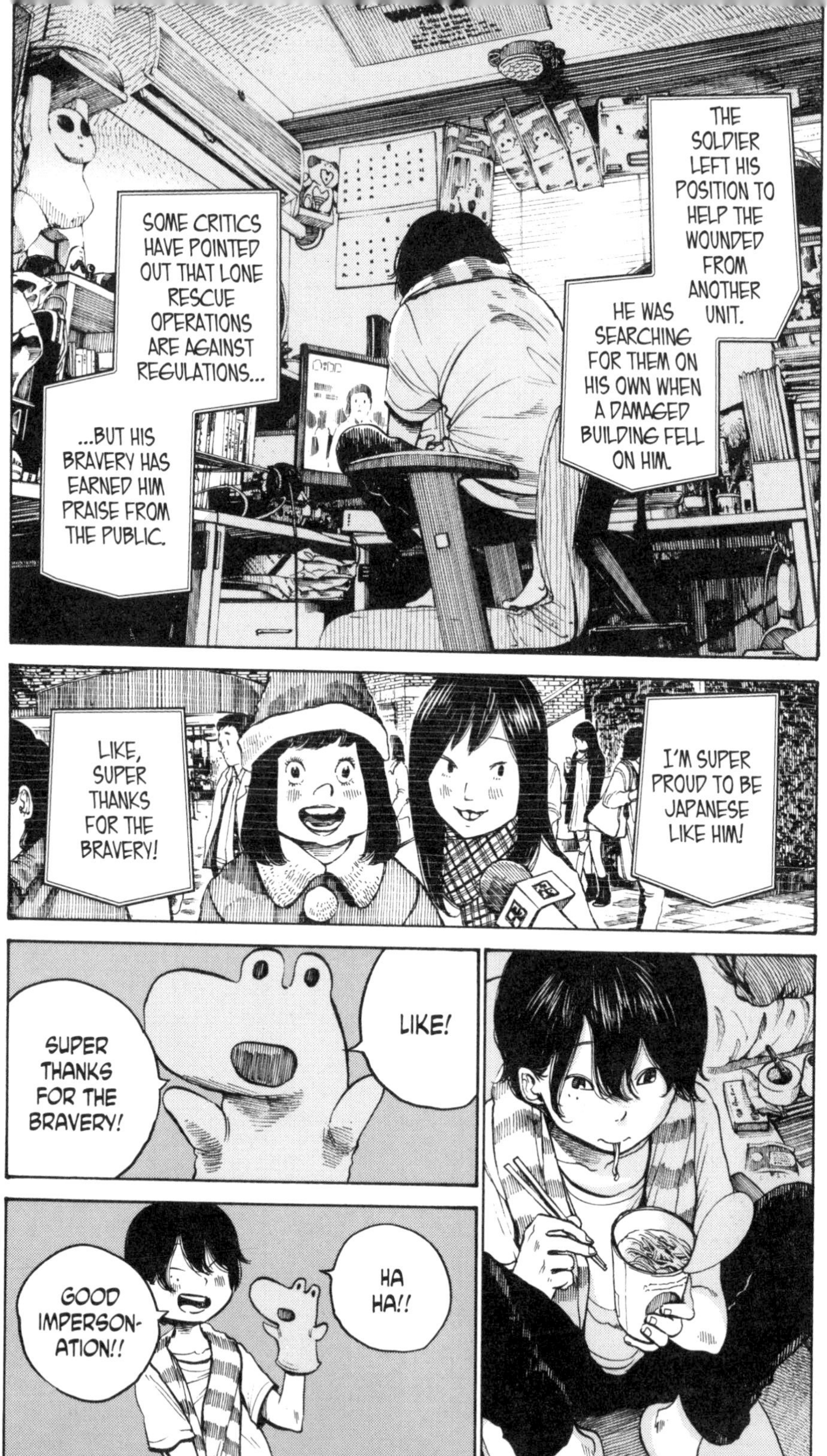
THE SOLDIER LEFT HIS POSITION TO HELP THE WOUNDED FROM ANOTHER UNIT.
HE WAS SEARCHING FOR THEM ON HIS OWN WHEN A DAMAGED BUILDING FELL ON HIM.
SOME CRITICS HAVE POINTED OUT THAT LONE RESCUE OPERATIONS ARE AGAINST REGULATIONS...
...BUT HIS BRAVERY HAS EARNED HIM PRAISE FROM THE PUBLIC.
I'M SUPER PROUD TO BE JAPANESE LIKE HIM!
LIKE, SUPER THANKS FOR THE BRAVERY!
LIKE!
SUPER THANKS FOR THE BRAVERY!
HA HA!!
GOOD IMPERSON-ATION!!

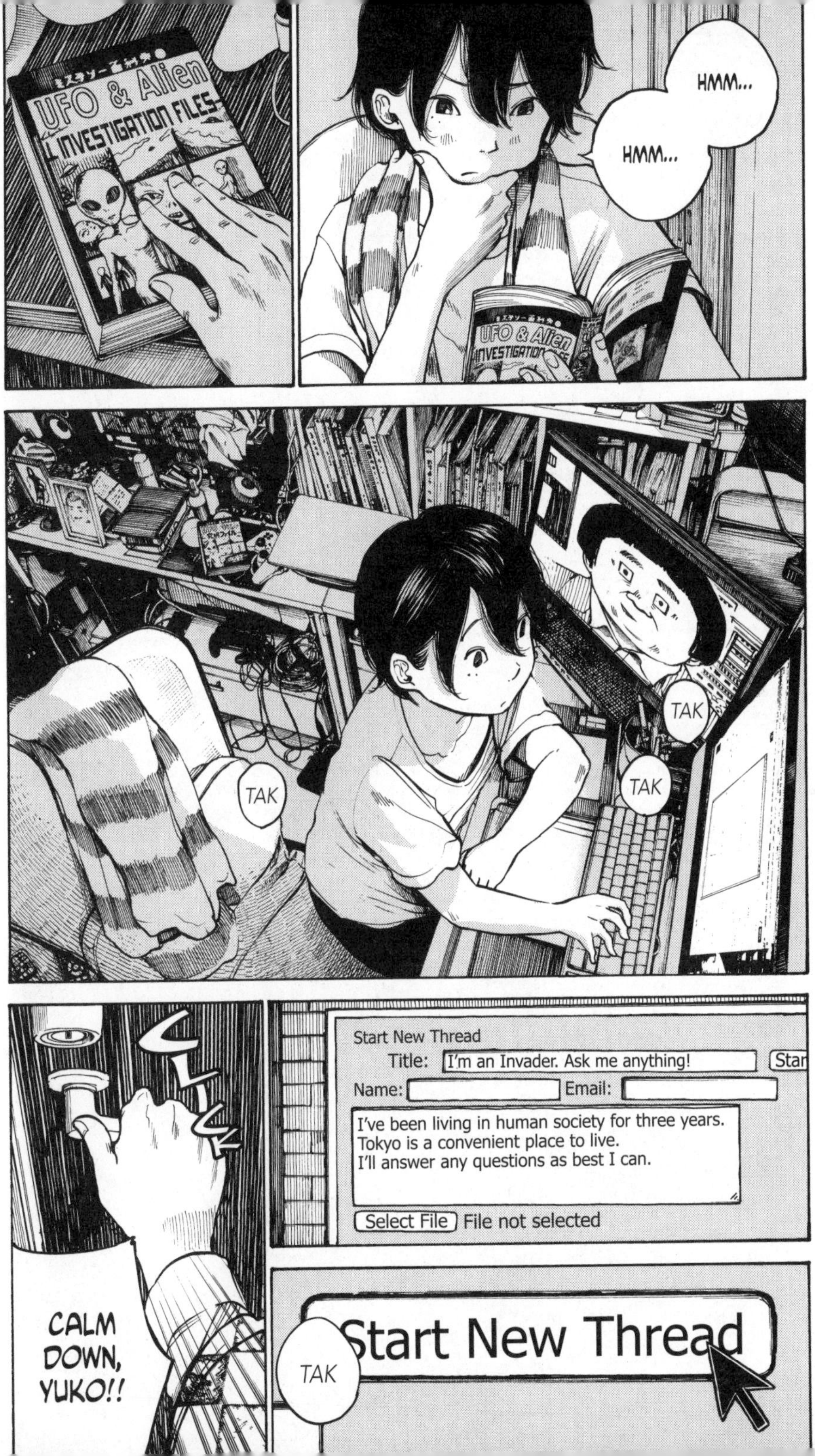
HMM...
HMM...
UFO & Alien
INVESTIGATION FILES
UFO & Alien
INVESTIGATION FILES
TAK
TAK
TAK
Start New Thread
Title: I'm an Invader. Ask me anything!
Name:
Email:
I've been living in human society for three years.
Tokyo is a convenient place to live.
I'll answer any questions as best I can.
Select File
File not selected
Start New Thread
TAK
CLICK
CALM DOWN, YUKO!!

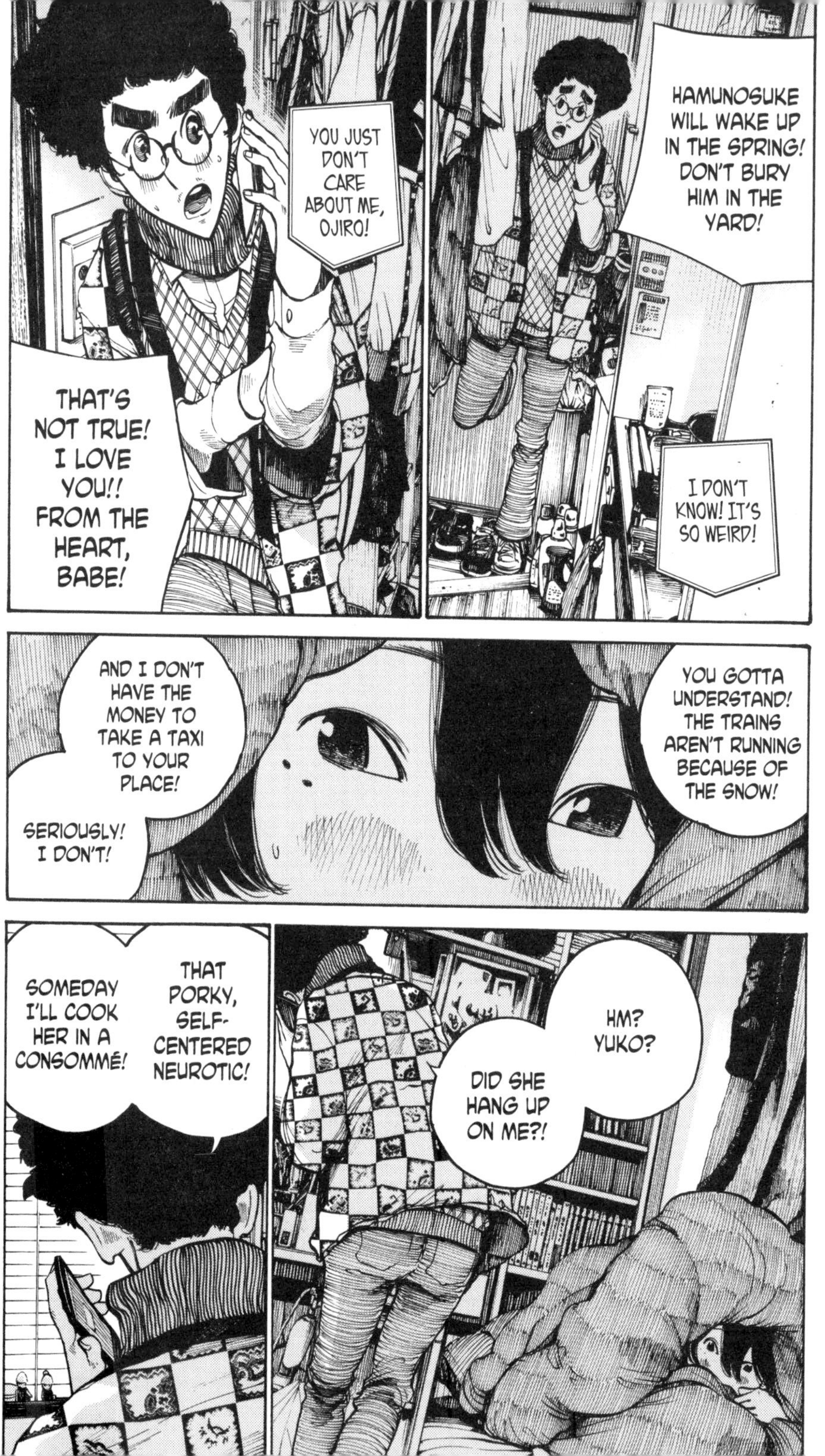
HAMUNOSUKE WILL WAKE UP IN THE SPRING! DON'T BURY HIM IN THE YARD!
I DON'T KNOW! IT'S SO WEIRD!
YOU JUST DON'T CARE ABOUT ME, OJIRO!
THAT'S NOT TRUE! I LOVE YOU!! FROM THE HEART, BABE!
YOU GOTTA UNDERSTAND! THE TRAINS AREN'T RUNNING BECAUSE OF THE SNOW!
AND I DON'T HAVE THE MONEY TO TAKE A TAXI TO YOUR PLACE!
SERIOUSLY! I DON'T!
HM? YUKO?
DID SHE HANG UP ON ME?!
THAT PORKY, SELF-CENTERED NEUROTIC!
SOMEDAY I'LL COOK HER IN A CONSOMMÉ!

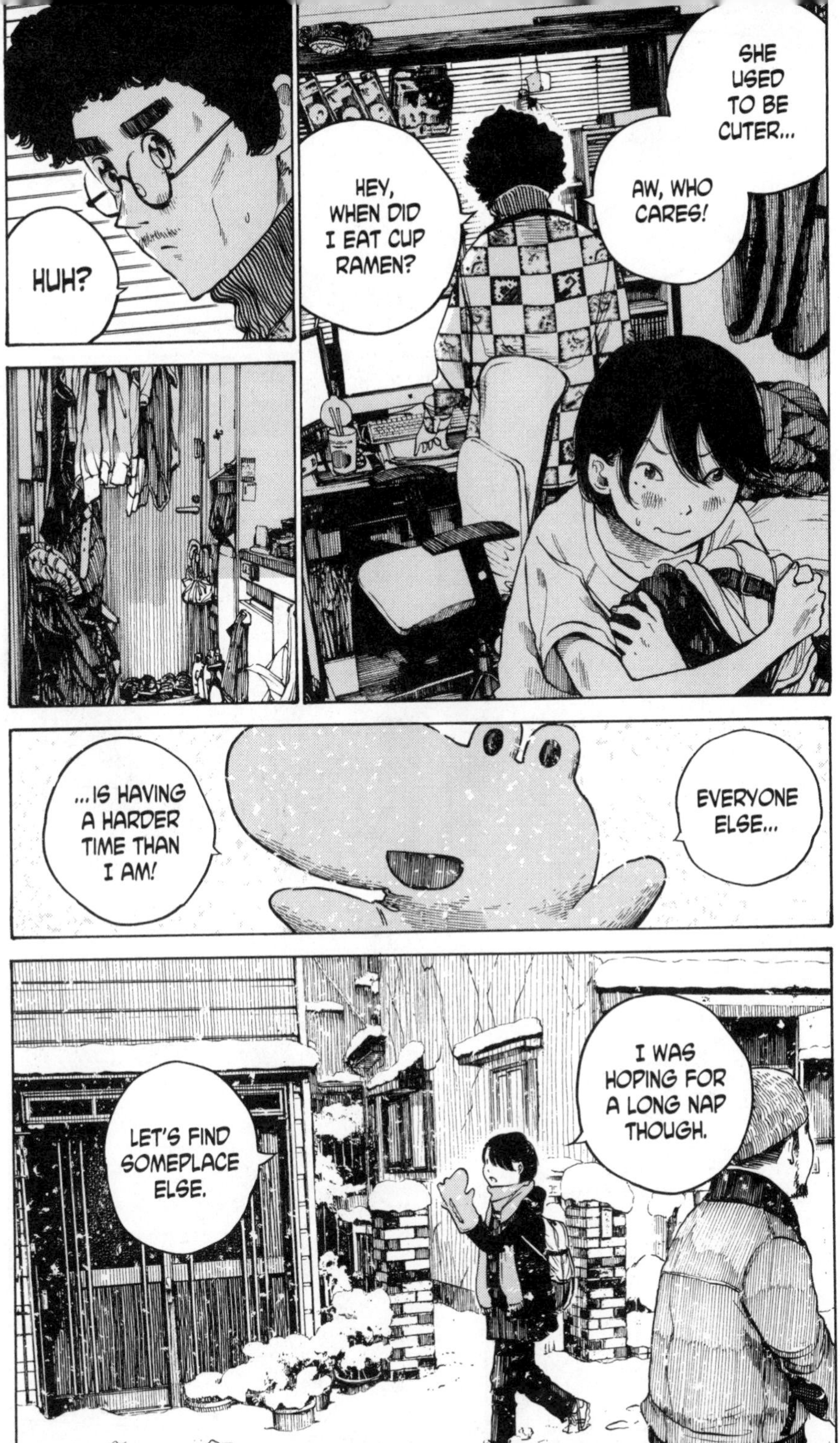
SHE USED TO BE CUTER...
AW, WHO CARES!
HEY, WHEN DID I EAT CUP RAMEN?
HUH?
EVERYONE ELSE...
...IS HAVING A HARDER TIME THAN I AM!
I WAS HOPING FOR A LONG NAP THOUGH.
LET'S FIND SOMEPLACE ELSE.

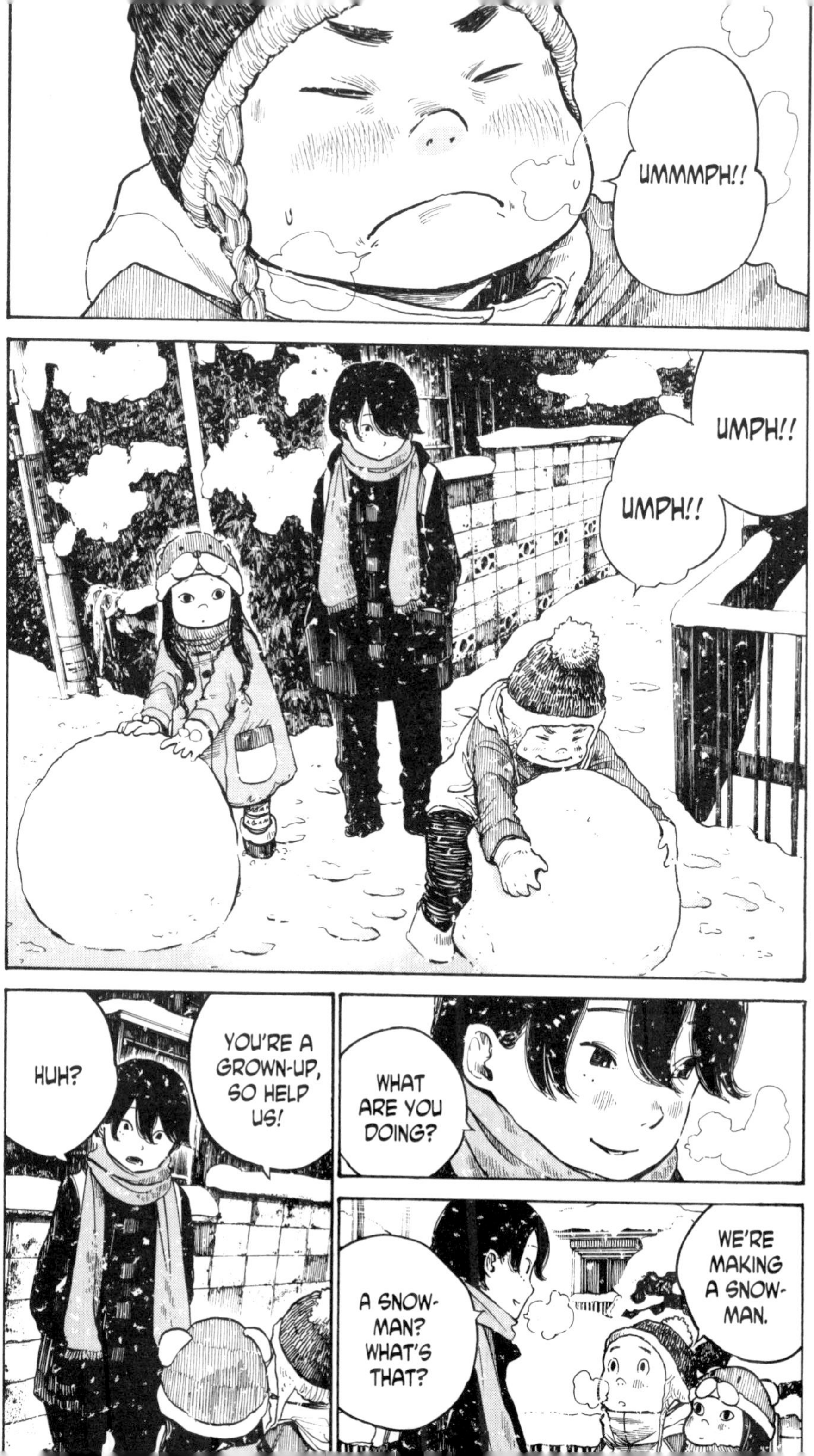
UMMMPH!!
UMPH!!
UMPH!!
WHAT ARE YOU DOING?
WE'RE MAKING A SNOW-MAN.
A SNOW-MAN? WHAT'S THAT?
YOU'RE A GROWN-UP, SO HELP US!
HUH?

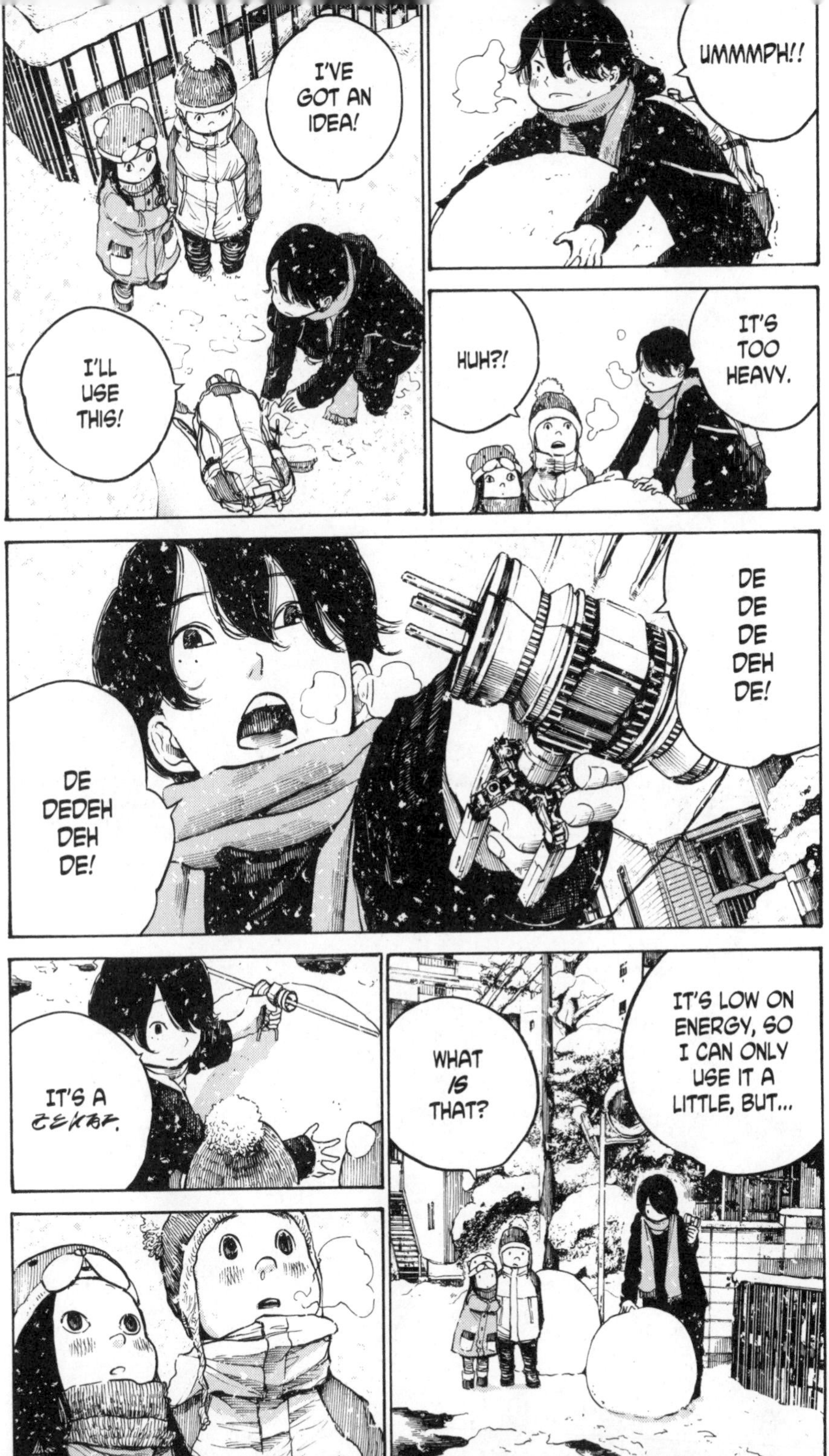
UMMMPH!!
IT'S TOO HEAVY.
HUH?!
I'VE GOT AN IDEA!
I'LL USE THIS!
DE DE DE DEH DE!
DE DEDEH DEH DE!
IT'S LOW ON ENERGY, SO I CAN ONLY USE IT A LITTLE, BUT...
WHAT *IS* THAT?
IT'S A

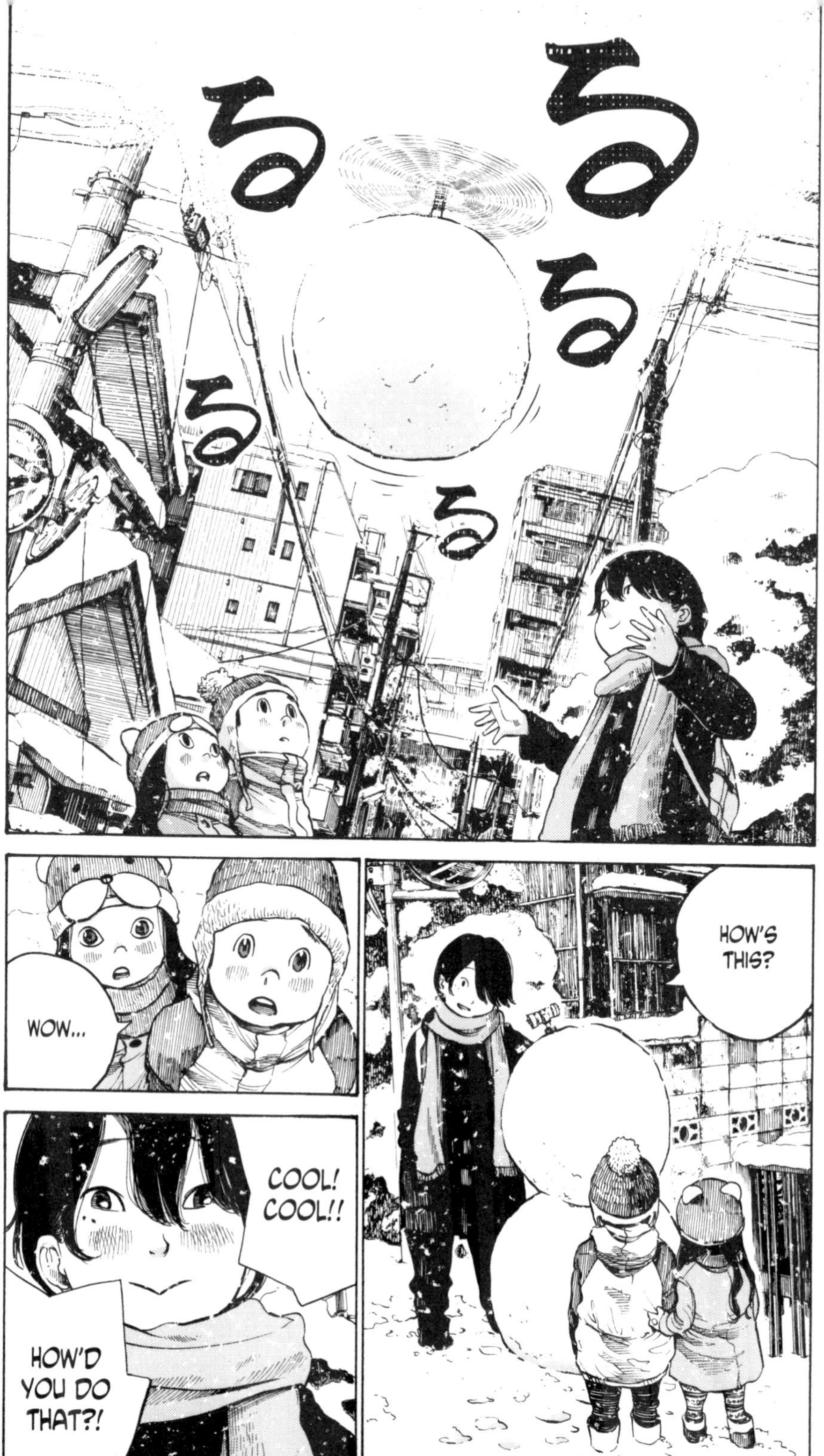
るる
る
る
る
HOW'S THIS?
WOW...
COOL! COOL!!
HOW'D YOU DO THAT?!

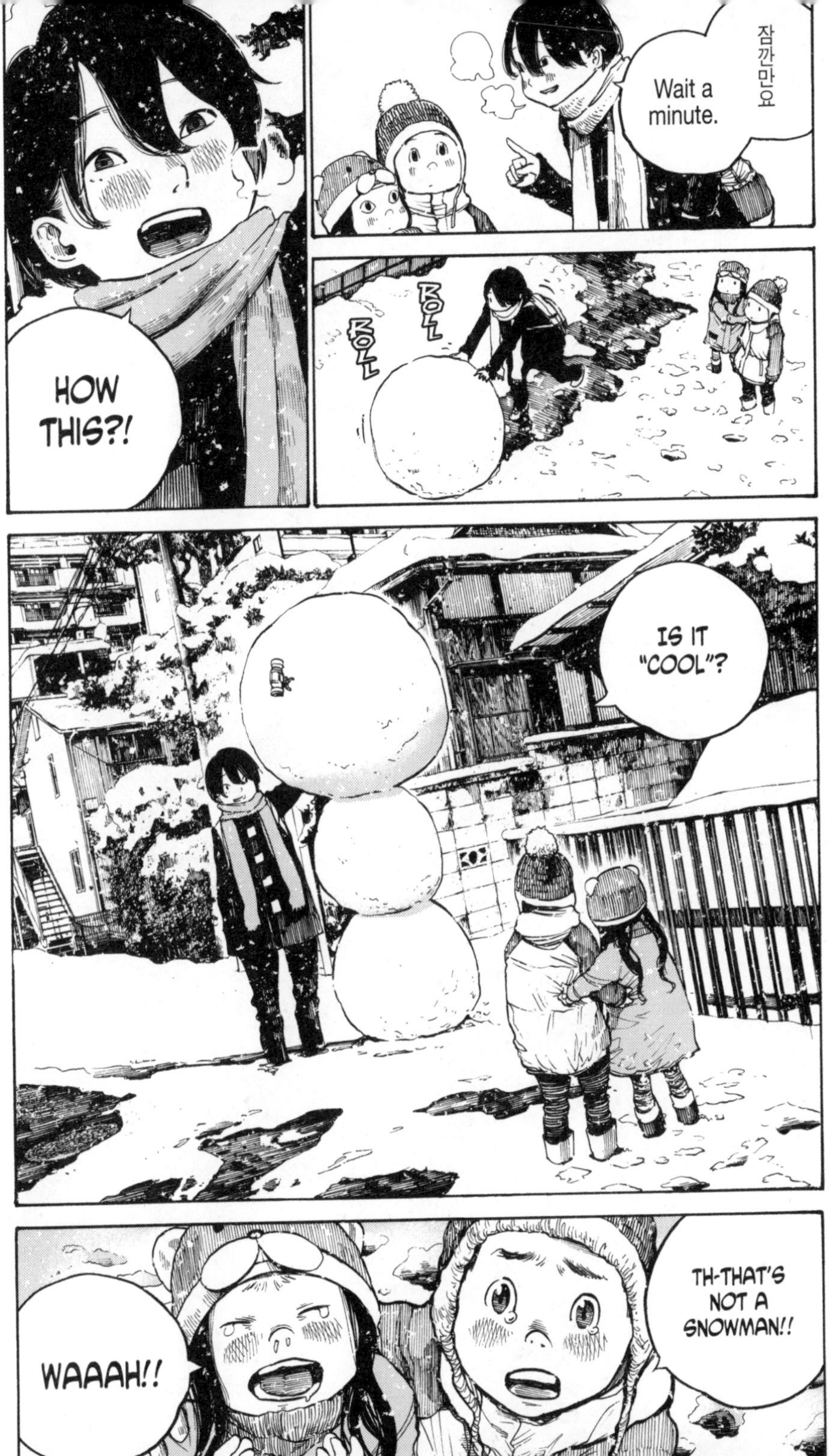
Wait a minute.
잠깐만요
ROLL
ROLL
HOW THIS?!
IS IT "COOL"?
TH-THAT'S NOT A SNOWMAN!!
WAAAH!!

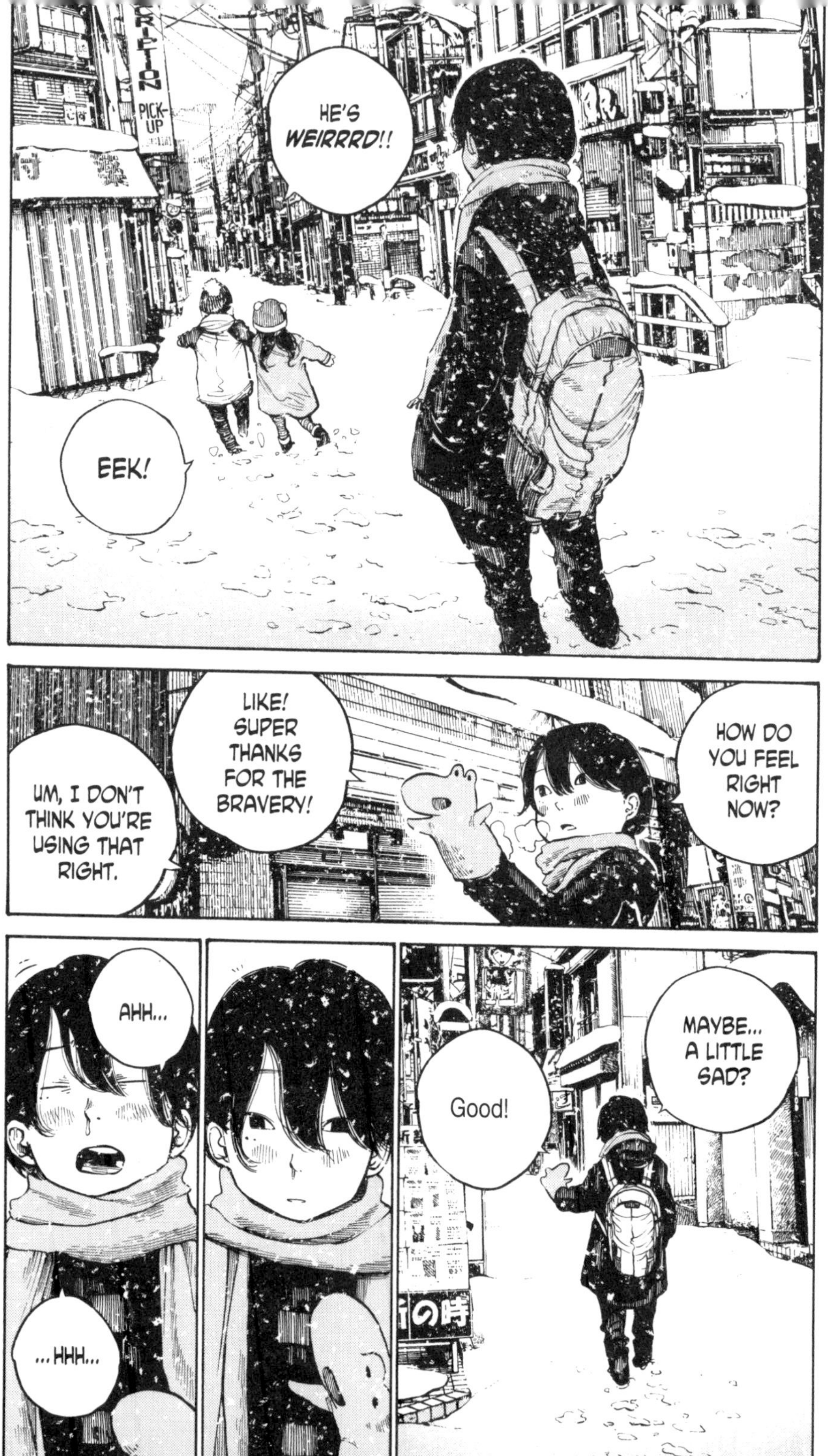
HE'S WEIRRRD!!
PICK-UP
EEK!
HOW DO YOU FEEL RIGHT NOW?
LIKE! SUPER THANKS FOR THE BRAVERY!
UM, I DON'T THINK YOU'RE USING THAT RIGHT.
MAYBE... A LITTLE SAD?
Good!
AHH...
...HHH...

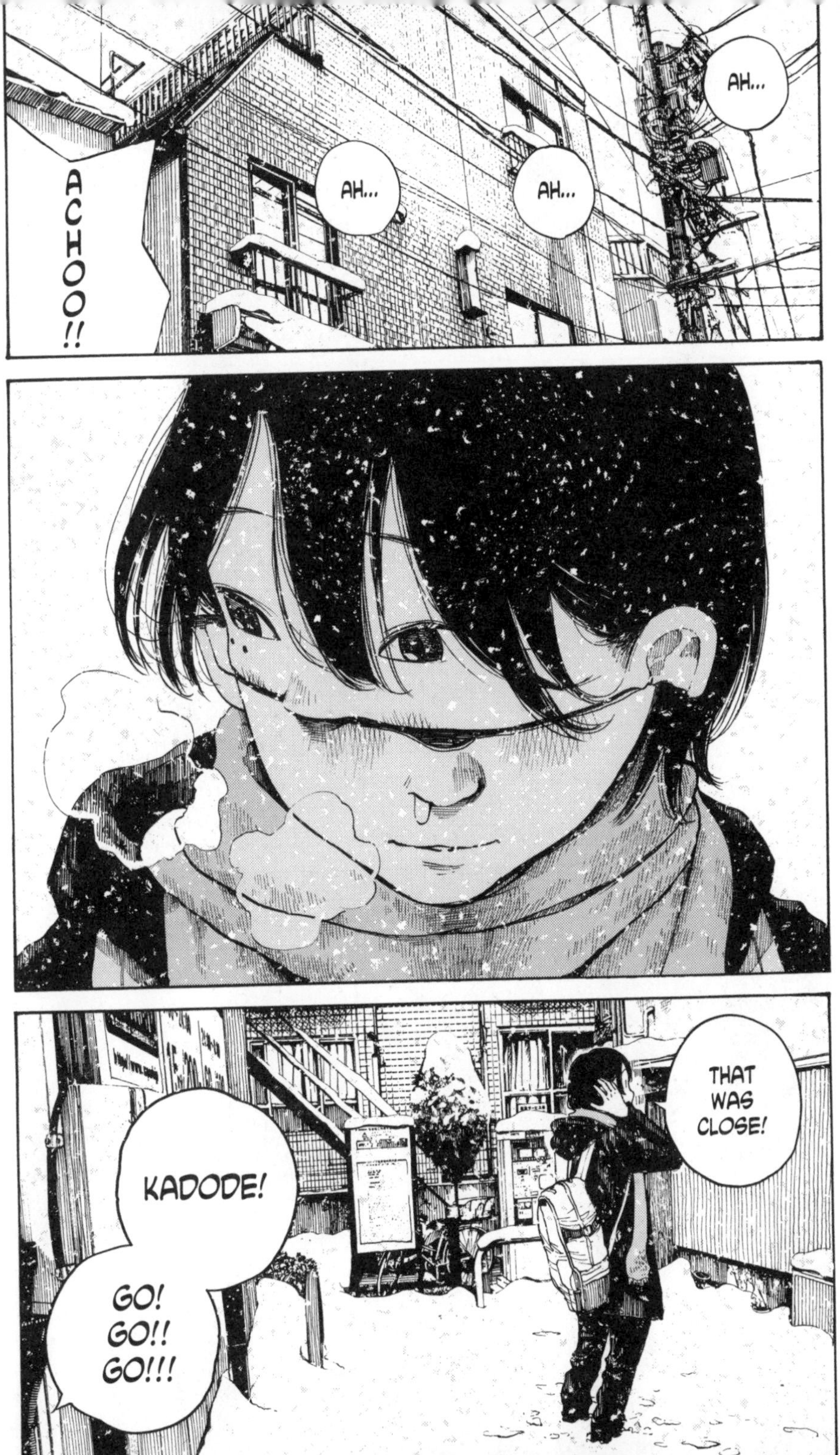
AH...
AH...
AH...
ACHOO!!
THAT WAS CLOSE!
KADODE!
GO! GO!! GO!!!

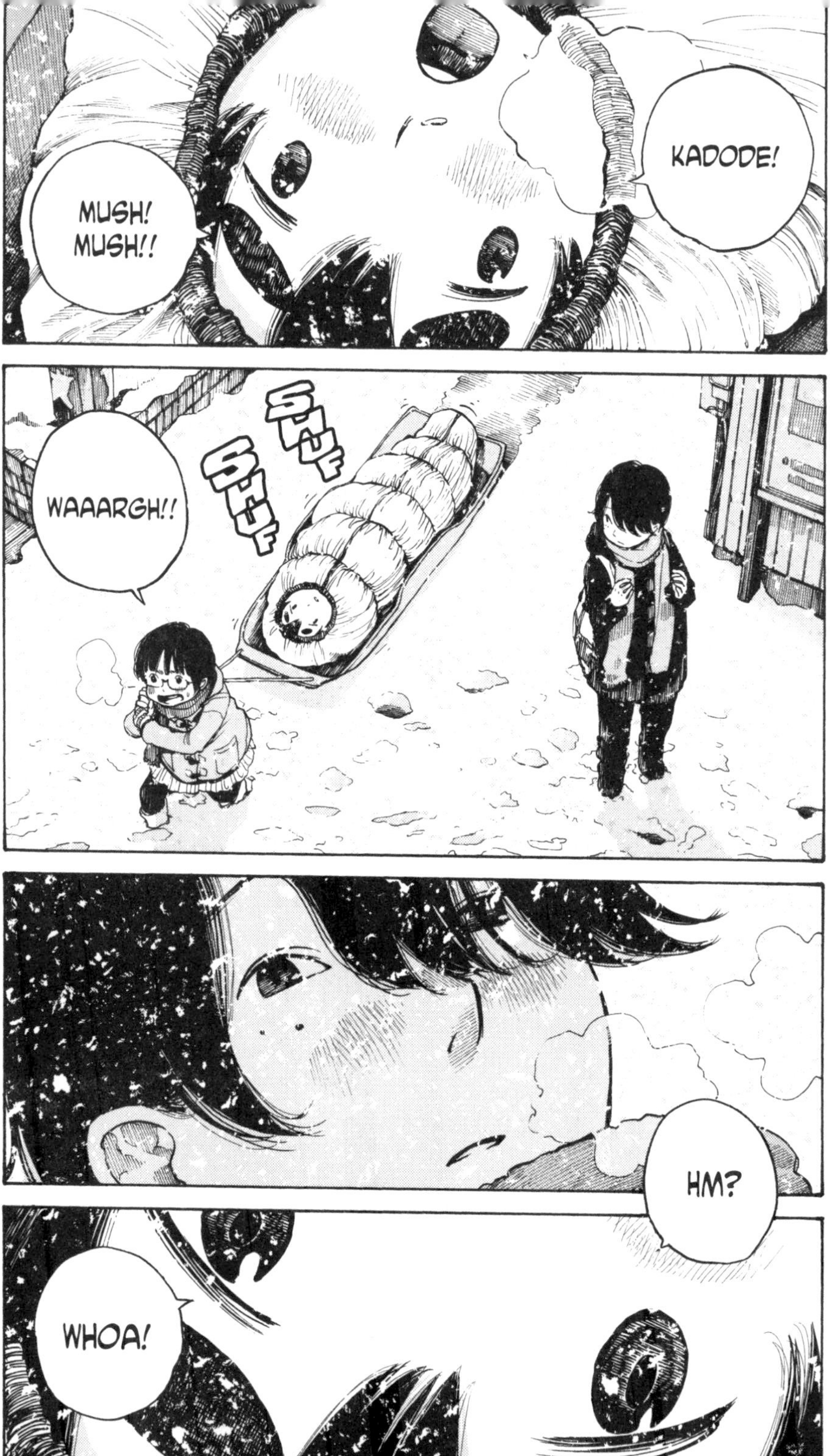
KADODE!
MUSH! MUSH!!
SNUF
SNUF
WAAARGH!!
HM?
WHOA!

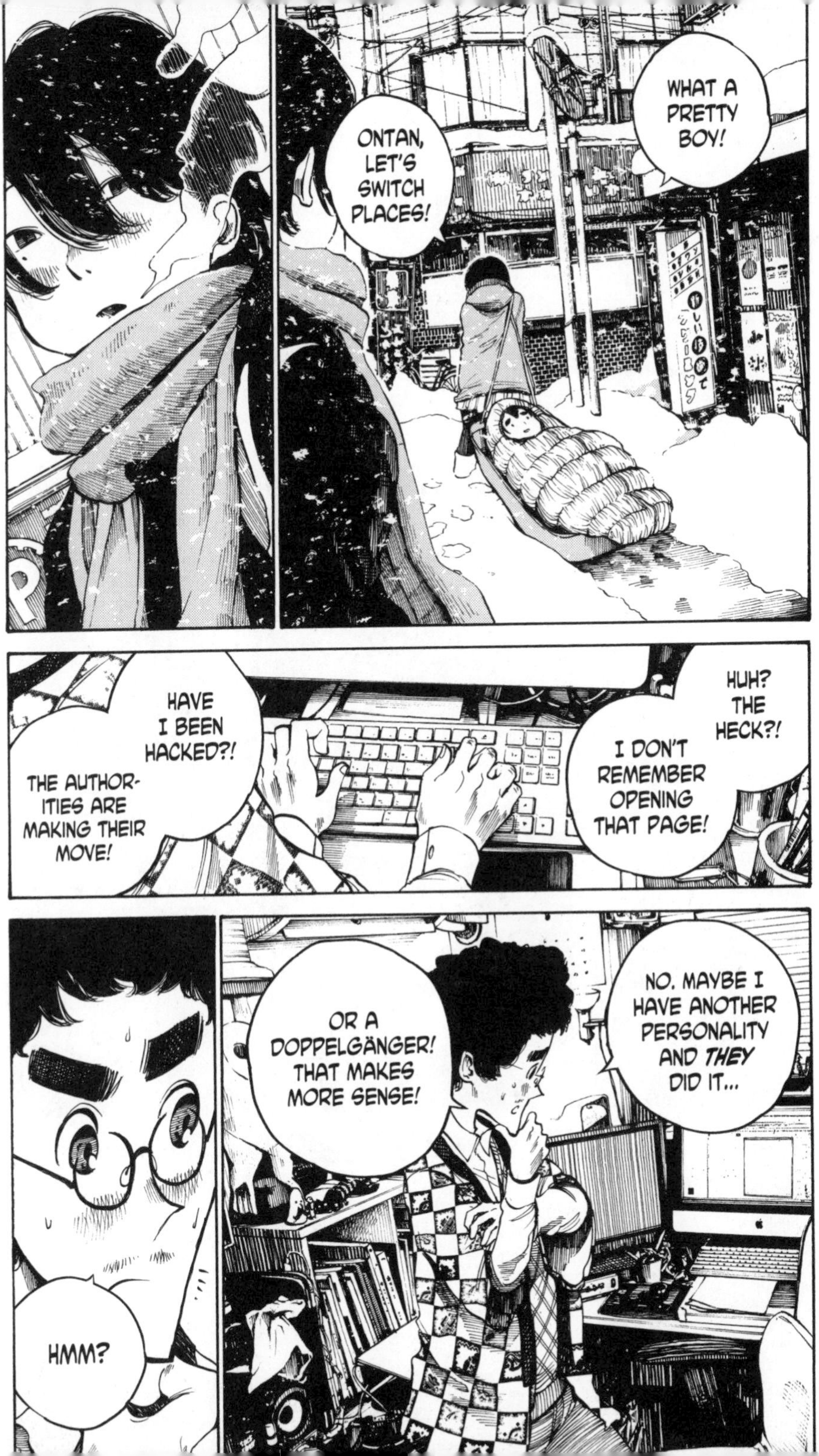
WHAT A PRETTY BOY!
ONTAN, LET'S SWITCH PLACES!
HUH? THE HECK?!
I DON'T REMEMBER OPENING THAT PAGE!
HAVE I BEEN HACKED?!
THE AUTHOR-ITIES ARE MAKING THEIR MOVE!
NO. MAYBE I HAVE ANOTHER PERSONALITY AND *THEY* DID IT...
OR A DOPPELGÄNGER! THAT MAKES MORE SENSE!
HMM?

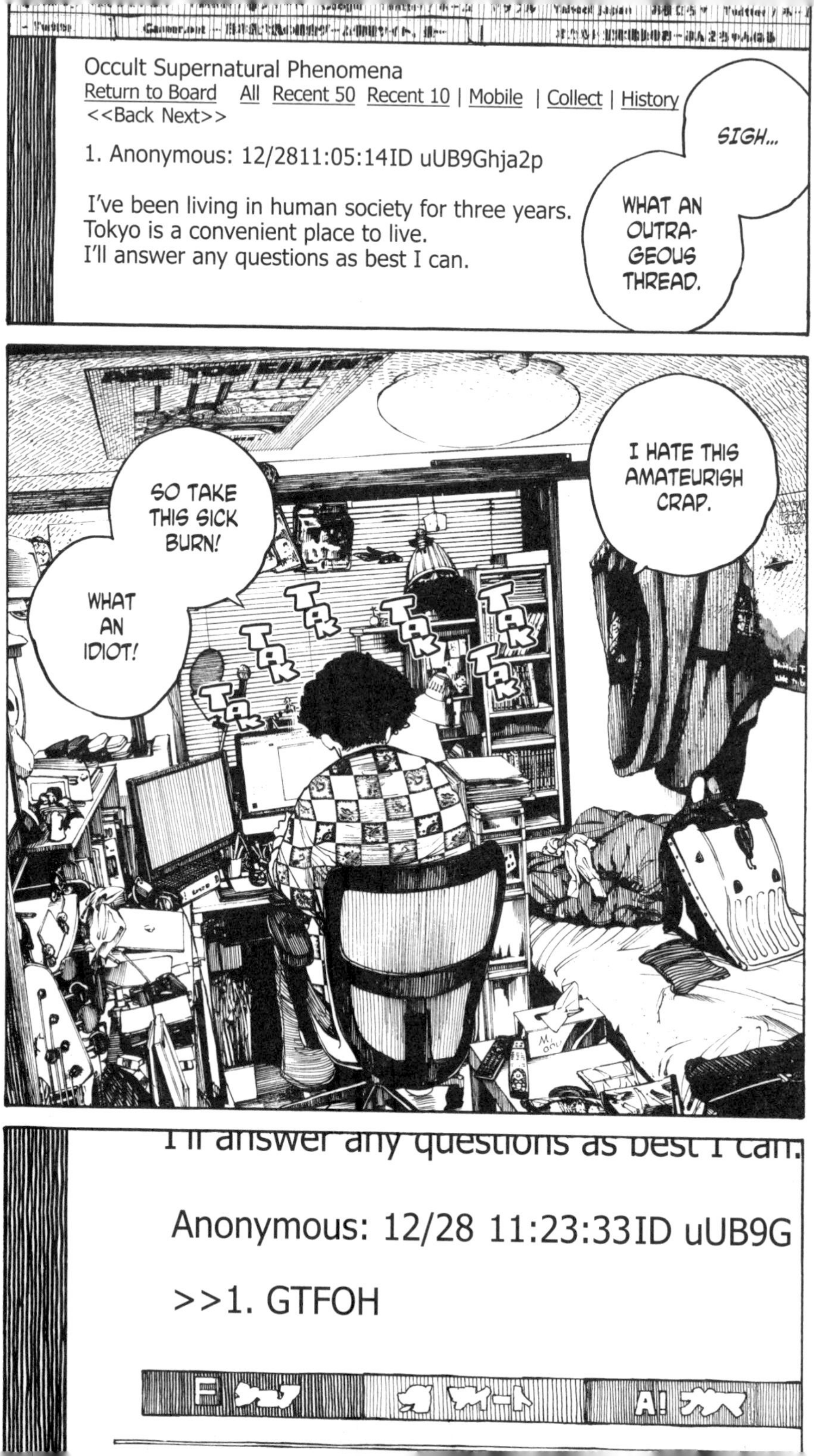
SIGH...
WHAT AN OUTRAGEOUS THREAD.
Occult Supernatural Phenomena
Return to Board All Recent 50 Recent 10 | Mobile | Collect | History
<<Back Next>>
1. Anonymous: 12/2811:05:14ID uUB9Ghja2p
I've been living in human society for three years.
Tokyo is a convenient place to live.
I'll answer any questions as best I can.
I HATE THIS AMATEURISH CRAP.
SO TAKE THIS SICK BURN!
WHAT AN IDIOT!
TAK TAK TAK TAK TAK TAK
I'll answer any questions as best I can.
Anonymous: 12/28 11:23:33ID uUB9G
>>1. GTFOH

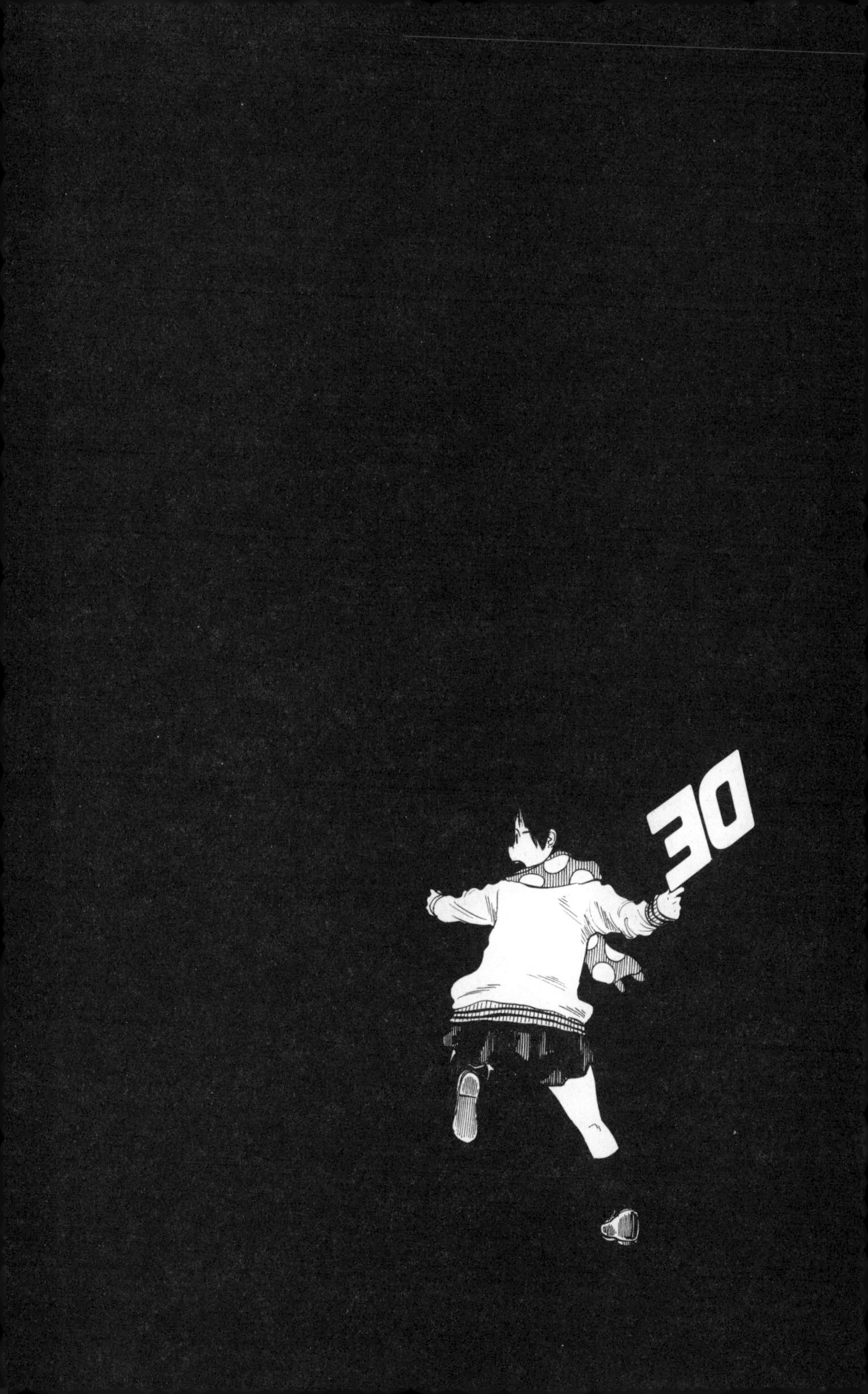
30

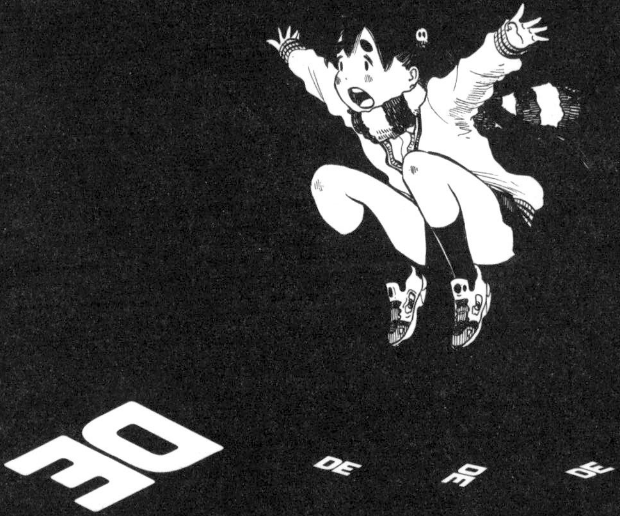
DE
DE
DE
DE

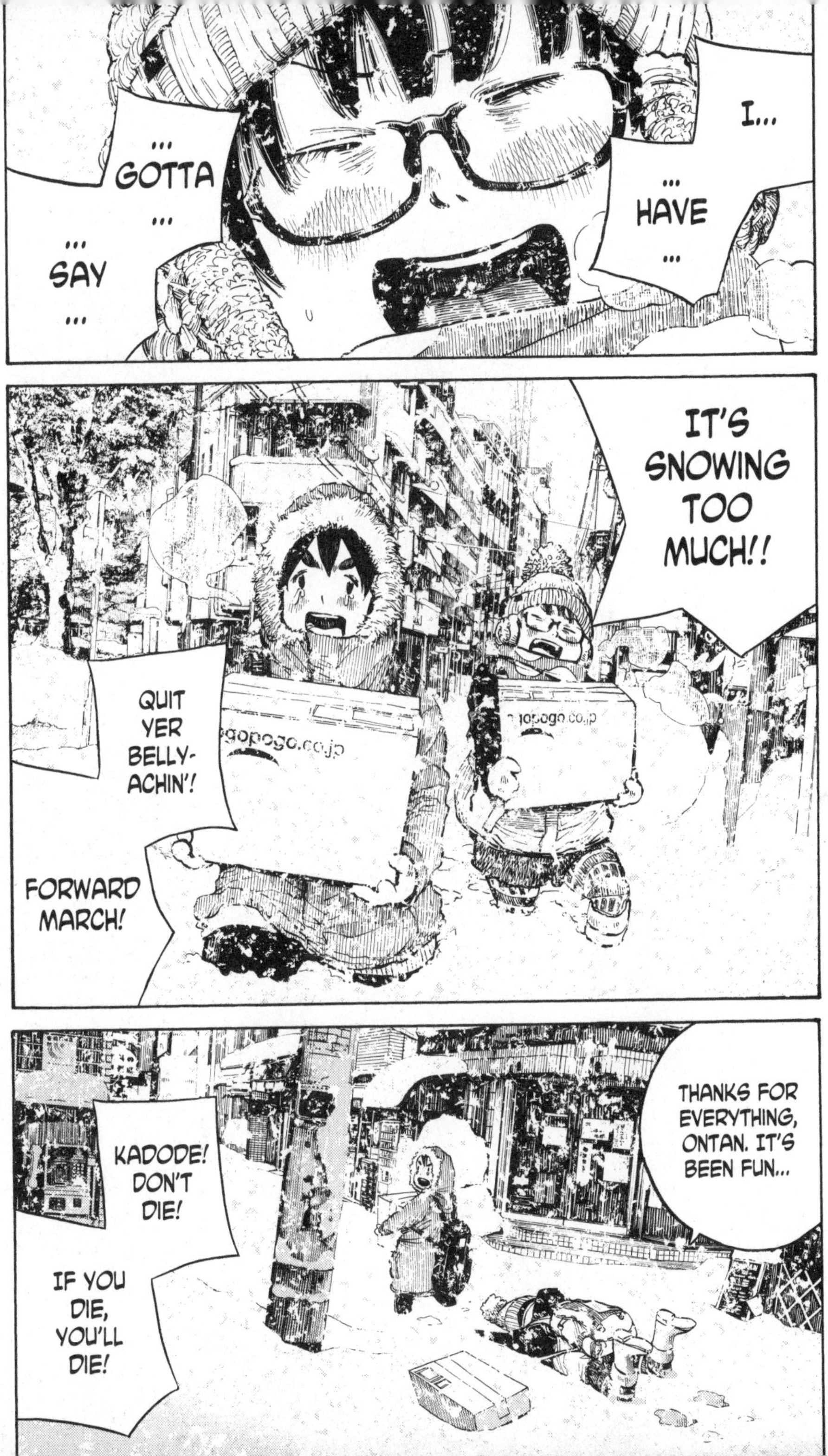
I... ...HAVE...
...GOTTA... ...SAY...
IT'S SNOWING TOO MUCH!!
QUIT YER BELLY-ACHIN'!
FORWARD MARCH!
THANKS FOR EVERYTHING, ONTAN. IT'S BEEN FUN...
KADODE! DON'T DIE!
IF YOU DIE, YOU'LL DIE!

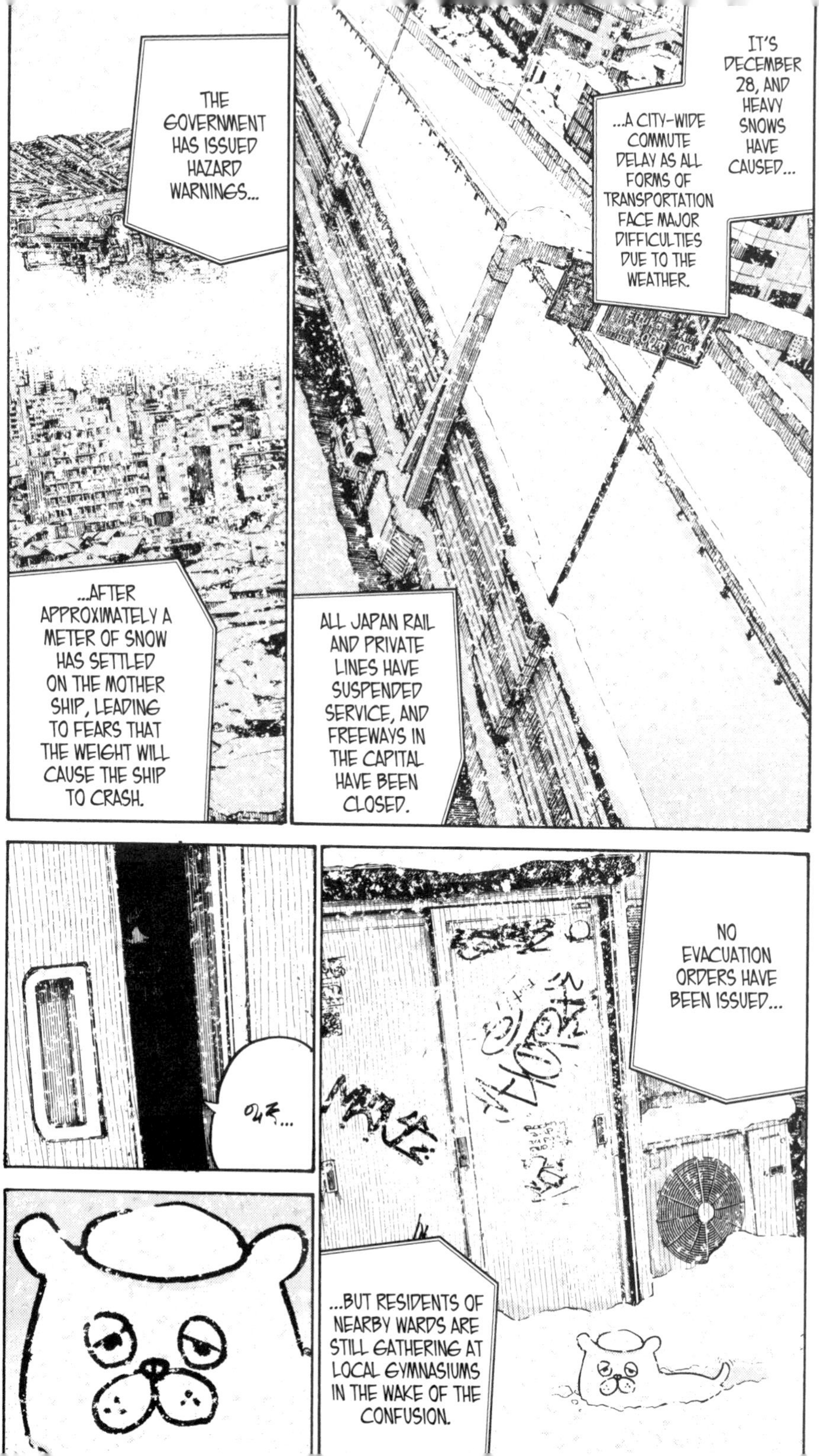
IT'S DECEMBER 28, AND HEAVY SNOWS HAVE CAUSED...
...A CITY-WIDE COMMUTE DELAY AS ALL FORMS OF TRANSPORTATION FACE MAJOR DIFFICULTIES DUE TO THE WEATHER.
ALL JAPAN RAIL AND PRIVATE LINES HAVE SUSPENDED SERVICE, AND FREEWAYS IN THE CAPITAL HAVE BEEN CLOSED.
THE GOVERNMENT HAS ISSUED HAZARD WARNINGS...
...AFTER APPROXIMATELY A METER OF SNOW HAS SETTLED ON THE MOTHER SHIP, LEADING TO FEARS THAT THE WEIGHT WILL CAUSE THE SHIP TO CRASH.
NO EVACUATION ORDERS HAVE BEEN ISSUED...
...BUT RESIDENTS OF NEARBY WARDS ARE STILL GATHERING AT LOCAL GYMNASIUMS IN THE WAKE OF THE CONFUSION.

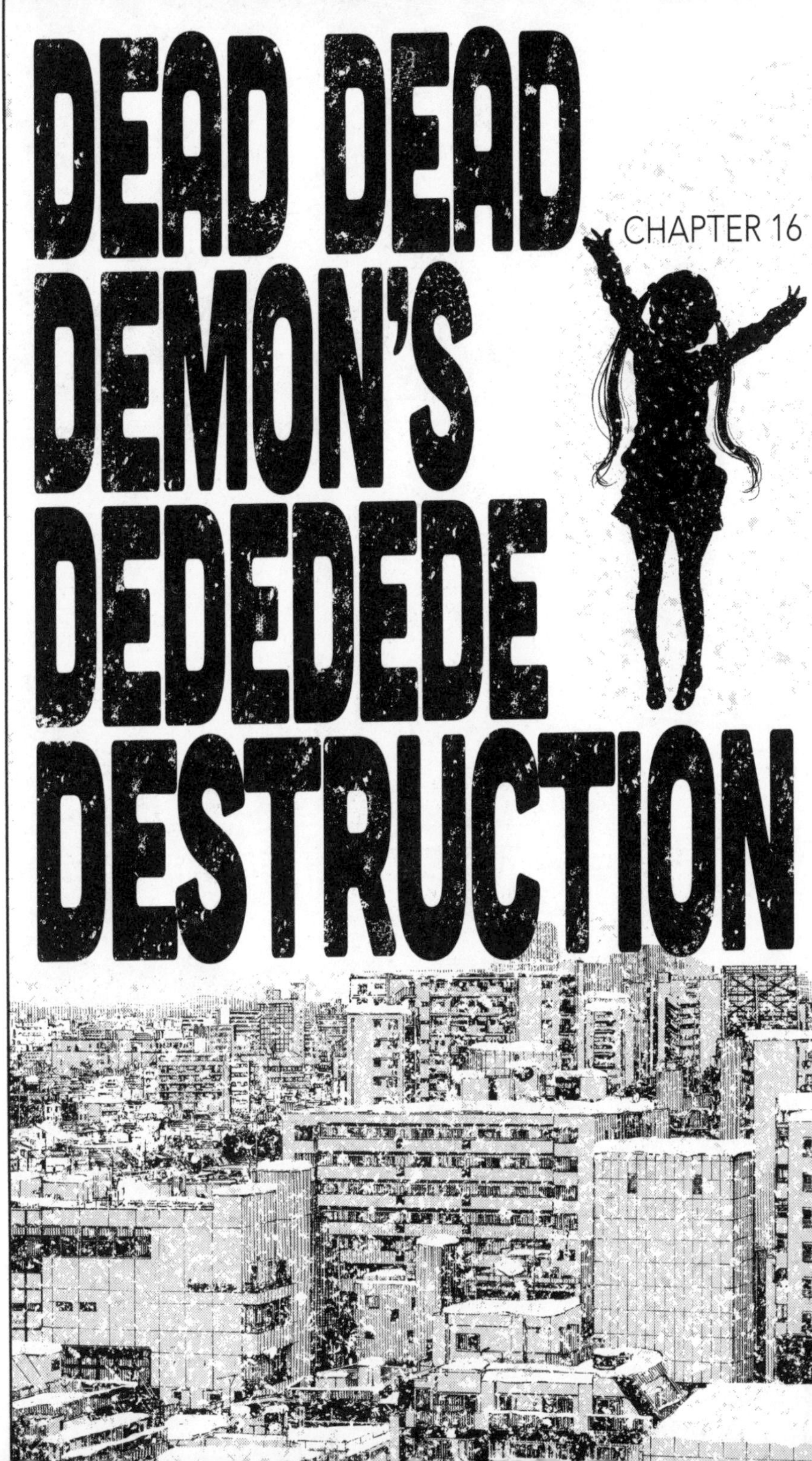

DEAD DEAD DEMON'S DEDEDEDE DESTRUCTION

CHAPTER 16

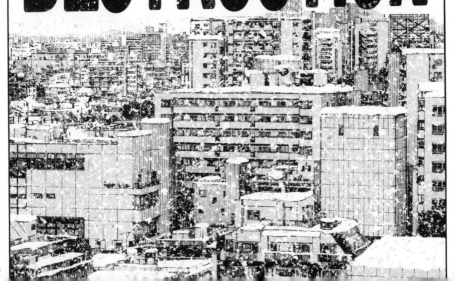

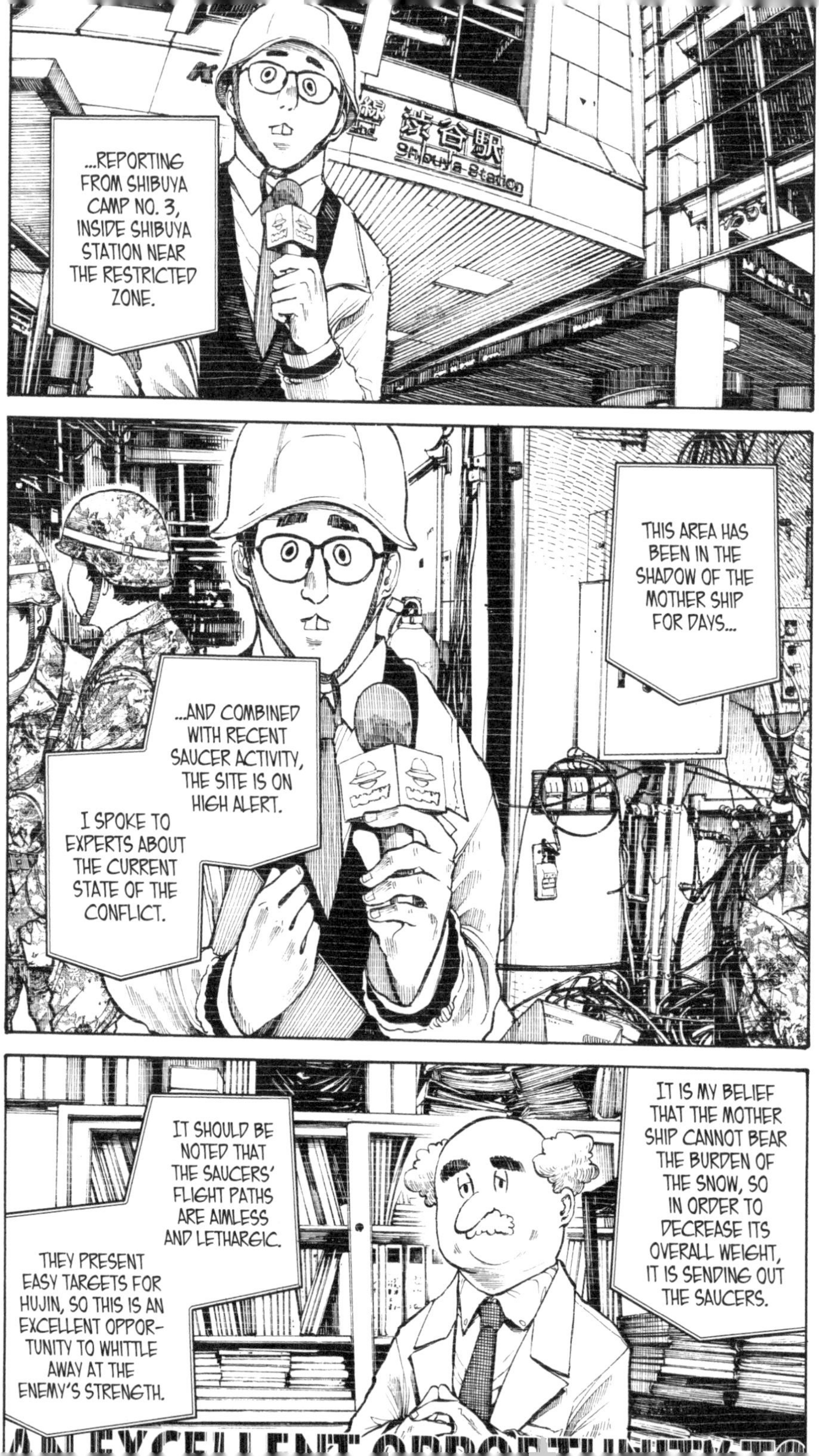

渋谷駅
Shibuya Station
...REPORTING FROM SHIBUYA CAMP NO. 3, INSIDE SHIBUYA STATION NEAR THE RESTRICTED ZONE.
THIS AREA HAS BEEN IN THE SHADOW OF THE MOTHER SHIP FOR DAYS...
...AND COMBINED WITH RECENT SAUCER ACTIVITY, THE SITE IS ON HIGH ALERT.
I SPOKE TO EXPERTS ABOUT THE CURRENT STATE OF THE CONFLICT.
IT IS MY BELIEF THAT THE MOTHER SHIP CANNOT BEAR THE BURDEN OF THE SNOW, SO IN ORDER TO DECREASE ITS OVERALL WEIGHT, IT IS SENDING OUT THE SAUCERS.
IT SHOULD BE NOTED THAT THE SAUCERS' FLIGHT PATHS ARE AIMLESS AND LETHARGIC.
THEY PRESENT EASY TARGETS FOR HUJIN, SO THIS IS AN EXCELLENT OPPORTUNITY TO WHITTLE AWAY AT THE ENEMY'S STRENGTH.

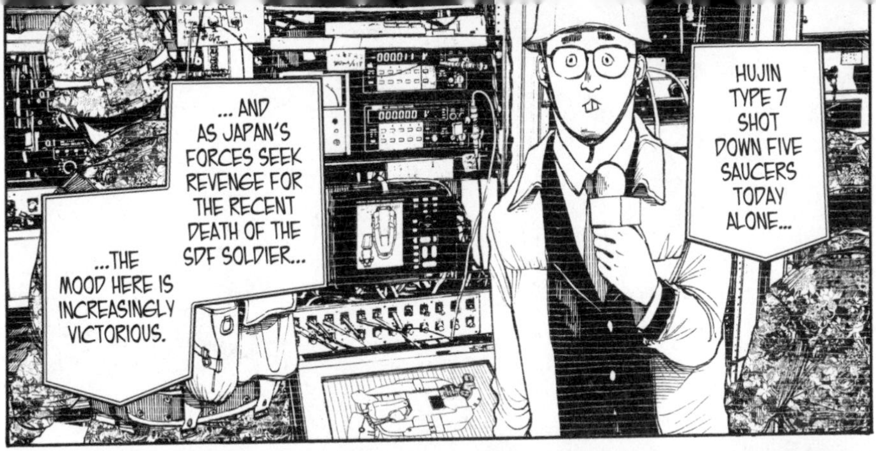
HUJIN TYPE 7 SHOT DOWN FIVE SAUCERS TODAY ALONE...
... AND AS JAPAN'S FORCES SEEK REVENGE FOR THE RECENT DEATH OF THE SDF SOLDIER...
...THE MOOD HERE IS INCREASINGLY VICTORIOUS.
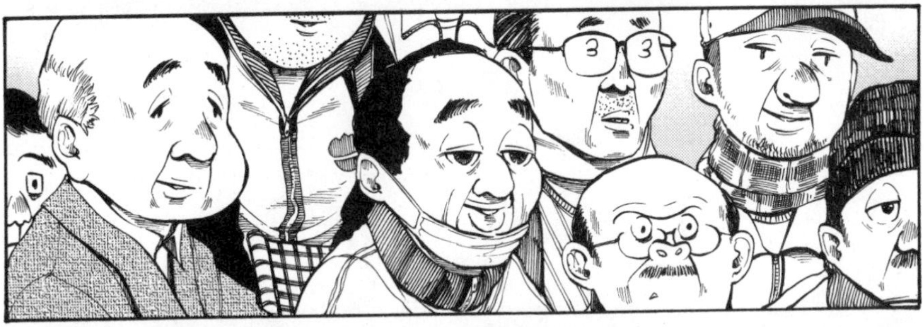
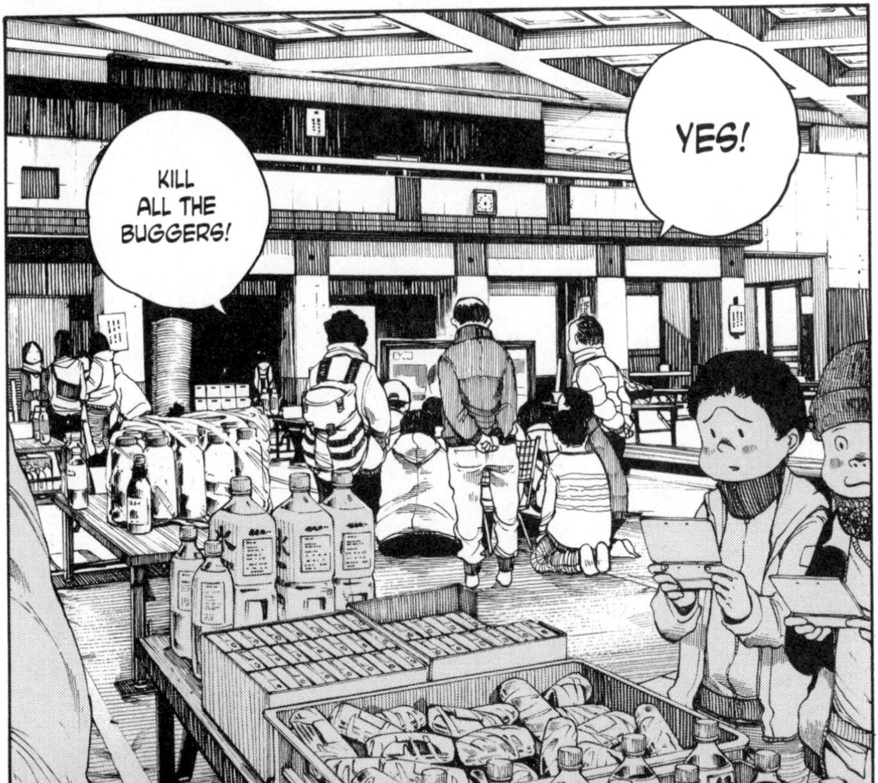
YES!
KILL ALL THE BUGGERS!

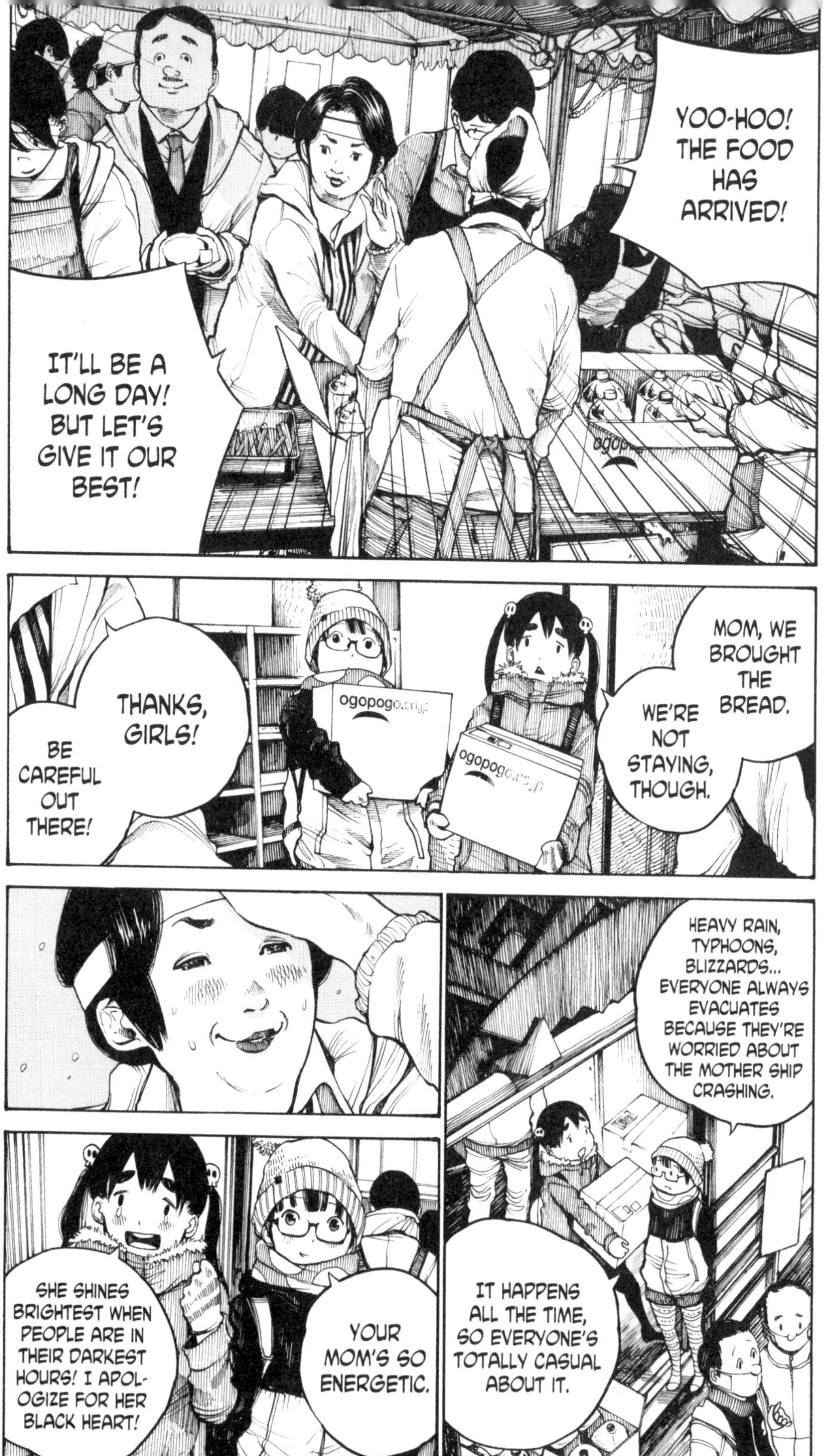
YOO-HOO! THE FOOD HAS ARRIVED!
IT'LL BE A LONG DAY! BUT LET'S GIVE IT OUR BEST!
MOM, WE BROUGHT THE BREAD.
WE'RE NOT STAYING, THOUGH.
THANKS, GIRLS!
BE CAREFUL OUT THERE!
HEAVY RAIN, TYPHOONS, BLIZZARDS... EVERYONE ALWAYS EVACUATES BECAUSE THEY'RE WORRIED ABOUT THE MOTHER SHIP CRASHING.
IT HAPPENS ALL THE TIME, SO EVERYONE'S TOTALLY CASUAL ABOUT IT.
YOUR MOM'S SO ENERGETIC.
SHE SHINES BRIGHTEST WHEN PEOPLE ARE IN THEIR DARKEST HOURS! I APOLOGIZE FOR HER BLACK HEART!

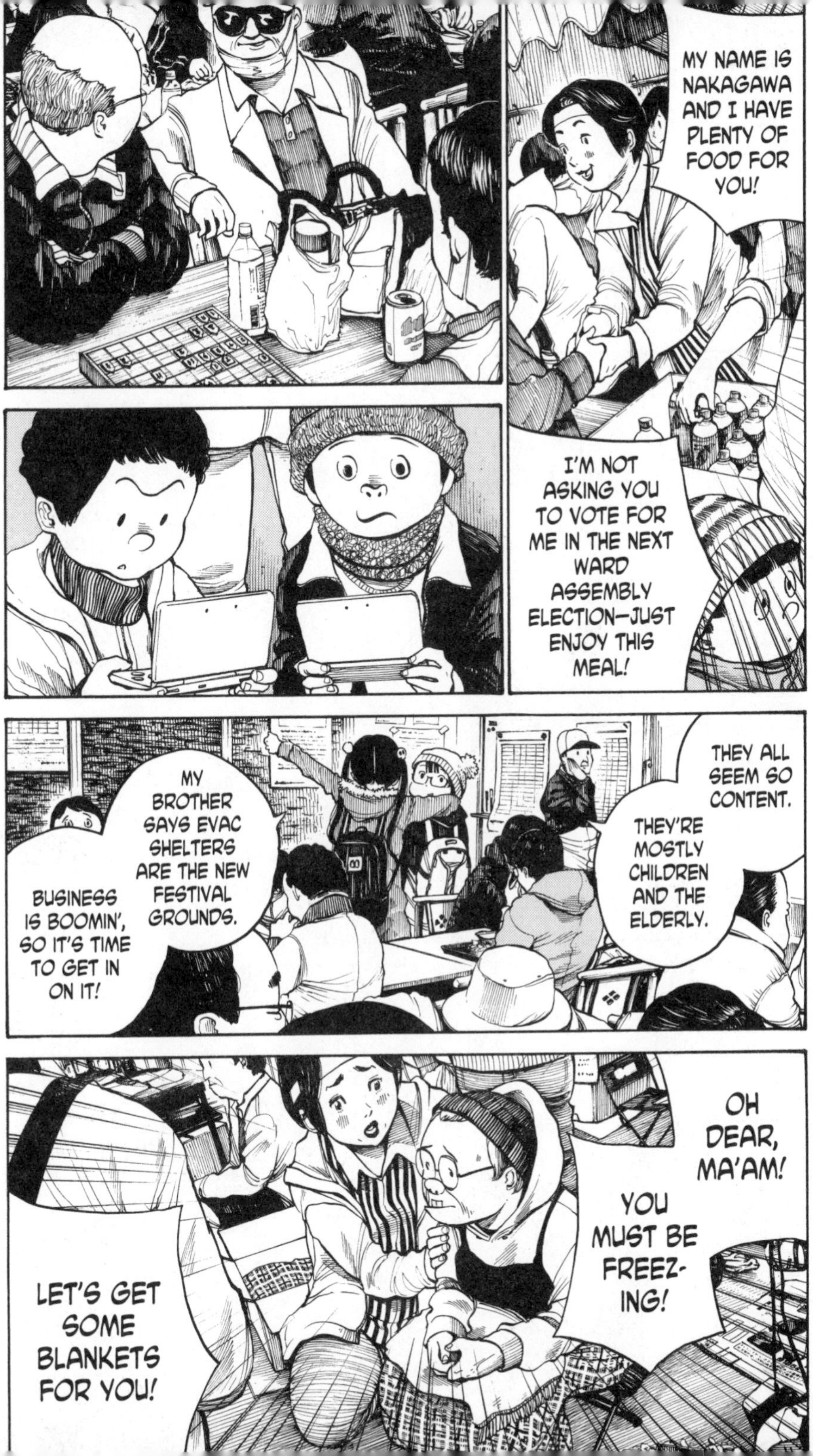
MY NAME IS NAKAGAWA AND I HAVE PLENTY OF FOOD FOR YOU!
I'M NOT ASKING YOU TO VOTE FOR ME IN THE NEXT WARD ASSEMBLY ELECTION—JUST ENJOY THIS MEAL!
THEY ALL SEEM SO CONTENT.
THEY'RE MOSTLY CHILDREN AND THE ELDERLY.
MY BROTHER SAYS EVAC SHELTERS ARE THE NEW FESTIVAL GROUNDS.
BUSINESS IS BOOMIN', SO IT'S TIME TO GET IN ON IT!
OH DEAR, MA'AM!
YOU MUST BE FREEZ-ING!
LET'S GET SOME BLANKETS FOR YOU!

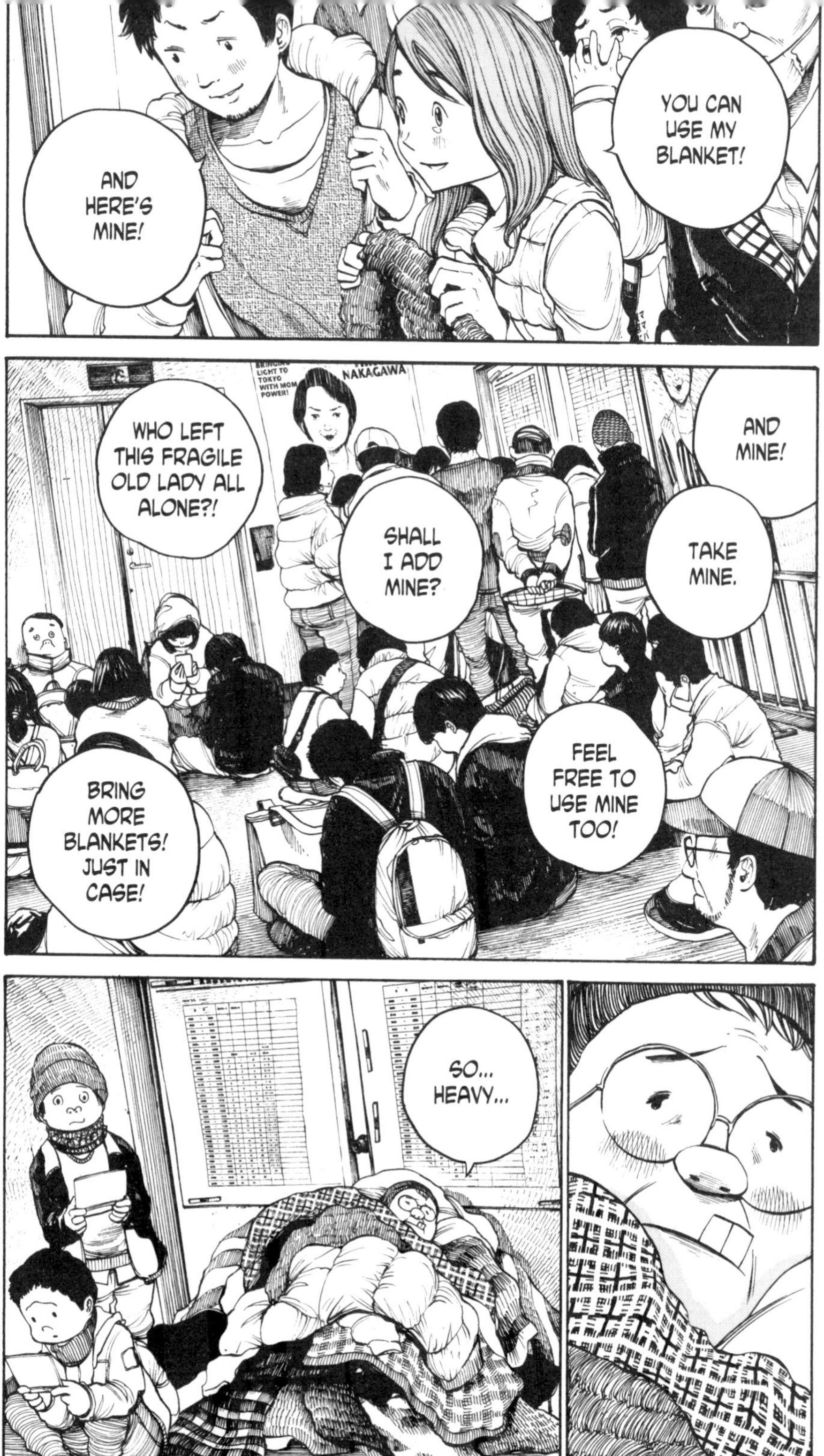
YOU CAN USE MY BLANKET!
AND HERE'S MINE!
NAKAGAWA
AND MINE!
TAKE MINE.
SHALL I ADD MINE?
WHO LEFT THIS FRAGILE OLD LADY ALL ALONE?!
FEEL FREE TO USE MINE TOO!
BRING MORE BLANKETS! JUST IN CASE!
SO... HEAVY...

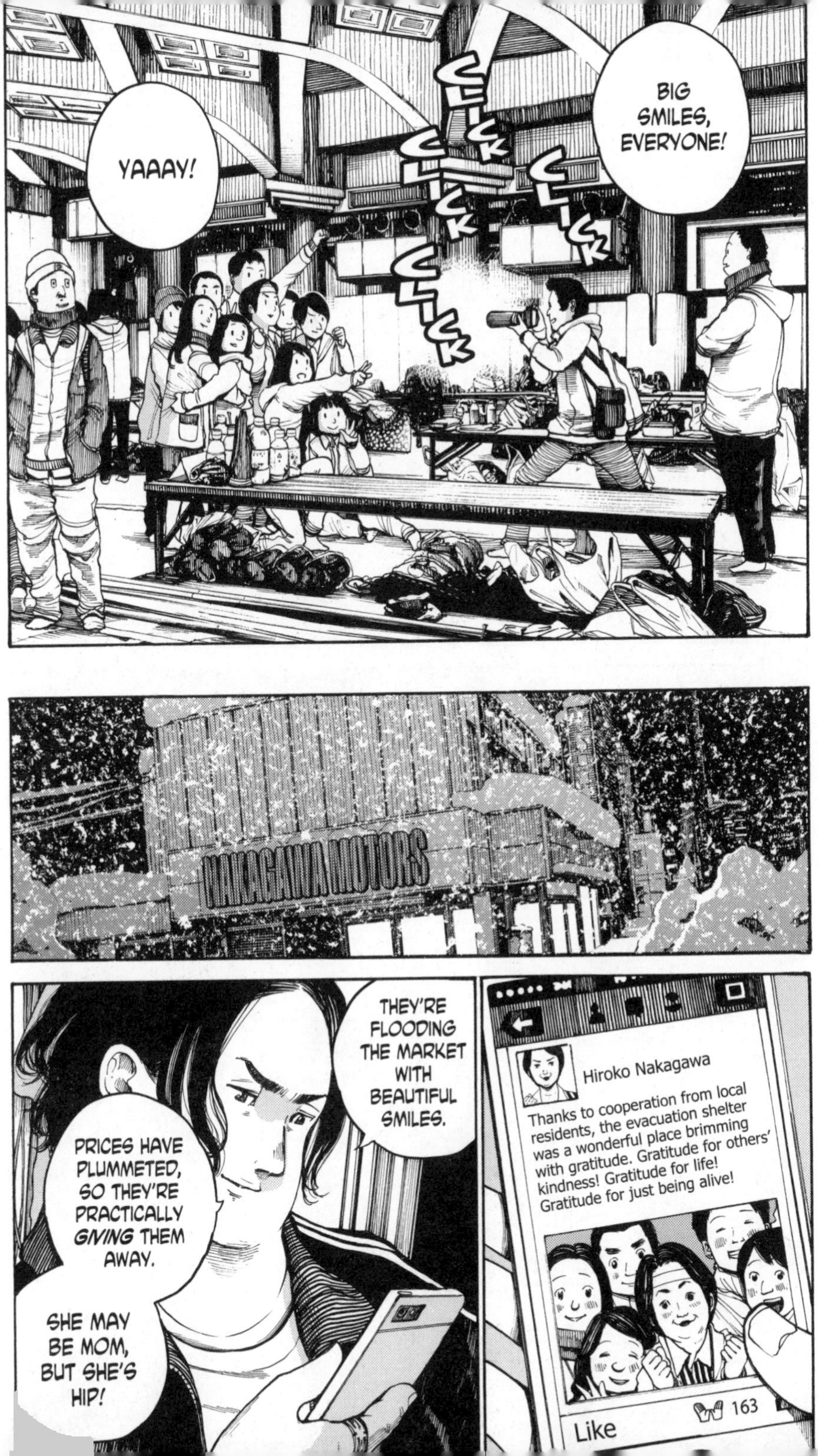
BIG SMILES, EVERYONE!
CLICK
CLICK
CLICK
CLICK
YAAAY!
NAKAGAWA MOTORS
Hiroko Nakagawa
Thanks to cooperation from local residents, the evacuation shelter was a wonderful place brimming with gratitude. Gratitude for others' kindness! Gratitude for life! Gratitude for just being alive!
163
Like
THEY'RE FLOODING THE MARKET WITH BEAUTIFUL SMILES.
PRICES HAVE PLUMMETED, SO THEY'RE PRACTICALLY *GIVING* THEM AWAY.
SHE MAY BE MOM, BUT SHE'S HIP!

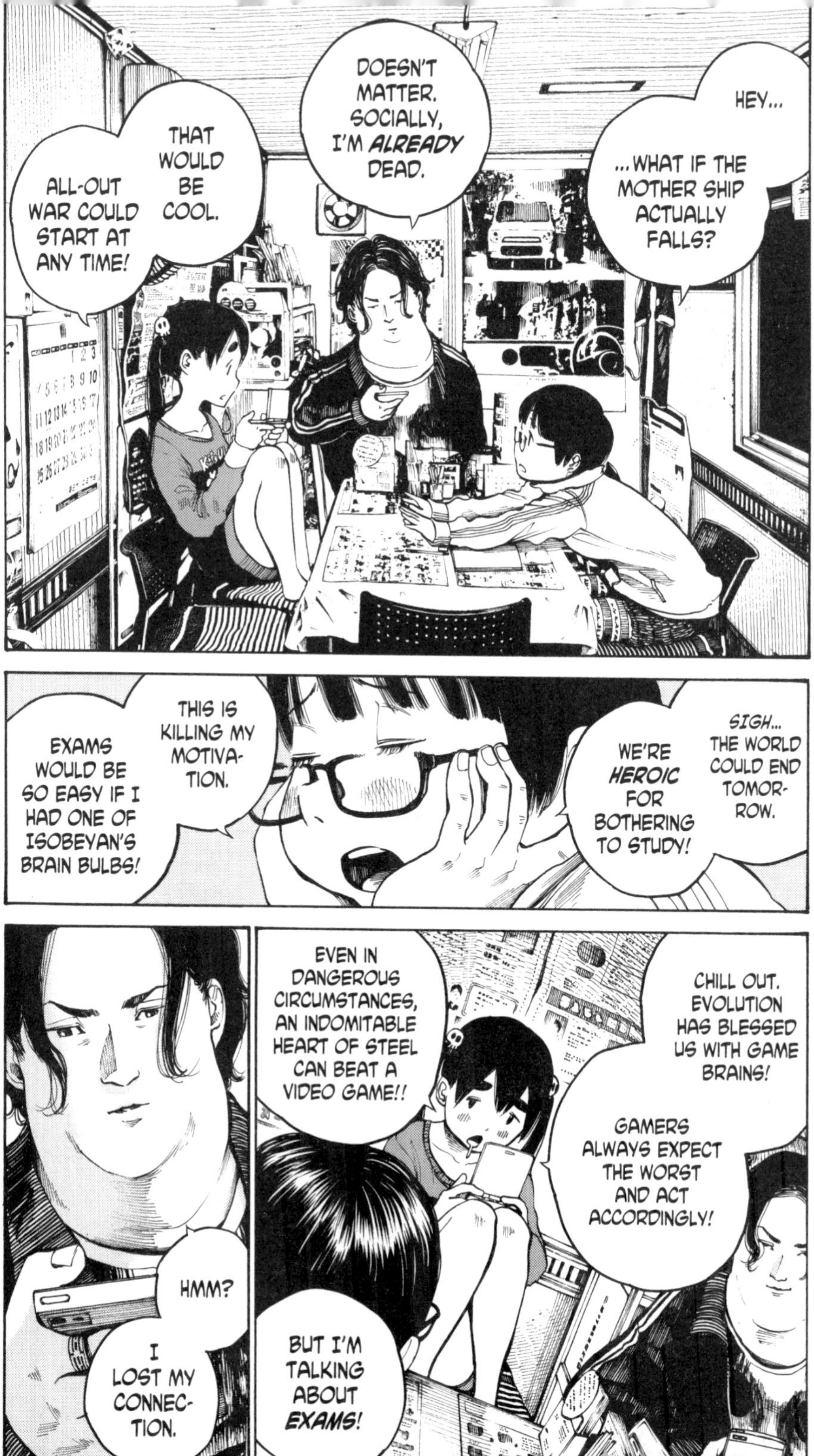
HEY...
...WHAT IF THE MOTHER SHIP ACTUALLY FALLS?
DOESN'T MATTER. SOCIALLY, I'M *ALREADY* DEAD.
THAT WOULD BE COOL.
ALL-OUT WAR COULD START AT ANY TIME!
SIGH... THE WORLD COULD END TOMORROW.
WE'RE *HEROIC* FOR BOTHERING TO STUDY!
THIS IS KILLING MY MOTIVATION.
EXAMS WOULD BE SO EASY IF I HAD ONE OF ISOBEYAN'S BRAIN BULBS!
CHILL OUT. EVOLUTION HAS BLESSED US WITH GAME BRAINS!
EVEN IN DANGEROUS CIRCUMSTANCES, AN INDOMITABLE HEART OF STEEL CAN BEAT A VIDEO GAME!!
GAMERS ALWAYS EXPECT THE WORST AND ACT ACCORDINGLY!
BUT I'M TALKING ABOUT *EXAMS!*
HMM?
I LOST MY CONNECTION.

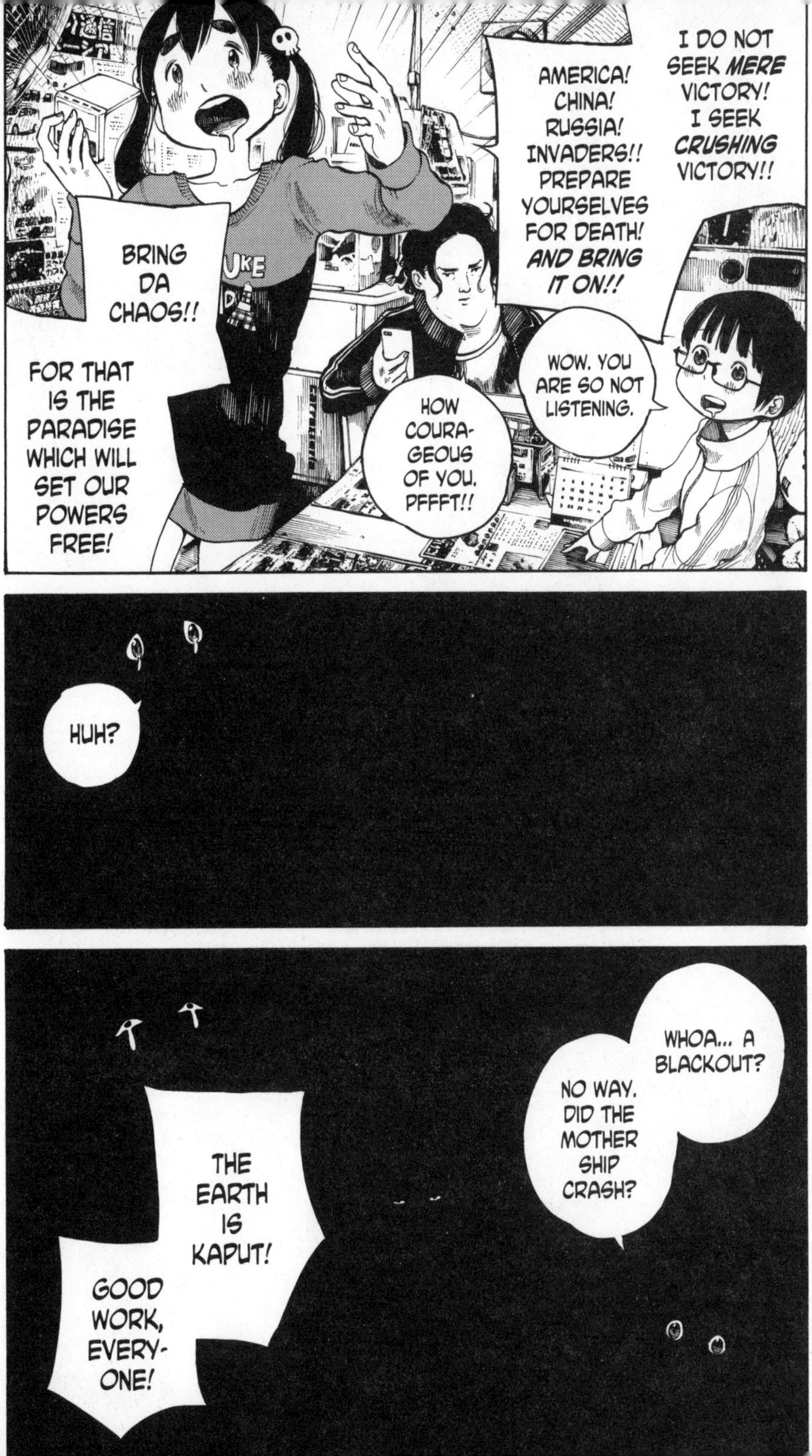
I DO NOT SEEK *MERE* VICTORY! I SEEK *CRUSHING* VICTORY!!
AMERICA! CHINA! RUSSIA! INVADERS!! PREPARE YOURSELVES FOR DEATH! *AND BRING IT ON!!*
BRING DA CHAOS!!
WOW. YOU ARE SO NOT LISTENING.
HOW COURAGEOUS OF YOU. PFFFT!!
FOR THAT IS THE PARADISE WHICH WILL SET OUR POWERS FREE!
HUH?
WHOA... A BLACKOUT?
NO WAY. DID THE MOTHER SHIP CRASH?
THE EARTH IS KAPUT!
GOOD WORK, EVERYONE!

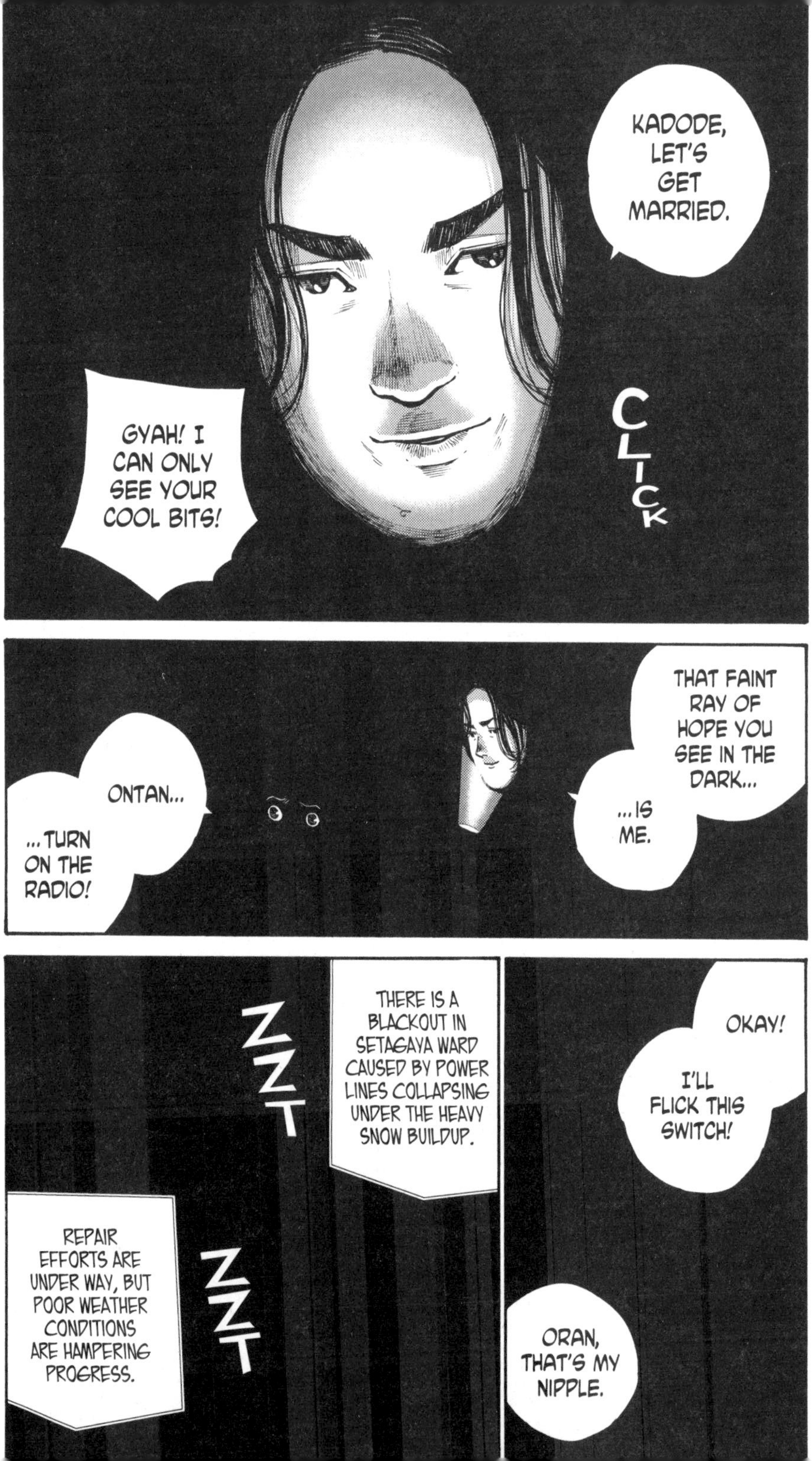
KADODE, LET'S GET MARRIED.
CLICK
GYAH! I CAN ONLY SEE YOUR COOL BITS!
THAT FAINT RAY OF HOPE YOU SEE IN THE DARK...
...IS ME.
ONTAN...
...TURN ON THE RADIO!
OKAY!
I'LL FLICK THIS SWITCH!
ORAN, THAT'S MY NIPPLE.
THERE IS A BLACKOUT IN SETAGAYA WARD CAUSED BY POWER LINES COLLAPSING UNDER THE HEAVY SNOW BUILDUP.
ZZT
REPAIR EFFORTS ARE UNDER WAY, BUT POOR WEATHER CONDITIONS ARE HAMPERING PROGRESS.
ZZT

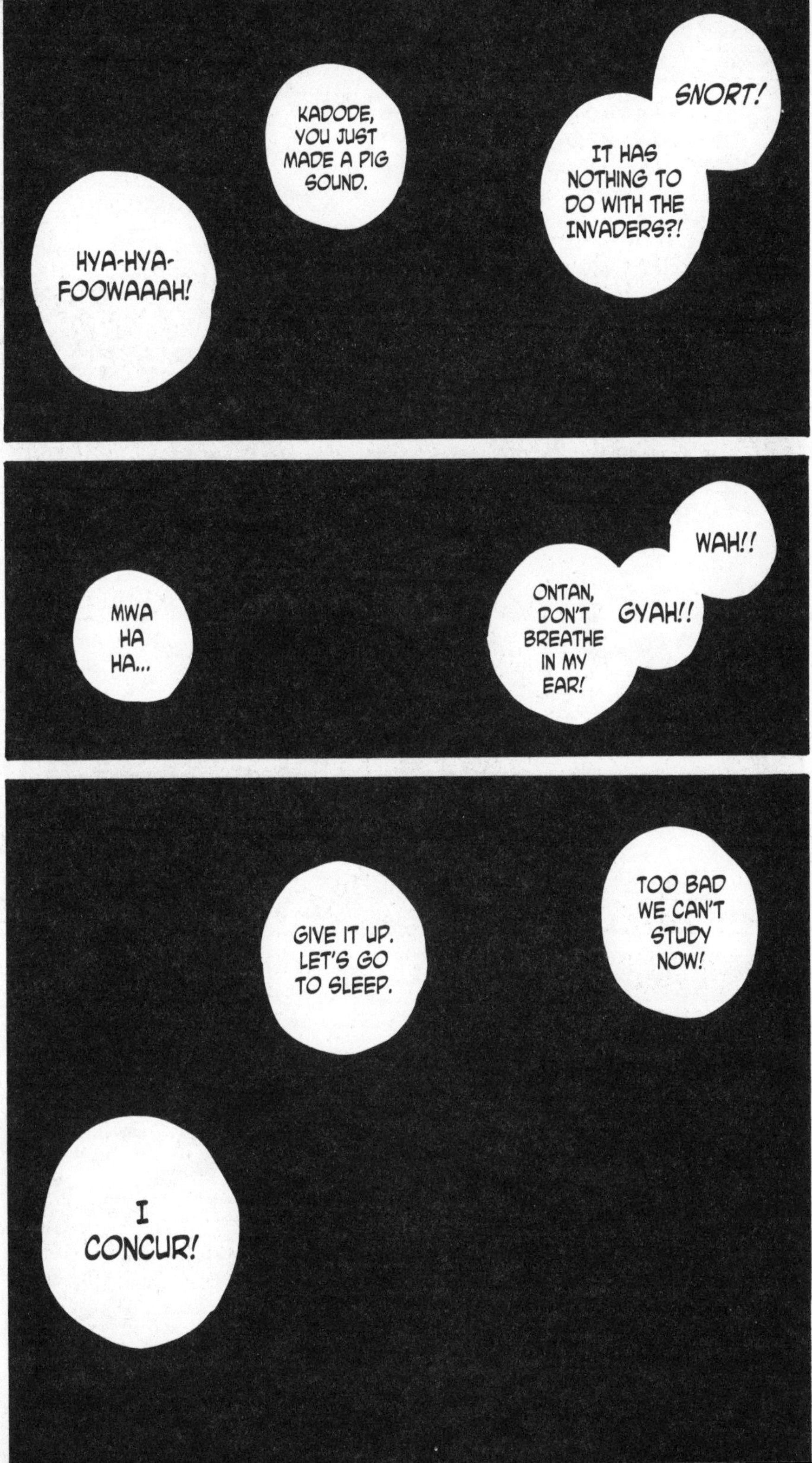
SNORT!
IT HAS NOTHING TO DO WITH THE INVADERS?!
KADODE, YOU JUST MADE A PIG SOUND.
HYA-HYA-FOOWAAAH!
WAH!!
GYAH!!
ONTAN, DON'T BREATHE IN MY EAR!
MWA HA HA...
TOO BAD WE CAN'T STUDY NOW!
GIVE IT UP. LET'S GO TO SLEEP.
I CONCUR!

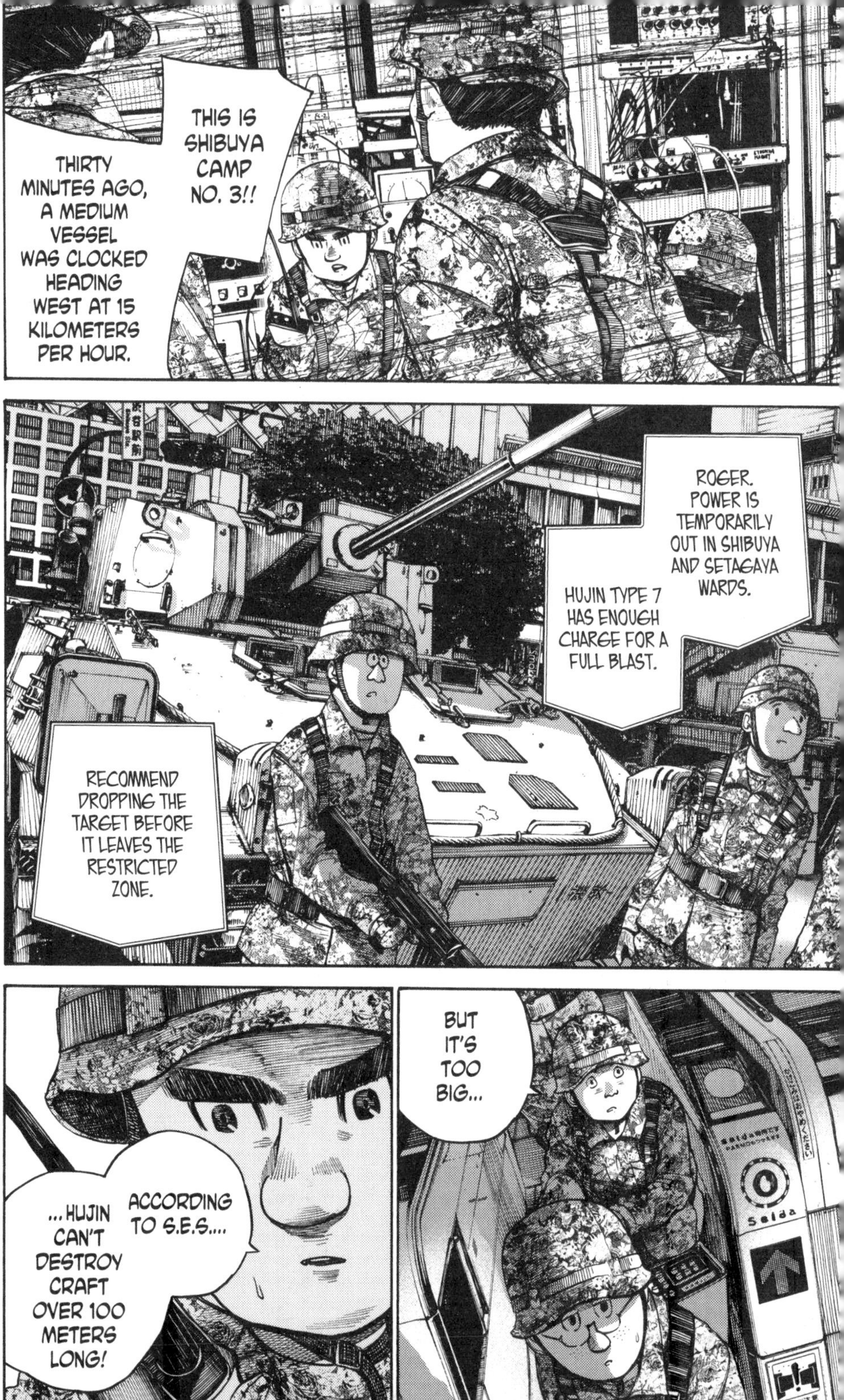
THIS IS SHIBUYA CAMP NO. 3!!
THIRTY MINUTES AGO, A MEDIUM VESSEL WAS CLOCKED HEADING WEST AT 15 KILOMETERS PER HOUR.
ROGER. POWER IS TEMPORARILY OUT IN SHIBUYA AND SETAGAYA WARDS.
HUJIN TYPE 7 HAS ENOUGH CHARGE FOR A FULL BLAST.
RECOMMEND DROPPING THE TARGET BEFORE IT LEAVES THE RESTRICTED ZONE.
BUT IT'S TOO BIG...
ACCORDING TO S.E.S....
...HUJIN CAN'T DESTROY CRAFT OVER 100 METERS LONG!

AT PRESENT, HUJIN IS JAPAN'S MOST POWERFUL WEAPON.
I THINK...
...YOU SHOULD BE CAREFUL ABOUT THIS.
WHAT SITE ARE YOU WITH?
DON'T RECORD THIS.
CIVILIANS, CLEAR THE AREA!
... THREE ...
I REPEAT!
RECOMMEND DROPPING THE TARGET BEFORE IT LEAVES THE RESTRICTED ZONE.
... TWO ...
... ONE ...

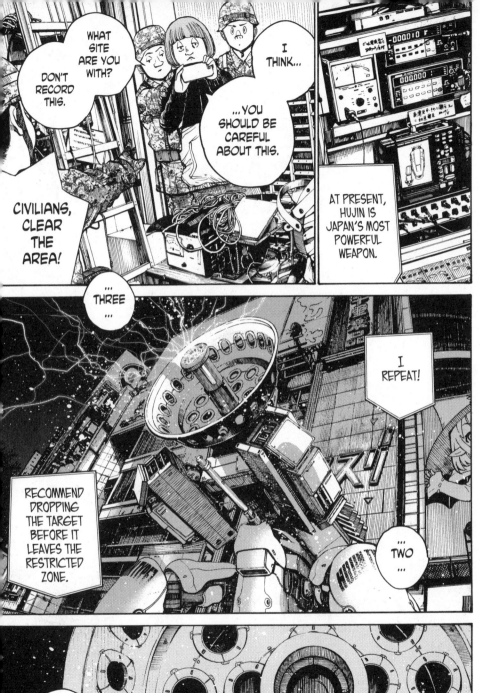

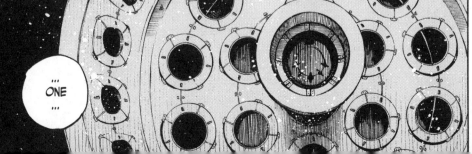

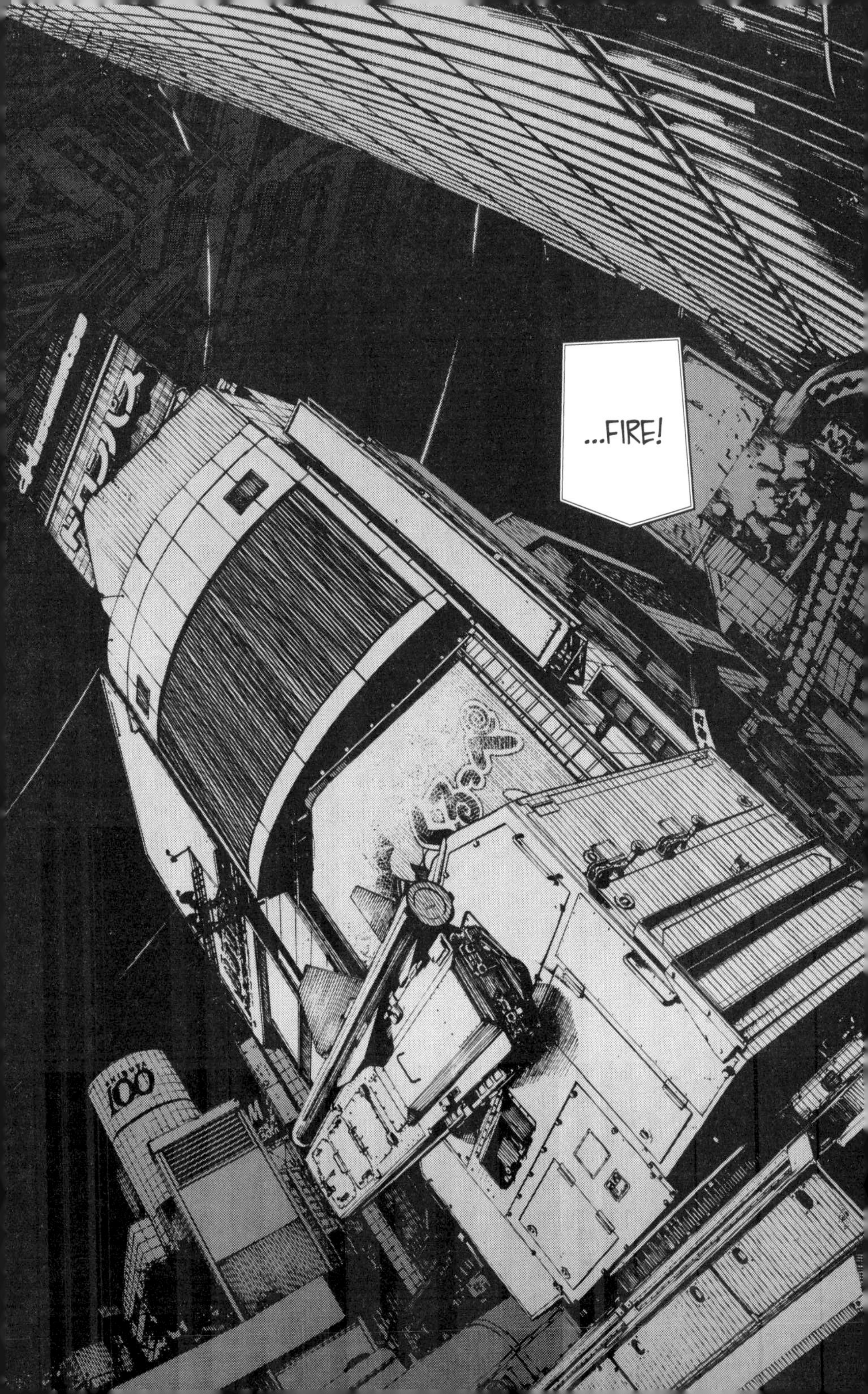
...FIRE!

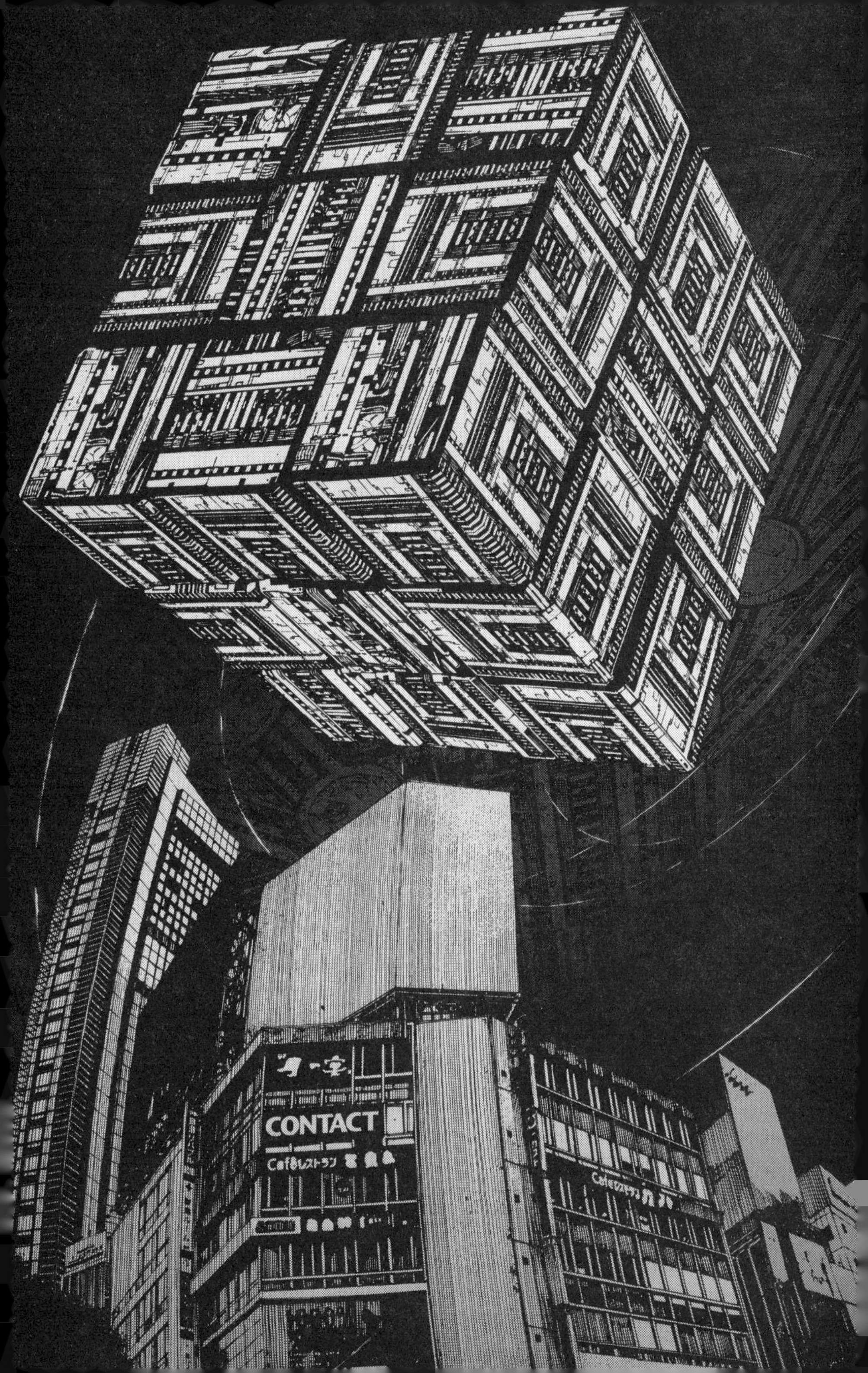
CONTACT
Caf&レストラン

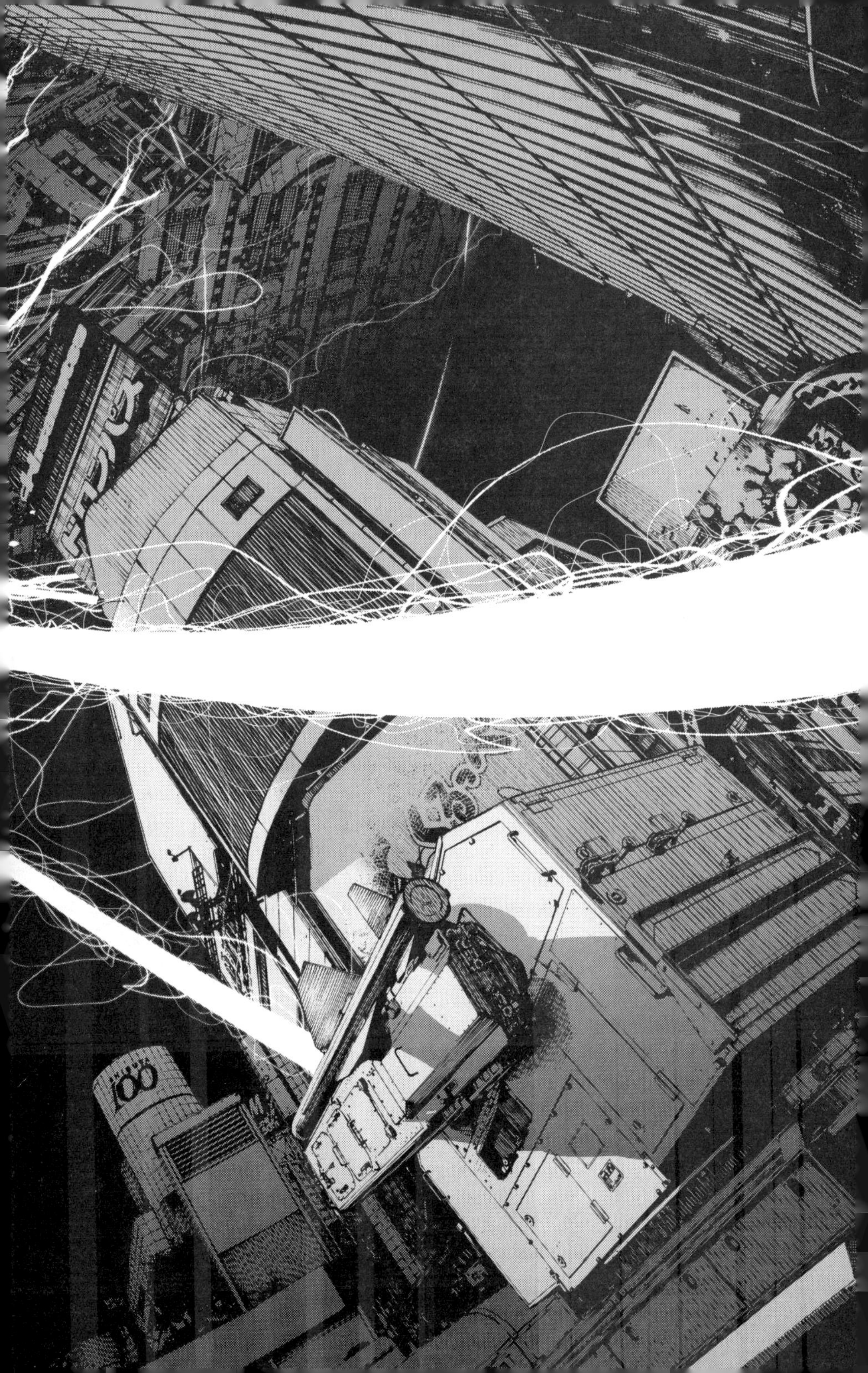

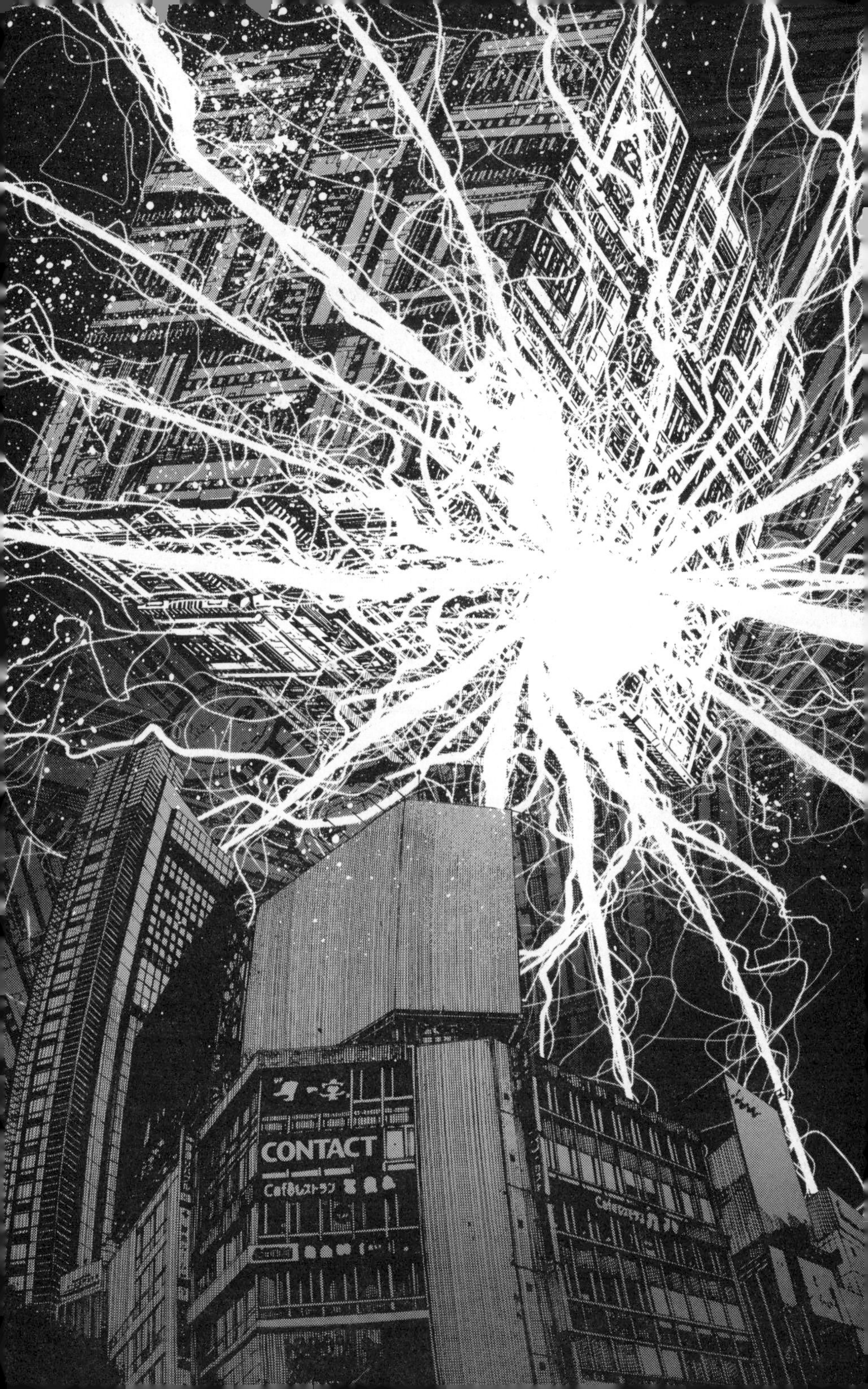
CONTACT

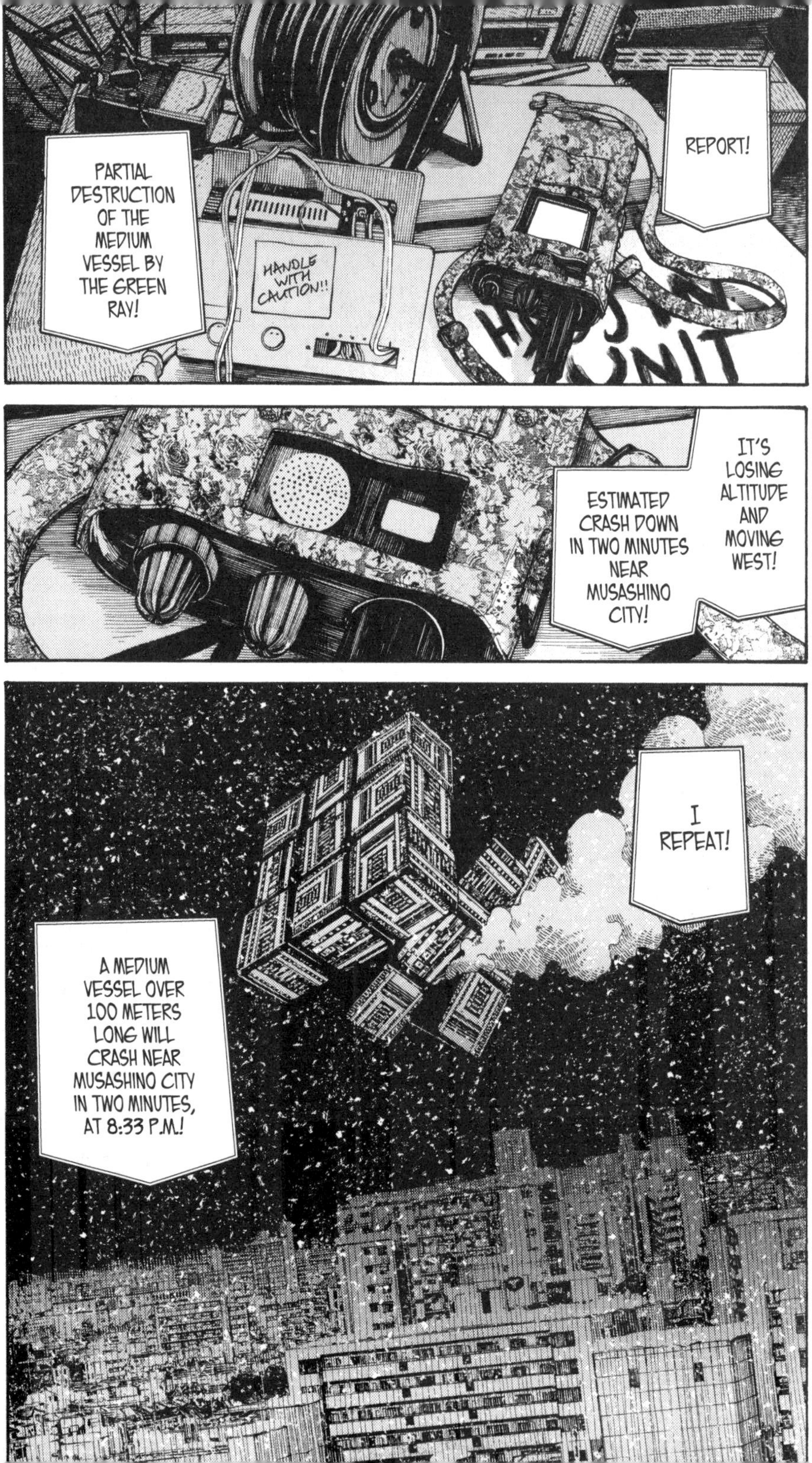
REPORT!
PARTIAL DESTRUCTION OF THE MEDIUM VESSEL BY THE GREEN RAY!
HANDLE WITH CAUTION!!
IT'S LOSING ALTITUDE AND MOVING WEST!
ESTIMATED CRASH DOWN IN TWO MINUTES NEAR MUSASHINO CITY!
I REPEAT!
A MEDIUM VESSEL OVER 100 METERS LONG WILL CRASH NEAR MUSASHINO CITY IN TWO MINUTES, AT 8:33 P.M.!

Dead Dead Demon's
Dededede Destruction Volume 2
Inio Asano

Background Assistants: Satsuki Sato
Ran Atsumori
Buuko

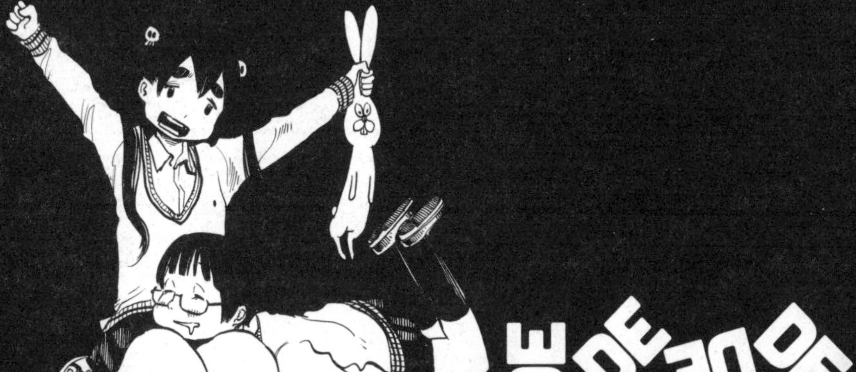
DE DE DE DE

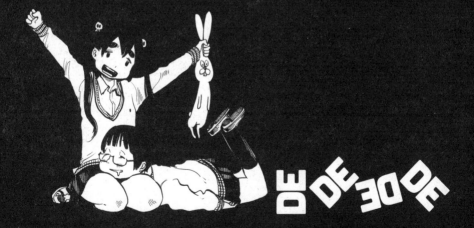

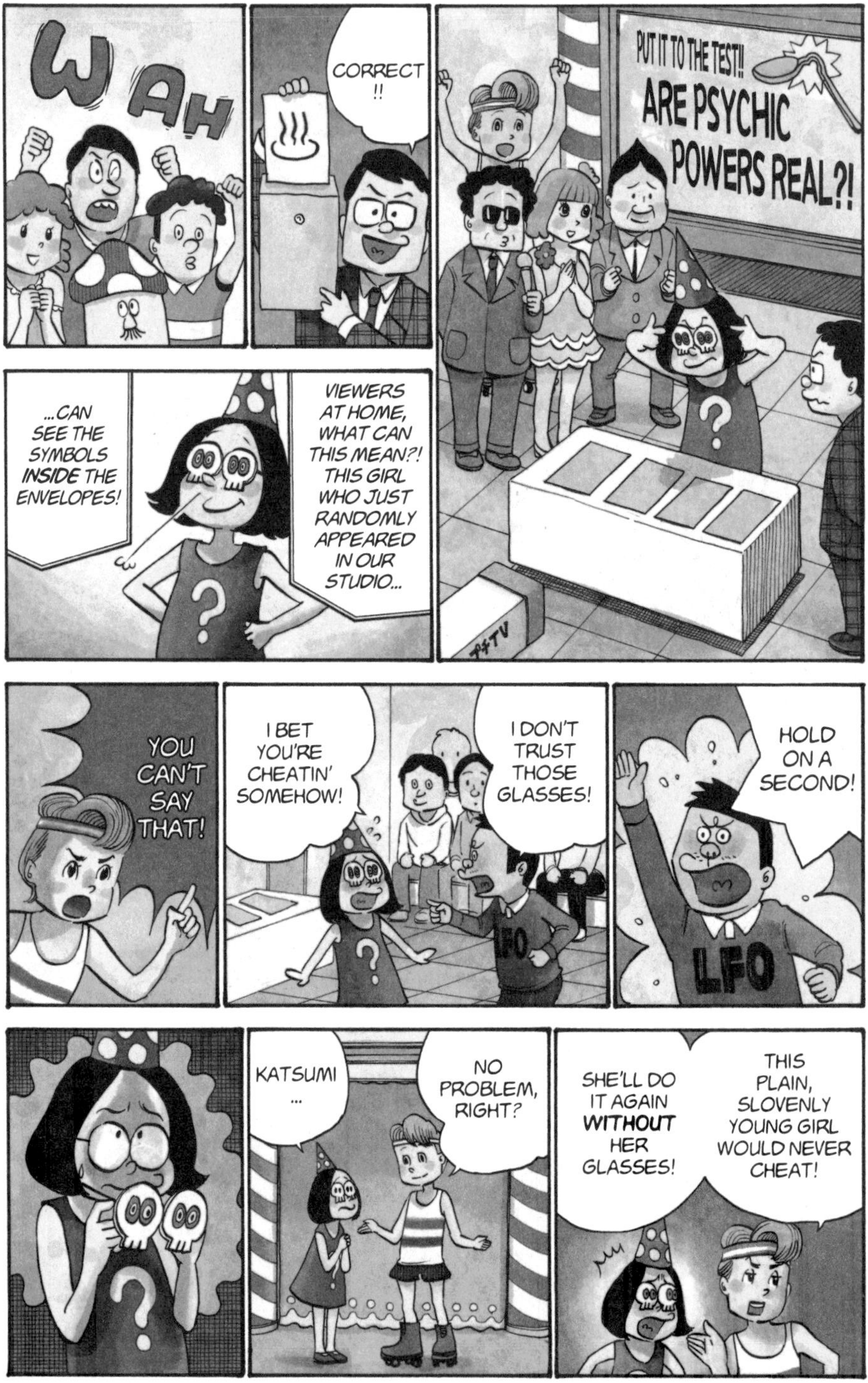
PUT IT TO THE TEST!!
ARE PSYCHIC POWERS REAL?!
CORRECT !!
WAH
VIEWERS AT HOME, WHAT CAN THIS MEAN?! THIS GIRL WHO JUST RANDOMLY APPEARED IN OUR STUDIO...
...CAN SEE THE SYMBOLS INSIDE THE ENVELOPES!
HOLD ON A SECOND!
I DON'T TRUST THOSE GLASSES!
I BET YOU'RE CHEATIN' SOMEHOW!
YOU CAN'T SAY THAT!
THIS PLAIN, SLOVENLY YOUNG GIRL WOULD NEVER CHEAT!
SHE'LL DO IT AGAIN WITHOUT HER GLASSES!
NO PROBLEM, RIGHT?
KATSUMI ...

☆Volume 3 goes on sale October 2018, so keep your eyes peeled!

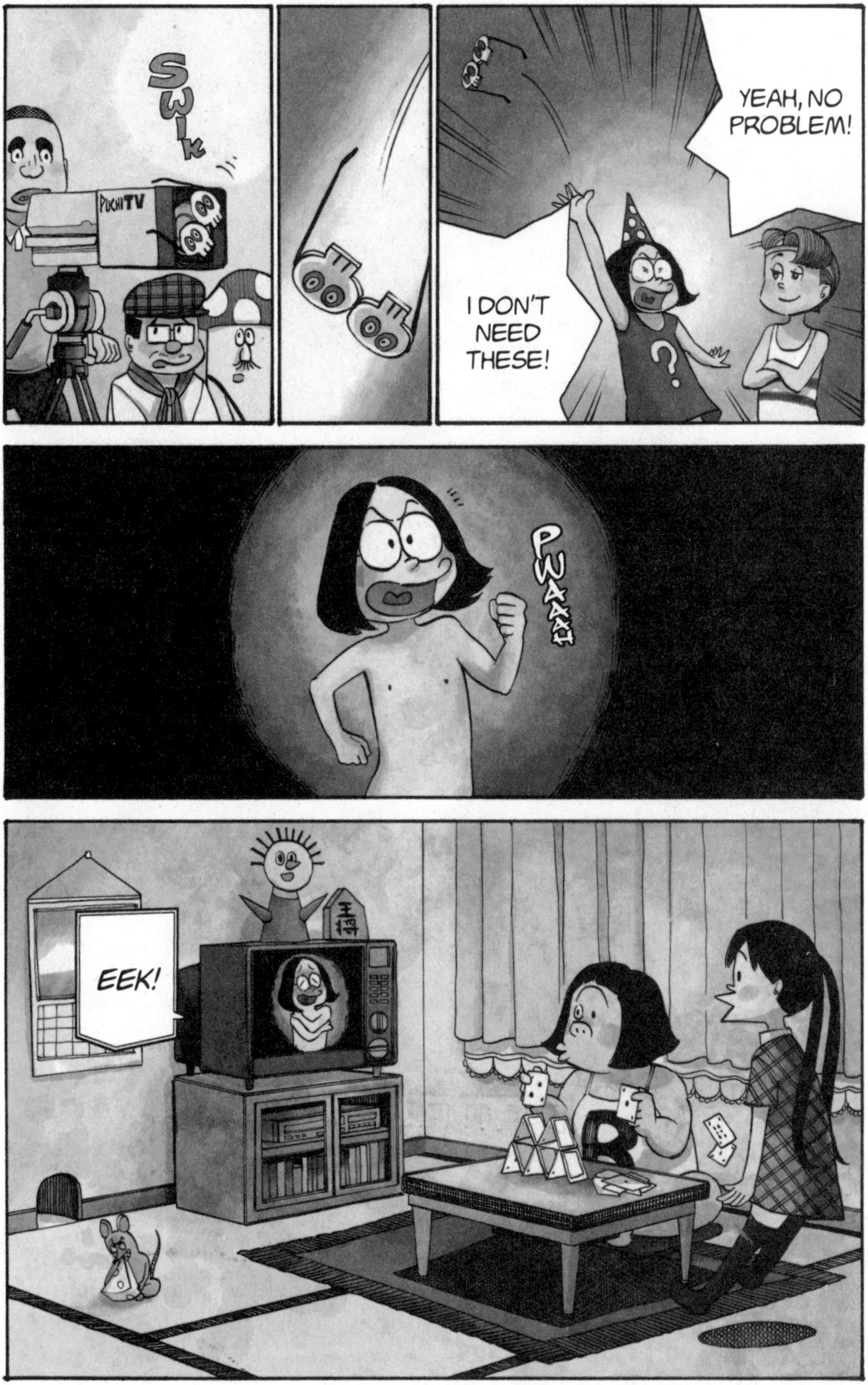

YEAH, NO PROBLEM!
I DON'T NEED THESE!
SWIK
PUCHI TV
PWAAAH
EEK!

DEAD DEAD DEMON'S
DEDEDEDE DESTRUCTION

Volume 2
VIZ Signature Edition

Story and Art by **Inio Asano**

Translation **John Werry**
Touch-Up Art & Lettering **Annaliese Christman**
Design **Shawn Carrico**
Editor **Pancha Diaz**

DEAD DEAD DEMON'S DEDEDEDE DESTRUCTION Vol. 2
by Inio ASANO
© 2014 Inio ASANO
All rights reserved.
Original Japanese edition published by SHOGAKUKAN.
English translation rights in the United States of America,
Canada, the United Kingdom, Ireland, Australia and
New Zealand arranged with SHOGAKUKAN.

Original Cover Design **Kaoru KUROKI+Bay Bridge Studio**

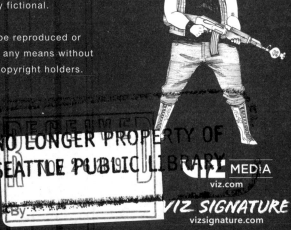

Printed in Canada

Published by VIZ Media, LLC
P.O. Box 77010
San Francisco, CA 94107

10 9 8 7 6 5 4 3 2 1
First printing, July 2018

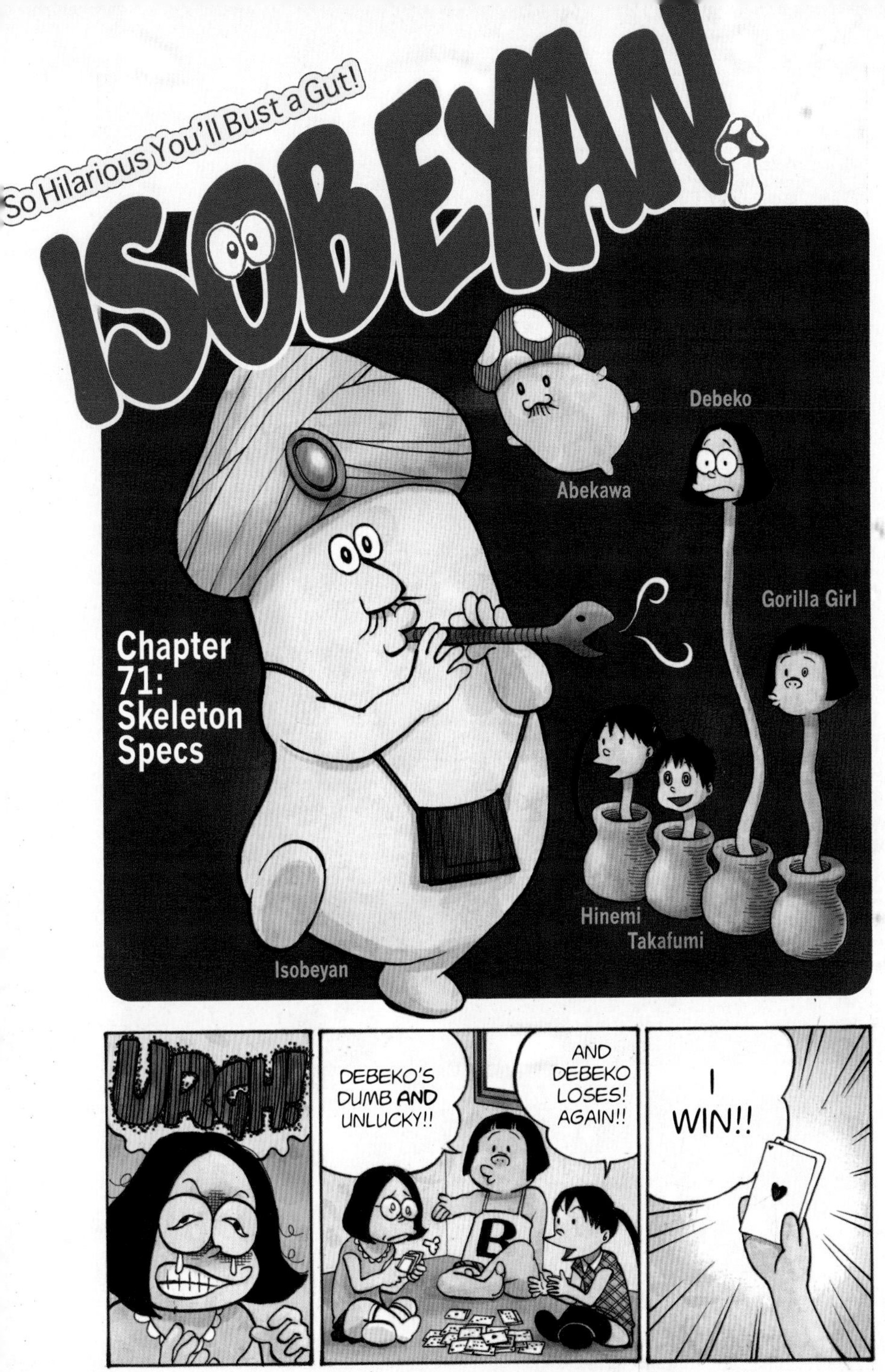
So Hilarious You'll Bust a Gut!
ISOBEYAN!
Chapter 71: Skeleton Specs
Abekawa
Debeko
Gorilla Girl
Hinemi
Takafumi
Isobeyan
I WIN!!
AND DEBEKO LOSES! AGAIN!!
DEBEKO'S DUMB AND UNLUCKY!!
URGH!

By Bonjiro Isofura

☆Since the new Mushroomian Abekawa showed up, *Isobeyan* chapters R even more interesting! I R going to keep reading for sure!

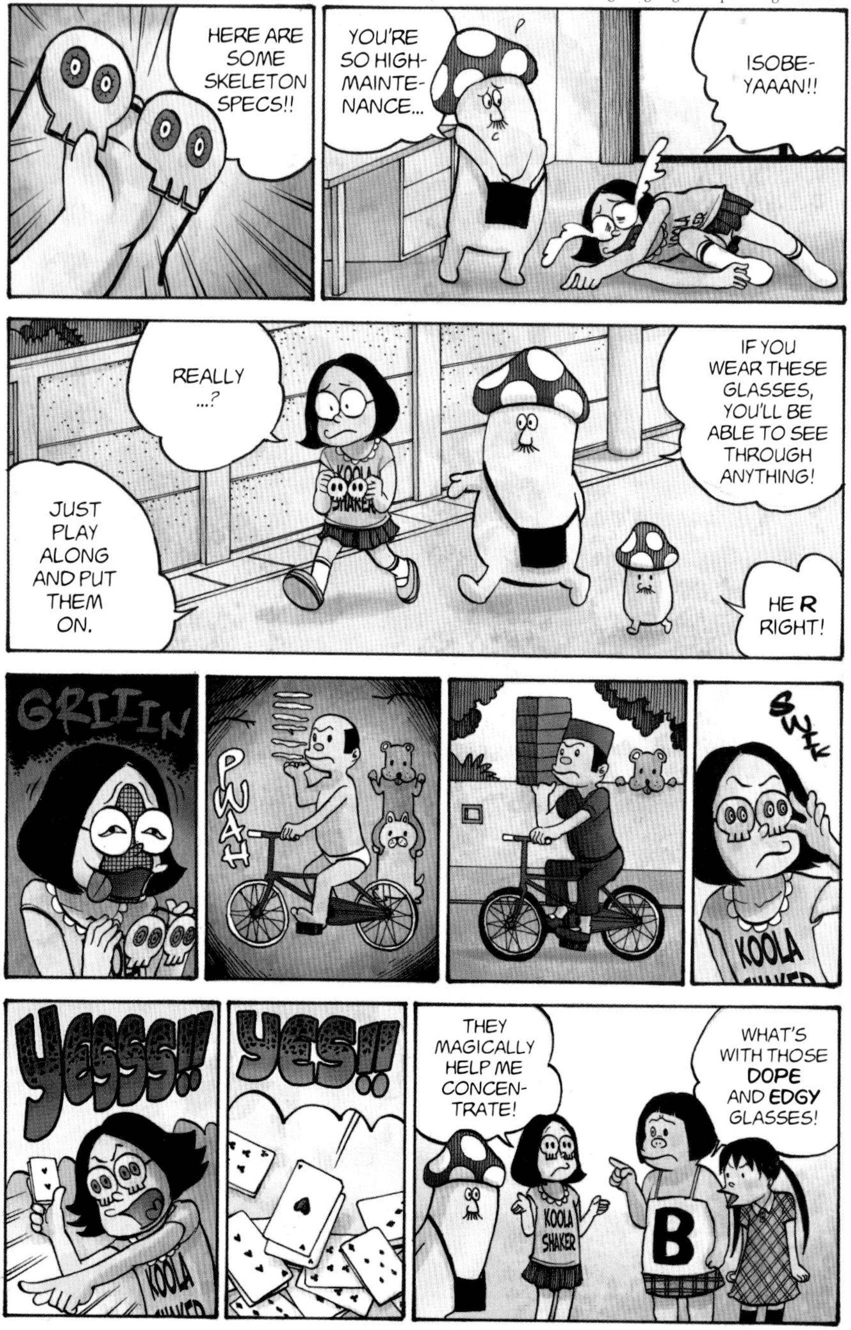

ISOBE-YAAAN!!
YOU'RE SO HIGH-MAINTENANCE...
HERE ARE SOME SKELETON SPECS!!
IF YOU WEAR THESE GLASSES, YOU'LL BE ABLE TO SEE THROUGH ANYTHING!
HE **R** RIGHT!
REALLY ...?
JUST PLAY ALONG AND PUT THEM ON.
SWIK
PWAH
GRIIIN
WHAT'S WITH THOSE **DOPE** AND **EDGY** GLASSES!
THEY MAGICALLY HELP ME CONCENTRATE!
YES!!
YESSS!!

SUPER-POPULAR MASTERPIECE COMEDY ISOBEYAN!

☆Bonjiro Isofura, the creator of *Isobeyan*, is waiting for your letters. So send 'em in!

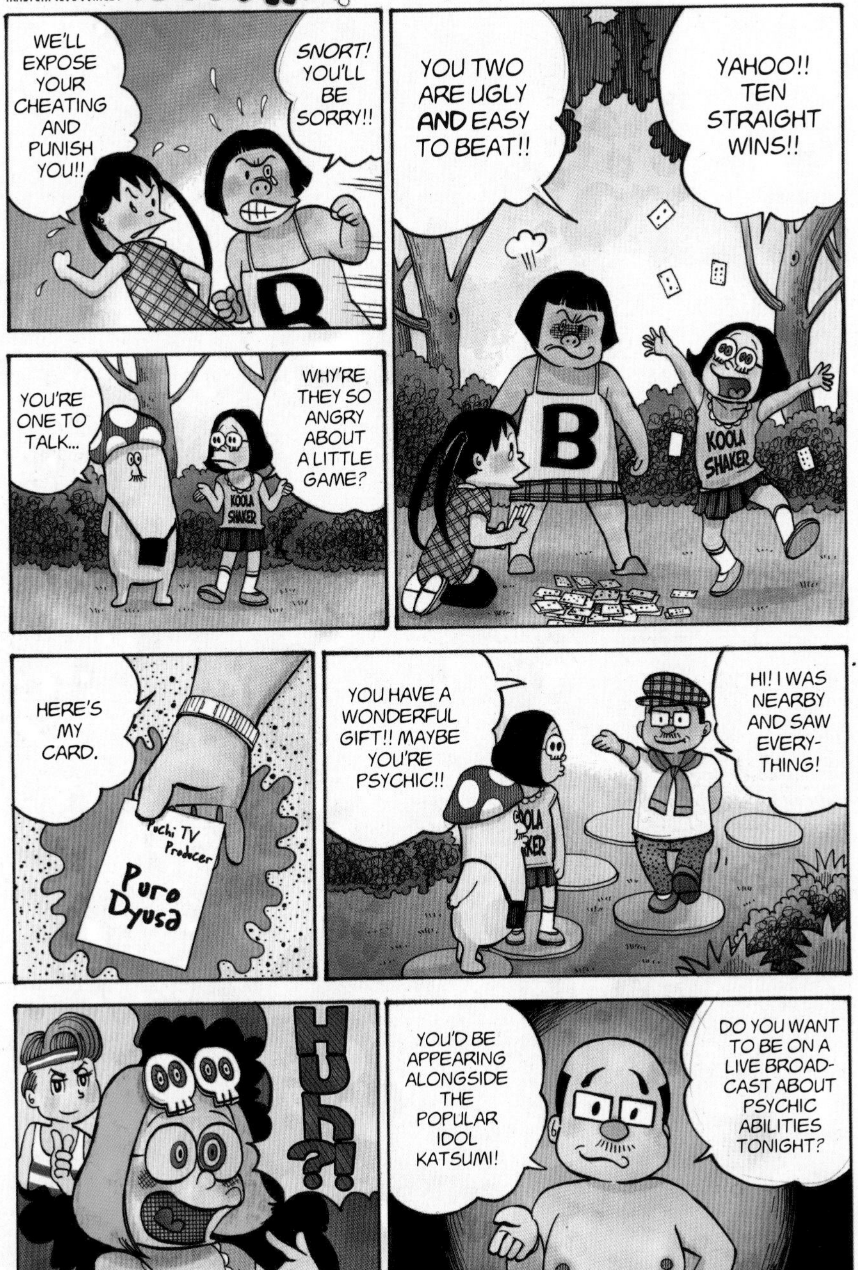

YAHOO!! TEN STRAIGHT WINS!!
YOU TWO ARE UGLY AND EASY TO BEAT!!
KOOLA SHAKER
B
SNORT! YOU'LL BE SORRY!!
WE'LL EXPOSE YOUR CHEATING AND PUNISH YOU!!
B
WHY'RE THEY SO ANGRY ABOUT A LITTLE GAME?
YOU'RE ONE TO TALK...
KOOLA SHAKER
HI! I WAS NEARBY AND SAW EVERY-THING!
YOU HAVE A WONDERFUL GIFT!! MAYBE YOU'RE PSYCHIC!!
HERE'S MY CARD.
Pochi TV Producer
Puro Dyusa
DO YOU WANT TO BE ON A LIVE BROAD-CAST ABOUT PSYCHIC ABILITIES TONIGHT?
YOU'D BE APPEARING ALONGSIDE THE POPULAR IDOL KATSUMI!
HUH?!

Uh-oh! Continued on page 162...

DEAD DEAD DEMON'S DEDEDEDE DESTRUCTION 2

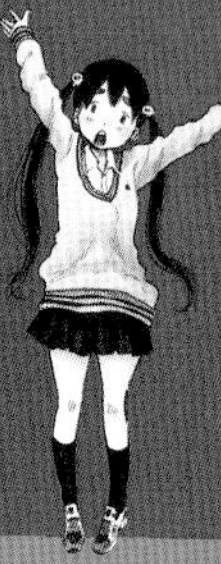